Roadmap to Bangalore? Globalization, the EU's Lisbon Process and the Structures of Global Inequality

ROADMAP TO BANGALORE? GLOBALIZATION, THE EU'S LISBON PROCESS AND THE STRUCTURES OF GLOBAL INEQUALITY

ALMAS HESHMATI
AND
ARNO TAUSCH

EDITORS

Nova Science Publishers, Inc.
New York

NOTICE TO THE READER

The Publisher has taken reasonable care in the preparation of this book, but makes no expressed or implied warranty of any kind and assumes no responsibility for any errors or omissions. No liability is assumed for incidental or consequential damages in connection with or arising out of information contained in this book. The Publisher shall not be liable for any special, consequential, or exemplary damages resulting, in whole or in part, from the readers' use of, or reliance upon, this material. Any parts of this book based on government reports are so indicated and copyright is claimed for those parts to the extent applicable to compilations of such works.

Independent verification should be sought for any data, advice or recommendations contained in this book. In addition, no responsibility is assumed by the publisher for any injury and/or damage to persons or property arising from any methods, products, instructions, ideas or otherwise contained in this publication.

This publication is designed to provide accurate and authoritative information with regard to the subject matter covered herein. It is sold with the clear understanding that the Publisher is not engaged in rendering legal or any other professional services. If legal or any other expert assistance is required, the services of a competent person should be sought. FROM A DECLARATION OF PARTICIPANTS JOINTLY ADOPTED BY A COMMITTEE OF THE AMERICAN BAR ASSOCIATION AND A COMMITTEE OF PUBLISHERS.

LIBRARY OF CONGRESS CATALOGING-IN-PUBLICATION DATA

Roadmap to Bangalore? : globalization, the EU's Lisbon Process and the structures of global inequality / Almas Heshmati and Arno Tausch (editors).
    p. cm.
Includes bibliographical references and index.
ISBN-13: 978-1-60021-478-3 (hardcover : alk. paper)
ISBN-10: 1-60021-478-9 (hardcover : alk. paper)
1. European Union countries--Economic policy. 2. Asia--Economic policy. I. Heshmati, Almas. II. Tausch, Arno, 1951-
HC240.R557   2007
338.94--dc22   2006100089

Published by Nova Science Publishers, Inc. ✛ *New York*

CONTENTS

AUTHORS AND CONTRIBUTORS
(IN ALPHABETICAL ORDER OF THEIR SURNAMES)

Adey Balinova, Dominique, language editor, is a graduate of Applied Language Studies from Ealing College of Higher Education and has worked with several international organizations. Contact: d_adey_balinova@yahoo.co.uk

Bhandari, Amit Kumar, doctoral student, Department of Economics, University of Kalyani, West Bengal–741 235, India, Phone: +9133-25825691, homepage: http://ideas.repec.org/e/pbh40.html. Contact: amitbhandari2@rediffmail.com

Ederveen, Sjef, is Research Coordinator at the Ministry of Economic Affairs, The Hague, Netherlands; Contact: S.Ederveen@minez.nl

Fitoussi, Jean-Paul, Observatoir Français de la Conjoncture Économique, Paris (France).

Heshmati, Almas, Professor of Economics, Hawler Institute for Economic and Policy Research and Department of Economics, University of Kurdistan Hawler, Hawler, Federal Region of Kurdistan, Iraq. Contact: almas.heshmati@hiepr.org and almas.heshmati@ukh.ac and homepages: http://www.hiepr.org and http://www.ukh.ac/

Holzmann, Robert, is Sector Director of the Social Protection & Labor Department at the World Bank, and former Professor of Economics and Head of the Euorpean Institute, University of Saarland, FRG. Contact: Rholzmann@Worldbank.org

Horst, Albert van der, is Researcher in the International Economics sector of CPB, Netherlands Bureau for Economic Policy Analysis, The Hague, Netherlands. Contact: a.van.der.horst@cpb.nl

Labini, Paolo Sylos, Università degli Studi di Roma "La Sapienza", Roma (Italy).

Mencinger, Joze, Professor of Economics, Ljubljana University, and former President, Ljubljana University, Slovenia; homepage: http://www2.arnes.si/aa/people/mencinger.html. During 1990-1991, Professor Mencinger served as Deputy Prime Minister of his home country. Current address: EIPF, Prešernova 21, Ljubljana, Slovenia. Contact: joze.mencinger@uni-lj.si

Modigliani, Franco, is the late Nobel Laureate in Economics (1985), and was – among others – Professor of Economics at the Massachussetts Institute of Technology (M.I.T.) in Cambridge, Ma., U.S.A.

Moro, Beniamino, is Professor of Economics and Director of the Department of Economics at the University of Cagliari, Italy. Contact: moro@unica.it

Oh, JongEun, doctoral student, Techno-Economics & Policy Program, College of Engineering, at Seoul National University. Contact: serapin7@snu.ac.kr

Snower, Dennis, Birkbeck College, London (Great Britain).

Solow, Robert, is the Nobel Laureate in Economics (1987), Massachussetts Institute of Technology, Cambridge, Mass. (USA).

Steinherr, Alfred, European Investment Bank, Basle (Switzerland).

Tang, Paul, is Member of Parliament, The Hague, Netherlands;
Contact: P.Tang@tweedekamer.nl

Tausch, Arno, Adjunct Professor of Political Science, Innsbruck University, Austria, homepage: http://www.getcited.org/mbrz/10134373.
Contact: arno.tausch@bmsk.gv.at

What would a different policy agenda for Europe look like?

First, it would modernize our social model. Again, some have suggested I want to abandon Europe's social model. But tell me: what type of social model is it that has 20 million unemployed in Europe, productivity rates falling behind those of the USA; that is allowing more science graduates to be produced by India than by Europe; and that, on any relative index of a modern economy - skills, R&D, patents, IT, is going down not up? India will expand its biotechnology sector fivefold in the next five years. China has trebled its spending on R&D in the last five.

Of the top 20 universities in the world today, only two are now in Europe. (...)

The purpose of our social model should be to enhance our ability to compete, to help our people cope with globalization, to let them embrace its opportunities and avoid its dangers. Of course we need a social Europe. But it must be a social Europe that works. (...)

And we've been told how to do it. The Kok report in 2004 shows the way. Investment in knowledge, in skills, in active labor market policies, in science parks and innovation, in higher education, in urban regeneration, in help for small businesses. This is modern social policy, not regulation and job protection that may save some jobs for a time at the expense of many jobs in the future. (...)

And since this is a day for demolishing caricatures, let me demolish one other: the idea that Britain is in the grip of some extreme Anglo-Saxon market philosophy that tramples on the poor and disadvantaged. (British Prime Minister Tony Blair, available at: http://www.number10.gov.uk/output/Page7714.asp)

In: Roadmap to Bangalore?   ISBN: 978-1-60021-478-3
Editors: A. Heshmati, A. Tausch, pp. 1-9   © 2007 Nova Science Publishers, Inc.

INTRODUCTION

The European Social Model is in the news again. British Prime Minister Tony Blair, not shying away from confrontations, has set the tone for this debate, to which this book wants to contribute. Nobody would deny that Europe, in one way or another, is in a crisis. 20 million unemployed people; productivity rates falling behind those of the USA; allowing more science graduates to be produced by India than by Europe; skills, R&D, patents, IT, going down not up. India will expand its biotechnology sector fivefold in the next five years. China has trebled its spending on R&D in the last five years. After the negative results of the constitutional referenda in France and the Netherlands, it would be foolish to deny the existence of such a crisis. But what are its causes? Too much globalization, too much distance from the average European citizen, or too heavy tax burdens, too much regulation? Or a shrinking demographic base and barriers to migration? Or the rigid policies of the European Central Bank and the Maastricht accords?

This book, written by a fairly globalized set of authors, leaves behind the trodden paths of transatlantic comparison US-EU and looks at the real global issues that cause some nations to stagnate while others rush forward. Among these nations, you find today China, India, and the new industrial giants of East Asia that recover from the effects of the "Asian Crisis" years ago.

This book studies the European crisis in a global, cross-national, quantiative and systematic way. The authors of this book include neoclassical economists, decision makers in the World Bank, Keynesian critics of Euro-monetarism, and dependency and world system theory authors that share one methodological belief in common: a thorough, comparative method is needed to look at the underlying issues of faltering economic growth and rising income inequality as well as the stagnating employment situation on the European Continent.

This volume now tries to answer some of these controversies and provide new and more solid evidence. What did the Europeans achieve and how and where did they fail in the 5 years of the Lisbon process since the European Summit in Lisbon in 2000? What is the real extent of globalization in the countries of the world system, including the European Union? What is the relationship between globalization and inequality? Would a Tobin tax and regulations against financial speculation be a way out? Are not globalization, but the rigid mechanisms of Maastricht and the European Central Bank to blame for the debacle experienced up to now? And what about the role of different Lisbon targets, like the leveling-down of relative price levels, in the process of stagnation in Europe? And what about the barriers against migration? Do they hinder, at the end of the day, long-run economic growth? And what alternatives are there?

In the first contribution, by **Sjef Ederveen, Albert van der Horst** and **Paul Tang**, the authors say that looking back at the first half of the Lisbon strategy, it has been difficult to improve simultaneously the central elements of the strategy: the economy, social cohesion and the environment. EU-Commission President Barroso has drawn the conclusion that Europe has to focus on its 'sick child', namely on the economy. In his view, 'growth and jobs' are essential for improving social cohesion and the environment. But that economic expansion contributes to maintaining social cohesion as well as the environment, is, according to the authors, a somewhat optimistic view. First, there are structural trade-offs among the central elements of the Lisbon strategy. Escaping these trade-offs temporarily is sometimes possible but requires policy changes (like pricing pollution). Second, higher productivity (growth) may not structurally provide more room for governments to manoeuvre. It leads to higher tax receipts but also to higher public expenditures since public sector wages and social security benefits are linked to productivity. In contrast, more employment (jobs) is associated with a smaller government. But to engineer the increase in employment changes in welfare state arrangements are needed. In other words, focusing solely on the sick child will probably harm the other children. How sick is the European economy really? In the last fifteen years participation on European labor markets has increased. Currently, labor productivity per hour is high in many European countries. It is perhaps troubling that the rate of productivity growth has fallen since the seventies and especially in the late nineties. The slowdown in productivity growth does not reflect a falling rate of investment in knowledge. Instead, the slowdown is explained by two European successes. First, the poor productivity growth in the late nineties reflects strong employment growth in that period. Second, the slowdown reflects high growth in the past: in the sixties and seventies the European countries have had 'the advantage of backwardness', i.e. the potential to increase productivity by imitating and implementing state-of-the-art technologies. Approaching the technology frontier, however, limits the relatively easy opportunities for technological progress.

At the same time that the European economies saw a sharp decline in productivity growth, the American economy showed acceleration in productivity growth, mainly prompted by the intensified use of ICT in services. The American acceleration does not make the European countries worse off, but shows a potential for increasing productivity growth. Some European countries like Finland and Sweden have already taken advantage of this potential. Whether other European countries will also take advantage in the near future is an open question.

The slowdown does not show a clear relation with investment in knowledge and technology, but to reverse it, more investment is needed. Higher investments in research and development, in education and possibly in ICT are likely to contribute to higher productivity growth in the medium run.

Is the European Union really a doctor? With the Lisbon strategy, a new mode of governance has been introduced: the Open Method of Coordination (OMC) aims at coordinating national policies by setting common targets, while accepting national sovereignty in policy design. In their review of the Lisbon strategy, Kok and Barroso lay the blame for the slow progress partly, if not fully, with the member states: they have not delivered. New proposals aim to increase the pressure on the member states to implement policies that stimulate growth and to pursue reforms that create jobs. These proposals will not put at ease the minds of those that find the powers of the Union already excessive. They do not view the Union as part of the solution but as part of the problem.

So, there are two antagonistic views on the role of the European Union. And one could argue that both views are correct. To argue this, one should apply the principle of subsidiarity: competences remain with the member states unless there are good reasons for coordination. A cross-border externality is the most common of these reasons. How does the subsidiarity principle work out for the two central elements in the renewed Lisbon strategy: jobs and growth?

Consider jobs. There is hardly any evidence of international spillovers from employment. The European labor markets hardly depend on each other, and barely affect production in other countries. This forms a rather weak basis for European employment targets and peer pressure on member states to engineer employment growth. The main value added of the OMC is that it stimulates policy learning in areas where coordination is unnecessary. However, even the potential to learn from each other should not be overestimated as the European member states differ markedly in their institutional design.

Consider growth. Productivity growth in one country does spillover to other countries, either by adding to knowledge and technology or through lower import prices. With this spillover, a classical problem of underinvestment arises: without coordination, countries do not internalize the benefits of their investments for other countries. This forms a relatively strong basis for European coordination in some form. Coordination is only successful if the member states are committed to the European goals. The past five years have shown that the OMC has not been able to deliver this. It does not have strong, formal sanctions and the informal pressure has not been enough to introduce effective policies to increase productivity growth, for example by raising R&D expenditures.

A National Action Programme and Mr. or Ms. Lisbon should make the sanctions stronger and the OMC more effective. For jobs, the need for stronger sanctions is not clear, however. For growth, a more effective OMC seems welcome. However, it is far from obvious that the renewed strategy will be able to deliver commitment. Either the targets are likely to become less ambitious when the political consequences of not reaching national targets become stronger, or the targets may remain overly ambitious and, thus, hardly credible. So, for growth the OMC may not be effective enough.

In their contribution, **Arno Tausch, Almas Heshmati** and **JongEun Oh** address the measurement of two composite Lisbon strategy indices ("one-glance, one click" indicators) that quantify the level and patterns of development for ranking countries. If we want to reduce the complexity of the 14 main Lisbon indicators, the usual ranking procedures, still popular among government bureaucracies in the EU, are by far insufficient. The new "Lisbon strategy index (LSI)" is composed of six components: general economics, employment, innovation research, economic reform, social cohesion and environment, each generated from a number of the 14 original main Lisbon indicators, each of which develops differently over time and across countries, covered by Eurostat. Sweden, Norway and the USA are ranked as highest. Bulgaria, Turkey and Malta are the lowest ranked countries in the new Index. The article, whose main results are reported in Text tables 1 to 3, also contains Lisbon process indicators results, based on principal components, reflecting the research and development process, social cohesion, the power of the freight lobby, and business investments. Again it is shown that the United States outperform most EU-member states. The investigations also allow us to show the dynamic changes taking place, as the countries of the Union struggle to achieve the

Lisbon goals. The necessity of a real reform agenda in Germany and in several new member and candidate countries again emerges from our analysis. The LSI Index ranks Korea as number 8, if Korea is introduced into the rankings of Table 2 of this study. This position is better than Japan's, and Korea has a higher score in innovation and research than the EU but lower than the USA and Japan. Also Korea's economic reform is quite high as a result of its lower price level than that of the EU and a higher business investment rate. Korea stabilized the economy very shortly after the 1997 economic crisis and the rate of rapid recovery after the crisis makes the country very interesting from the perspectives of reform, growth and development strategy. Thus many aspects of its policy can serve not only as a model for economic development, but also as an experiment field for development of new industries such as telecommunication, and to achieve high innovativeness and competitiveness to both developing and developed countries as well.

Amit Kumar Bhandari and **Almas Heshmati** show in their essay that the process of globalization is an international economic order which has led to the progressive integration of the world economy through pulling down the barriers of trade and enabling greater mobility of factors of production. In addition, technological innovation also provides an impetus to the progressive integration of nations. Features of globalization include the free movement of goods and services, flow of capital, movement of labor and the transfer of technology. Many transitional and developing countries have benefited from liberalization. Apart from the economic benefits, globalization also indicates the flow of ideas, norms, information and peoples. There is, however, a large heterogeneity in the degree of globalization over time and across countries and regions of the world, as well as within countries. The present study is an attempt to measure globalization by using both parametric and non-parametric approaches. The data cover a wide range of industrialized, transition and developing countries on the basis of their international integration. Bhandari and Heshmati identify the factors influencing globalization among the countries in the form of economic integration, personal contact, technology and political engagement. They isolate the contribution of the factors by quantifying the individual factor contribution to overall integration. Finally, they investigate the links between globalization and labor market in the Indian manufacturing industry.

Preceding the present boom, India embarked on integration with the world economy on a much bigger scale through the removal of various directives, regulations and controls. However, the necessity of reform had arisen out of the pressure to rescue the economic system from financial and external payment crisis. Other political factors also provided the motivation. Thus, at the behest of the IMF and the World Bank, India sincerely followed a structural adjust program, which contained loaded prescriptions like trade liberalization, lifting up restrictions on foreign direct and portfolio investments, current account convertibility in phases and partial capital account liberalization, shifting towards a market-determined exchange rate regime, beginning the privatization process and measures to pass on a substantial portion of the domestic market to the transnational corporations (TNCs).

Since independence, India followed a mixed economy structure with major emphasis on a state owned public sector nurtured in a relatively closed or protected environment, with trade and foreign investment playing a limited role and a significant agrarian sector marked by low per capital income and income inequality. Still, agricultural growth is the major force in stimulating domestic demand for industrial products. The organized manufacturing sector in India includes all public sector enterprises and all non-agricultural establishments employing ten or more workers. The post-globalization phase of Indian manufacturing industries is facing various challenges. A segment of manufacturing is now getting linked with global capital and technology. This has posed a significant challenge for domestic industry, its self-reliant industrial development and the industrial growth. Firstly, domestic industry irrespective of size and class is encountering the problem of demand deficiency. It is to be noted here that unlike the industries in East and South-East Asia, India's share in world industrial output and export is not commensurate with its size and potentiality. India accounts for less than a 1 per cent share in world trade. Hence, the major demand for industry stems from the domestic market. The decade of the nineties were characterized by large volatile fluctuations in market demand. Secondly, domestic industry has been facing stiff competition in the domestic market from foreign firms and products in terms of price, brand names and attributes. With trade liberalization and implementation of rationalization of tariff and non-tariff barriers, the Indian market is now infested with cheap imports of both consumer and intermediate products. These are now posing serious threats to the market share and profitability of Indian industry. Lastly and most importantly, domestic as well as global financial surplus are now no longer geared to the requirements of Indian industry. Financial liberalization has de-linked the finance from industrial investment.

Bhandari and Heshmati show that the process of globalization is not witnessing a steady growth, and that rather it is fluctuating throughout the time period. There is large heterogeneity in the degree of globalization across countries and regions. West European countries dominate the top ten positions in the world, with Ireland leading the group. The bottom of the group is dominated by countries belonging to the region of Sub-Saharan Africa and South Asia. The position of low ranking countries is not only associated with internal and external conflicts, but also the socio-political environment holds back its growth and development, which would seem to reduce the globalization prospects of the countries concerned. The breakdown of the globalization index into major components offers the possibility to identify the sources of globalization. Of all components, political engagement is the biggest contributor, followed by economic integration, personal contacts and technology. It is interesting to note that during the current phase of globalization, the least globalized countries emerge as the best performers. Right now, both China and India are the fastest growing economies but they are way behind in globalization. They are integrating their economy at a faster pace, clearly holding a lesson for many other developing countries. In India high population growth coupled with a complex cultural geography and continuing geopolitical tensions jeopardize the equitable development of globalization.

In his second paper, **Almas Heshmati** examines the causal relationship between inequality and a number of macroeconomic variables frequently found in the inequality and growth literature. These include growth, openness, wages, and liberalization. Heshmati reviews the existing cross-country empirical evidence on the effects of inequality on growth and the extent to which the poorest in society benefit from economic growth. The linkage between growth, redistribution and poverty are also analyzed. In the review of literature, mainly empirical examples from 1990s are taken. In addition the author tests the conditional and unconditional relationship between inequality and growth in the post World War II period using the WIDER inequality database. Regression results suggest that income inequality is declining over time. Inequality is also declining with the growth of income. There is a significant regional heterogeneity in the levels and development over time. The famous Kuznets hypothesis represents a global U-shape relationship between inequality and growth.

There exists a comprehensive body of literature investigating the relationship between openness, growth, inequality and poverty. In general there exists a positive relationship between openness and growth. The effect is declining over time and different in its impact on the distribution of income.

However, there is no indication of a systematic relationship between trade and inequality. One major shortcoming of the literature on the link between growth, openness, inequality and poverty is that the direction and simultaneous causal relationships between these key variables has been neglected. An establishment of the linkage and direction of causality will have major impacts on the relevance of results and inferences made based on such results. Empirical findings, based on a large sample of countries and relatively long time periods, indicate the presence of convergence in per capita income but divergence in income inequality in the world system. There is evidence of a strong convergence among more homogenous and integrated advanced countries but also divergence among less developed countries or regions of countries and the world. The between country contribution is much higher than the within country contribution to the world inequality. Democratization in Western countries has led to institutional changes and changes in taxation and redistribution, too, to reduce inequality. Other paths are the East Asian Miracle with low inequality and high growth, while Sub-Saharan Africa is characterized by high inequality and low growth. There is a conflicting viewpoint about the causal effects of inequality on growth. The new empirical results on the relationship between growth, inequality and poverty show that outcomes of policy measures are heterogeneous. Depending on the initial position of the poor and the diversity of the impact of policies, the poor might gain more from redistribution, but also suffer more from economic contraction. Globalization, openness and technical change have been biased to skilled labor in industrialized countries, widening wage differentials and suggesting a positive association between openness and wage inequality. However, the pattern is seen to be more complex.

For developing countries, these changes reduce wage inequality by narrowing the wage gap between skilled and unskilled workers. The relative demand for skilled labor and wage inequality has been developed differently across countries. Regression results based on the WIID database suggest that income inequality is declining over time. Inequality is also declining with the growth of income. There is significant regional heterogeneity in the levels and development over time.

Joze Mencinger maintains that modern societies and governments are preoccupied with efficiency and growth; it is taken as limitless due to enhanced total factor productivity and prevalence of services over production of goods. The EU, which had condensed this passion in the Lisbon strategy 2000, admitted that it failed. In February 2005, the old strategy was replaced by a new one. The realization of new, less firmly defined goals, however, does not seem to be assured; the strategy relies on empty talks and new institutions. The "scientific" pillar of the strategy is production function; growth is to be attained by increasing total factor productivity. However, reorganization of science and creation of a multitude of institutions, regardless of financial resources, do not guarantee scientific discoveries. Even if they did, discoveries do not guarantee growth and jobs. Technological changes are predominantly labor saving; they may but do not necessarily create new jobs in other sectors, predominantly in services. Also this path is in Europe threatened by the globalization which swiftly turns its activities with high value added jobs into activities with low value added jobs.

European countries have shifted a large part of globalization challenges from the national to EU level. The EU, however - even if it becomes a knowledge based society – is unable to compete with much more ruthless societies. The Achilles' heel of Lisbon strategy is the overall neglect of aggregate demand. Very high economic growth is not a lasting phenomenon; it is often based on country specific features, and co-determined by shifts in aggregate demand. Long running and uniform economic growth cannot be assured by reductions of budget deficits or public expenditures. Indeed, the new Lisbon Partnership for Growth and Jobs of 2005 is threatened by the old Stability and Growth Pact of 1997.

The late Nobel Laureate in Economics, Franco Modigliani, and **Beniamino Moro** (initiators), together with **Nobel Laureate in Economics, Robert Solow** and the other signatories of the famous 1998 Economists' Manifesto on Unemployment in Europe, which we are glad to be able to reprint here in view of the terrible problem of European unemployment, believe that the EU unemployment problem needs to be attacked on two fronts: through a broad spectrum of supply side policies and the demand management policy. The expansion of aggregate demand is necessary to increase both investment and employment. However, unless supply side measures are also taken, demand expansion can result in more inflation instead of more employment, because of the mismatch between the demand and supply of labor. What is important to stress is that both demand and supply side policies must be adopted together by all European countries, in order both to avoid beggar-my-neighbor problems, and, at the same time, to catch all the possible complementary effects of these policies.

Arno Tausch, starting from the current debate about the European social model, undertakes a radical new assessment of the deficits of the European social model. His approach underlines the – until now - neglected effects of the lack of industrial policy and structural dependence on economic growth and social development in Europe. Much of the re-ascent of Europe and Japan after 1945 was due to import substitution. When that ended, Europe and Japan began to slide back again vis-à-vis the United States, thus re-affirming the old wisdom of development history research in contrast to "pure" free trade economic theory (Senghaas, 1985). Senghaas' analysis of the development history of European states today finds its confirmation in global development statistics summarized by the United Nations (2002). Re-analyzing the existing data for the 1990s clearly shows that the winners and losers of globalization were indeed distributed very unevenly around the globe. In a significant portion of the countries of the globe, inequality and globalization – the inflow of foreign direct investments per host country GDP - are on the increase since 1980, as the author confirms here, based on the data series of the ILO, the UTIP project at the University of Texas, and the World Bank. These analyses of the dynamics in the world system calculated the time series correlations of globalization, economic growth (Global Development Network Growth Database, William Easterly and Mirvat Sewadeh, World Bank) unemployment (Laborsta ILO), and inequality (UTIP, University of Texas Inequality Project, Theil indices of inequality, based on wages in 21 economic sectors).

Within this framework the author then analyzes falling relative price levels (Eurostat, Lisbon indicators) or unequal exchange. A lowering of the price level will, according to the underlying Commission logic, mean "price reform", while a hypothetical movement upwards on the indicator will mean a "setback". With the UNDP Human Development Indicators from the year 2000 the author shows that a high price level (in the terminology of Eurostat) is exceptionally highly and positively correlated with positive indicators of the development performance of a nation, and very highly negatively correlated with indicators of human misery. Contrary to the Commission's assumptions, it would have to be expected that movements in the direction of a "lower price level" lead indeed to social imbalances and crises. Pushing Europe towards even more "price reform" will mean a Yotopoulos cycle of backwardness and stagnation. Tausch's analyses show the dramatic world shifts in price levels relative to the United States in recent years. Contrary to what European policy makers expected with their Eurostat politically binding price level indicator, which is, after all, one of their 14 main Lisbon targets, the United States as the Lisbon competition target country was a high price region throughout much of the late 1990s and the early 2000s. By and large, it is shown that the member countries of the "old" EU-15 are on the losing side in that transnational equation. No "old" European country improved its position, on the contrary, "old Europe" becomes a region that is itself a victim of price reform (unequal exchange, low international price level).

Starting with the writings of Perroux, Prebisch and Rothschild in the 1930s, he then shows that there is no empirical support for the thesis that globalization is good for the poor. By using latest (United Nations and other data) and multivariate techniques, investigating the determination of 14 indicators of development in 109 countries with complete data by 12 determinants of development, the author shows that a reliance on the "Washington Consensus" alone will not "fix" the performance of the EU-25. The most consistent consequence of the "dependency" analysis of Tausch's essay is the realization that a reliance on foreign capital in the short term might bring about positive consequences for employment – especially female employment – but that the long-term negative consequences of dependence in the social sphere, but also for sustainable development, outweigh the immediate, positive effects. His threefold empirical understanding of the process of globalization – reliance on foreign savings, MNC penetration and unequal transfer/price reform (ERDI) - goes beyond the average analysis of the workings of dependency structures and shows how different aspects of dependency negatively affect development performance.

EU membership, by contrast, fails to have sufficiently dynamic effects and its democratic deficits become ever more clear. What is more, the unweighted average dependency rates of the EU-25 are much higher than in India, the US and China. Among the EU countries, only Turkey, Italy, Greece had a lower MNC penetration rate than the US, and Slovenia (see Mencinger in this volume) is the country with the lowest MNC penetration rate among the countries of the "new Europe" and at the same time the most successful one in social policies. Indeed, one could say that we are confronted with *"Dependencia y desarrollo en Europa"*

In the final paper, written by **Robert Holzmann**, the author investigates the demographic alternatives for dealing with the projected population aging and low or negative growth of the population and labor force in the North. Without further immigration, the total labor force in Europe and Russia, the high-income countries of East Asia and the Pacific, China, and, to a lesser extent, North America is projected to be reduced by 29 million by 2025 and by 244 million by 2050. In contrast, the labor force in the South is projected to add some 1.55 billion, predominantly in South and Central Asia and in Sub-Saharan Africa. The demographic policy scenarios to deal with the projected shrinking of the labor forth in the North include moving the total fertility rate back to replacement levels, increasing labor force participation of the existing population through a variety of measures, and filling the demographic gaps through enhanced immigration. The estimations indicate that each of these policy scenarios may partially or even fully compensate for the projected labor force gap by

2050. But a review of the policy measures to make these demographic scenarios happen also suggests that governments may not be able to initiate or accommodate the required change.

Not all answers, of course, could be given. But the present volume tries to be an honest, cross-nationally argued collection of essays that look at some of the real issues of the contemporary European malaise. And a steering compass for all those who really want to re-construct the European Social Model that is under real strain.

April 25, 2007
Hawler and Vienna
Almas Heshmati and Arno Tausch (Editors)

In: Roadmap to Bangalore?
Editors: A. Heshmati, A. Tausch, pp. 11-51

ISBN: 978-1-60021-478-3
© 2007 Nova Science Publishers, Inc.

Chapter 1

IS THE EUROPEAN ECONOMY A PATIENT AND THE UNION ITS DOCTOR? ON JOBS AND GROWTH IN EUROPE

Sjef Ederveen[1], Albert van der Horst[2] and Paul Tang[3]

ABSTRACT

A stronger focus on jobs and growth is part of an effort to renew the Lisbon strategy. This will not contribute to social cohesion and the environment. For example, higher productivity is not likely to add to the financial sustainability of the public sector.

Looking back, employment (jobs) keep expanding in the European Union whereas the productivity growth rate is falling. The latter is not easily explained by (falling) investment in knowledge. Instead, the current relatively low productivity growth rate largely reflects success in the past: many European countries have caught up with the United States and have seen relatively fast employment growth in the late nineties. Looking forward, the combination of the Open Method of Coordination (OMC) with National Action Plans is both too little and too much. European interference with national employment polices has a weak basis, whereas OMC may not provide the member states with strong enough commitment to pursue an innovation agenda.

Key words: Jobs and growth, Lisbon agenda, productivity slowdown, Open Method of Coordination.

[1] Ministry of Economic Affairs, P.O. Box 20101, 2500 EC The Hague, The Netherlands, email: s.ederveen@minez.nl.
[2] CPB Netherlands Bureau for Economic Policy Analysis, P.O. Box 80510, 2508 GM The Hague, The Netherlands, email: A.van.der.Horst@cpb.nl.
[3] Dutch house of representatives, P.O. Box 20018, 2500 EA The Hague, The Netherlands, email: p.tang@tweedekamer.nl.

1. A FOCUS ON GROWTH AND JOBS

Much cited is the phrase 'to become the most competitive and dynamic knowledge-based economy'. It summarises the Lisbon declaration of government leaders drafted some five years ago. According to the declaration, the European Union and its member states should improve economic performance without deteriorating the environment or damaging social cohesion. A wide variety of actions and targets have been proposed at the same time to achieve this, and together they form the Lisbon strategy.

One immediate success has been to put economic performance on the top of the policy agenda in Europe. Quite a few observers find the Lisbon strategy overambitious and/or ineffective, but do not seem to disagree that reforms of various markets and government policies have the potential of boosting European economic performance considerably. The fear is that even without reforms Europe will fall behind.

The Lisbon strategy covers many aspects of economic life; it ranges from increasing participation to 70% of the potential labour force to completing the internal market for services, and from raising R&D expenditure to 3% of gross domestic product to reducing the administrative burden on companies. The Lisbon strategy is worked out in detail. The broad aim of increasing overall participation in the European labour markets is supplemented with explicit targets for participation rates of females and workers older than fifty-five. Similarly, the aim to improve education is translated into targets for early school leavers, for graduates in mathematics, science and technology, and for literacy for 15-year olds.

In short, Lisbon aims to improve economic performance in Europe but not at any cost. Europe is looking for its own ways to increase employment and raise productivity. It is not only concerned with improving economic performance, but is also eager to maintain non-economic qualities of life: economic performance should not harm the environment or break up social cohesion.

Five years after its start, the Lisbon strategy has not brought a clear change in the relative position of Europe in the world economy. Even after the collapse of the internet bubble and during an economic recession, productivity growth in the United States has remained impressive, i.e. higher than in the European Union. Lisbon has not delivered, Barroso concludes.

Kok and others (2004) have reviewed the Lisbon strategy and put forward several proposals to rejuvenate it. Building on this review, Barroso has recently clarified the position of the new European Commission. Both Kok and Barroso seek to renew the Lisbon strategy in two ways. The first way is to give the Lisbon strategy a clearer focus: growth and jobs must take centre stage. The stronger emphasis on the economy seems to imply less emphasis on the environment and on social cohesion. But Barroso and Kok see growth and jobs as essential for achieving sustainable development and for financing the European welfare states in the future. Clearly, this seems to be an important change in view between 2000 and 2005. Whereas in the Lisbon declaration economic growth is made conditional on social cohesion and the environment, Barroso, as well as Kok seem to put forward the view that one cannot go without the other. This raises the question whether there is a trade-off or not. In the next section, 1.1, we address this question.

The priority on jobs and growth is also seen to reflect the urgency of these problems in European economies. Specifically, Barroso argues: "I have three children: the economy, our social agenda, and the environment. Like any modern father, if one of my children is sick, I'm ready to drop everything and focus on him until he is back to health. But that does not mean I love the others any less."[4] Barroso is a modern father but perhaps also another overwrought parent. The Europeans economies are among the most well-off in the world, how sick can they really be? The next section deals with this simple and yet complex question. Not surprisingly, the factors behind employment (jobs) and productivity (growth) are rather different and hence, are discussed separately.

The second way to renew the Lisbon strategy is to put pressure on member states to reform. Both Kok and Barroso lay the blame for the lack of progress partly, if not fully, with the member states, in which the political will to reform is considered too weak. The national governments and parliaments must therefore adopt a national action programme how to increase the rate of growth and the number of jobs in their countries. Not 'naming and shaming' by the European Commission, but rather the fear of losing political reputation, should induce national policy makers to implement the programmes. Moreover, the idea seems to be that if countries undertake reforms at the same time, these reforms become less painful: 'after all, everyone will benefit from the future that the Lisbon agenda is trying to shape' Barroso (2005, p. 13) writes. The renewed Lisbon strategy should thus commit national policy makers to reform and help them to internalise the spillovers of national reforms to European partners. Is the Open Method of Coordination, that is central in the implementation of the Lisbon strategy, necessary and effective in bringing commitment, and changing the national perspective into a European perspective? The last section deals with this method and the underlying principle of subsidiarity. Also in that section, the distinction between jobs and growth is essential.

1.1. The Price to Pay for Jobs and Growth:
Social Cohesion and Environment

Up to now the aim of raising economic growth in the European Union has been conditional in the Lisbon strategy. Two broad conditions have been recognised: economic growth should not come at the expense of social cohesion and should not bring damage to the environment. These conditions reflect the idea that welfare is not identical to economic production and income. More specifically, the two conditions reflect the concern that boosting economic growth may be at odds with maintaining social cohesion and the environment. Barroso's European Commission seems to sweep this concern aside. Jobs and growth are explicitly put centre stage. Moreover, the Commission seems to argue that jobs and growth will only help European countries to achieve the other non-economic goals. Growth is regarded essential for keeping the European welfare states sustainable. With regard to sustainability, investing in a clean environment is not seen as a drag on economic growth, but rather is assumed to provide a boost to innovation. Is the concern for a trade-off relevant or is Barroso right to sweep this concern aside? This section discusses separately two possible trade-offs: between economic growth (predominantly jobs) and social cohesion; and between economic growth (mainly productivity) and the environment. As Figure 1.1 shows, a trade-off

---

[4]   See: http://www.telegraph.co.uk/news/main.jhtml?xml=/news/2005/02/03/weu03.xml&sSheet=/news/2005/02/03/ixworld.html

between productivity and employment growth is discussed in the next section. The relation between social cohesion and the environment is left out, as we consider them to be hardly related.

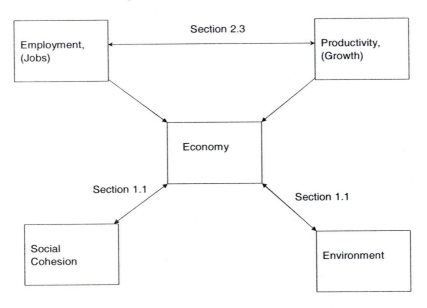

Figure 1.1. Trade-offs between the four essential elements of the Lisbon strategy.

1.1.1. Economic Growth Versus Social Cohesion

In the Lisbon strategy the aim of maintaining social cohesion has been worked out in various ways.[5] Central to the concept of social cohesion is income inequality, and income redistribution to keep inequality limited. European economies are characterised by an elaborate welfare state: social security, tax, and other systems, that aim to protect individuals against unforeseen shocks in income, and that aim to redistribute purchasing power from rich to poor. As a result, income distributions in European economies are more equal than in the United States. For example, income of the richest 10% is at least three times higher than income of the poorest 10% in the Netherlands and Sweden, whereas in the United States it is five and a half times higher. This income redistribution comes at a cost: it distorts individual decisions to work, to save, and to invest. Some find this cost too high or fear that it will become too high.

Barroso is not alone in thinking that economic growth is essential for maintaining the European welfare states. Sapir et al. (2003), for instance, maintain that to keep the financial position of the public sector sustainable the European countries need to see faster growth. In this view economic growth does not come at the expense of the welfare state, but is an instrument to limit income inequality and to maintain social cohesion. One argument within this view is that with a higher income the same number of workers are better able to pay the same – or a growing – number of social security benefits.

---

[5] In the Lisbon agenda, it comprises the distribution of income, the risk of poverty, unemployment, the regional dispersion of employment rates and the fraction of early school leavers.

The financial burden on workers becomes less, however, only if wages rise (much) faster than social security benefits. A crucial assumption is thus a decoupling of benefit income from wage income. The relative income difference between workers and benefit recipients must become (much) larger in the future than it is now. This may trigger demand for higher social security benefits, which may partly or fully undo the effect of economic growth on the financial burden. Similar reasoning holds for other aspects of public expenditure, like old-age pensions and expenditures on labour intensive health care. When higher productivity (per worker) and higher wages translate into higher public expenditure, the financial position of the public sector may not improve at all, even though total income is higher. The tax revenue grows, but public expenditure grows as well. So it is an empirical question whether allocating the pie is easier when the pie is larger.

To see whether productivity growth changes the balance between the private and the public sector, Figure 1.2. plots the relation between the share of public expenditure in production, and the growth rate of labour productivity. A negative relation may arise for two reasons. First, with higher productivity, growth wages (and other income) in the private sector outpace expenditure in the public sector. Second, a smaller public sector may imply a stronger incentive for the private sector to invest, innovate, and grow. The difference between the two reasons is the chain of causation. According to the first, higher productivity growth leads to a smaller government, whereas according to the second, it is exactly the other way around. Not only a negative relation may arise, but also a positive relation is possible. For instance, higher productivity growth may bring about a shift in demand in favour of public goods and services (Baumol's Law).

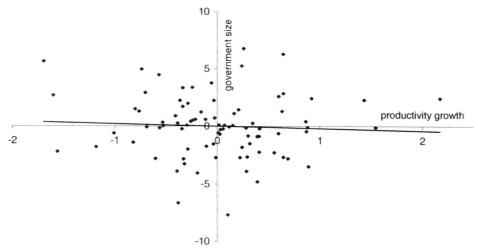

[a] Government size is measured by (log of) total public expenditure as percentage of gross domestic product. The five-year averages of all variables have been corrected to take account of country-specific and period-specific fixed effects. Data are from Ameco and cover an unbalanced sample of 19 OECD countries in 1978-2003 (with 5-year intervals).

Figure 1.2. Higher productivity growth is not associated with less public expenditure[a].

A clear relation does not emerge from the data (once country-specific and period-specific fixed effects are allowed for). An increase in the productivity growth rate is not associated with a relative decrease in government spending within the same five-year period. This emphasizes that productivity growth is an obvious way to keep the European welfare states in tact.

A more obvious way to lower the tax burden on workers than increasing productivity levels is raising participation rates. Figure 1.3. plots the relation between public expenditure as a percentage of gross domestic product and employment growth. A clear and negative relation emerges, implying that employment growth may indeed contribute to keeping the European welfare states sustainable. This should not come as a real surprise. When European governments are able to bring down unemployment and increase participation among, for example, older workers, they will see the tax revenue increase as well as expenditure on social security benefits go down. The relation between employment growth and social expenditures will not make political choices easier, however. To understand this, we turn to the question how to raise employment rates structurally.

To structurally reduce unemployment and permanently increase participation, labour market institutions need to be reformed. Shorter and lower unemployment benefits, less employment protection or combinations thereof are proposals in that direction. With reform comes the concern that more employment comes at the price of more inequality. The labour market institutions in Europe are intended to protect workers against the whims of the markets by providing them income or job security. Reforming these institutions may then lead to larger income differences. Indeed, empirical work by de Groot, Nahuis and Tang (2004) confirm a trade-off between participation and inequality. They find that lower and shorter unemployment benefits, a lower tax wedge and less coverage through collective wage is associated with higher participation but also leads to more income inequality. Interestingly, countries have partly escaped the trade-off through active labour market policies. Spending on things like training, matching and public jobs has had the impact of reducing inequality and raising employment. Similarly, de Mooij and Tang (2004) provide evidence that raising upper secondary education of the labour force has allowed countries to score well on both counts.

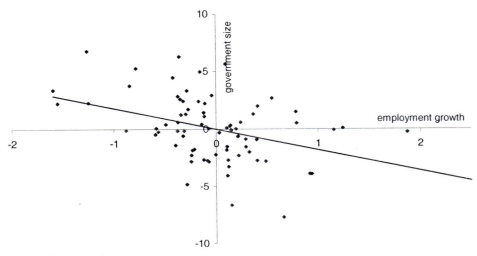

[a] See Figure 1.2. for an explanation.

Figure 1.3. Higher employment growth goes hand in hand with a smaller government[a].

The empirical work thus suggests that there is a trade-off between employment and equality. At same time, some countries may have the possibility to escape this trade-off by putting more emphasis on active labour market policies and/or on secondary education.

Does Higher Participation Lead to More Unemployment?

Some fear that boosting participation is useless as higher participation will simply lead to more unemployment. Behind this fear is the idea that total employment is fixed. This is rather popular and persistent fallacy. To some extent it may be true in the short run (due to hiring and firing costs and labour hoarding), but in the long run it is clearly wrong. First, unemployment rates fluctuate only temporarily, but are bounded in the long run. This implies that employment and labour supply grow hand in hand. In Europe both have grown by about 1.1% annually in the last two decades. Second, less participation of elderly workers has not led to less youth unemployment. The figure below shows instead that the opposite is true (where once again country-specific and period-specific fixed effects are taken into account). An increase in participation of relatively old workers is associated with a decrease, and not an increase, of unemployment among the relatively young workers. The negative relation indicates that non-participation of elderly workers and unemployment among young workers are driven by similar factors, most likely the labour market institution in interaction with macroeconomic shocks. Policies aimed at reducing youth unemployment by limiting elderly participation have at best been only temporarily successful.

The idea that total employment is fixed, does not find much support. If the Lisbon agenda has led in some countries to a break in economic policy, from discouraging to encouraging labour supply, that alone is an important success.

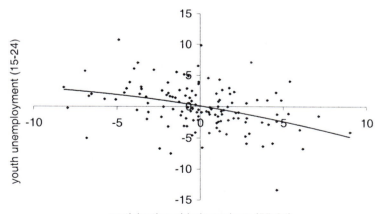

participation elderly workers (55-64)

[a] Both unemployment (among the young) and employment (among the old) are scaled with the labour force in the relevant age group. The five-year averages have been corrected for country-specific and period-specific fixed effects. The data are from the Labour Force Statistics of the OECD and covers an unbalanced sample of 28 OECD countries in 1968-2003 (with 5-year intervals).

Higher participation of the old is associated with lower unemployment among the young[a]

1.1.2. Economic Growth Versus the Environment

Economic growth may come at the expense of the environment. Higher production is usually associated with higher energy use, higher emissions of greenhouse gasses and more local pollution. Until 1980 this link between economic growth and pollution clearly applies, as Figure 1.4. shows for the emissions of sulphur dioxides (SO_2), nitrogen oxides (NO_x) and carbon dioxides (CO_2) in Europe.

This negative relation between the economy and the environment is not an invariable law. In fact, some environmental problems have become less when countries have grown richer, as Figure 1.4. illustrates for recent decades. The emissions of sulphur dioxides (SO_2) in the EU25 had reached a peak in the eighties, whereas the emissions of nitrogen oxides (NO_x) had attained a maximum level in the nineties. Thereafter the emissions of both have fallen even though the European economy has continued to grow.

This non-monotonic relation between the economy and the environment is known as the Kuznetz-curve. At the initial stages of development the economy has a clear priority over the environment. At those stages, reducing poverty is essential and economic growth is instrumental in achieving this, at the expense of the environment. At later stages social preferences shift from the economy to the environment. Once poverty is under control, the concern for the environment builds up and the wish for good living conditions becomes dominant. Still, economic growth leads to more pollution, but now societies make an effort to reduce emissions. These reductions in emissions do not come automatically, but are a deliberate choice. Policies that lead towards forms of sustainable economic growth, become eventually socially and politically feasible.

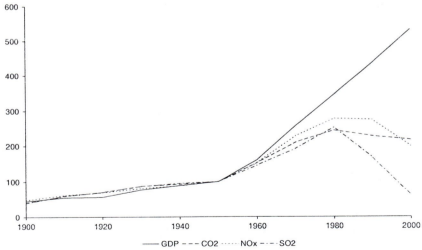

^a Source: RIVM (2004).

Figure 1.4. Emissions of CO_2, NO_x and SO_2 have not followed production in the EU25 (1950 = 100)[a].

Policies to decouple the economy and the environment are not always feasible. First, national decision makers do not take into account the international benefits from national environmental policies. This is the classical problem of collective action. Countries benefit directly from reducing local pollution like smog, stench and noise. Indeed, as indicated before, national and European policies have been effective in reducing emissions of local pollution, like sulphur dioxides and nitrogen oxides (SO_2 and NO_x respectively). However, the incentives for individual countries to reduce their emissions with global environmental externalities, like greenhouse gasses (CO_2) are much weaker. Figure 1.4 shows that the CO_2 emissions have not fallen as fast as the emission of SO_2 and NO_x, and are projected to increase in 2020. Second, competition among governments may stop them from effectively fighting even local problems. The difference between energy taxes on households and on firms is telling. The competition among government to attract firms with favourable conditions will only grow in the future. Both reasons imply that a reduction of emissions at higher stages of development is not an automatic process. In fact, rich countries do not always optfor a cleaner environment, while poorer countries do, which implies that the empirical evidence for the Kuznets-curve is not very strong (see for example de Bruyn, 2000).

Limited coordination is one threat to sustainable growth, the costs of environmental policy are another. Some claim that the costs of Kyoto are prohibitively high and are a drag on economic growth. This is exaggerated. CPB (2004a), for example, calculates for different scenarios the costs of stabilizing greenhouse gas emission (at 550 ppmv) for the EU15 under the assumption of international emission trade. In 2040, these costs range from 2.2% of national income in the scenario Strong Europe, to 6.2% in the scenario Global Economy. This boils down to foregoing one or two years economic growth. Clearly, these costs are not negligible but they are not prohibitive either. Others claim that eco-efficient innovations stimulate, rather than deter, future economic growth, by saving on inputs which will likely become scarcer and, therefore, more expensive. Of course, this would make the costs of the environmental policy negligible. The empirical support for this view is weak or even lacking.

The past experience suggests that discussing the trade-off between economy and environment is not appropriate. Different environmental problems have developed differently over time. Looking at the future, policies to break the link between the economy and the environment, i.e. to escape the trade-off between the two, are not self-evident. They will require more than before international and/or European coordination. Particularly the emissions of greenhouse gasses are likely to grow, although not at the rate of economic growth, unless effective action is taken. It is still an open question whether Kyoto provides a strong framework for international agreements and will lead to European action that effectively breaks the link between economic production and greenhouse gas emissions. It is also necessary that research and development be adequately directed towards the main economic problems in relation to the environment.

Conclusion

Barroso's claim that jobs and growth are essential for maintaining social cohesion and the environment, does not seem realistic. Economic growth will come at the expense of the environment unless policies are implemented to break the link between the two. These policies do not seem to thwart economic growth, but are not free either. The main problem is perhaps the organisation of these policies; particularly if these require international and/or European coordination.

Economic growth does not ensure that the European welfare states are sustainable in the future. Employment growth is required (and not productivity growth). This is possible but will necessitate reform in these welfare states. Employment growth as a result of these reforms is likely to come at the expense of higher income inequality. However, some countries may avoid this trade-off up to a point, for example by shifting from passive to activating social security.

2. GROWTH AND JOBS

Ever since the European leaders formulated the ambition of becoming the most competitive economy in the world, economic growth in Europe has faltered. This partly reflects a cyclical downturn. Some unexpected factors, like the stock market collapse and the sudden threat of terrorism, may have prolonged this downturn. Nevertheless, an upturn usually follows a cyclical downturn.

However, the poor growth rates in recent years partly reflect structural problems.[6] First, labour markets in many European economies are considered sclerotic. Symptomatic are high unemployment benefits, strong employment protection and powerful trade unions. Moreover, governments find it difficult to reform labour market institutions as they often require interventions in the social security system. Second, productivity growth is a concern: it had been high until the seventies, but has fallen since. Several explanations have been put forward. Some think that Europe invests too little in knowledge, in particular in R&D and education. Some think that Europe does not benefit enough from the new possibilities of ICT. Others think it is a combination of the two. Whatever the explanation, the slowdown in productivity growth will make the Lisbon ambition unfeasible, even in the long run.

There is a second reason why the ambition to become the most competitive economy has become more difficult to realise: the economic performance of United States has improved in the last ten years. With the problems of imperfect labour markets and poor productivity growth in mind, the credo of Barroso's European Commission 'growth and jobs' does not seem odd.

The next section compares the performance of several European economies over time and with the track record of the United States. Section 2.1 shows that the European employment rate in persons has grown faster than the American in the last 15 years. In section 2.2 we argue that future trends, rather than past performance, will require reforms of European labour markets. Section 2.3 will show that productivity in Europe is relatively high but that its rate of growth is falling over time since the 1970s. We argue that the European slowdown is not directly related to investment in knowledge. The slowdown is rather the logical outcome of European successes. The American acceleration, on the other hand, is driven by investment in ICT, especially in services.

2.1. Growing Number of Jobs but Falling Rates of Growth

Americans are richer than Europeans. Production per head of the population is roughly 30% higher on the other side of the Atlantic than it is in Europe. No wonder that economic performance of the United States is often put forward as an example for the European Union and its member states.

---

[6] Sapir et al. (2003) forcefully point at these structural problems.

Production as a measure for economic performance does not take into account whether it is the result of high productivity or much effort. Hard but not smart work implies long working hours and little leisure. Needless to say leisure is also important for the economic welfare of households and individuals, even though it is not reflected in the usual statistics of income and production.

To roughly distinguish between hard and smart work, Figure 2.1. decomposes production per capita into productivity per hour and total hours worked per capita. The variables for 8 European economies and the average for the European Union (of 15 members) are expressed as percentage difference with the United States and are ranked according to GDP per capita. In France, for example, GDP per capita is 28% behind the United States: the difference in hours per capita is 36%, which is partly compensated by a 12% higher production per hour.

An important observation from Figure 2.1. is that productivity per hour worked is *not* uniformly lower than in the United States. Workers in Ireland, the Netherlands, Germany and France produce more per hour than their American colleagues. Even the EU-15 average, including the relatively low-productive countries Greece, Portugal and Spain, is only moderately behind.

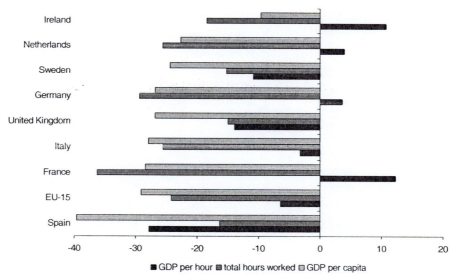

■ GDP per hour ▨ total hours worked ▱ GDP per capita

Source: GGDC (Total Economy Database, August 2004, http://www.ggdc.net) and own calculations for the EU-15.
[a] Decomposition of GDP per capita in 2003 by productivity (GDP per hour worked) and employment (hours worked per capita) in percentage deviation of the United States.

Figure 2.1. European productivity per hour is high but hours worked are low (percentage difference with USA)[a].

The income gap between the two economic blocs is largely explained by the difference in hours worked per capita: annual hours worked in European countries are relatively low, lagging 5% to 35% behind the United States. Within Europe, working hours are relatively high in countries with relatively low productivity levels (per hour), like Spain, Portugal and Greece. Shortest hours are observed in France, Germany and the Benelux. This suggests a negative relation between working hours and productivity per worker, even in the long run.

Are Western-European economies productive, for example because unproductive workers are excluded from the labour market? We turn to a possible trade-off in section 2.3.

New Member States

This study focuses on the 15 member states that have formed the European Union up to 2003. In contrast to the new member states, a fair comparison for these countries with the United States is possible for two reasons. First, both the EU-15 countries and the United States have known fairly similar conditions for several decades: they are market economies with good access to the world markets. New member states from Eastern Europe have been competitive at similar conditions only recently. Second, reliable statistics for productivity for a couple of decades are not available for the new member states.

To give a brief indication of the situation in the new member states, the figure below presents the level of GDP per capita, decomposed in employment (in hours) and productivity per hour in deviation of the European Union of 15 members.

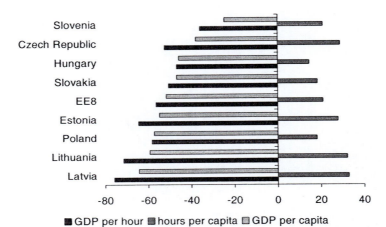

[a] In deviation of Figure 2.1., the percentage deviation of the EU-15 is shown. EE8 is the average of the 8 new member states from Eastern Europe.

Eastern Europeans work more but less efficient than in the EU-15[a]

The picture is clear: labour productivity per hour clearly lags behind the EU-15 average, and is fully responsible for the lag in income per capita. In terms of employment, however, workers in almost all of the 15 member states work on average less than their Eastern European colleagues.

Developments over the Period 1989-2003

Productivity per hour is high in many European countries. That productivity is below the US average in other European countries is not an immediate cause for concern. Typically, these countries like Greece and Portugal, have joined the European Union relatively late. As long as they catch up to the high-productive European countries, the European average will come close to or even exceed the American level of productivity in due course.

Figure 2.2. shows the growth rates within the European Union in the period 1989-2003, in deviation of the growth rate in the United States.[7] Again, GDP per capita is decomposed in productivity per hour and total hours worked per capita.

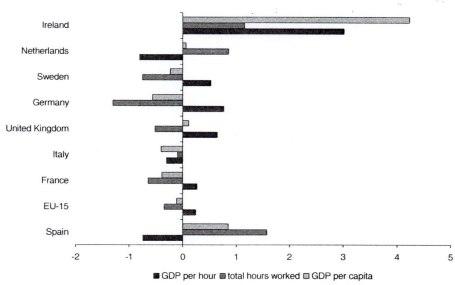

[a] Decomposition of the growth rate (%) of GDP per capita in deviation of the growth rate in the United States (1989-2003), see Figure 2.1 for data definition and source.

Figure 2.2. Over the last 14 years the growth difference between the EU and the USA is small[a].

For the European Union growth of GDP per capita was 1.7% annually and roughly kept pace with the United States. Whereas employment growth was relatively low in the period 1989-2003, productivity growth in the European Union was clearly higher than the United States.

The differences across European countries were, however, huge. Ireland performed remarkably well, especially in terms of productivity: the growth differential for GDP per hour was on average 3% during the 14 years, and was enough to close the initial productivity gap with the United States of 30%. However, the performance of Spain (and also Portugal and Greece) was disappointing: Spain was able to reduce the gap in GDP per capita, but not the difference in GDP per hour worked. These countries were not able to raise their productivity levels, even though they had the advantage of backwardness (i.e., improving productivity by adopting technologies from the most advanced economies).

In the period 1989-2003 the gap of EU-15 with the United States in production per capita grew, for which the difference in employment growth was responsible. Behind this lagging growth in hours worked per capita, two developments can be observed. First, European economies created more jobs than the United States, as shown by the bars for 'workers per capita' in Figure 2.3. Indeed, in the latter the fear of jobless growth emerged. In contrast, European countries like Ireland, the Netherlands and Spain, and to a lesser extent France and

---

[7] The GGDC (2004) data set is balanced for the period 1989-2003, including united Germany.

Italy, saw a remarkable growth in participation rates in the period 1989-2003.[8] Second, the working weeks of European workers declined, with Sweden as the single exception. Working weeks became on average shorter and the number of part-time jobs grew. Europeans opt for a different combination of work and leisure than Americans. CPB/SCP (2005) study this difference in detail and explore the underlying reasons.

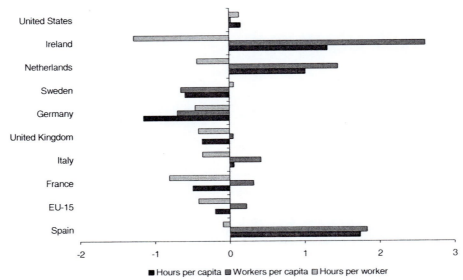

[a] Source: GGDC (2004) and own calculations for the European Union. Population is restricted to the working-age.

Figure 2.3. In Europe, more workers that work fewer hours (annual growth in 1989-2003)[a].

The Break in the Mid Nineties

The discussion thus far does not provide much reason to be gloomy about the productivity performance of the European economy or to praise the American dynamics. In many European countries productivity is higher than or close to the American level, and for the European Union it has grown on average somewhat faster than in the United States. Yes, the United States could be said to outperform the European Union in terms of employment, considering both the levels and the growth rates of total working hours. Whether or not this is a problem for Europe is not immediately clear. First, it might be a matter of choice: Europeans use their prosperity to enjoy more leisure. Second, it might be a matter of division of labour, and therefore a measurement issue: Americans hire a cleaning lady, whereas Europeans clean their houses themselves: the first activity is measured in the employment statistics, unlike the second.[9]

One has to focus on the period after 1995 to understand the gloom about the European economy and the optimism about the American ability to innovate: after 1995 productivity growth has accelerated in the United States, whereas growth is slowing down further in the European Union. Figure 2.4. visualises this by showing the growth acceleration or

---

[8] The Lisbon agenda pays special attention to the participation of women and elderly. Readers interested in the European scores should consult CPB/SCP (2003).

[9] CPB/SCP (2005) looks further into the divisions of time between work, household production and leisure.

deceleration of GDP per capita . Note that it is different from the previous figures: it does not directly compare the performance in the European Union and the United States but rather cuts the period, 1989-2003, in two and compares the later period, 1997-2003, with the earlier period, 1989-1996.

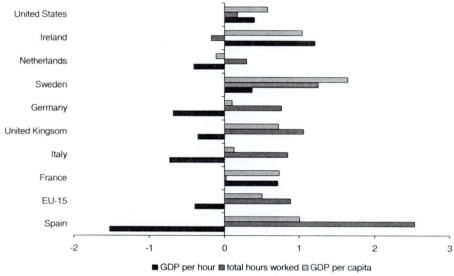

[a] Decomposition of the acceleration of GDP-per-capita growth between 1989-1996 and 1997-2003, see Figure 2.1.

Figure 2.4. Productivity growth slows down in Europe, but accelerates in the United States[a].

Both economic powers saw the growth rate of GDP per capita increase. The United States hardly accelerated more than the European Union of 15 countries, but the sources of growth differed remarkably. In Europe, faster growth in total hours worked, especially in the number of workers (per capita), compensated for the slowdown in productivity growth. In the United States, both sources were responsible for the acceleration. In other words, after 1995 the main difference between the two economic blocs was the *change* in productivity growth.

The acceleration in US productivity growth and the slowdown in EU productivity growth are widely documented in the growth-accounting literature[10], though the particular numbers vary from study to study, depending on the country sample (Euro area versus European Union), the time span and the data source. Our measure for the slowdown, a decline from 1.5% to 1.1%, is at the lower bound of what can be found in the literature. Much more dramatic are the figures of Fiani (2004), who observes a slowdown in the growth of hourly productivity for the Euro area of 1.6 percentage points (1991-1996 versus 1997-2001).

A Structural Decline in Productivity Growth Since the Seventies

Productivity growth in Europe has not slowed down all of a sudden, but rather shows a structural decline, see Figure 2.5. In the seventies, the European countries clearly outperformed the United States in terms of productivity growth. Even in the eighties, US commentators (see Baumol et al., 1989, Dollar and Wolff, 1993, and Nordhaus, 2004) were very concerned about the poor productivity growth in their country. Indeed, with the exception of France and the Netherlands, the average European rate of productivity growth was still higher than the American rate at that time. The lead of Europe gradually declined, however. In recent years, productivity growth in Europe was what it used to be in the United States in the seventies and eighties.

For the United States, Figure 2.5. shows that the acceleration of productivity growth since 1995 occurred after a long period of stable growth. Until about 1995 growth in productivity per hour was on average 1.3% annually, but then it speeded up. The growth rate accelerated from 1.5% in 1995-1999, to 1.8% in 2000-2003. In the last period the growth rate in the United States was about a half percentage point higher than in the European Union of 15 countries.

From Figure 2.5. the concerns about the European performance become clear. The difference in productivity growth between the United States and the European Union is perhaps not large, but the direction of change is worrisome. In the 'old world' the rate of productivity growth goes downhill, whereas in the 'new world' the pace has picked up. Of course, this does not bode well for the Lisbon ambition. Would the change be structural and extend in the next decades, the United States soon becomes – again – the unchallenged productivity leader in the world.

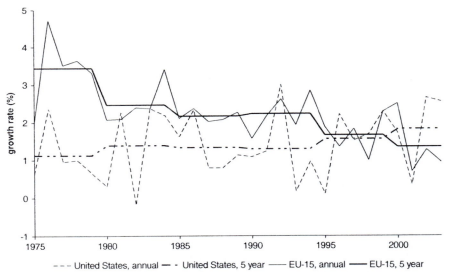

--- United States, annual — · United States, 5 year —— EU-15, annual —— EU-15, 5 year

[a] Growth rate of productivity per hour 1975-2003, both annual and their 5-year averages, running from 1975-1979, 1980-1985 etc; the final period 2000-2003 covers only 4 years. Source: GGDC (2004).

Figure 2.5. The productivity slowdown in Europe (EU-15) is structural[a].

Conclusion

In the period 1989-2003 the European Union was able to raise employment. Indeed, in 2003 quite a few countries score equally well or better than the United States on participation in persons. (Since a few large member states have a relatively poor employment record, making the Lisbon target for participation difficult to meet in the near future.) Whereas the

---

[10] See Daveri (2004), Denis et al. (2004), Gordon (2004) and O'Mahony and Van Ark (2003).

European economies have not been bad in creating jobs in the past period, we will argue in the section 2.2 that in the near future even more jobs are needed: participation has to increase to relieve the growing pressure on the European welfare states.

Looking back, the main problem with the economic performance of the European Union has not been 'jobs' but 'growth'. European productivity growth is slowing down. At the same time, the American rate of productivity growth has jumped, i.e. has increased after a period of stable and relatively low growth. In section 2.3 we will go deeper into the reasons behind the European slowdown and America's acceleration.

2.2. Future Trends and Employment Growth

In the past years the European Union (of 15 members) has seen its employment in persons grow faster than its population. Employment in hours has grown less rapidly: hours worked per worker have continued to fall. Europeans spend thus relatively much time on leisure and household activities. The employment growth in the past is not an immediate reason to worry. Rather, the future gives rise to concern. There are several trends that threaten the financial sustainability of the public sector in European economies. In other words, they put the public sector under pressure. Employment growth is essential for relieving this pressure (see section 1.1).

Pressure on the Welfare States

Structural trends put pressure on the public sectors in Europe, leading to similar problems in different European countries. According to De Mooij and Tang (2003), these trends together will in particular make the European welfare states in their current forms unsustainable, forcing national government to choose for change. In particular four trends are relevant:

- *Ageing populations* raise public expenditures on old-age pensions and health care. Besides, relatively slow productivity growth and high income elasticities will lead to extra demand for publicly provided services (i.e. Baumol's Law).
- The position of high-skilled workers on labour markets is steadily improving relative to *low-skilled workers*. That the income differences between the two groups have not grown (fast) in the recent past, is a result of the fast increase in supply of high-skilled workers. When the increase levels off, as is expected during the coming decades, the income differences may start to grow. Higher benefit levels prop up wages of the low skilled, but also lead to more unemployment among them.
- Society has become more heterogeneous. Individualisation as well as immigration has contributed to that. More *heterogeneity* makes economic policy less effective. Some specific transfers, for example, not only benefit those who need support, but are also provided to those with high incomes. Heterogeneity also raises the demand for diversity, which the public sector often fails to deliver.
- The choice set of individuals has expanded, which has increased the response to income taxes and income transfers and has amplified the distortionary consequences of taxation. Adding to this is the increasing mobility of capital and firms. With

further integration of capital and good markets, this mobility will only increase. This also increases the *costs of taxation*.

International Integration and the Welfare State

Is globalization not one of the important threat to the European welfare state? As a result of integration, firms can escape the relatively high tax burden in Western European countries by relocating their activities to countries with relatively low taxes. These countries can no longer afford extensive and thus expensive social security systems. International integration and the welfare state do not seem to mix.

The logic is flawless but the analysis is not. Firstly, it assumes that firms are extremely mobile, whereas in fact they are not. Proximity to consumers and suppliers is an important aspect of location (see Brakman et al., 2005). Indeed, the rich European countries offer good access to a large output market and specialised input markets, making firms reluctant to leave. Second, the analysis is incomplete. When firms tend to relocate their activities, employment tends to fall as well. To restore equilibrium on the labour market, wages must fall (or grow for some time at a lower pace). In equilibrium the relatively high taxes, partly in the form of social security contributions, are compensated by relatively low wages. This situation confirms a general rule in the economic literature on taxation saying that the immobile factor bears the burden of taxes in the end, although formally the mobile factor, i.e. the firm, may pay them. The implication of this rule is that European and international integration shifts the burden of taxation, from the (more) mobile factor to the immobile factor. European countries can afford extensive social security systems as along as they can afford a higher tax burden on labour. Summing up, since firms are not fully mobile and lower wages may compensate higher taxes, the impact of integration on social spending may not be as negative as a simple partial analysis seems to suggest.

Rodrik (1998) argues that the impact of international economic integration on social spending could even be positive. As a result of integration, economies become more vulnerable to external shocks. This raises the demand for (public) insurance. Governments may respond to this demand and extend, rather than downsize, the social security systems. A first look at the data seems to corroborate Rodrik's view. Figure 2.6 plots openness, defined as the average of exports and imports as a ratio of gross domestic product, against two measures of public spending, namely the share of transfers in public expenditure and the GDP-share of total public expenditures. The figure suggests that openness is associated with more transfers (as a percentage of total public expenditure) and that openness leads to more public spending (as a percentage of total production). A better look at the data learns that just a few observations give rise to a positive relation and that for the bulk of the observations a clear relation does not seem to emerge. Clear is, however, that integration does not necessarily lead to downsizing of the European welfare states.

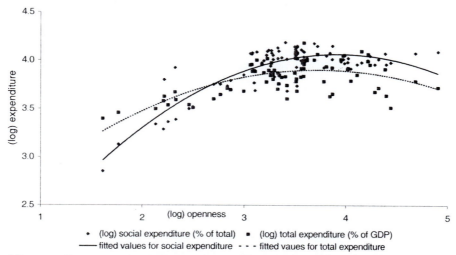

^a Social public expenditure concerns transfers both in money terms and in kind, and is expressed as a percentage of total public expenditure. The government size is measured by total public expenditure as a percentage of gross domestic product. Five-year averages are shown. The data are taken from Ameco.

Figure 2.6. Open economies do not show lower income transfers or a smaller government^a.

Conclusion

Four trends – ageing, changing skill composition, increased heterogeneity, rising costs of taxation – put pressure on the welfare state: public expenditures increase, become less effective and more costly to finance. One way to bring down public expenditure and to relieve the pressure, is to increase the employment rate. Jobs should therefore be high on the policy agenda in the different European countries. Of course, more jobs may require changes in the current welfare state arrangements.

2.3. Determinants of Productivity Growth in the Past

2.3.1. Europe's Slowdown: Victim of its Own Success

By trying to invigorate the European economy, the Lisbon strategy is meant to fight pessimism about the economy. The gloom about Europe's performance is wide-spread. One reason is the trend of falling productivity growth rates. In the late nineties European economies have shown, according to several sources, a significant decline in the productivity growth rate. This continues a trend that has started after the first oil crisis. The trend suggests that Europe will see its relative position in the economic league of nations deteriorate, especially since a country like China sees its income double in every 10 years and the American economy has surprised observers by showing an acceleration in productivity growth rates.

This section challenges pessimism not by promising a glorious future but rather pointing to a glorious past. The slowdown, we will argue, is partly the inevitable consequence of Europe's success. First, high employment growth – one of the objectives within the Lisbon strategy – is partly responsible for disappointing productivity growth in the late nineties. Second, many European countries have caught up with the United States and have exhausted their potential to grow by imitating state-of-the-art technologies. The logical implication is that their rate of productivity growth has fallen. Furthermore, structural reasons for the slowdown do not seem strong. Yes, nowadays the European Union invests relatively less in R&D and spends relatively less on education than the United States, but this was also true ten, twenty or thirty years ago. Moreover, the European Union has not seen its expenditure on R&D and on education, as share of GDP, fall. Only in interaction with catching up might R&D and education play a role: the low expenditure levels might contribute less to productivity growth when countries approach the productivity frontier. Even in this case is Europe's slowdown the mirror image of its own success: high employment growth in recent years and catching up in recent decades.

In the Short Run Employment Growth Hurts Productivity Growth

In many European countries productivity growth in the second half of the nineties was significantly lower than in the first half. At the same time, the growth of employment (in persons) recovered markedly from −0.35% in the first half to 0.65% in the second half. In the United States the concern was exactly the opposite: the country showed a remarkable increase in productivity growth but was not able to create jobs. There was fear for jobless growth.

The different country experiences suggest a trade-off between employment growth and productivity growth, at least in the short run. One explanation is that irrespective of the economic conditions high-productive workers are employed and that depending on these conditions the low-productive workers are invited to enter or forced to leave the labour market. With fast(er) employment growth, like in the second half of the nineties, the low productive workers enter, reducing the average productivity of workers. This effect of productivity through the composition of the labour force has been studied for the Netherlands, with the spectacular employment growth in the nineties. The effect exists, but is quantitatively small (CPB, 2004b). Another, more relevant explanation for the short-run trade-off is the delayed response of capital growth to a change in employment growth, such that the available stock of capital per worker falls when employment expands. As a result, labour productivity slows down as production becomes less capital intensive. Below we clarify in two steps why this explanation is relevant for the nineties.

The first step relates the change in labour productivity growth (from the first to the second half of the nineties) to the change in capital deepening. Capital deepening contributes to labour productivity growth. The more capital goods are available for a worker, the higher the productivity of this worker. Figure 2.7. shows for several countries the change in labour productivity growth and the contribution of capital deepening to that growth. The difference between the two is usually referred to as total factor productivity.

Countries in continental Europe saw the growth rate of labour productivity fall. At the same time these countries saw (the growth of) the capital-labour ratio decline. In France and Spain a lower contribution of capital explained the growth slowdown completely, in Germany and Italy for a significant part.

The second step relates fluctuations in capital deepening to fluctuations in employment growth. Figure 2.8. shows the four-year averages of the growth in total working hours (left panel) and in the capital-labour ratio (right panel)[11]. A quick look already reveals that capital-deepening is weak in periods of high employment growth (like in 1988-1991 and 1996-2003).

This apparent relationship is confirmed by a panel regression for 16 OECD countries in the period 1970-2003, where we regressed the pace of capital deepening on the growth of employment (measured as total hours worked). The dotted line in Figure 2.8. reveals that the explanatory power of this regression is very high: a very large part of fluctuations in capital deepening is induced by fluctuations in employment growth. This implies that the slowdown in productivity growth, insofar it stems from a slower pace in capital deepening, is temporary. It is the flip side of a strong increase in employment growth. Would employment growth in the near future, say in 2004-2011, return to its average over 1970-2000, capital deepening is expected to recover. This is indicated by the dotted lines in both panels for 2004-2011.

Capital deepening is, however, only part of productivity growth. For the other part – growth of total factor productivity (TFP) – a similar story does not hold: TFP growth hardly slowed down in the late nineties – the period of accelerating employment growth – but all the more in the early years of the 21st century. Indeed, a panel regression confirms that TFP growth and employment growth are hardly related, not even in the short run. TFP growth has its own dynamics, hardly related to fluctuations in employment growth.

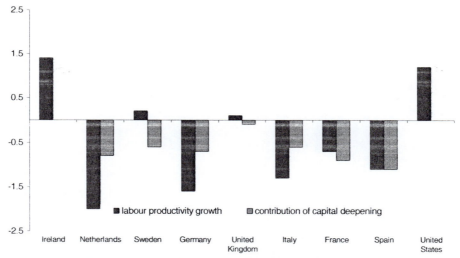

[a] The figure shows the difference between the period 1996-2000 and the period 1989-1995. For Ireland and the United States, the change in the contribution of capital deepening is negligible. Source: Economic Outlook (2004).

Figure 2.7. A falling capital-labour ratio largely explains the slowdown in the late nineties[a].

---

[11] Figure 2.7 shows the composite of 9 European economies: Belgium, Denmark, Spain, France, Germany, Italy, Netherlands, Sweden and the UK. The panel of 16 OECD countries includes in addition Australia, Canada, Finland, Japan, Norway, New Zealand and the US. Data source: Economic Outlook (2004).

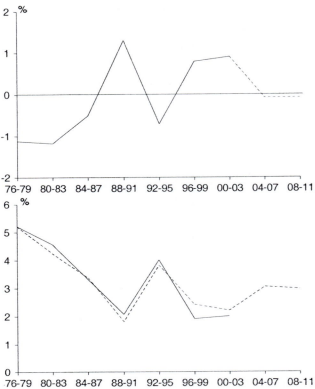

[a] The left panel shows the growth (4 year average) of total hours worked including a projection for 2011; the right panel shows capital deepening (4 year average, straight line) , the fit from a panel regression and a forecast based on the same regression and the projection for employment.

Figure 2.8. Growth of total hours worked and the capital-labour ratio in Europe.

The trade-off between employment and productivity growth (or capital deepening) applies to the short run but most likely not to the long run. Barro and Sala-i-Martin (1995) show for many OECD economies that, unlike population growth, the growth rates of real GDP per capita do not have a secular tendency to decline.[12]. From a different angle, countries like France and the United Kingdom experienced similar productivity growth of nearly 2%, despite their diverging population growth (0.3% in France and 1.5% in the United Kingdom). Van Ark et al. (2004) show that over the past two centuries productivity and employment growth are positively related, though a trade-off clearly exists for one or two decades. Finally, EC (2004) uses a (SVAR) model for the European Union in which an employment shock has a negative but small impact on the level of labour productivity, but not on its long-run growth rate.

Summarizing, high employment growth has contributed to the slowdown in productivity growth via a temporary reduction in capital intensity. It is unlikely, however, that a trade-off persists in the long run.

---

[12] Theoretical models are often silent about the relation between productivity and population growth. The latter has a positive, and not a negative, effect on economic growth in some models. In these models more researchers generate more knowledge, which is non-rival and contributes to the productivity of *each* worker (Jones, 2004).

Europe's Potential for Catching-up Is Exhausted

The high productivity growth rate in Europe after the Second World War derived partly from the possibility to learn from the leader in productivity, i.e. United States. By copying and adapting state-of-the-art technologies most of the European countries could augment productivity at a rather rapid pace. At the same time the possibility to learn from the United States diminished. This may explain the structural slowdown in productivity growth, at least for some countries.

France and Spain are illustrative of how European countries have caught up with the United States. Figure 2.9. shows the decomposition of GDP per capita – in deviation of the United States – into GDP per hour and hours per inhabitant. The figure shows that in the early seventies France and Spain needed to increase GDP per capita with 30% and 70% to draw level with the United States. In terms of GDP per hour France succeeded and Spain came halfway, but both lost ground in terms of hours per capita.

France is illustrative of several advanced countries in Europe, like Germany, Italy, the Netherlands, Belgium, Denmark and Austria. Until the eighties or nineties, these countries enjoyed high growth rates, catching up to the United States. This potential for catching up has been exhausted, as their GDP per hour has come at par with the productivity leader. They still lag behind in terms of GDP per capita. This does not reflect a gap in ability, but stems from a different choice between labour and leisure, see section 2.1.

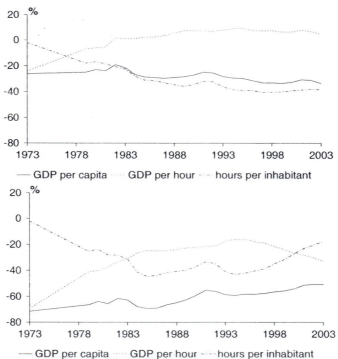

[a] Source: computations by De Groot et al. (2004) based on the GGDC (2004) dataset.

Figure 2.9. Catching up in France (left) and Spain (right): difference with the United States[a].

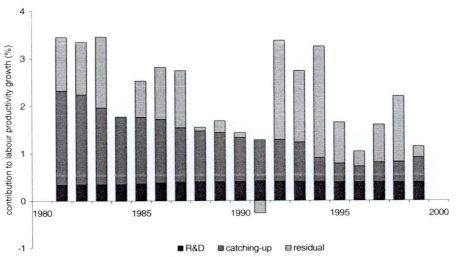

[a] Contribution of R&D and catching up to labour productivity growth in 7 European countries, see footnote 11.

Figure 2.10. Catching-up is behind the productivity slowdown[a].

Spain is illustrative of a few lagging economies, like Greece and Portugal, with substantially larger productivity gaps.[13] Convergence in GDP per hour has been substantial until the seventies (Greece and Portugal) or eighties (Spain), but has stopped in the nineties. In Spain, it has turned into divergence since 1995. At the moment none of these countries converges to the United States, despite their productivity gap of 30% to 60%.

Intermediate positions are taken by the United Kingdom, Sweden and Finland, still lagging 10% to 20% behind. Remarkable outliers are Ireland and Luxembourg. Due to its specialization in financial services, Luxembourg has a sky-high productivity level. Ireland has shown an extraordinary growth spurt. It has become at par with the United States, both in GDP per hour and per capita, despite the gap of 80% in 1970.

Productivity in level mainly West-European countries has come close to that in the United States. These countries operate at the technology frontieR&Do no longer have the 'advantage of backwardness'. Can gradually losing this potential of learning explain (part of) the European slowdown in productivity?

To answer this, we have run a panel regression in which labour productivity growth is 'explained' by R&D expenditure and by the productivity gap with the United States.[14] The

---

[13] Carvalho and Harvey (2004) apply a multivariate time series model and observe two possible convergence clubs in the Euro zone. The first club including France is at par with the US. The second club including Spain will remain almost 30% below the high group in terms of per capita income.

[14] A panel regression forms the basis for the decomposition of productivity growth into the impact of R&D and catching up, for 7 EU countries (Denmark, Finland, France, Italy, Netherlands, Sweden and UK).The panel includes 12 OECD countries and 12 industries in 1981-1999. We regress the growth rate of value-added per hour in country i and industry j ($YH_{i,j}$) on the productivity gap with the United States (per sector), the growth rate in the United States (per sector) and the share of R&D expenditures (R/Y) and include a full set of industry and country dummies. The resulting equation is:

$$g\left(YH_{i,j}\right) = 0.15g\left(YH_{US,j}\right) + 0.07\left(YH_{US,j} - YH_{i,j}\right) + 0.31\left(R_{i,j}/Y_{i,j}\right) \qquad R^2 = 0.15$$

Following Griffith et al. (2000), we also included a cross-term (productivity-gap * R&D-share) measuring the decreasing return to R&D in sectors close to the productivity frontier, but this cross-term is insignificant.

effect of the gap measures the advantage of backwardness. In Figure 2.10 the regression result is illustrated for an average of 7 EU member states. Labour productivity growth is attributed to R&D expenditure and to catching-up. The growth rate falls on average over years. Similarly, the catch-up effect becomes smaller over time, as the gap with the United States grows smaller. The effect is one and a half percentage point at the beginning of the sample period and only a half percentage point at the end. Catching-up is behind the structural slowdown in productivity.[15]

2.3.2. America's Success: Using ICT

The usual measures like access to internet or access through a broadband connection show that ICT has much more infiltrated economic life in the United States than it has in the European Union. Moreover, the technological breakthrough seems to have benefited especially American companies like Microsoft, Cisco and Dell a great deal. Indeed, ICT is behind America's success after 1995, and is often regarded a recipe for Europe's ailing productivity growth. But, how important is the contribution of ICT to economic growth on either side of the Atlantic? First, ICT is more important in the United States than in the European Union, simply because the share of ICT capital is much higher (5.2% of GDP in the United States versus 3.3% of GDP in 4 EU countries).[16]

Table 2.1. Growth Accounting Decomposition of Labour Productivity Growth[a]

	EU-4		United States	
	1979-1995	1995-2000	1979-1995	1995-2000
Labour-productivity growth	2.30	2.02	1.21	2.46
ICT producing sectors	0.44	0.65	0.51	0.89
ICT using sectors	0.62	0.59	0.36	1.43
Non-ICT sectors	1.21	0.83	0.48	0.23
Non-ICT capital	0.70	0.25	0.35	0.43
ICT producing sectors	0.08	0.03	0.05	0.06
ICT using sectors	0.18	− 0.03	0.12	0.10
Non-ICT sectors	0.44	0.25	0.17	0.26
ICT capital	0.33	0.53	0.46	0.86
ICT producing sectors	0.04	0.07	0.06	0.11
ICT using sectors	0.21	0.35	0.28	0.57
Non-ICT sectors	0.08	0.11	0.11	0.18
TFP growth	0.94	1.07	0.26	1.05
ICT producing sectors	0.30	0.53	0.35	0.71
ICT using sectors	0.17	0.19	− 0.15	0.68
Non-ICT sectors	0.48	0.35	0.06	− 0.34

[a] EU-4: France, Germany, the Netherlands and United Kingdom.
Source: Inklaar, O'Mahony and Timmer (2003).

---

[15] Figure 2.9. also shows that R&D contributes to productivity growth, but not to its slowdown, see section 2.2.3.
[16] The ICT-decomposition of productivity growth is made by Inklaar et al. (2003) for four European countries (Germany, France, UK and Netherlands) and the US.

The share reflects investment in ICT goods in past and present. It has increased in the recent decades in Europe but much faster in the United States. The growth of ICT capital has contributed positively to the acceleration of productivity growth in both regions. This is shown by the contribution of ICT capital in Table 2.1.

Second, two elements in the contribution of ICT to economic growth can be distinguished, stemming from the production of ICT or from its use in other sectors. Table 2.1 shows that the ICT producing sectors of the economy (like electronic equipment and communications) have contributed to higher productivity growth in both the 4 European countries and the United States. Although productivity growth rates of more 10% are no exception, direct impact of these sectors on aggregate productivity growth is limited, given their relative size: 0.2 percentage points in the European countries and 0.4 percentage points in the United States. This does not exclude, however, the possibility of spillovers to other sectors. The acceleration of productivity growth in the United States is concentrated in ICT using industries (like wholesale trade, retail trade and financial intermediation): TFP-growth in these service-sectors has been up to 5% in 1995-2000, about 3%-points higher than in the decades before (1979-1995). This contrasts sharply with the European experience in these sectors showing a modest TFP-growth of 1% both before and after 1995.

Does this evidence lead to the conclusion that ICT fully explains, not only the acceleration of productivity growth in the United States, but even the whole gap between the America's upswing and the European slowdown (Van Ark et al. 2003)? This conclusion is not clear-cut, however. Several qualifications are in order. First, ICT related sectors in the United States are not uniformly outperforming their EU counterparts. Figure 2.11. shows the growth differential for selected ICT related sectors in the period 1995-2001.

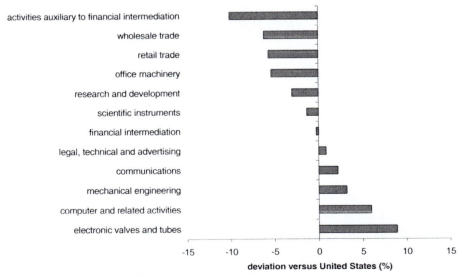

[a] Source: O'Mahony and Van Ark (2003).

Figure 2.11. Growth differential of labour productivity for ICT-sectors between the EU-15 and the United States (1995-2001)[a].

It clearly shows that labour productivity in some sectors has grown much faster in European Union than in the United States, especially in services like communication and computer services. However, three large sectors – wholesale trade, retail trade and (part of) financial intermediation – have grown relatively fast in the United States. These three sectors are able to account for almost all of the productivity growth difference between the two economic blocs. The question arises, which is the second qualification, how much of the growth spurt in these sectors is related to the introduction of ICT. Gordon (2004) points at the spatial component of productivity growth in the retail sector. The retail sector in the United States has grown fast by using ICT intensively *and* by concentrating retail in the sparse suburbs of large cities. Daveri (2004) points at the limited use of ICT in retail trade. He shows that the share of ICT capital in this sector is smaller than in the total economy. Leaving this sector out of the set of ICT using sectors, he shows that ICT use explains only 55% instead of 90% of the US acceleration, and 40% instead of 60% of the productivity gap between the United States and the European Union.

Why has the United States benefited more from ICT than the European Union?

We distinguish between two aspects of ICT-related productivity growth, namely ICT investment and TFP growth in ICT-intensive industries. In this box, we survey some of the arguments, but are unable to give a conclusive answer.

ICT-investments are and have been higher in the United States than elsewhere. Inklaar et al. (2003) investigate whether this reflects a relative cost advantage, but the evidence is hardly supportive. It is also unlikely to be a matter of insufficient access to new technologies in the European Union, as the market for ICT goods and software is essentially global (Van Ark et al., 2003). An alternative explanation starts with the observation that ICT investments are relatively risky. Bartelsman and Hinloopen (2004) argue that the share of firms investigating in a risky technology increases as competitive pressure becomes more intense and as firms are able to flexibly adjust complementary production factors like labour. In a panel for 13 OECD countries, they show that employment protection legislation (EPL) in particular, but also various measures of product market regulations, significantly reduce the share of ICT investment in total investment. Van Ark et al. (2003) also point to structural impediments in product and labour markets hampering the ICT adoption in Europe. They quote recent research for U.S. retail trade, which has shown that entry of high-productive firms and exit of low-productive firms is responsible for almost all of labour productivity growth in this sector.

TFP-growth in ICT-using industries has been relatively high in the United States since 1995. The success-story of retail trade in the United States suggests that conditions like the scale and geography of the economy might determine the return to ICT adoption. Alternatively, Jovanovic and Rousseau (2005) argue that the adoption of a general-purpose technology like ICT in recent years or electronics in the late 19th century requires a lengthy learning process, resulting in temporary lower productivity growth preceding the boom. The United States has gone through this learning process in the eighties and early nineties; many European countries are still in it. An important aspect of this learning process is the implementation of ICT through experimentation and innovation. Pilat (2004,p52) argues that "without this process of "co-invention", which often has a slower pace than technological invention, the economic impact of ICT may be limited". Van Ark et al. (2001) concludes that "(..) one must be careful not to embrace a simple story that is based only on excessive European regulation. The more rapid take-off of wireless technology in Europe suggests that some regulation, for example, setting standards can be productivity enhancing as well."

Within Europe, the differences in impact of ICT across member states are huge and depend highly on the sources of growth (capital deepening or total factor productivity growth) and types of industries (ICT producers versus ICT users). The share of ICT capital in Sweden and Finland comes close to the American rate of 6% of GDP, about twice as high as in Germany and Spain (Timmer et al. 2003). A different pattern, and again wide variation, can be observed in productivity growth of ICT producing industries: it has accelerated strongly in Germany and Finland, but slowed down in Sweden. This contrasts with productivity growth in ICT using industries, showing an acceleration in Sweden, but a downturn in Italy (Daveri, 2004).

The differences across countries, including European success stories, and the high growth rates of many ICT sectors in Europe, make one point clear: Europe has not missed the ICT train completely (cf. Gordon, 2004). Some countries and several sectors have been able to produce or adopt ICT successfully. Why shouldn't other sectors and other countries be able to copy this? In other words, ICT is a potential source for Europe to raise its productivity growth. It has been unable to overcome the productivity slowdown in the past, but might be an opportunity for acceleration in the future.

2.3.3. Growth to Come: Investment in Knowledge and Technology

The poor productivity growth is often seen as evidence that the European Union and its member states lack the ability to innovate. Lacking, the reasoning goes further, is investment in knowledge. Europe spends less on R&D than the United States. Europe spends less on (tertiary) education than the United States. Investment in knowledge is the key to come up with new ideas and to find ways to implement these ideas; it is the key to innovation.

We agree that investment in knowledge, via education and R&D, is beneficial for economic growth. We do not dismiss the thesis that more investment in knowledge will boost European productivity growth, as Barroso, Kok and Sapir put forward. This does not imply, however, that lack of investments explains the productivity slowdown in Europe. Neither investments in R&D nor in education have declined. As such, they did not contribute to the productivity slowdown. It might be, however, that the current shares of R&D and education have been sufficient in the past for the adoption of technology, but inadequate for future innovations.

Research and Development

R&D is important for discovering new products and production methods. In their brief survey of the literature Jones and Williams (1998) conclude that the social return to R&D is likely to exceed 25%. Given that a normal rate of return on investment is often set equal to 10%, this is high. Positive externalities explain that the return on R&D is higher than normal: investment by one firm increases not only productivity of that firm but also of other firms, within or outside the same sector and within or outside the same country. The large difference in return prompts Jones and Williams to conclude that the United States should spend more on R&D. In fact, much more: they claim that the United States should quadruple its expenditure. From this perspective the Lisbon target that the European Union should increase R&D expenditure from roughly 2% to 3%, does not even seem ambitious.

R&D contributes to growth, but is it also part of the story behind the productivity slowdown in Europe, or the acceleration in the United States? To start with the latter, Figure 2.12. shows that the United States has slightly raised, but no more than slightly, their R&D

expenditures. For any reasonable estimate of the return on R&D, this increase has only marginally contributed to the productivity acceleration in the United States. Moreover, a large role for R&D is in conflict with the observation that the R&D-intensity is quite low in successful ICT using service sectors, like wholesale and retail trade.

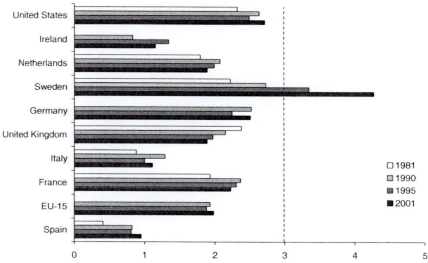

[a] Source Eurostat.

Figure 2.12. R&D expenditures (% of gross domestic product)[a].

With the exception of Sweden and Finland, in European economies expenditures on R&D have been stable. In Sweden and Finland, higher R&D investments are likely to have contributed to an acceleration of productivity growth; in other countries, however, a change in R&D has not occurred, and cannot therefore explain the change in productivity growth. The total contribution to productivity growth depends not only on R&D expenditures but also on the return on these expenditures. This return may have declined since European economies have shifted towards the technology frontier. R&D to absorb state-of-the-art technologies becomes less important when fewer technologies are left to absorb. But this line of reasoning is not essentially different from that in the previous section, where we argued that potential for catching up is exhausted and that this is a structural reason for the productivity slowdown.

Where do these differences in R&D expenditures stem from? Bottazzi (2004) shows that country-level variations in R&D expenditures cannot be explained by differences in sector compositions. Low R&D expenditures at the national level reflect low expenditures within each sector. Unfortunately, little is known about the determinants of R&D expenditures within countries, sectors or firms. Several explanations are put forth in the literature to explain variations in these R&D expenditures. First, a recent paper by Bloom et al. (2002) shows that the user costs of R&D are a significant determinant of R&D expenditures, and likely explain part of the cross-country variation. They show that countries with low tax burdens on R&D, i.e. with low corporate taxes and substantial R&D tax credits, tend to have higher R&D shares. Second, not only costs, but also revenues are a likely determinant of R&D expenditures. These returns are likely to be higher for countries able to learn from the productivity leader. In other words, catching-up reduces the return to R&D (Acemoglu et al.

2004). Third, both private firms and governments invest in R&D. It could be that public R&D stimulates firms to raise their private expenditures by reducing marginal costs. Alternatively, it is also possible that public R&D makes private expenditures redundant, as new technologies are invented anyway. Unfortunately, the empirical literature does not give a clear answer whether public R&D raises or reduces private expenditures, as Garcia-Quevedo (2004) concludes from an extensive meta-analysis[17]. Finally, differences in regulations or in the scale of the economy might affect the R&D intensity, but again it is yet unsettled how. It is even unclear whether univocal conclusions will ever be reached, as different types of R&D in different sectors have to deal with specific sources of market failures (Martin and Scott, 2000).

Looking backward, R&D cannot explain the productivity slowdown in Europe: if anything R&D expenditures have increased. Looking forward, the empirical literature supports the idea that a higher R&D intensity raises productivity growth, but is less conclusive about how expenditures can be raised.

Education

An educated population is a prerequisite for high income per worker. This statement undoubtedly holds at the global level, comparing western economies with developing countries. Sala-i-Martin et al. (2004) show in a world-wide cross-section that primary schooling is among the most important determinants of economic growth in the post-1960 period. Focusing on advanced economies, it is less obvious whether education is a critical factor behind productivity differences. Does education, possibly of a particular type, matter for economic growth in Europe and the United States? If so, has it contributed to the productivity slowdown?

Intuitively, education matters for growth or at least for the level of productivity. Do empirical studies confirm this intuition? The economic literature does not provide unequivocal evidence for the impact of education on productivity growth. Yet, both De la Fuente and Domenech (2002) and Krueger and Lindahl (2001) emphasise that the contribution of investment in education to productivity growth is sizable, once education is correctly measured.

Might education also be a reason behind the productivity slowdown? It might be if the growth rate of human capital have slowed down. Unfortunately, observations for the recent decades are scarce. The picture for the period up to 1995, in figure 2.13., gives little indications of a European slowdown in education. First, European countries lag behind the United States in terms of its expenditures on education (as a share of GDP), but they are catching up. Second, Europeans have had better scores than Americans on an internationally comparable literacy test – measuring both language and math skills – already in 1975, but even more so in 1995.

Summarizing, educational attainment did not slow down in recent years (or even decades) in Europe. Therefore, the productivity slowdown does not follow from reductions in education expenditures or performance.

---

[17] A meta-analysis can be briefly defined as a quantitative survey of the literature, taking differences in data sources or estimation methods into account.

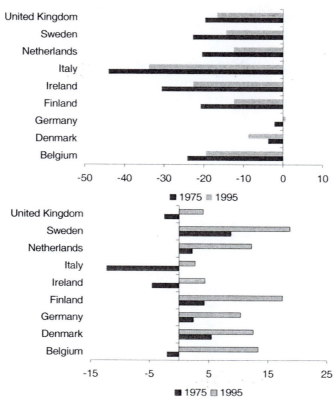

[a] Schooling years (left panel) are OECD figures, as summarised by De la Fuente and Domenech (2001); Literacy of the working-age population (right panel) is taken from the 1994 International Adult Literacy Survey (IALS).

Figure 2.13. Schooling years and literacy in 1975 and 1995 (percentage deviation of the United States)[a].

R&D and Education in Combination with ICT

The fall in productivity growth rates in Europe cannot follow from a decrease in investments in R&D, education or ICT. The latter is, however, identified as the engine of the accelerating productivity growth in the United States. Does the Europe benefit too little from ICT because the level of investment in R&D and education is too low?

Griffith et al. (2003) point out that R&D has two sides. Investment in R&D is not only essential for the introduction of new technologies but is also conducive to the absorption of existing technologies. They show for a panel of 13 advanced OECD economies that this latter effect of R&D is stronger in less advanced economies, since for them there are more existing technologies to absorb. For countries at or near the productivity frontier, the possibilities of absorption are exhausted, or at least diminished. They have to come up with new technologies, like ICT. Is it a coincidence that R&D-intensive countries - like the United States, Sweden and Finland (see figure 2.11.) have been successful in ICT-production and adoption?

Similarly, the fact that education sec has not contributed to the productivity slowdown, does not dismiss the possibility that a highly educated population is essential in the transformation of European economies from technology-adapting to inventing economies, cf. Sapir et al. (2003). The empirical evidence on this topic is inconclusive. Krueger and Lindahl

(2001) conclude that "(T)he positive effect of the initial level of education on growth seems to be a phenomenon that is confined to low-productivity countries." This view is challenged by a recent study of Vandenbussche et al. (2004), who find that skilled human capital (i.e. a highly educated population) statistically matters for technological progress in the advanced OECD economies. Tertiary education in particular is good for growth in these countries. Being at or close to the productivity frontier, these countries are less able to adopt technology from more advanced economies, so they have to invent new technologies or production methods themselves. This requires an educated population.[18] If tertiary education mattered, the United States would have a lead: its share of workers with a tertiary degree has increased from 30% to 38% of the working-age population in recent years (1991-2002).[19] Only a few European countries like the United Kingdom have been able to mimic this growth spurt, though at a lower level (from 16 to 27%). In other countries, like Germany, the gap with the United States has widened. Most European countries, however, have shown a significant increase in the share of the working-age population with a upper-secondary degree in recent years (1991-2002), which contrasts with the United States, where this share declined from 54 to 49% (OECD, 2004, pp. 72-73).

Summarizing, large R&D expenditures and a highly educated population may have contributed to the successful development and implementation of ICT in the United States, Sweden and Finland, and might be a prerequisite for innovation of new technologies in the future.

2.3.4. Conclusions

Pessimism about the performance of European economies seems exaggerated. In many economies the level of productivity is high. The growth rate of productivity shows a decline, but this a logical consequence of success. First, employment growth in the late nineties has been much higher than in the early nineties by historical standards (although it has not been high enough to reach the Lisbon targets for participation). As a result, less capital goods have been available per worker, leading to a fall in labour productivity growth. As such, this fall in productivity growth between the early and the late nineties is temporary. Second, many European countries have caught up with the United States. As a result, the potential for catching-up – by imitating and adapting state-of-the-art technologies and products – has become exhausted. This largely explains the downward trend in European productivity growth over a longer period than the nineties. It implies that Europe will not return to its historically high productivity levels, but should be able to mimic productivity growth in other frontier economies like the United States.

At the same time that the European Union saw a sharp decline in productivity growth, the growth rate in the United States stepped up. The American economy has benefited from the ICT revolution more than European economies on average. Mainly the introduction ICT technologies in services like retail and wholesale trade has contributed to the growth spurt. These service sectors are not known for their spending on R&D.

More generally, there are not many indications that Europe's slowdown or America's acceleration are related to changes in investment in R&D or in education. On both sides of the

---

[18] In contrast, economically successful adoption of technologies by less advanced economies requires a substantial amount of lower-skilled labour.
[19] Source: OECD (2004), Education at a Glance, pp. 72-73.

Atlantic R&D expenditures have been a stable fraction of GDP over the years. A change in education is also not an obvious candidate to explain the slowdown in Europe and acceleration in America. Over the years average schooling years and average test scores have improved in Europe much faster than in America.

The fact that education, R&D and ICT do not explain the productivity slowdown in the past does not dismiss the opportunity they might offer for future productivity growth in Europe.

2.4. Conclusions

Looking backward, the European economies score well on some aspects of economic performance. First, participation on the European labour market has on average increased, although the rates of participation remain rather low in the largest EU member states. Second, the level of productivity is high by international standards. That its growth rate has fallen over time, especially in the late nineties and ever since the seventies, is partly the consequence of economic successes. The fall in the late nineties is related to surge in participation in that period. The decrease since the seventies is related to pas growth: many European economies have caught up with the United States in terms of productivity.

The European slowdown does not follow from decreasing investment in R&D, education or ICT. The possibility is that investment in knowledge may not have been enough to fully exploit the opportunities from ICT. The evidence for this possibility is scarce as well as mixed.

In this section we have focused on the proximate causes of productivity: investments in R&D, education and ICT. We left out the deeper causes, like institutions, regulations and preferences, without wanting to suggest in any way that they are unimportant for economic growth. On the contrary, removing international barriers to trade in goods and productive factors could be one of the spearheads of European policy. Similarly, we have largely ignored the determinants of employment growth, but only pointed at the likely role of the welfare state. For a thorough study of why participation rates went up or why Europeans work shorter hours than Americans we refer to other publications, like CPB/SCP (2003, 2005).

3. OPEN METHOD OF COORDINATION: TOO MUCH AND TOO LITTLE

3.1. Introduction

In Lisbon the head of states formulated a common ambition for the member states of the European Union. To fulfil the common ambition, a common approach seemed logical. The problem for the European Union was to agree upon reforms without favouring one type of welfare state over the other. The solution for this problem was a method of governance, with which the European Union and its member states had already experience, the Open Method of Coordination (OMC). This method brackets political conflict as it does not impose a single, European vision on the ideal welfare state design or other policy areas. Instead, it was positioned as a 'means of spreading best practices and achieving greater convergence towards the main EU goals' (European Council, 2000).

The OMC is a combination of national policy and informal European coordination, where decisions are based on consensus. Specifically and according to the Conclusions of the European Council in Lisbon March 2000, it involves:

- 'Fixing guidelines for the Union combined with specific timetables for achieving the goals which they set in the short, medium and long terms;
- Establishing, where appropriate, quantitative and qualitative indicators and benchmarks against the best in the world and tailored to the needs of different member states as a means of comparing best practice;
- Translating these European guidelines into national and/or regional policies by setting specific targets and adopting measures, taking into account national and regional differences;
- Periodic monitoring, evaluation, and peer review takes place, organised as mutual learning processes.'

The OMC does not want to impose one, single standard on all member states, but takes into account the diversity among them. That the OMC accommodates diversity among member states, has allowed it to spread to various areas. Currently, the method is employed both in the areas of 'jobs' (e.g. the European Employment Strategy) and 'growth' (e.g. innovation). The next section will further explore the arguments for an European role in both areas, whereas section 3.3 will go deeper into the functions of the OMC. This analysis leads us to the conclusion that differential approaches to jobs and to growth are needed. Whether these approaches are part of a renewed OMC or not, is of secondary importance.

3.2. The European Role in Stimulating Jobs and Growth

The Subsidiarity Principle

Within the European Union the allocation of competences between the community of member states and the member states themselves is subject to the subsidiarity principle. Competences remain exclusively with the member states unless there are good reasons for some form of European coordination or centralisation.

The subsidiarity principle is in itself neutral about the direction to take: decentralisation or centralisation. There are at least two good reasons to assign competences to the most decentralised, in this case national level of decision making. First, the distance between decision makers and voters is relatively small. This is important for making decision makers accountable for their actions. Local environmental problems should preferably be handled locally. Second, decision makers can relatively easily incorporate in their actions country-specific preferences or institutions, as for instance prevalent on the labour market. Country-specific policies might be preferable over a unifying as well as restrictive framework.

Similarly, there are two good reasons for delegating powers to the European level or for sharing powers between the community and its member states. The first derives from cross-border externalities. A policy change in one member states may have positive (R&D) or negative (pollution) effects on other member states. The second reason derives from economies of scale. It is for example an important reason behind the harmonisation or mutual recognition of standards: firms do not need to comply with many different standards but rather with only one.

European involvement in policies to stimulate jobs and growth is generally defended on the grounds of cross-border externalities. It is often argued that together the European countries are stronger than on their own. The Kok report for instance states: '... *a jointly created economic tide would be even more powerful in its capacity to lift every European boat*'. The stake in economic success elsewhere is assumed to be large. One would like to know, rather than assume, how large this stake actually is. To gauge this we need to distinguish between both sources of economic growth: employment and productivity.

Employment Growth

In a variety of ways employment growth in one country has an impact on other (neighbouring) countries. First, the country with employment growth sees its production and income increase and will demand more goods and services from the other countries. Through export growth the other countries benefit from employment growth in one country. This mechanism is valid in the short run, specifically if there is slack capacity. Gros and Hobza (2001) look at the short-run cross-border effects of fiscal expansion in Germany, based on simulations with different macro-econometric models. The overview of simulation results learns that the effects are small or often even negative. A negative effect may arise when a German expansion retriggers an interest rate increase in the Euro area. Second, imbalances on labour markets could be resolved by an in- or outflow of workers. SER (2001) shows, however, that in the short run the net flow is small, in particular between European countries: a member state with a low unemployment rate attracts more immigrants, not from other member states but from outside the Union. For the long run, there is little evidence that employment rates depend significantly on migration flows. The (un)employment rate is structurally determined by country-specific institutions (see Nickell et al., 2005, and the rich literature on structural unemployment).

To identify other structural spillovers from employment growth, we resort to simulations with the general-equilibrium model WorldScan. Important is that the model considers only long-run effects of changes in policy or in the economic environment, by assuming that labour- and product markets are in equilibrium, both in the initial situation and after the changes have been completed. The model captures two relevant cross-border effects, one positive and the other negative. The positive effect works through the terms of trade. Higher employment in one country raises the export demand for others. In the short run, this could spur production, using slack capacity, and reduce unemployment. In the long run, higher export demand will be accommodated by higher export prices, as slack capacity is not structural. Higher employment in one country therefore benefits others through terms-of-trade gains. The negative spillover works through the (rental) price of capital. A member state will see capital leave and the investment rate fall temporarily, when economic success elsewhere brings an increase in the return on capital. This will have a negative effect on productive capacity in the future.

The simulations assume that in Germany employment increases with 10% and show the effects on other European countries. From the results in Table 3.1 it is clear that other countries share in the German success, but the spillovers of employment growth are rather small. The income gain is only 1% to 3% of the income gain for Germany (the first column in Table 3.1.). Put differently, 1 Euro extra income in Germany leads to about 1 Euro cent extra income in the countries and regions in Europe. These effects cannot be characterised as a rising tide, but rather as a drop in the ocean. A member state can therefore expect far more from increasing its own employment rate than from higher employment in other member states.

Table 3.1. The Effects in Europe from an Employment Increase in Germany, Change as a Result of the 10% Increase in Employment

	Real national income Percentage change	Absolute change (Germany = 100)	Terms of trade Percentage change
Germany	9.04	100.00	− 1.55
France	0.12	0.92	0.23
Italy	0.12	0.62	0.20
United Kingdom	0.09	0.71	0.19
Spain	0.10	0.36	0.21
Netherlands	0.18	0.49	0.12
Belgium	0.27	0.47	0.20
Eastern Europe	0.28	0.90	0.29

Source: simulations with WorldScan.

Productivity Growth

Investments in better products and production methods are important for the levels and growth rates of productivity. Typically, they involve externalities, i.e. investments by one firm increase the production possibilities of other firms. The reason is that knowledge of products and production methods resembles a public good. Its use is non-rival and is − to some extent − non-excludable.

The spillovers of knowledge investments are international. Investments in one country have an impact on the productivity of other countries. Empirical work linking these two is large (see for an overview Keller, 2004). In particular, R&D investments are found to have important external effects on productivity outside the country in which the investments occur.

Knowledge is, however, not a global public good. Distance matters for the transfer of new technologies. The effect of knowledge investment on productivity becomes smaller, the farther a country is from the place of investment. Table 3.2, based on Keller (2002), shows that R&D in the United States contributes much less to total factor productivity in small European economies like Finland, Italy and the Netherlands, than German, French or British R&D, even though the US expenditures are more than six times larger. Keller's estimates imply that for every 1200 kilometres the effect of R&D investments is reduced by a half. He also finds support for the popular notion that world has become smaller: in the late 70s the decay with distance was larger than in early 90s. But, even in 90s distance is far from dead.

Table 3.2. European R&D is Important for Domestic Productivity (TFP), Percentage Change in TFP Due to a 10% Increase in R&D-Expenditures

	Finland	Italy	Netherlands
Domestic	0.01	0.06	0.03
France	0.11	0.12	0.11
Germany	0.17	0.16	0.16
United Kingdom	0.16	0.15	0.17
Japan	0.01	0.00	0.00
United States	0.08	0.05	0.06
Aggregate	0.53	0.53	0.53

Source: own calculations based on Keller (2002).

In short, spillovers from knowledge investment are international but are confined to neighbouring countries. This seems to make the European Union well suited to coordinate and even perhaps to implement measures to stimulate knowledge investments. It seems likely that each member states has a stake in the success with which other member states stimulate investments in new products and production methods.

3.3. The Functions and Flaws of OMC

The cross-border externalities of more jobs and higher growth differ markedly. More employment has virtually no international spillovers, whereas faster productivity growth may lead to significant gains elsewhere. Based on the first observation, one could argue that the European Union has too many competences: the main argument for European involvement with national employment policies is not very strong. At the same time, one could argue that the European Union has too few competences: the community of member states has little influence on national policies to stimulate investments in technologies and know-how, even though these investments have clear international spillovers.

Except for internalising international spillovers, European coordination could also provide countries better opportunities to learn from each others' experiences. This is a possible motivation for European involvement with national employment polices. How well has the OMC served these functions? And will the new proposals improve any of these functions? Five years of experience with the Lisbon strategy should help us to answer these questions.

International Spillovers

Coordination is a necessary condition for internalising international spillovers. As such, the OMC is potentially useful for policies to stimulate knowledge investments or to boost innovation. However, the common European goals in these areas have not been translated into different national targets. It is therefore hardly possible to enforce commitment of national governments to the common goals. The introduction of National Action Programmes may change this practice, though.

Even with national targets, one could question whether countries can credibly be forced to comply with their obligations. In the OMC formal sanctions do not exist. The main sanction mechanism is informal and relies on peer pressure and public opinion. Furthermore, the Lisbon targets are set without addressing the costs of reaching these targets. What are the costs of increasing R&D expenditure with roughly 1% of GDP? When these costs are too high, the target is not credible, whether the sanction mechanism is formal or informal.

Since the sanctions are not strong and the targets not credible, the OMC does not seem to solve the problem of free-riders. Countries then fail to take into account that the benefits of productivity growth spill over to other European countries.

Learning

An important argument for a soft coordination method as the OMC is the potential for policy learning, both bottom-up and cross-national. The idea is that through the process of participation, exchanging information and peer reviews policy learning is stimulated. A problem in obtaining the optimal results for learning is that there is a tension between diversity and learning on the one hand and targeting for convergence and EU wide results on the other hand. Whereas policy learning is a unpredictable, cooperative process, progress on the Lisbon strategy is measured with targets and timetables and is forced by peer pressure.

From the preliminary evidence we can draw some lessons regarding the potential for learning. The overall impression emerges that the results have been very limited till now. According to De la Porte and Pochet (2004), the European Employment Strategy has at best sparked national-level discussions. Also cross-national and bottom-up policy learning has been limited.

One seemingly successful result is convergence at the level of ideas in some policy areas (ideational convergence; Radaelli, 2003). This may be an important development, as the convergence at the level of ideas may point the way towards a European model. Radaelli (2003) for instance describes the emergence of an 'EU desirable model' in employment policy, which is a hybrid of Anglo-Saxon and Scandinavian instruments. However, these elements of ideational convergence are still embryonic; furthermore, convergence in 'talk' may not produce convergence in decisions.

A Single Method for Both Jobs and Growth?

In some policy areas, like innovation policy, international spillovers warrant coordinated action. Member states should raise investment in R&D beyond their national ambition, to let other countries benefit from their inventions, and vice versa. The experience of the past five years has, however, shown that the OMC is not capable of generating the necessary commitment. Although a greater involvement of national governments is a step forward towards more commitment of national governments, we still should not expect too much in this direction. Without formal sanctions there is no way to enforce that the member states improve productivity growth by raising their investments in R&D. Ideally, the decision-making power in innovation policy should be delegated to the European Union in order to optimally benefit from its potential.

In other policy areas where international spillovers are weak, like in 'jobs', the OMC may already contribute by fostering mutual learning. This learning might be pursued further, in particular in policy areas where member states are faced with similar challenges. Neither the emphasis on national action plans, nor the use of quantitative targets will be very helpful in this respect. Maybe, OMC in its current weak form is most appropriate to serve the task of learning, although the huge diversity within the EU reduces the potential to imitate policies.

Overall, it seems impossible to serve both jobs and growth with one single governance method. Especially when applied to policy areas with strong international spillovers, like growth, the OMC does not seem the most appropriate method.

REFERENCES

Acemoglu, D., P. Aghion and F. Zilibotti, 2004, *Distance to frontier, selection, and economic growth,* Mimeo MIT.

Ark, B. van, E. Frankema and H. Duteweerd, 2004, *Productivity and employment growth: an empirical review of long and medium run evidence,* GGDC Research Memorandum GD-71.

Ark, B. van, R. Inklaar and R.H. McGuckin, 2003, ICT and productivity in Europe and the United States; Where do the differences come from?, *CESifo Economic Studies* 49: 295-318.

Barro, R.J. and X. Sala-i-Martin, 1995, *Economic Growth,* McGraw-Hill, New York.

Barroso, J.M., 2005, Working together for growth and jobs; A new start for the Lisbon Strategy, *Communication to the spring European Council.*

Bartelsman, E. J. and J. Hinloopen, 2004, Unleashing animal spirits: investment in ICT and economic growth, in *The economics of the digital economy,* eds. Soete, L. and B. ter Weel, Edward Elgar.

Baumol, W.J., S.A.B. Blackman and E.N. Wolff, 1989, *Productivity and American Leadership, The long view,* MIT Press, London.

Bloom, N., R. Griffith and J. van Reenen, 2002, Do R&D tax credits work? Evidence from a panel of countries 1979-1997, *Journal of Public Economics* 85: 1-31.

Brakman, S., H. Garretsen, J. Gorter, A. van der Horst and M. Schramm, 2005, *New economic geography, empirics, and regional policy,* CPB, The Hague.

Bottazzi, L., 2004, R&D and the financing of ideas in Europe, *CEPS Working Document* 203.

Bruyn, S. de, 2000, *Economic Growth and the Environment: an empirical analysis,* Thela Thesis, Amsterdam

Carvalho, V.M. and A. Harvey, 2004, Convergence and cycles in the euro zone, CEPR Discussion Paper 4726.

Castello, A. and R. Domenech, 2002, Human capital inequality and economic growth: Some new evidence, *Economic Journal* 112(127): C187-C200.

CPB/SCP, 2003, *Social Europe,* European Outlook 1, Annex to State of the European Union 2004, The Hague.

CPB/SCP, 2005, *European Times, Public opinion on Europe / Working hours, compared and explained,* European Outlook 3, Annex to State of the European Union 2006, The Hague.

CPB (2004a), *Four futures for energy markets and climate change,* Special Publication 52.

CPB (2004b), *Macro Economische Verkenning* 2005, Sdu Publishers, The Hague.

Daveri, F., 2004, Why is there a productivity problem in Europe? *CEPS Working Document* 205.

Denis, C., K. McMorrow and W. Röger, 2004, An analysis of EU and US productivity developments (a total economy and industry level perspective), *European Economy, Economic Papers* 208.

Dollar, D. and E.N. Wolff, 1993, *Competitiveness, convergence, and international specialization*, MIT Press, London.

EC (2004), EU Economy 2004 Review.

European Council, 2000, *Presidency conclusions*, Lisbon European Council, 23-24 March 2000.

Fiani, R., 2004, *Europe: a continent in decline?*, Mimeo Universita di Roma Tor Vergata.

De la Fuente, A. and R. Domenech, 2001, Schooling data, technological diffusion, and the neoclassical model, *American Economic Review* 91(2): 323-27.

De la Fuente, A. and R. Domenech, 2002, Human capital in growth regressions: How much difference does data quality make? An update and further results, *CEPR Discussion Paper* 3587.

García-Quevedo, J., 2004, The public subsidies complement business R&D? A meta-analysis of the econometric evidence, *Kyklos* 57: 87-102.

Griffith, R., S. Redding and J. van Reenen, 2000, Mapping the two faces of R&D: productivity growth in a panel of OECD industries, *CEPR Discussion Paper* 2457.

Griffith, R., S. Redding and J. van Reenen, 2003, R&D and absorptive capacity: Theory and empirical evidence, *Scandinavian Journal of Economics* 105(1): 99-118.

Gordon, R.J., 2004, Why was Europe left at the station when America's productivity locomotive departed?, *NBER Working Paper* 10661.

Groot, H. de, R. Nahuis and P. Tang, 2004, Is the American model miss world?, *CPB Discussion Paper* 40.

Gros, D., and A. Hobza, 2001, Fiscal policy spillovers in the Euro area: *Where are they? CEPS Working Document* No. 176

IMF, 2004, Fostering structural reforms in industrial countries, *World Economic Outlook* 2004.

Inklaar, R., M. O'Mahony and M. Timmer, 2003, ICT and Europe's productivity performance: Industry-level growth account comparisons with the United States, *GGDC Research Memorandum* 68.

Jones, C.I. and J.C. Williams, 1998, Measuring the social return to R&D, *Quarterly Journal of Economics* 113(4): 1119-1135.

Jones, C.I., 2004, Growth and ideas, *NBER Working Paper* 10767.

Jovanovic, B. and P.L. Rousseau, 2004, General purpose technologies, *NBER Working Paper* 11093.

Keller, W., 2002, The geographic localization of international technology diffusion, *American Economic Review*, 92: 120-142.

Keller, W., 2004, International technology diffusion, *Journal of Economic Literature*, 42: 752-782.

Kok, W., 2004, *Facing the challenge; the Lisbon strategy for growth and employment*.

Krueger, A.B. and M. Lindahl, 2001, Education for growth: Why and for whom?, *Journal of Economic Literature* 39(4): 1101-1136.

Martin, S. and J.T. Scott, 2000, The nature of innovation market failure and the design of public support for private innovation, *Research Policy* 29: 437-447.

Mooij, R. de, and P. Tang, 2003, *Four futures of Europe*, Koninklijke De Swart, The Hague.

Mooij, R. de, and P. Tang, 2004, Reforming the public sector in Europe: reconciling equity and efficiency, paper presented at ECFIN Workshop "Fiscal Surveillance in EMU".

Nickell, S., L. Nunziata and W. Ochel, 2005, Unemployment in the OECD since the 1960s. What do we know?, *Economic Journal* 115: 1-27.

Nordhaus, W., 2004, Retrospective on the 1970s productivity slowdown, NBER Working Paper 10950.

OECD, 2004, Education at a Glance. Paris

O'Mahony, M. and B. van Ark, 2003, EU productivity and competitiveness, an industry perspective: Can Europe resume the catching-up process? DG Enterprise, European Union, Luxembourg (downloadable from http://www.ggdc.net/pub/EU_productivity _and_competitiveness.pdf).

Pilat, D., 2004, The ICT productivity paradox: insights from micro data, OECD Economic Studies 38.

Porte, C. De la, and P. Pochet, 2004, The European Employment Strategy: existing research and remaining questions, *Journal of European Social Policy* 14(1): 71–78.

Radaelli, Claudio M., 2003, *The Open Method of Coordination: A new governance architecture for the European Union?*, Rapport nr 1, Swedish Institute for European Policy Studies, Stockholm.

RIVM, 2004, Outstanding environmental issues; *A review of the EU's environmental agenda*, Bilthoven.

Rodrik, D., 1998, Why do more open economies have bigger governments?, *Journal of Political Economy* 106(5): 997-1032.

Sala-i-Martin, X., G. Doppelhofer and R.I. Miller, 2004, Determinants of long-term growth: A bayesian averaging of classical estimates (BACE) approach, *American Economic Review* 94(4): 813-835.

Sapir, A. (2003), An agenda for a growing Europe; *Making the EU economic system deliver*, Report to the European Commission.

SER, 2001, *Arbeidsmobiliteit in de EU*, Advies nr 01/04.

Timmer, M.P., G. Ypma and B. van Ark, 2003, IT in the European Union: Driving productivity divergence?, *Research Memorandum GD-67*, Groningen.

Vandenbussche, J., P.Aghion and C. Meghir, 2004, *Growth, distance to frontier and composition of human capital*, Mimeo Harvard University.

In: Roadmap to Bangalore?　　　　　　　　　　　　ISBN: 978-1-60021-478-3
Editors: A. Heshmati, A. Tausch, pp. 53-68　　　　　© 2007 Nova Science Publishers, Inc.

Chapter 2

THE LISBON DEVELOPMENT PROCESS: A NOTE ON A NEW COMPOSITE LISBON STRATEGY INDEX[1]

Arno Tausch[2], Almas Heshmati[3] and JongEun Oh[4]

ABSTRACT[5]

As is well known, in March 2000 the EU Heads of States and Governments agreed to make the EU "the most competitive and dynamic knowledge-driven economy by 2010". Although some progress was made on innovating Europe's economy, there is growing concern that the reform process is not going fast enough and that the ambitious targets will not be reached. This joint Austrian-Swedish/Kurdish-Korean study now addresses the measurement of two composite Lisbon strategy indices ("one-glance, one click" indicators) that quantify the level and patterns of development for ranking countries. If we want to reduce the complexity of the 14 main Lisbon indicators, the usual ranking procedures, still popular among government bureaucracies in the EU, are by far

---

[1] The opinions expressed in this paper are strictly private academic opinions, and do not necessarily reflect the opinions of Governments or International Organizations. The authors would like to thank Dr. Ewald Walterskirchen from the Austrian Institute of Economic Research for his useful comments on the draft.

[2] Adjunct Professor of Political Science at Innsbruck University, Austria. Website: http://www.mylitsearch.org/mbrz/10134373. e-mail address: arno.tausch@bmsg.gv.at. Available book titles at: http://www.campusi.com/

[3] Professor of Economics, Hawler Institute for Economic and Policy Research and Department of Economics, University of Kurdistan Hawler, 30m Zaniary, Hawler, Federal Region of Kurdistan, Iraq Homepages: http://www.hiepr.org and http://www.ukh.ac/ and Contact: almas.heshmati@hiepr.org and almas.heshmati@ukh.ac

[4] Doctoral student, Techno-Economics and Policy Program, College of Engineering, at Seoul National University. Contact: serapin7@snu.ac.kr

[5] The authors would like to emphasize that lots of imputations (by using countries own lag values and average EU-25 with a of minimum impact on the index results) were necessary in view of the limited Eurostat data since around 1995, especially for the new members among the EU-25, to get the data balanced, which is required for the normalization of the indicators before computing the composite LSI index (Lisbon Strategy Index). In our EXCEL data file, entitled "Heshmati Lisbon" etc. lag imputations are marked in yellow color, imputations by using the value of the EU-25 are marked by red color, etc. The original data as well as other EXCEL files about the LSI Index are all available from http://www.gallileus.info/gallileus /members/m_TAUSCH/publications/110978567308/ upon registration at the Gallileus Scientific Network in Berlin (sponsored by PricewaterhouseCoopers and the German Ministry of Economics and Labor) by sending a short e-mail to feedback@gallileus.de.

insufficient. Our new "Lisbon strategy index (LSI)" is composed of six components: general economics, employment, innovation research, economic reform, social cohesion and environment, each generated from a number of the 14 original main Lisbon indicators, each of which develop differently over time and across countries, covered by Eurostat. Sweden, Norway and USA are ranked as highest. Bulgaria, Turkey and Malta are the lowest ranked countries on the new index. The article – see Text tables 1 to 3 for the main results - also contains Lisbon process indicators results, based on principal components analysis, reflecting the research and development process, social cohesion, the power of the freight lobby, and business investments. Again it is shown that the United States outperform most EU-member states. Our investigations also allow us to show the dynamic changes taking place, as the countries of the Union struggle to achieve the Lisbon goals. The necessity of a real reform agenda in Germany and in several new member and candidate countries again emerges from our analysis. The LSI Index ranks Korea as number 8, if Korea is introduced into the rankings of Table 2 of this study. This position is better than Japan's, and Korea has a higher score in innovation and research than EU but lower than USA and Japan.

Key Words: Economic Development, Index Numbers, Economic Integration, Comparative Country Studies, and Lisbon Agenda.

1. INTRODUCTION

As it is well known, in March 2000 the EU Heads of States and Governments agreed to make the EU "the most competitive and dynamic knowledge-driven economy by 2010". Although some progress was made on innovating Europe's economy, there is growing concern that the reform process is not going fast enough and that the ambitious targets will not be reached[6]. As it is also widely known that the 14 main structural "Lisbon" agenda indicators, created to measure progress in meeting the Lisbon targets, play an important role in European policy making[7]. The Lisbon lists of indicators, apart from the highly publicized debt-related ... Maastricht criteria of the European Monetary Union, are perhaps the most important checklists for government success or failure in Europe today. They are omni-present in the public political as well as scientific debate and are defined by Eurostat as:

1. GDP per capita in PPS (purchasing power standard)
2. Labor productivity
3. Employment rate
4. Employment rate of older workers
5. Educational attainment (age 20-24)
6. Research and Development expenditure

---

[6] for a short survey of the Lisbon process, see also: http://www.euractiv.com/Article?tcmuri=tcm:29-117510-16andtype=LinksDossier
[7] http://epp.eurostat.cec.eu.int/portal/page?_pageid=1133,1403427,1133_1403432and_dad=portaland_schema=PORTAL

7. Comparative "price levels" (developed on the basis of the ERD-Index Yotopoulos et al.)[8] (the Commission maintaining that a low value is a good result)
8. Business investment
9. At risk-of-poverty rate (low value = good result)
10. Long-term unemployment rate (low value = good result)
11. Dispersion of regional employment rates (low value = good result)
12. Greenhouse gas emissions (low value = good result)
13. Energy intensity of the economy (low value = good result)
14. Volume of freight transport (low value = good result)

It is assumed that a good performance on one indicator is causally linked to a good performance on the other indicators. Or in the words of Professor Romano Prodi, the former Commission President:

"The Lisbon Strategy remains the right course for an enlarged European Union. It is the best way of delivering what concerns our citizens most - prosperity, more and better jobs, greater social cohesion and a cleaner environment - and making sure that they are achieved sustainably for future generations." (http://www.socialdialogue.net/en/en_lib_068.htm)

But a recent study by the European Commission (2005, Literature survey) warns that it is very difficult to quantify the impact of the reforms because of the "heterogeneity" of individual reform measures, time lags in implementation and complementarities and trade-offs between reforms. The Commission classifies the Lisbon reforms into five categories:

1. product and capital market reforms;
2. investments in the knowledge-based economy;
3. labor market reforms;
4. social policy reforms;
5. environmental policy reforms.

Their study underlines[9] that "product and labor market reforms alone in the second half of the 1990s resulted in an increase in annual GDP growth of almost one half percent point over the medium term. When also taking into account the potential contribution of increased investment in knowledge, the increase in EU potential growth could reach 3/4 of a percentage point. Over a ten-year period, this would imply an increase in the GDP level of up to 7 or 8%". As is well known, their study says that the costs of not achieving a better environment may be felt in a reduced quality of life, negative health impacts, lost economic opportunities, and economic costs as a result of a poor environment. "This would add to the costs of deviating from the Lisbon goals." The Commission working paper points to the need for further research to establish what 'flanking policies' are needed to maximize the benefits of Lisbon while minimizing the adjustment costs.

---

[8] It can be shown that the Eurostat data series GDP PPP per capita/GDP exchange rate per capita (EU-25=100), used for the "price level", in reality measure GDP exchange rate per capita/GDP PPP per capita (EU-25=100). For more on that, see Appendix A of the full Internet version of our paper at http://www.insightturkey.com/
[9] http://www.euractiv.com/Article?tcmuri=tcm:29-136834-16andtype=News

Our note now presents results from the computation of two composite indices corresponding to the Lisbon structural development strategy. Without a proper methodological handling of the statistical observations, provided by Eurostat so far on the Lisbon process, little progress will be made in the political debate as to who performed better or worse in the Lisbon process and why. Surprisingly, there is little serious, cross-national and quantitative social science research available on the results of the *"Lisbon process"* and the *"Lisbon indicators"* provided by Eurostat. The usual but totally useless *"beauty contests"*, understandably performed in the state chancelleries around Europe and based on mere average rankings, to show where member country x or y is situated along the Lisbon indicators, are unacceptable from a methodological viewpoint because they simply aggregate the Lisbon indicators on a 1:1 basis for a ranking of the EU-member countries.

Our paper would like to apply serious cross-national indicator and development research to the problems raised by the Lisbon process, based on methodological advances mainly achieved in the framework of the United Nations. Our first indicator is based on the methodology of the human development index (HDI) of the United Nations, *developed by the Economics Nobel Laureate of the year 1998,* Amartya Sen and the Kearney *"Foreign Policy magazine"* index types[10], and the second is obtained from principal component analysis, well known in technical literature on social indicators of development[11]. Such composite indicators inform us about the individual countries' level of development and patterns of changes among the countries and over time in their efforts to achieve the Lisbon goals. Our Kearney type index is composed of six components: general economics, employment, innovation research, economic reform, social cohesion and environment, each generated from a number of indicators. A breakdown of the composite index into major components provides possibilities to identify the sources of (under)development at the country level and associate it with economic policy measures. *The empirical results show that by accounting for non-technology factors US and Japan are not superior to several European nations.*

2. A COMPOSITE INDEX

Kearney (2002, 2003) is the first attempt to construct a database and to compute a composite globalization index. The index is composed of four major components: economic integration, personal contact, technology, and political engagement, each generated from a number of determinant variables, 13 in total (see also Heshmati 2006). This index can serve as a model for computation of a Lisbon strategy index (LSI). The LSI is computed based on the *normalization* of 14 individual indicators and the subsequent *aggregation* using an *ad hoc* and equal weighting system.

---

[10] It should be noted that this HDI type index differs from the state chancelleries' approach of simple aggregation of the Lisbon indicators on a 1:1 basis. In the HDI type index the individual indicators are normalized prior to the aggregation. Thus, in addition to the ranks the distance to the best in the HDI is quantitatively measured as well.

[11] For surveys and new results based on that approach, and the work carried out by the United Nations World Institute for Development Economics Research, based in Helsinki, see, among others http://www.wider.unu.edu/publications/publications.htm, Discussion Paper 2003:69 and Arno Tausch (with Fred Prager), *'Towards a Socio-Liberal Theory of World Development'* Basingstoke, London and New York: Macmillan's and Saint Martin's Press.

The component's weights are chosen on an ad hoc basis and are in general constant across countries and over time. However, it can be generalized to accommodate necessary variations reflecting differences in importance of development factors and changing conditions. This LSI index can be used as a benchmark index. Lockwood (2001), in computing the globalization index, finds the ranking of countries to be sensitive to the way the indicators are measured, normalized and weighted. The index is similar to the commonly used human development index (HDI), which is based on educational attainment, life expectancy and real GDP per capita (see Noorbaksh 1998).

There are at least two other alternative approaches to the LSI for computing a Lisbon strategy index; using the principal component (Heshmati 2006) or factor analysis (Andersen and Herbertsson 2003); for a survey of literature on the use of composite indices in development research see also Heshmati and associates, 2001–2006; Tausch and associates, 1986-2006). Principal component analysis is a multivariate technique for examining relationships within a set of quantitative variables. Given a dataset with p numeric variables, at most p principal or factor components can be computed; each is a linear combination of the original variables with coefficients equal to the eigenvectors of the correlation of the covariance matrix. The principal components are sorted according to the descending order of the *eigenvalues,* which are equal to the variance of the components. *So for the readers, not familiar with mathematical statistics*, it might suffice to say: *PC analysis can be viewed as a way to uncover approximate linear dependencies among variables.*

3. THE DATA AND VARIABLE DEFINITIONS

The database created by Eurostat[12] is used for the computation of the Lisbon strategy index. The part of the database used here constitutes a small balanced panel covering 33 countries observed for the period 1995-2003. There were several missing units and missing observations. These are imputed, when available, using lag values for the same country, and when not available the missing units were imputed using average EU-25. The imputation was undertaken to avoid the use of unbalanced data and subsequent distortions in reference points for the normalizations. It has a minimum effect on the index results. The data contain 14 structural indicators that are expected to proxy the countries' development towards the Lisbon agenda goals. The 14 indicators are *grouped into 6 groups* including: *general economics, employment, innovation research, economic reform, social cohesion and environment*, each generated from a number of indicators.

4. VARIATION IN THE LISBON STRATEGY INDEX

The normalized indicators ranging in the interval 0 and 1 were used in the computation of the non-parametric Lisbon strategy index (in the form of country mean values). Sweden, Norway, the USA and Austria are ranked highest. Despite the high ranking, Sweden has quite

---

12

http://epp.eurostat.cec.eu.int/portal/page?_pageid=1133,1400891,1133_1402816and_dad=portaland_schema= PORTAL low scores in the "price level" and business investment component, Norway in prices and freights, and the USA in the regional distribution of employment and emissions. Japan is ranked very low as number 12. Bulgaria, Turkey and Malta, despite their low prices and their low levels of energy intensity and freights, are amongst the lowest ranked countries. The summary main results are given in our text Table 1.

Table 1. The Lisbon Strategy Index – The Final, Main Result of Our Study

Rank and Country	LSI (Lisbon Strategy Index)
1. Sweden	**9.736**
2. Norway	*9.557*
3. USA	***9.037***
4. Austria	**8.800**
5. Netherlands	8.778
6. Denmark	8.705
7. Czech Republic	8.692
8. Finland	**8.514**
9. Luxembourg	8.494
10. Germany	8.413
11. UK	8.233
12. Japan	*8.144*
13. France	7.758
14. Belgium	7.672
15. Slovenia	7.388
16. Hungary	6.976
17. Ireland	6.962
18. Romania	*6.926*
19. Slovakia	6.799
20. Cyprus	6.785
21. Portugal	6.770
22. Iceland	*6.615*
23. Poland	6.497
24. Greece	6.316
25. Estonia	6.315
26. Croatia	*6.162*
27. Spain	6.059
28. Latvia	6.022
29. Lithuania	6.021
30. Italy	5.718
31. Malta	5.684
32. Turkey	*5.276*
33. Bulgaria	*4.839*

Note: Countries printed in *indented letters* are included in the Eurostat Lisbon statistics but were not (yet) members of the EU at the time of writing this essay.

In geographical terms, the success or failure of the Lisbon process up to now, as measured by our indicator, is presented in Map 1.

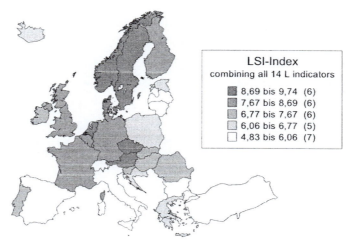

Note: "bis" is shorthand for "ranging from ... to". 8,69 = 8.69; 9,74 = 9.74 etc. Only countries with complete data are represented in the map.

Map 1. The LSI Index at one glance.

Table 2. The Combined Principle Components Index (Based on the Weighted Averages of the 4 Principal Components[13])

Rank and Country	PCI-2[14]-Index based on the method of principle components
1. Norway	*2.388*
2. Sweden	2.300
3. Austria	2.039
4. Denmark	2.036
5. Netherlands	1.999
6. Finland	1.891
7. USA	1.888
8. Japan	1.795
9. Germany	1.679
10. Luxembourg	1.632

---

[13] http://www.insightturkey.com/

[14] See our general remarks in the footnote above. We also calculated a PCI index that does not take into account that factors 2 and 3 reflect a socially negative development. For readers interested in the mathematical details of our investigation, the PCI results are included in the longer web-site version of this publication. Only the PCI-2 index should be interpreted.

Table 2. (Continued)

Rank and Country	PCI-2-Index based on the method of principle components
11. Czech Republic	1.592
12. France	1.447
13. Belgium	1.424
14. UK	1.381
15. Slovenia	1.326
16. Ireland	1.286
17. Iceland	1.101
18. Cyprus	1.093
19. Croatia	0.955
20. Portugal	0.936
21. Greece	0.908
22. Italy	0.873
23. Spain	0.855
24. Hungary	0.849
25. Slovakia	0.721
26. Malta	0.679
27. Poland	0.651
28. Estonia	0.641
29. Romania	0.540
30. Lithuania	0.456
31. Latvia	0.412
32. Turkey	0.229
33. Bulgaria	0.129

Note: Countries printed in *indented letters* are included in the Eurostat Lisbon statistics but were not (yet) members of the EU at the time of writing this essay.

If we, instead of the non-parametric Lisbon strategy index (LSI), rank countries by the *parametric principal component (PCI-2) index (where the index is based on weighted averages of the first 4 principal components)*, the rank of the countries does not differ significantly. *Norway* is the highest ranked followed by *Sweden, Austria and Denmark.* The correlation between the two scales is very large and allows us to say that the results could claim validity in favor of them. The Netherlands and Finland also outperform the US.

The results of our PCI-2 index do not differ systematically from the LSI-Index, as is also shown in the following map.

The PCI-2 index

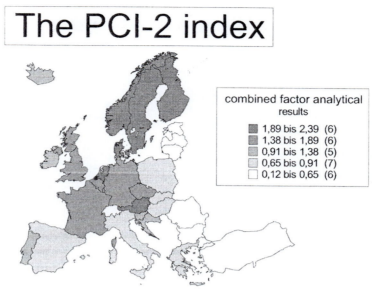

combined factor analytical
results

■ 1,89 bis 2,39 (6)
■ 1,38 bis 1,89 (6)
□ 0,91 bis 1,38 (5)
□ 0,65 bis 0,91 (7)
□ 0,12 bis 0,65 (6)

Note: see Map 1. "bis" is again shorthand for "ranging from … to".

Map 2. The factor analytical combined PCI-2 index – results for Europe at one glance.

The very highly correlated relationship between the two main results – the new LSI Index and the principal component index – is shown in Graph 1.

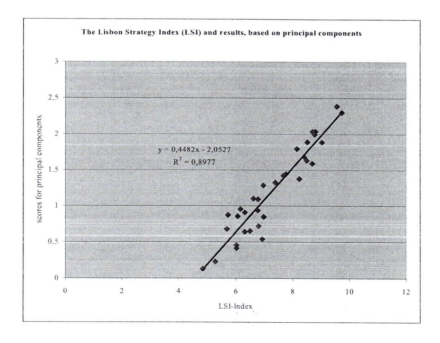

Graph 1. The relationship between the two new Lisbon Strategy synthetic indicators.

The performance of the EU-15, and the EU-25 in comparison with the United States:

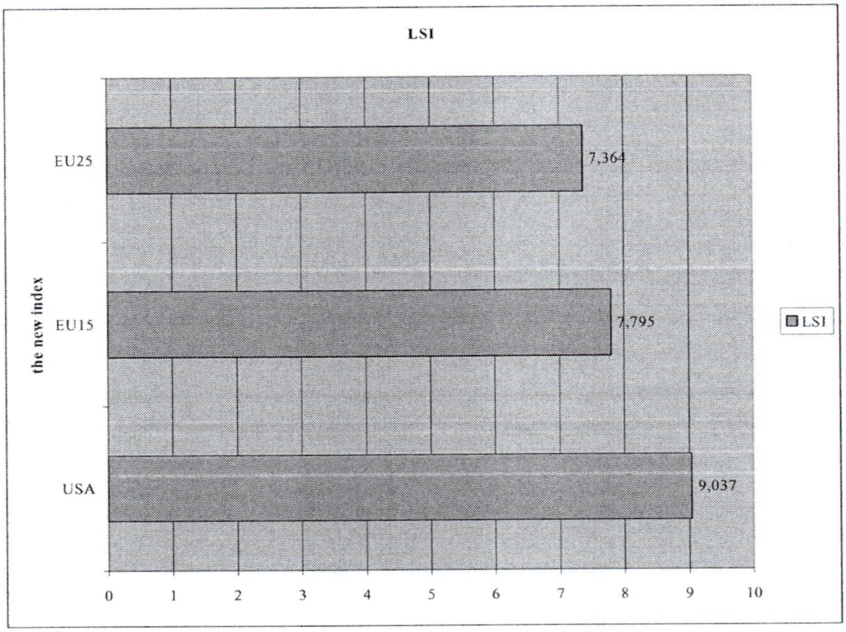

Graph 2. The LSI-index values for the EU-15, the EU-25 in comparison with the United States

The position of the respective countries on the 4 Lisbon Strategy Index principal components is seen from Table 3.

Herewith Turkey has a better performance on these factors than several Eurostat Lisbon process comparison countries:

Factor 1:   development of productive forces: *Turkey* better values than Bulgaria, Slovakia, Poland and Romania

Factor 2:   social exclusion: smaller values for Turkey (better values) than Italy and Malta.

Factor 3:   freight lobby: smaller values (better values) for Turkey than Cyprus, Lithuania, Norway, Greece, Spain, Latvia, Ireland, Portugal, Estonia

Factor 4:   business investment and neo-liberal investment climate: Turkey has better values than: Malta, Iceland, USA, Bulgaria, UK, Cyprus, Japan, Sweden.

Our investigations also allow us to show the dynamic changes taking place, as the countries of the Union struggle to achieve the Lisbon goals. Spain, Ireland and Hungary had the most rapid changes to the better to report, while the precarious situation in *Germany* and in several new member (like Poland) or candidate countries (like Romania) again emerges from our analysis. Turkey again outperforms several EU-25 member countries, including Germany.

Table 3. The Factor Scores and the Performance of the 33 Eurostat Countries

	Factor 1 development of productive forces	Factor 2 social exclusion	Factor 3 freight lobby	Factor 4 business investment and neo-liberal investment climate
AUSTRIA	0.725	-0.840	0.088	1.532
BELGIUM	0.517	0.111	-1.147	0.681
BULGARIA	-1.701	-0.716	-1.966	-0.958
CROATIA	-0.488	0.687	-0.932	0.294
CYPRUS	0.412	0.327	0.943	-1.168
CZECH REPUBLIC	-0.387	-1.673	0.025	1.100
DENMARK	1.237	-0.920	-0.238	-0.791
ESTONIA	-0.799	-0.038	3.344	0.687
FINLAND	1.152	-0.980	-0.807	-0.503
FRANCE	0.629	-0.111	-0.656	0.136
GERMANY	0.574	-0.415	-0.760	-0.075
GREECE	-0.118	0.540	1.322	1.424
HUNGARY	-0.492	-0.558	-0.652	0.660
ICELAND	0.824	1.041	-0.478	-0.921
IRELAND	0.786	0.835	1.757	0.414
ITALY	-0.024	1.567	-0.596	-0.402
JAPAN	1.146	-0.267	0.141	-1.241
LATVIA	-0.878	0.064	1.713	0.407
LITHUANIA	-1.008	-0.179	0.959	-0.779
LUXEMBOURG	1.021	0.589	-1.006	-0.046
MALTA	0.069	1.820	-0.400	-0.866
NETHERLANDS	0.943	-1.061	-0.272	-0.011
NORWAY	1.576	-1.260	1.082	-0.806
POLAND	-1.265	0.244	-1.243	-0.236
PORTUGAL	0.202	0.680	1.943	-0.265
ROMANIA	-1.237	-0.555	0.710	-0.194
SLOVAKIA	-1.513	-0.223	-1.031	1.286
SLOVENIA	-0.215	-0.439	-0.735	1.278
SPAIN	0.122	1.171	1.508	1.029
SWEDEN	1.653	-1.732	-0.554	-1.648
TURKEY	-1.175	1.283	0.823	-0.847
UK	0.846	-0.668	0.124	-1.087
USA	1.245	-0.292	-0.066	-0.955

As to the factor analysis, see also http://classic.lalisio.com/members/m_TAUSCH/publications /110978567308/112487315866/?use_session=True&browser_type=Explorer&-C=&language=en

Table 4. Dynamic Changes in the Lisbon Strategy
Index (LSI) over the Entire Period Since 1995

Country	% change in the LSI
Spain	4.75
Bulgaria	*3.90*
Ireland	3.50
Hungary	3.06
Latvia	3.00
Greece	2.62
Italy	2.59
UK	2.55
Belgium	2.47
Finland	**2.42**
Netherlands	2.19
Slovenia	2.12
Portugal	1.98
Denmark	1.88
Luxembourg	1.79
France	1.51
Lithuania	1.49
Slovakia	1.40
Iceland	*1.33*
Japan	1.32
Malta	1.30
Austria	**1.23**
USA	*1.22*
Turkey	*1.12*
Sweden	**1.05**
Croatia	*0.90*
Estonia	0.53
Germany	0.38
Norway	*0.32*
Czech Republic	0.21
Cyprus	0.15
Romania	*-0.02*
Poland	-0.49

Map 3 now pinpoints the results of text table 4 above in a geographical fashion.

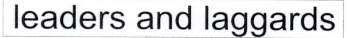

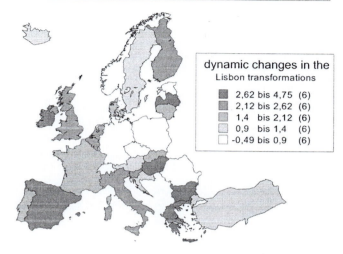

In this and in all other maps, missing data for Switzerland, the West Balkans and countries of the former USSR. "bis" is again shorthand for "ranging from … to". Other notes: see maps above

Map 3. The reform leaders (dark color) and reform laggards (white) in Europe.

5. Europe and the Asian Economies – the Case of Korea

As was shown by Heshmati and Oh (2006), Korea is ranked as number 8 by the LSI Index, if Korea and Japan are introduced into the rankings of Table 2 of this study. This position is better than Japan's, and Korea has a higher score in innovation and research than the EU but lower than that of USA and Japan. Also Korea's economic reform is quite high as a result of its lower price level than in the EU and a higher business investment rate. Korea stabilized the economy very shortly after the 1997 economic crisis and the rate of rapid recovery after the crisis makes the country very interesting from the perspectives of reform, growth and development strategy. Thus many aspects of its policy can serve not only as a model for economic development, but also an experiment field for development of new industries such as telecommunication, and to achieve high innovativeness and competitiveness to both developing and developed countries as well.

There are several key factors deriving the Korea's dramatic economic development. The World Bank reports that the reason for the high investment ratio in Korea is to be found in the structure of demand. The investment ratio is defined as the ratio of gross domestic investment to gross domestic product. From 1965 to 1990 Korea's investment ratio rose from well below to well above the group average with 23-24 percent. This was supported by a high saving rate and low borrowing cost. The Korean government's planning and industrial policy both reduced future uncertainty, while the rapid growth has offset investors' error.

Korea's investment in education and technology to enhance its human resources and technological capabilities as infrastructure for its economic development started from the mid 1960s. From 1962-1972, Korean economic development was based on an export-led growth strategy, in 1973-1981 it was focused on the heavy and chemical industry, while 1982-1992 is the period of stabilization and liberalization to promote competition and efficiency of firms and industries.

Korea focused on technology development from from the early 1980s. Since the 1980s, Korea has rapidly modernized its industrial structure by promoting capital investment and technology development and a policy to adjust toward high value-added and technology intensive production technology. From this time onwards, R&D investment increased dramatically. Korea is committed to technology based on innovation as the primary source of economic transformation to realize the goal of reaching the level of the G7 group members' development in the early 21st Century. The Korean government's fiscal commitment to annually increase R&D investment by 25-30% is one measure to achieve this vision. As the result of such policy measures, GDP per capita grew from $300 in 1955 to more than $10000 before the economic crisis in 1995 and to more than $15000 in 2006.

Kuznets (1994) stated that the key characteristics of South Korea's economic development since the mid 1960s are: high investment rates, labor market competition, export orientation and a strong interventionist government. Indices of human resource development based on post-primary school enrolment ratios for 112 countries in 1960 and 1965 show that Korea's educational attainment was the same as that of semi-advanced countries like Italy and Spain and much higher than that of other countries with equally low per capita GNP. What is unique about Korean development from 1945 is that a high level of human resources was developed early and despite a low per capita income. The high level of investment in education was an important driving force of Korean economic development. Education influenced development by increasing skills and expanding learning capacity, which in turn resulted in a higher productivity, investment and welfare.

From the data for the empirical analysis, we can see that Korea obtained a high score in education, R&D expenditure and business investment as compared to the other Lisbon race countries. The ranking by education is better than that of EU despite a lower level of GDP per capita. This indicates that although the role of state and industrial policy changed markedly after the crisis, the key deriving factors of Korea economic development remain the same.

It is to be noted that the rank of Korea by the principal component analysis is lower. The results show that, despite its great progress in recent decades, Korea has a high risk of poverty and a higher regional dispersion of employment than in the EU, in Japan and in the USA, as well as a lower labor productivity measured as GDP per employed person (see Heshmati and Oh, Table 8). The high risk of poverty and dispersion in employment are a direct consequence of the deep economic crisis. The gradual increases in the level of GDP per capita post crisis and the corresponding improvement in the employment rates suggest a significant gain?.

In sum, the results suggest that Korea has advanced to become a technologically advanced country with great improvement in development capability, competitiveness, and it competes with the highly developed nations like the EU, Japan and USA. However, Korea lags behind in social cohesion compared to the developed countries and in particular to Europe. The results show that (see Heshmati and Oh, Table 10) Korea's dynamics of social cohesion in the aftermath of the economic crisis are also negative. However, the changes in environment performance are very impressive compared to other countries suggesting effectiveness of investment in environmentally friendly technologies both for domestic consumption and for competitive export markets.

REFERENCES

Official Documents

Commission: Report: "The economic costs of non-Lisbon. A survey of the literature on the economic impact of Lisbon-type reforms", SEC(2005) 385 (15 March 2005) available at: *http://europa.eu.int/growthandjobs/pdf/SEC2005_385_en.pdf.*

Eur-Lex: Communication to the Spring Council: "Working together for growth and jobs - A new start for the Lisbon Strategy " , COM (2005) 24 (Febr. 2005) [FR] [DE] available at: *http://europa.eu.int/eur-lex/lex/LexUriServ/site/en/com/2005/com2005_0024en01.pdf.*

European Commission (2005), 'A new start for the Lisbon Strategy', available at: *http://europa.eu.int/growthandjobs/index_en.htm.*

Further References

Addison T. and A. Heshmati (2004), "The New Global Determinants of FDI Flows to Developing Countries: The Impacts of ICT and Democratization", *Research in Banking and Finance* 4, 275-297.

Andersen, T. M., and T. T. Herbertsson (2003). *'Measuring Globalization'.* IZA Discussion Paper 2003: 817.

Cooper R. (1999), 'The Asian Crisis: Causes and Consequences" *World Bank-Brookings Institution Conference "Emerging Markets and Development",* Department of Economics, Harvard University, available at:

Heshmati A. (2001), "On the Causality between GDP and Health Care Expenditure in the Augmented Solow Growth Models", *Swedish Working Paper Series in Economics and Finance* 2001:423, Stockholm School of Economics.

Heshmati A. (2006), 'Measurement of a Multidimensional Index of Globalization', *Global Economy Journal* 6(2), Paper 1.

Heshmati A. and J-E. Oh (2006), 'Alternative Composite Lisbon Development Strategy Indices: A Comparison of EU, USA, Japan and Korea', *The European Journal of Comparative Economics* 3(2), 133-170.

Kearney, A. T., Inc., and the Carnegie Endowment for International Peace (2002). 'Globalization's Last Hurrah?'. *Foreign Policy,* January/February: 38-51.

Kearney, A. T., Inc., and the Carnegie Endowment for International Peace (2003). 'Measuring Globalization: Who's up, who's down?'. *Foreign Policy,* January/February: 60-72.

Kravis I. B., Heston A. and Summers R. (1981), 'New Insights into the Structure of the World Economy' *The Review of Income and Wealth,* 4, available at http://www.roiw.org/1981/339.pdf.

Kuznets S. (1955), Economic growth and income inequality, *American Economic Review* 45, 1-28.

Kuznets P.W. (1994), *"Korean Economic Development",* Westport, Connecticut, London: Praeger.

Lockwood, B. (2001). '*How Robust if the Foreign Policy/Kearney Index of globalization?*'. CSGR Working Paper 79/01.

Noorbakhsh, F. (1998). 'The Human Development Index: Some Technical Issues and Alternative Indices'. *Journal of International Development*, 10: 589-605.

Rao J. M. (1998), '*Development in the time of Globalization*' UNDP Working Paper Series, Social Development and Poverty Elimination Division, February 1998, available at http://www.undp.org/poverty/publications/wkpaper/wp2/RAO-Rf1.PDF.

Sawada, Yasuyuki, and Yotopoulos, Pan A. (1999). "*Currency Substitution, Speculation, and Financial Crisis: Theory and Empirical Analysis.*" SIEPR Policy Paper Series No. 99- 5.

Tausch A. (1986), 'Positions within the Global Order, Patterns of Defense Policies, and National Development: Austria and Pakistan Compared' in '*Security for the Weak Nations. A Multiple Perspective. A Joint Project of Pakistani and Austrian Scholars*' (S. Farooq Hasnat and Pelinka A. (Eds.)), pp. 245 - 55, Lahore: Izharsons.

Tausch A. (1989, appeared 1991), 'Armas socialistas, subdesarrollo y violencia estructural en el Tercer Mundo' *Revista Internacional de Sociologia, CSIC, Madrid,* 47, 4: 583 - 716.

Tausch A. (1990) 'Quantitative aspects of a socio-liberal theory of world development'. *Economic Papers,* Warsaw School of Economics, Research Institute for Developing Countries, 23: 64 – 167.

Tausch A. (1991), '*Jenseits der Weltgesellschaftstheorien. Sozialtransformationen und der Paradigmenwechsel in der Entwicklungsforschung*' Munich: Eberhard.

Tausch A. (1993, with Fred Prager as co-author), '*Towards a Socio - Liberal Theory of World Development*' Basingstoke and New York: Macmillan/St. Martin's Press.

Tausch A. (2003) (Editor) '*Three Pillars of Wisdom: A Reader on Globalization, World Bank Pension Models and Welfare Society*'. Hauppauge, New York: Nova Science.

Tausch A. (2003) 'The European Union: Global Challenge or Global Governance? 14 World System Hypotheses and Two Scenarios on the Future of the Union' in 'Globalization: Critical Perspectives' (Gernot Kohler and Emilio José Chaves (Editors)), pp. 93 – 197, Hauppauge, New York: Nova Science Publishers.

Tausch A. and Köhler G. (2001) *Global Keynesianism: Unequal exchange and global exploitation.* Huntington NY, Nova Science.

Tausch A. and A. Heshmati (2006), 'Turkey and the Lisbon process. A short research note on the position of Turkey on a new Lisbon Strategy Index', *Insight Turkey* 8(1), 7-18.

United Nations Development Programme (2005), *"Human Development Report".* New York and Oxford, Oxford U.P.

Walterskirchen E. (2004), '*Die Position Österreichs im internationalen Strukturwettbewerb. Die neuen EU-Strukturindikatoren*' Materialien zu Wirtschaft und Gesellschaft, 86, available at http://www.arbeiterkammer.at/pictures/d9/MWuG_86.pdf?PHPSESSID =aead8ae613e86a68e0a681cf20a02766.

Yotopoulos P. (1996), '*Exchange Rate Parity for Trade and Development: Theory, Tests, and Case Studies.*' Cambridge, UK: Cambridge University Press, 1996.

Yotopoulos P. and Sawada Y. (2005), "Exchange Rate Misalignment: A New test of Long-Run PPP Based on Cross-Country Data" *CIRJE Discussion Paper* CIRJE-F-318, February 2005, Faculty of Economics, University of Tokyo, available at: http://www.e.u-tokyo.ac.jp/cirje/research/dp/2005/2005cf318.pdf.

In: Roadmap to Bangalore?
Editors: A. Heshmati, A. Tausch, pp. 69-108

ISBN: 978-1-60021-478-3
© 2007 Nova Science Publishers, Inc.

Chapter 3

MEASUREMENT OF GLOBALIZATION AND ITS VARIATIONS AMONG COUNTRIES, REGIONS AND OVER TIME

Amit K. Bhandari[*] and Almas Heshmati[+]

University of Kalyani

Hawler Institute for Economic Policy Research and University of Kurdistan Hawler

ABSTRACT

The process of globalization is an international economic order which has led to the progressive integration of the world economy through pulling down the barriers of trade and enabling greater mobility of factors of production. In addition, technological innovation also provides impetus to the progressive integration of nations. The main features of globalization include free movement of goods and services, flow of capital, movement of labor and the transfer of technology. Many transitional and developing countries have benefited from globalization and liberalization. Apart from economic benefits, globalization also indicates the flow of ideas, norms, information and peoples. There is, however, a large heterogeneity in the degree of globalization over time and across countries and regions of the world, as well as within countries. The present study is an attempt to measure globalization by using both parametric and non-parametric approaches. The data cover a wide range of industrialized, transition and developing countries on the basis of their international integration. We identify the factors influencing globalization among the countries in the form of economic integration, personal contacts, technology and political engagement. We isolate the contribution of each factor by quantifying the individual factor contribution to the overall integration. Finally, we investigate the link between globalization and labor market in Indian manufacturing industries.

[*] Amit Kumar Bhandari, Department of Economics, University of Kalyani, West Bengal–741 235, India, Phone: +9133-25825691, E-mail: amitbhandari2@rediffmail.com I am grateful to Prof. Rabindra N. Bhattacharya for his valuable comments and suggestion.

[+] Corresponding author: Almas Heshmati, Hawler Institute for Economic and Policy Research and Department of Economics, University of Kurdistan Hawler, 30m Zaniary, Hawler, Federal Region of Kurdistan, Iraq. E-mail: almas.heshmati@hiepr.org and almas.heshmati@ukh.ac

Keywords: Globalization, economic integration, composite index, manufacturing, India.

1. INTRODUCTION

The proper meaning of globalization is a debatable issue. The meaning of globalization is different to different people and to different disciplines. In general, globalization is a process in which the combined forces of different elements lead to an increase in dependence of countries on the interactions with the rest of the world. For economists, the process of globalization is an international economic order that leads to the progressive integration of the world economy through weakening restrictions on trade, exchange rate and the greater mobility of factors of production. Apart from that, globalization is a process of geographical reorganization of economic activities by which people's lives have been shaped and reshaped all over the world. It could also be thought of as the extent and legitimate fabric of a highly diverse world (see Rowntree et al., 2000). Although economic interconnectedness is the prime mover of globalization, the conflicting behavior of environment, culture, and political and social development antecedes the contemporary development process. The contemporary process of globalization is characterized by unevenness on a global scale. In different parts of the world, globalization is experienced in different ways. There is a large heterogeneity in the degree of globalization over time, across countries and economic and geographic regions of the world, as well as regions within countries. There is a mismatch between costs and benefits where the costs are easily identifiable and the benefits are often delayed and occur over a longer period of time.[34] The heterogeneity in the degree of globalization points to the need to develop the sources of indicators to quantify its magnitude.

There are vast amounts of empirical literature discussing various aspects of the recent wave of globalization in developing countries. Several special issues on globalization have been published in Oxford Development Studies, the Journal of World-Systems Research and the Journal of African Economies. Editorial introductions to these special issues are provided by Woods (1998); Manning (1999); Bata and Bergesen (2002a, 2002b); and Bevan and Fosu (2003). In addition, a number of books on the issue have been published. Dollar and Collier (2001) and the World Bank (2002) explore the relationship between globalization, growth and poverty; James (2002) analyses technology, globalization and poverty, Aghion and Williamson (1998) examine the relationship between globalization, growth and inequality, while Khan and Riskin (2001), focusing on history and policies, limit their study to the development in China. O'Rourke and Williamson (2000) look at the evolution of the 19th century Atlantic economy, and Tausch and Herrmann (2002) analyzed globalization and European integration.

The present study attempts to investigate the measurement of different approaches of globalization based on Kearney (2002) and the principal component analysis covering a wide range of industrialized, transitional and developing countries on the basis of their international integration. We have identified the factors influencing globalization in those countries in the form of economic integration, personal contact, technology and political engagement. The study also investigates the contribution of these factors by quantifying each individual factor's contribution to overall integration and its variations in different

---

[34] See Tanzi (2004) and Stiglitz (2002).

dimensions. Currently, there is a lack of data and standards to measure globalization. The study is an attempt to fill the gap. It is an attempt to analyze the very diverse aspects of globalization and subsequently to discover the different channels through which it can affect the process of globalization significantly. Finally, we investigate the link between globalization and labor market in India with the focus on the manufacturing industry.

The study is organized as follows. In the next section we discuss globalization and review the various issues involved in globalization, particularly those relating to the poor. In Section 3 we describe the data used in computing the globalization indices. The methods of computation of the globalization index are presented in Section 4 where two alternative parametric and non-parametric approaches are used to compute globalization index and decompose it into economic, technology, personal and political sub-components. Distribution of the indicators is presented in section 5. In section 6 the relationship between the four different components are investigated. In section 7 the empirical results are discussed, where the focus is on the variations in the degree of globalization across countries, geographic and economic regions, as well as over time. In section 8, an attempt is made to link the globalization to the labor market in Indian manufacturing industries. The final section concludes and provides policy measures and also suggestions for future advances in research on globalization.

2. GLOBALIZATION

The exact time frame of globalization is a matter of debate. Its roots are to be found in the Industrial Revolution of 1789. Industrialization is normally portrayed as an illustration of European and British exceptionalism. O'Rourke and Williamson (2000), O'Rourke (2001), Maddison (2001) and Williamson (2002) split the period of globalization (1870-2000) into four distinct phases: the first wave of globalization 1870–1913, the de-globalization period of 1913-1950, the golden age of globalization 1950-1973 and the second wave of globalization from 1973 onward.

Broadly, the four decades of globalization up to the First World War were largely driven by the strong growth of trade and intercontinental financial and migratory flows. These years were dominated mainly by European colonialism, by their proficiency in innovative transportation and communications. The role of technology has massive capacity to generate huge profits, which played a crucial role in rapid interconnectiveness of the human society. But the societies to benefit most from industrialization were those involved in the earliest version of the globalization race.

In the first wave of globalization, the dismantling of mercantilism and the worldwide transport revolution worked together to produce truly global markets. That was a long period when the flow of factors was limited and trade was dominated mainly by a few European investors. They believed in the strong growth prospects of oversees markets, but collapsed due to the outset of world war. Instead of adopting mechanisms of global cooperation and development, the period was marked by nationalism and the creation of national empires. So, in the second phase inward looking policies dominated in almost all industrial nations, which were aggravated after the second round of world war. The third phase of globalization was marked as the period of decolonization and saw the creation of multilateral institutions, which managed to liberalize trade and prevented the return of national economic cooperation. But colonialism had left the independent countries poorly equipped to survive in the globalized world. The current wave of globalization has been driven by a new set of factors, such as: deregulation of financial services, emergence of modern transportation and communication technologies, collapse of Eastern Bloc and the demonstration of the success stories of East Asia.

2.1. Globalization, Trade and Development

The importance of trade liberalization is the most significant manifestation and also constitutes the prime component of globalization. Trade liberalization came first during the so-called golden age of globalization (1950-1973) with the unprecedented expansion of international trade. After the Second World War, on average trade has grown at roughly double the rate of growth of GDP. The growth in trade is connected with the emergence of Multinational Corporations (MNCs) and Transnational Corporations (TNCs). As a result, attracting FDI of the corporations assumes a special significance for improving the performance of nations. This development coincided with the upsurge in international investment that began in the late 1960s.

The mid-eighties and the nineties are characterized by greater openness in the form of international trade, which accelerated the adoption of technological innovations originating from the industrial countries. Openness to trade provides access to imported inputs which embody new technology and increases the size of market facing producers, which in turn raise the level of investment and affect a country's specialization in research intensive production. Thus, a country's openness leads to an improvement in domestic technology and helps the production process to become more efficient and enhances productivity improvement. The pattern of world trade has experienced major changes during the current phase of globalization. Drastic reductions in the barriers to international trade have opened the door for export led growth.

The common perceptions on trade liberalization as an integral part of globalization are that a nation that opens its economy to the outer world experiences a rapid economic growth. However, the trade growth nexus remains a contentious issue. Dollar and Kraay (2002) proposed that trade is more important for medium-term growth. Bolaky (2004) proposed that the contribution of trade is limited for highly regulated countries. Economic growth in some parts of the world has been unprecedented over the recent decades. With increased competition, domestic firms start utilizing resources more efficiently and improve their productivity. However, little evidence is available in support of the long run effect of trade liberalization on economic growth. Rodrik (2002) suggests that institutions matter more for growth in the long run. The effect of increased trade on growth is absent in highly regulated countries. Excessive regulations restrict growth because resources are prevented from moving into the most productive sectors and to the most efficient firms within sectors. Strict regulations prevent some firms from entering, others from exiting, and labor from moving across sectors or across firms.

The complex nexus between openness and agriculture should be highlighted. In several developing and least developed countries a large number of people are dependent on agriculture. Primary sectors often face adverse terms of trade movement. Like India, in the majority of developing countries, the primary sectors are relatively labor intensive. Their market share of agriculture exports have not improved in a significant way. The real culprit is the protectionist measures taken by some developed countries, which benefit from shutting the door on imports from developing countries. In this way, trade liberalization has failed to keep its promise, generating unemployment, poverty and provoking strong opposition.

The percentage changes in export and import volumes by level of development are presented in Table 1. Variations in the growth rate of developing countries are higher than those of developed and transition countries. For 2001 both export and import growth rates are negative. Two other exceptions are the growth rate of export from transition countries in 1999 and the import growth rate of developing countries in 1998. The growth rate in 2000 is found to be the highest.

Table 1. Percentage Changes Over the Previous Years in Export and Import Volumes by Region and Economic Grouping of Countries

	Regions	1990-1995	1996	1997	1998	1999	2000	2001
Export Volume	World	6.0	6.1	10.7	5.0	4.8	10.8	-0.9
	Developed Economies	5.3	4.9	10.0	4.6	4.3	9.2	-1.2
	Developing Economies	9.0	6.9	12.5	5.6	7.1	13.9	-1.5
	Transition Economies	5.0	6.5	10.4	5.1	-1.7	13.0	8.7
Import Volume	World	6.5	6.9	9.9	4.3	6.0	10.2	-1.0
	Developed Economies	5.6	5.3	9.4	7.7	7.0	6.4	-1.6
	Developing Economies	10.1	6.4	10.5	-3.8	5.6	19.6	-1.1
	Transition Economies	2.5	16.0	13.7	4.7	-8.8	15.0	12.7

Source: Various issues of Trade and Development Report, UNCTAD.

2.2. Globalization and Finance

The contemporary discussion on the economic integration of nations is dominated by financial globalization. Historically this is not a new phenomenon, which has its roots long back (see Obstfeld and Taylor (1998), Baldwin and Martin (1999), Collins and Williamson (1999)). At that time only few countries participated in this process. The first setback was received in the form of the Great Depression just after the First World War until the beginning of the Second World War and continued for a couple of decades till the 1960s. 1970s was marked by a new era of financial globalization with the collapse of the Breton Wood System and the oil shock. The oil shock forced/prompted international banks to come up with fresh funds to invest in developing countries. These funds were used mainly to finance public debt in the form of syndicated loans. This incidence was the clear manifestation of the opening up of financial systems to the developing countries. During the last decade, the investment boom in the form of foreign direct investment (FDI) and portfolio flows to the emerging markets mushroomed with deregulation, privatization and technological renovation.

In general, FDI should follow those sectors and technologies, which are capable of generating sizable growth in productivity, value added and employment. However, much of the FDI is being diverted to the special route of service sectors, which have little impact on exports. Free markets (or free market policies) may not always lead foreign investors to transfer enough technology or to transfer it effectively and at the depth desired by the host countries. But appropriate policy can induce investors to act according to the ways that enhance the developmental impact by building local capabilities, using local suppliers, upgrading local skills, technological capabilities and infrastructure. Attracting FDI is important when tempting foreign affiliates to transfer technology to the domestic firms to create local research and development capacity. Apart from FDI, portfolio investment, banks and trade related transfers are playing a crucial role in the financial integration. Advances in information and communication technology facilitate the transfer of resources in a lightening speed. The rapid financial and capital market mobilization is often associated with 'contagion effect'. The higher role of private capital is associated with a higher degree of volatility, which has made countries more vulnerable as evident from the East Asian Crisis.

The effect of financial integration with the rest of the world is a debatable issue. Financial globalization has been associated with both risk and benefits.[35] When a country first opens its financial sector, volatility and crisis might arise in the short run if the domestic financial sector is not prepared to regulate and/or is not supervised properly. In the long run, with the development of the financial sector, volatility tends to decrease following liberalization and integration with world markets. Despite risk, the net benefits of financial globalization can be large if they are well managed. The diversity of the source of funding reduces the risk of credit crisis. Borrowers can now raise funds by issuing stocks or bonds in the domestic security markets or by seeking other financing sources in the international capital markets. The most important thing to the global investor is the development of local infrastructure, which is crucially absent for most of the developing countries. Two unfavorable comparisons emerge between India and China on account of the role of FDI. In the 1990s, after almost two decades of liberalization, China started getting the benefits of FDI for its economic development. But in China, domestic investment as a share of national income is estimated as 40 per cent of GDP whereas in India it is barely 20 percent at present, making the investment regime friendlier for potential investors.[36] So, there needs to be a serious alteration of policy regime to appropriate the benefits of FDI on overall development.

In the open financial market borrower and investor can now finance physical investment more cheaply and investors can more easily diversify internationally and modify portfolio risk to their preferences. This encourages investment and saving, which facilitate real economic activity and growth and improve economic welfare. But in the more integrated world with weakly regulated banks and financial institutions, this leads to more vulnerable financial markets. Thus, a sound macroeconomic fundamental is the key to managing crises more efficiently. Countries with a very low degree of integration with the world market and underdeveloped financial markets should ensure a shock absorbing capacity. Governments

---

[35]See Kindleberger (1996) and Bordo, Eichengreen, and Irwin (1999) for detailed account of crises.
[36] See Balakrishnan (2003)

are left with fewer policy instruments to manage the internationalization of financial services. Another view is that underdeveloped financial markets would benefit from full financial liberalization if there were fewer intervention and policy instruments.

2.3. Information and Telecommunication Technology and Globalization

The sudden prominence of the worldwide wave has changed the way of international relations in the era of globalization. Now the global communication system links all regions on the planet instantly along with the revolution of the global transportation system. The evolution of communication through information technology is one of the key elements of globalization. The inventions of modern communication devices have made the communication network much cheaper and more accessible to the common people. The efficient commutation network changed the way of integration of countries, which played a vital role in growth, productivity and new employment opportunities. The microprocessor and cheap memory revolutionized the communication industry in 1980s. The rapid decline in the real price of telecommunication provides an impetus in the global networking of computing through Internet. The tele density and connectivity gap between middle income and low-income countries has also been rising, rapidly deteriorating the growing digital divide between developed and developing countries as well as within developing countries. In many countries the communication industry has been transferred from public ownership to private through the increased waves of privatization. So, global communication networks have challenged the policy makers to get used to new international relations. Faster and quicker delivery of information shifts the attention of the people, organization and government to any particular global event (Baylis, 2001).

The WTO Negotiation on the Basic Telecommunication successfully mandated on the liberalization of telecommunication markets starting from January 1st, 1998. Sixty-nine countries agreed in the negotiation. Many of them agreed to lower or remove domestic barriers to intervene on competition in the area of local and long distance and satellite services. It was agreed on market access, the adoption of a regulatory principle, liberalization of FDI rules and satellite offers. Fifty-nine countries agreed to adopt transparent, pro competitive regulatory principles, representing a majority of the WTO telecommunication market. Forty-four countries agreed to permit significant inward foreign direct investment (FDI). Fifty countries guaranteed market access for all domestic and international satellite services and facilities. Investment in information and communication technology (ICT) infrastructure is found to positively affect the inflow of FDI to the developing countries. The flow of FDI also affects positively the ICT infrastructure development. Thus, there is a two-way causal relationship between flow FDI and ICT infrastructure (see Addison and Heshmati, 2004).

Outsourcing acts as a mitigating factor of the debate of international migration. Outsourcing reduces the need for cross-border migration, which can help to overcome the battle between labor exporting and labor importing countries. It was based on the assumption that a competitive advantage would be gained if external suppliers were contracted to carry out non-core processes more efficiently and effectively (McCarthy, 2004). As a result of the evolution of information technology, many of the services, which in the past had to be managed at the host location, can now be spread to and delivered from remote locations.

These types of services include IT enable services (ITeS), business process outsourcing (BPO), which are for the most part facilitated by information technology. Some developing countries, especially India, benefited because of a competitive advantage to deliver quality business services at a lower cost.

2.4. Globalization and the Poor in Developing Countries

There is considerable attention to the effects of globalization on the world distribution of income in general and its impacts on the poor in developing countries in particular. However, there is no clear consensus yet on whether globalization can hurt the poor or provide recuperative power for them. It is true that poor countries, which embrace globalization, witnessed faster growth in the prosperity level than countries which have stayed away from this process. For example, some Asian countries have been able to reduce the gap between themselves and some western countries. The strongest claim on the debate of income distribution and poverty has emanated from World Bank (2002) research covering the recent phase of integration of the world economy. The report shows that during the past two decades the total number of poor in the world has come down by 200 million. However, the decline in poverty is not surprising considering the two fastest growing countries (India and China) in terms of poverty reduction, where large numbers of poor reside. The high rates of economic growth have helped those countries to pull significant numbers of poor out of poverty. Nevertheless, even today huge numbers of people live in abject poverty and hunger.

Trade liberalization enables firms to import high technology, which in turn benefits their operation and productivity in the long run. Higher technology requires a highly skilled workforce. However, for most of the developing countries trade liberalization is often associated with labor-intensive sectors. Such industries employ a high percentage of low skilled workers. So the average return to their skill decreases and their demand is bound to decline as mentioned by Winters (2002). Low skilled workers are the most vulnerable in the process of globalization unless their skills are improved adequately. Therefore, the low-skilled workers are more likely to oppose freer trade and immigration than their counterparts. Empirical estimates on the impact of international trade on wages concludes that trade has played a major role in the rise in skill premium which is primarily driven by skill based technological change. Sectors that had the highest protection before reform experienced the smallest wage premium. There is a shift in the labor force towards the informal sector where wages are relatively low. Miller (2001) demonstrates that globalization explains a significant increase in earning inequality for declining relative wages of unskilled workers in the US since the late 1970s. Eckel (2003), in analyzing the role of wage inequality in labor market adjustment to international trade and biased technological progress shows that changes in relative wages are independent of wage rigidities, but wage inequality is affected by capital market integration.

The failure of government policies coupled with widespread corruption are considered a stumbling block for the development of human resource. Who suffers from the poor state of governance? The answer is the poor, because of corruption in governance and politics. The accommodation of global business interests is often portrayed in terms of surrendering national sovereignty. Giffen (2003) stressed the need for global economic development provided that it is achieved by democratic institutions of global governance. But there is a conflict between greater market led globalization and democracy. There needs to be a redefinition of the economic role of the state in relation to the market. The state must create the preconditions for more equitable development, bargain with outside capital to improve the distribution of gains from cross border transactions, prudent macro economic management of the economy so as to reduce vulnerability and take active steps to minimize the social cost associated with globalization. (Nayyar, 2001) A number of measures could reduce the negative impact of the rapid globalization process. Nayyar and Court (2001) identified the main ways in which the need for good governance and the strengthening of policies for the world economy can be achieved. They proposed that a new structure of governance, reforms and new institutions are required to protect the poor peoples in the developing countries. Some of the successful redistributive policy cases include – Nordic social democracy, East Asian land reform, the Costa Rican welfare state, egalitarian distribution of health services and nutrition in Sri Lanka, and wage compression in Singapore.[37] Two Indian states, Kerala and West Bengal were successful in land reforms, which resulted in improving the well-being of the poor (Besley, 1998).

2.5. Other Effects of Globalization

Empirical literature lends support to the fact that globalization gives a premium to the people with high levels of skill, high levels of education and high entrepreneurship. The skill biased technological change in manufacturing in developing countries has definitely had an adverse effect on the demand for unskilled, uneducated and marginalized workers. For developing countries, on the other hand, the fall in demand for low skilled workers has coincided with the emergence of an informal economy. There is a growing shift from 'formal' jobs to the informal sector, which provides the majority of employment opportunities (ILO, 2004). The same trend is found in the industrialized countries too.

There has been an intense link between globalization and income inequality. Lindert and Williamson (2001) and O'Rourke (2001) highlighted that increased world inequality has been driven by between-country rather than within-country inequality. It follows therefore, that globalization will have very different implications for within-country inequality. The direction of impact of globalization on within-country inequality depends on the participating country's policy orientation to exploit it. If globalization factors are taken out, the source of within-country inequality in the lagging countries might be their poor governance and non-democracy.

There arises a worldwide polarization of income distribution. Rich countries reap most of the benefits of globalization leading to the inequality and potential conflicts among nations (Intriligator, 2004). Some argued that nations that gained most from globalization are those of poor ones that changed their policies to make use of it, while the ones that gained the least did not (Lindert, 2001). Although some remarkable achievements by some East Asian countries are comparable to those of rich nations. At the national level, a particular group of people - because of better education, past training, personal contacts and access to modern financial system - is able to take advantage of globalization. Thus, groups which are economically better off earlier are in a better position to take advantage of the globalization process.

---

[37] See Bowles (2001)

One of the major sources of discontent about globalization is the failure to free movement of labor facilitated by the regulatory regimes of the nations.[38] The forces of globalization don't allow labor to play freely. Only selective migration is encouraged in the form of skilled workers (e.g., software professionals), whereas the movement of unskilled or semi-skilled workers is controlled by the immigration laws of the rich countries. The most important reason to put a ceiling on the free movement of labor is the desire on the part of the rich countries to preserve their own labor through tighter immigration policy. An increased mobility of labor would enhance knowledge and technology acquisition and welfare equality by its equalization effects on wages. The conscious and explicit state intervention prevents the emergence of a global labor market. On the other hand, capital is freely mobile by the virtue of ownership of large financial multinationals by the developed countries. This contradiction needs to be resolved to get the maximum benefits of globalization across the world.

Gomory and Baumol (2004) pointed out that globalization may suffer from economic damage for some groups of people including developed ones. Nevertheless, the increased competition pressure resulting from globalization enhances innovation and growth leading to a beneficial effect in the long run for every nation. Bhagwati (2004) pointed to two main groups of critics of globalization. Some have a deep antipathy of globalization composed of an anti-capitalist, anti-globalization, and acute anti-cooporation mind-set. There are others who consider economic globalization is the cause of several social ills today, such as poverty in poor countries and deterioration of the environment worldwide. However, it can be demonstrated that globalization advances rather than holds back various social causes such as gender equality and the reduction of poverty.

Stiglitz (2004) argued that developing countries which manage the globalization process well have received benefits in the form of rapid economic growth. But the most common phenomenon is that globalization has not been well managed, which may have adversely affected growth and poverty for some countries. Increased financial arrangements increased risk and force the developing countries to absorb risk. But developed countries enjoy a comparative advantage in absorbing risk at the cost of developing countries with their comparative disadvantage. The increased risk those developing countries are likely to face is from mismanaged globalization, which can have an adverse effect on their growth. Thus, nations should design policies to mitigate risks.

The success story of China and Korea demonstrated that with tactful governing and regulation, the globalization process could avoid the potential harmful effects and reap the full advantages. China achieved its aim of quadrupling its GDP in the two decades from 1980 to 2000 and is trying to hold it for the next two decades (Klein, 2004). India was able to achieve an annual growth rate just above 5% level just after the reform but its growth rate is susceptible to agricultural production. Now, India excels in software and finance and strives for an annual growth rate of 7% most years. Tanzi (2004) highlighted the need for increasing public spending to upgrade a country's infrastructure, improve institutions, finance eventual costs of correcting policies and replacing the traditional primitive and inefficient system of social protection with a minimum, modern safety net.

---

[38] See Castells (1996)

3. THE DATA SOURCES

The database created by Kearney/Foreign Policy magazine (2002)[39] is used for the computation of the globalization index. It constitutes a small balanced panel covering 62 countries observed for the period 1995-2001. It was originally collected from national sources, international organizations and financial institutions. In this paper we examine the process of globalization through the lens of four major components: economic integration, personal contacts, communication technology, and political engagement. For each sample of countries the data cover these four groups of indicators which are expected to act as a proxy for most of the channels through which globalization affects the nations' economies.[40] Before computation of the index let us consider each of these factors in turn.

Economic factors underlying the globalization process consist of four variables: trade, FDI, portfolio capital flows, and income payments and receipts. All four variables are given as a share of GDP. The trade variable includes total trade and is measured as the sum of trade of goods and services. Equally important is the FDI measured as a net inflow in a year. Portfolio flows are measured as the sum of portfolio inflows and outflows. Income payments and receipts include the compensation of non-resident employees and income earned and paid on assets held abroad.

Under the component of personal contact the best possible ways through which it occurs among the countries are: international telephone traffic, international travel and tourism, and transfer of payments and receipts. Telephone traffic is defined as the per capita sum of incoming and outgoing calls. It is obtained from the International Telecommunication Union (TU) and the World Telecommunication Indicators database. Travel and tourism includes the share of travelers entering and leaving a country in relation to its total population. The variable for transfers and payments is measured as the total of in and out transfer payments as a share of total GDP produced.

The third component is technology transfer. Technology transfer takes many forms. Due to non-availability of data this component is built on three variables: Internet users, Internet hosts and secure Internet servers. These components are communication specific and do not adequately reflect technology in broad terms. The Internet user variable is measured in terms of its share of total population, while Internet hosts and secured servers are measured in per capita terms.

Finally, the political component consists of political engagement, which is based on three variables - the number of embassies in a country, the number of memberships in international organizations, and the number of UN Security Council missions undertaken by a country during a calendar year. It may be noted that the personal and political components should ideally account for the domestic political situation and the flows of information supplied by the media. Detailed summary statistics of the complete set of variables are shown in Table 2.

---

[39] The data sources can be viewed at web sites: www.foreignpolicy.com and www.atkearney.com.
[40] A number of components such as financial market, environment, cultural, technology and innovation, and labor market could be added to the set of components. No data on these components are currently available.

Table 2. Summary Statistics of Globalization Data, 1995-2001, 62x7=434 Observations

Variable	Mean	Std Dev	Minimum	Maximum
A. Economic Integration				
1. Trade (w=1)	75.770	49.012	10.500	340.500
2. Foreign direct investment (w=2)	4.830	5.934	0.000	44.210
3. Portfolio investment (w=2)	6.021	16.572	0.000	193.120
4. Income payment and receipts (w=1)	9.100	9.869	0.670	78.390
B. Personal Contacts				
1. International telephone traffic (w=2)	101.575	133.333	0.850	738.320
2. International travel and tourism (w=1)	77.389	94.888	0.300	515.60
3. Transfer payment and receipts (w=1)	3.434	2.774	0.000	15.490
C. Technology				
1. Internet users (w=2)	8.020	12.038	0.000	59.950
2. Internet hosts (w=1)	0.015	0.034	0.000	0.381
3. Secure internet servers (w=1)	0.016	0.040	0.000	0.335
D. Political Engagement				
1. Embassies in country(w=1)	70.444	33.947	13.000	172.000
2. Membership in intel. organization (w-1)	48.732	11.008	6.000	77.000
3. Participation in UNSC missions (w=1)	26.545	21.261	0.000	81.300

Note. w indicates weights attached to each indicator.

4. EMPIRICAL FRAMEWORK

The present study attempts to quantify the level of globalization of different countries from different parts of the world. Kearney (2002, 2003) attempted first to construct a database and computed a composite globalization index. The basic component of the index is comprised of economic integration, personal contact, communication technology, and political engagement. The globalization index (hereafter denoted as KEARNEY) is based on the normalization of individual variables as well as the subsequent aggregation using an ad hoc weighting system. The equation used to describe globalization index takes the form

$$KEARNEY_{it} = \sum_{j=1}^{J} \omega_j \sum_{m=1}^{M} \omega_m \left[\frac{X_{jmit} -}{X_{jmt}^{max} -} \right]$$

1)

where i and t stands for the country and time periods, m and j are within and between major component variables, ω_j and ω_m are the weights attached to each within group and between group variables, min and max are minimum and maximum values of respective variables across countries in a given year. The index is similar to that of human development index (HDI).

We consider this index as a benchmark index where the weights of the components are chosen on an ad hoc basis and are constant across countries and over time. In the basic index, each of the 13 determinants of the index is given equal weight (w=1). In the alternative case, a number of variables are given double weights (w=2). Using a smaller set of countries, Lockwood (2001) finds the ranking of countries based on the above index to be sensitive to the way the indicators are measured, normalized and weighted together to a composite index.

Apart from the Kearney index, which is non-parametric, there are two alternative parametric approaches to measure the level of globalization: using the principal component (Heshmati 2003 and 2006) or factor analysis (Andersen and Herbertsson 2003). Principal component analysis is a multivariate technique. Agénor (2003) used trade and financial openness to compute a simple economic globalization index based on PC analysis. In this study we use the Kearney index, the weighted globalization index and the principal component index with variation in the weights in all dimensions. It should be noted that an aggregation of the statistically significant principal and factor components, where in the aggregation process the share of total variance is explained by each index component or factor is used as weight in the overall aggregation results in identical rankings of countries. In the analyses we use only principal component and Kearney based indices.

In principal component analysis we estimate the globalization index using least square solutions. For a given dataset of P numeric variables at most P-1 principal components can be computed. Each component is linearly combined with the original variables with coefficients equal to the eigenvectors of the correlation of the covariance matrix and is sorted according to the descending order of the *eigenvalues*, which are equal to the variance of the components. The empirical estimate of the solution of principal component is:

$$Y_{it} = BX_{it} + E_{it} \qquad (2)$$

where Y_{it} is an PxN matrix of the centered observed variables for country i in period t, X_{it} is the JxN matrix of scores of the first J principal components, B is a PxJ matrix of eigenvectors, E_{it} is an PxN matrix of residuals, N is the number of observations, P the number of partial variables and J is the number of variables or indicators of globalization. Here we minimize the sum of all the squared residuals, which are measured as distances from the point to the (first) principal axis. In the least squares case, the vertical distance to the fitted line is minimized. The globalization indices indicate the level and progress of globalization for different countries over time. A breakdown of the index into its major components provides the possibility to identify the sources of globalization, and to quantify the impact of each sources on the global integration of countries.

5. DISTRIBUTION OF THE DATA

Trade, the driving force behind a nation's economic integration, having an average value of 76% of GDP with a large standard deviation of 49%, indicating wide variation of the trade share across counties. (see Table 2) The average values of FDI and portfolio, as a share of

GDP are about 5 per cent and 9 percent respectively. The maximum values of these variables are 44 per cent and 193 per cent respectively and the minimum share is found to be zero.

The most important item among the personal components is international telephone traffic. Average per capita sum of incoming and outgoing call is 101.5 with a large standard deviation of 133.3. A wide gap is found between the minimum (0.85) and maximum (738.3) values. On average, 77 per cent of the travelers entered and departed a country in relation to its population (standard deviation 95) whereas the maximum and minimum values are 0.30 per cent and 515.6 per cent respectively. The average value of the share of in and out transfer payment is 3.43 per cent of GDP, with the minimum and maximum value 0 and 15 per cent respectively.

As far as technological components are concerned the average share of population using Internet is 8.02 per cent with the standard deviation of 12.03 per cent. The maximum value is found to be 60 per cent and countries with no Internet connection are also found in our sample. The values for the per capita Internet host and secure Internet server variable are 0.015 and 0.016 respectively.

The average number of embassies in the country is found to be 70 with a wide gap in the minimum (13) and maximum (172) values. As far as the number of memberships in international organizations is concerned, on average each country has 49 such memberships. The minimum and maximum values are 6 and 77 respectively. On average each country participates in 27 UN Security Council Missions, with a large standard deviation of 21.26.

6. THE RELATIONSHIP BETWEEN THE COMPONENTS

Correlation coefficients among the various index components are presented in Table 3. As expected, the various components are positively and mostly significantly correlated among themselves. The economic integration component is negatively correlated with time, while technology is positively correlated with time. The remaining personal and political components as well as the two Kearney globalization indices are weakly correlated with time.

Economic integration consists of four variables, defined largely by trade and the indicators of capital flows. There was a major East Asian financial crisis at the end of 1997 and a crisis in the emerging Russian and Brazilian markets in 1998. These resulted in a major decline in capital flows to the emerging-market countries as well as high volatility in the East Asian financial markets. This could be a possible explanation of the negative correlation between economic integration and time trend.

The application of different weights does not change the rank of the countries much. The overall Kearney index is dominated by political and economic integration.

We have not decomposed the principal component index into its underlying four components. Such decomposition would require, first, the application of PC analysis on each component separately, and then the aggregation of the components into a single globalization index by assigning some weights to each component, or, alternatively, the use of canonical correlation analysis looking at the correlation relationship between two or more sets of variables.

Table 3. Pearson Correlation Coefficients, 434 Observations

	Year	Eco	Eco(w)	Persl.	Persl(w)	Tech	Tech(w)	Political	GIndex(k)	GIndex(kw)	PC
Year	1.000										
Economic	-0.161	1.000									
Economic(w)	-0.200	0.988	1.000								
Personal	0.043	0.626	0.601	1.000							
Personal(w)	0.035	0.682	0.660	0.981	1.000						
Technology	0.169	0.307	0.329	0.387	0.473	1.000					
Technol(w)	0.205	0.314	0.333	0.400	0.484	0.992	1.000				
Political	0.067	0.045	0.103	0.099	0.136	0.397	0.385	1.000			
GIndex (K)	0.041	0.708	0.725	0.731	0.793	0.765	0.763	0.573	1.000		
GIndex(KW)	0.023	0.756	0.777	0.734	0.806	0.767	0.772	0.496	0.991	1.000	
PC	0.297	0.353	0.392	0.426	0.490	0.699	0.704	0.802	0.832	0.796	1.000

Notes. Kearney (K), Kearney Weighted (KW), and Principal Component (PC) globalization index (GIndex).

Table 4 reports the summary statistics of different indices and their components. The unweighted mean economic component is 0.642 with the standard deviation of 0.560. Except economic component all other index components are positively related with time (see Table 4). The economic component is decreasing (-0.161) over time, the weighted coefficient decreased further to -2.00. The maximum and minimum values vary widely between 0.050 and 3.588. The average values of other components are 0.590, 0.390 and 1.397 for personal contacts, technology and political engagements respectively. They are positively related over time (personal contacts (0.043), technology (0.169) and political engagements (0.067)). The coefficients of personal components come down from 0.043 to 0.035 by attaching weights. However, technology component increased from 0.169 to 0.205 by attaching weights to Internet users. The economic component is highly correlated (0.625) with personal engagements, moderately (0.307) with technology transfer and weakly correlated (0.045) with political components. The mean value of personal component is 0.590 with the standard deviation of 0.455. Personal and technology transfer are positively correlated (0.387), while personal and political components are weakly correlated (0.099).

Table 4. Summary of Statistics of Globalization Indices and their Components, 434 Oobservations

Variable	Mean	Std Dev	Minimum	Maximum
Economic Integration	0.642	0.560	0.050	3.588
Economic Integration (w)	0.943	0.875	0.057	5.588
Personal Contacts	0.590	0.455	0.015	2.420
Personal Contacts (w)	0.758	0.647	0.025	3.335
Technology	0.390	0.557	0.000	2.856
Technology (w)	0.583	0.795	0.000	3.713
Political Engagement	1.397	0.551	0.006	2.695
Unweighted Kearney Index (K)	3.019	1.471	1.150	7.937
Weighted Kearney Index (KW)	3.682	2.088	1.227	11.004
Principal Component Index (PC)	0.000	0.642	-1.347	2.532

Note. w= weights.

7. VARIATIONS IN GLOBALIZATION

7.1. Comparison of Different Approaches

As mentioned earlier the globalization index as measured on the basis of Kearney and principal component are computed for each of 62 countries covering for seven years 1995-2001. The Kearney index is computed with equal weights and considered as benchmark model. Following Kearney's approach a number of economic, personal and technology factors are given higher weights. The logic for this argument is to go for a sensitivity analysis. The differences in levels of the two indices are due to differences in normalization of the variables. The range of principal component-based indices differs from those of Kearney-based indices. The mean unweighted globalization index is 3.019 with standard deviation of 1.471 whereas by using weighted system the mean value increased to 3.682 with higher standard deviation of 2.088. So the dispersion around the mean is significantly higher in the weighted index (Table 4).

In Table 4 we can observe large variations in the variables underlying the calculation of the index and its components. The distribution of the index components is not uniform. Political component comprised 47.27% of the unweighted index, followed by economic integration (21.27 per cent), personal contacts (19.54 per cent) and technology transfers (12.92 per cent). As far as weighted index is concerned, the components are distributed as political engagement (37.95 per cent), economic integration (25.62 per cent), personal contact (20.59 per cent) and technology transfers (15.84 per cent).

Globalization is positively correlated with time for each index where the highest value is found for principal component index (0.297). There is a decrease in the value of correlation coefficients from 0.041 to 0.022 using weighted globalization index (see Table 3). Our analysis is based on weighted globalization and its components which gives more stress on some crucial components of globalization. Unweighted index components are highlighted in the analysis. Such a provision enables us to compare the change in the position of the country after different weights are attached.

Since the expected effects from each indicator on the composite index are the same in each of the indices, each of the three indices is suitable for analysis. However, they differ in a number of respects. The parametric principal component is more flexible by not assuming any weights on an ad hoc basis rather than estimating them. A disadvantage of principal component is that it does not allow decomposition of the total composite index into underlying 4 major components, unless each component is computed separately and then assuming some weighing system aggregated into a singe composite index. The two versions of the non-parametric Kearney index are flexible in decomposition, but suffer from ad hoc aggregation of the indicators. In this paper we avoid to select any of the indices, and instead try to analyze the results based on each index in parallel. In doing so, we account for their benefits and limitations.

7.2. Globalization by Country

Country wise analysis of the globalization index reveals that indices are highly correlated with each other.[41] The countries are ranked in a descending order according to the weighted Kearney index (see Appendix A and Figure 1). As mentioned earlier following Kearney's approach a number of economic, personal and technology factor are given higher weights.

The positions of the countries with both categories - weighted and unweighted are almost the same. Ranking of the countries differs to some extent by principal component index (see Appendix A and Figure 2).

---

[41] Spearman rank correlation coefficient: K-KW: 0.975, K-PC: 0.828, KW-PC: 0.795

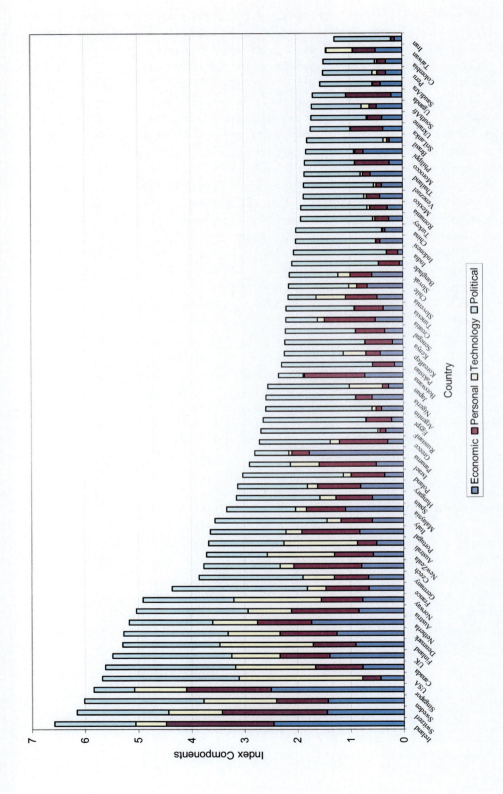

Figure 1. Unweighted Kearney Globalization index (K) decomposed by components.

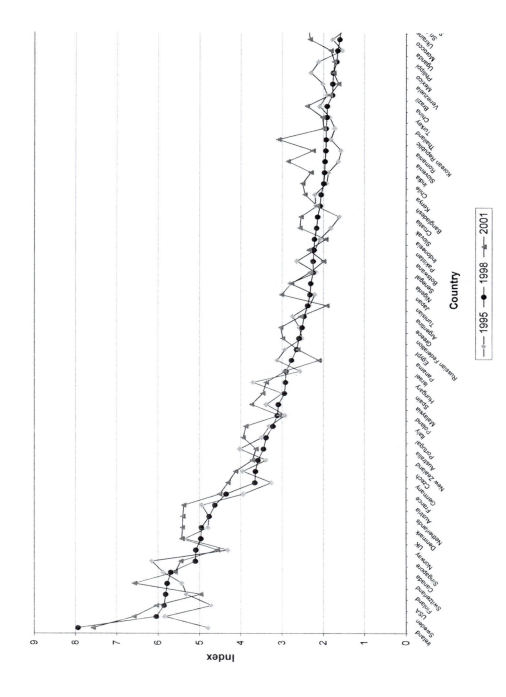

Figure 2. Kearney index by country (Ranked by 1998 position.

The top ten position of globalization is dominated by West European countries, with Ireland (8.829) leading the group. Singapore is the second highest globalized country in the world with an index value of 8.321, followed by Switzerland (8.238), Sweden (8.125), Canada (7.175), the UK (7.064), Netherlands (7.032), Finland (6.919), Denmark (6.860) and the USA (6.844). The three non European countries qualified in the group are Singapore, Canada and the USA. Good overall performance of the components goes together in forming highest positions. In terms of factors influencing their globalization no similar trend is found among them. For Ireland and Singapore economic and political component dominated the globalization process. While in Switzerland personal component influenced more than other factors. In Sweden both economic and political components have more influence.

Iran, Colombia, Peru, Uganda and Saudi Arabia are among the least globalized countries in the world. The low ranking is mainly due to low technological and economic components. Very likely, lack of policy coordination due to their political setup, limited resources and internal conflicts may have caused such imbalances in the first four countries. Republic of Korea, Russia, Slovenia, Croatia and Chile are among the average five globalized countries. The economic component has identical influence among these countries but differ as far as other three components are concerned.

Except Singapore no other Asian countries showed a satisfactory level of globalization. From individual country's perspective it is worthwhile to compare China and India, looking at their different political setup and almost identical population size. China has a single party rule while India is a multiparty democracy. Ranked 42nd in the world, China is marginally (0.128) ahead of India in terms of the computed globalization index. China is well ahead in economic integration compared to India, which enjoys better advantage in personal and political engagements. Figure 3 shows the breakdown of the indices into the four components for two countries.

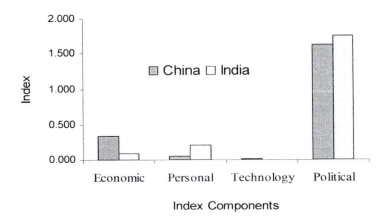

Figure 3. Globalization and its components for China and India.

By far the largest category is political engagement, which makes up 84.77% and 80.24% for India and China respectively. In terms of components influencing globalization political factors have contributed much for both countries. In China political factor of globalization is followed by economic, personal and technological components (see Table 5). In India, political factor is the second highest component of globalization (see Table 6).

Table 5. Globalization Index and its Components in China

Year	Economic	Personal	Technology	Political	K	KW	PC
1995	0.494	0.031	0.000	1.566	2.092	2.473	-0.167
1996	0.432	0.038	0.001	1.545	2.015	2.316	-0.178
1997	0.404	0.058	0.001	1.490	1.953	2.233	-0.208
1998	0.315	0.044	0.005	1.545	1.909	2.123	-0.193
1999	0.239	0.055	0.015	1.468	1.778	1.926	-0.206
2000	0.226	0.059	0.035	1.641	1.961	2.101	0.001
2001	0.248	0.044	0.043	2.063	2.398	2.544	0.288
Mean	0.337	0.047	0.014	1.617	2.015	2.245	-0.095

Table 6. Globalization Index and its Components in India

Year	Economic	Personal	Technology	Political	K	KW	PC
1995	0.127	0.176	0.002	1.571	1.876	1.965	-0.192
1996	0.153	0.281	0.003	1.549	1.986	2.094	-0.207
1997	0.128	0.269	0.002	1.725	2.124	2.202	-0.129
1998	0.070	0.169	0.004	1.731	1.974	2.005	-0.137
1999	0.053	0.215	0.005	1.829	2.103	2.127	-0.040
2000	0.050	0.201	0.008	1.813	2.073	2.098	0.041
2001	0.090	0.186	0.010	2.016	2.301	2.329	0.229
Mean	0.096	0.214	0.005	1.748	2.062	2.117	-0.062

India and China adopted different types of strategy on FDI for their industrial development. India followed import substitution policy which relied heavily on domestic resource mobilization and domestic firms were given protection in production.[1] To quote from World Investment Report 2003, FDI has contributed to the rapid growth of China's merchandise export. At an annual rate China's export grew by 15% between 1989 and 2001.

In 2000-2001, about two third of the FDI to China went to the manufacturing sectors. Differences are there in FDI performance of the two countries relating to timing, progress and the contents of FDI liberalization. China opened its economy in 1979 and since then has been progressively liberalizing its investment regime. Since its opening, China has liberalized FDI in export oriented sectors. India didn't take comparable steps towards liberalization, instead followed a combination of legal and institutional infrastructure and restrictive FDI policies until 1991. (see Nagaraj, 2003). FDI has been much less important in driving India's export growth except in high technology activities. The low effect is due to low inflow of FDI to India. Even after a significant liberalization of FDI policies, internationalization is not necessary a dominant factor.

---

[1] See (Sarma, 2002)

7.3. Globalization by Region

Regionally we divide the sample countries into nine broad groups. Their mean globalization is presented in Table 7. The mean index components by region are presented in Table 8.

Table 7. Globalization Index by Region: Ranked in Descending Order of the Weighted Globalization Index

Political	K	Rank (K)	KW	Rank (KW)	PC	Rank (PC)
West Europe	4.748	1	6.129	1	0.699	2
North America	4.672	2	5.876	2	0.748	1
South East Asia	2.974	3	3.731	3	-0.275	5
East Europe	2.529	4	2.941	4	-0.253	4
East Asia	2.061	7	2.600	5	-0.339	8
Middle East and N. Africa	2.180	5	2.434	6	-0.320	6
Latin America	2.011	8	2.393	7	-0.235	3
Sub-Saharan Africa	2.131	6	2.309	8	-0.496	9
South Asia	1.893	9	1.943	9	-0.339	8

Table 8. Globalization Index by Region: Ranked by Descending Order of Unweighted Index

Region	Eco	Eco (w)	Persl.	Persl (w)	Tech	Tech (w)	Political	Gindex (w)	Ginde (kw)	PC
West Europe	1.060	1.661	1.039	1.417	0.793	1.196	1.856	4.748	6.129	0.699
North America	0.575	0.906	0.584	0.926	1.619	2.150	1.894	4.672	5.876	0.748
South East Asia	1.078	1.467	0.542	0.754	0.250	0.405	1.105	2.974	3.731	-0.275
East Europe	0.510	0.701	0.600	0.709	0.178	0.289	1.241	2.529	2.941	-0.253
East Asia	0.389	0.576	0.216	0.274	0.390	0.684	1.066	2.061	2.600	-0.339
Middle East and N. Africa	0.342	0.447	0.523	0.619	0.103	0.155	1.212	2.180	2.434	-0.320
Latin America	0.572	0.856	0.171	0.215	0.072	0.126	1.196	2.011	2.393	-0.235
Sub-Saharan Africa	0.428	0.564	0.584	0.606	0.030	0.050	1.089	2.131	2.309	-0.496
South Asia	0.168	0.208	0.342	0.348	0.003	0.007	1.379	1.893	1.943	-0.339

The ranking of regions differs over the methods applied in the measurement of globalization, i.e. whether an identical or different weighting system of the non-parametric Kearney type index is applied or whether the parametric principal component is employed.

The mean index value showed wide variations across regions ranging from a high level of 4.748 in West Europe to the low level of 1.893 for South Asia. West Europe has the highest score in both Kearney and weighted Kearney method whereas North America ranked highest in terms of Principal component index. Top four positions (West Europe, North America, South East Asia and East Europe) of the regions are the same in both Kearney and weighted globalization index.

As a result of attaching higher weight to the technology factor the position of East Asia has moved up from the seventh to the fifth position in ranking of the weighted Kearney index. Conversely, the ranking of Sub-Saharan Africa moved down from the sixth to the eights position after attaching weights to some individual indicator variables. The ranking of South Asia stands in the bottom in both unweighted and weighted Kearney indices while in the case of the principal component index Sub-Saharan Africa holds got the lowest rank.

West Europe, North America and South East Asia constitute the three highest globalized regions (see Figure 2, 4 and 8). Also these three regions differ in terms of individual index components. Political component is the dominant factor for all of these three regions, followed by economic, personal and technological factor for majority of the regions. In general these three regions enjoy advantageous positions in any of the index components. In particular the large countries with embassies in all countries and strong positions in the US system organizations and the UN Security Council are attached quite high political index components.

Table 8 shows the contribution of the factors both in terms of Kearney and weighted Kearney methods. For instance, South East Asia has got the highest advantage in economic globalization, West Europe has the highest expediency in personal contacts and North America enjoys most commendable position in technology transfers. East Europe, Middle East and North Africa and East Asia are identified at the medium level of globalization. East Europe has the advantage in all index components in the group.

The index component differs among the other two regions where Sub Saharan Africa has the advantage in economic and personal engagements than Middle East Africa which has better position in technology and political components. Lastly, East Asia, Latin America and South Asia are amongst the bottom three in terms of the lowest degree of progress in globalization. East Asia enjoys better advantage in technology transfer whereas for South Asia's globalization has been impacted by low economic and nearly absent technology factor. Sub Saharan Africa enjoys better progress in economic and personal factors and Latin America shows progress in technology and political engagements.

As far as other factors of globalization are concerned political component is more dominant for the least globalized regions. The reverse trend is found for technological components, where South Asian and Sub-Saharan African region ranks low in technological transfer. North America has better advantage in technology transfer followed by East Asia and West Europe countries. In terms of political engagement they are also different. The South East Asian and Latin American region shows high economic integration, but its level of globalization is limited by relatively low personal contacts and technology transfer.

If we take out Spain and Greece all the other West European countries belong to top 20 most globalized countries. Good overall functioning of index components especially in economic and political components made them the leader. West Europe was the place of origin of Industrial Revolution and continues its position as industrial leader even today. Ireland, Netherlands, Sweden, UK, Denmark and Finland witnessed a modest presence in economic integration. Economic integration and personal contacts are the driving forces of Ireland's globalization, while they have mixed effect for other countries in the group. Switzerland ranked up the second position in the world and in the group, achieves good overall performance in all of its components. Being founded on technology transfer Finland outranked others in the group (1.756) and is the second in the world.

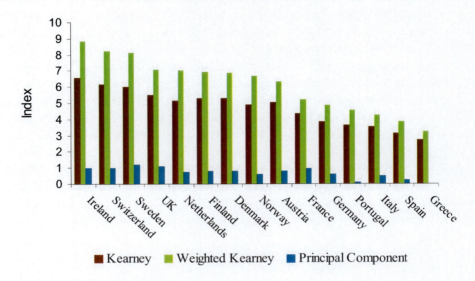

Figure 4. Globalization by region, West Europe.

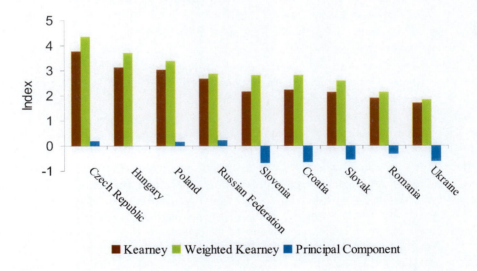

Figure 5. Globalization by region, East Europe.

East Europe did not fare so well in global integration placed as medium globalized region. Czech Republic leading the group ranked 18th position in the world followed by Hungary, Poland, Russia, Croatia, Slovenia, Slovakia, Romania and Ukraine. The total collapse of Soviet Union in 1990s landed the region into a period of chaotic economic, political and social transition.

In North America resides the world's most powerful economy, contributed by its size, geography, diversity and abundant natural resources. Countries belonging to this region play a pivotal role in global economic scenario. Canada leads the group, followed by the USA with its supreme power in the world of technology transmits (2.323), while New Zealand and Australia are not as strong as the former.

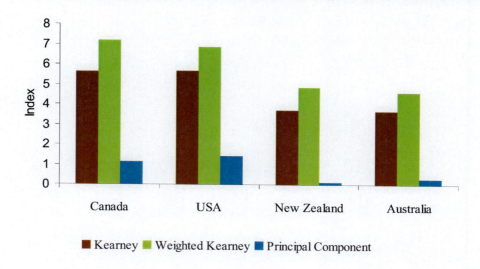

Figure 6. Globalization by region, North America and Pacific.

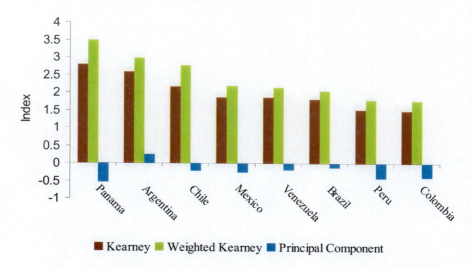

Figure 7. Globalization by region, Latin America.

In Latin America, Panama and Argentina have maintained a considerable lead over the other countries (see Figure 7). Brazil, the tenth largest economy in the world ranked 6th in the region and 54th in the world, is the largest debtor in the world. In the 1960s, Brazil, Mexico and Argentina showed remarkable advancement in industrial position. Oil wealth also helped to nurture the economy of Venezuela and Mexico. But these countries were badly shaken by the debt crisis in 1980s and have failed to recuperate.

Middle East and North Africa played a crucial role in the process globalization (see Figure 8). Israel is ahead in the group with good overall performance of the components of globalization followed by Egypt, Tunisia, Turkey, Morocco and Saudi Arabia. Political conflict across the region played a crucial role in disrupting the process of economic development. Civil war and conflicts across the states have jeopardized their greater international integration. Sub Saharan Africa - the poorest and the least developed regions of the world have limited connectedness with rest of the world (see Figure 9). Nigeria is in the lead with good achievement in political and economic components.

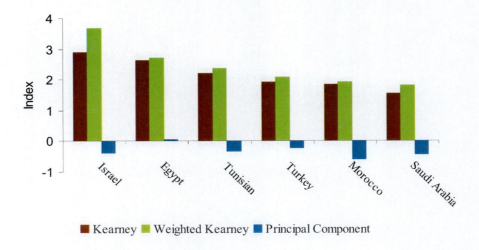

Figure 8. Globalization by region, Middle East and North Africa.

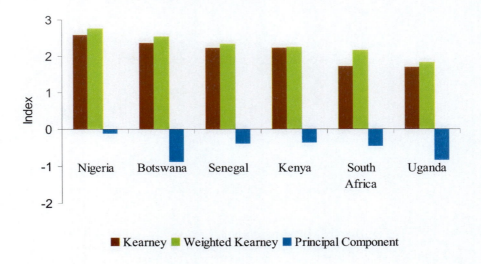

Figure 9. Globalization by region, Sub Saharan Africa.

Botswana, second position in the group, has a stable, democratic setup, enjoys strong and growing economic base is leading in economic integration and personal contacts. South Africa is known as economic powerhouse and has well balanced industrial economy within the region. But failed to do well in economic integration but placed first in technology transfers within the group. The population growth emerges as a severe problem which has been outstripping economic expansion. Moreover, ethnic conflicts and the spread of AIDS exasperate the regions problem.

   Most heterogeneous development in globalization is found among Asian regions and countries. On the one side there are South East Asian countries, most dominant in the recent globalization process. Singapore and Malaysia are the two leading countries in the group. Singapore placed second in the world is now the communication cum financial hub thriving with high tech manufacturing centre. Singapore experienced mild economic recession in 1990s. The government of Singapore encouraged investment by multinationals and invested heavily in the social and physical infrastructures. Malaysia, well behind Singapore, shows better performance of political and economic components. Economic development in Malaysia is centered around primary sector and on the extraction of natural resources. The Philippines placed at the bottom of the group is one part of the region hardly hit by the Asian Economic crisis of the late 1990s. The once highly developed Philippines experienced biggest economic disappointment in South Asia.

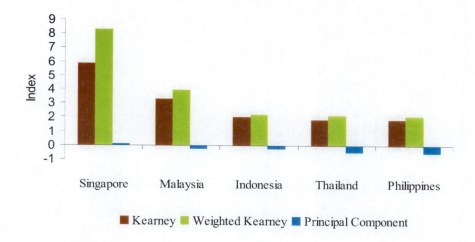

Figure 10. Globalization by region, South East Asia.

   Countries belonging to the East Asian region made successful strides in the path of globalization. Japan, the leading country in the group with their supremacy in technology transfers. This followed by Korean Republic with dominant in economic and technology transfers. China placed third in the group, with better performance in economic and political engagement. With weak political engagement Taiwan placed bottom of the group. The success story of all these countries owe much to their export-led development policy success after dismantling protectionist and illiberal domestic policies in 1970s.
   The most unsuccessful among the regions is South Asia. Countries belongs the region failed to take advantage of globalization where political components play a crucial role in their globalization campaign (see Figure 12). In countries belonging to this region globalization worsened very much by a near absence in technology transfer. Pakistan is leading the group with better economic and political components, followed by Bangladesh, India, Sri Lanka and Iran. The continuing geopolitical tension between Indian and Pakistan is deteriorating the globalization process in this region. Ethnic violence in Sri Lanka also appended the problem.

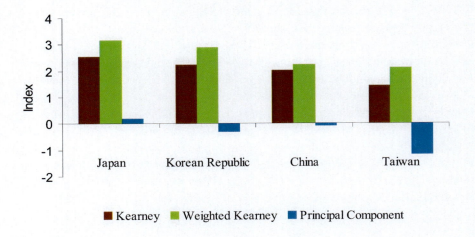

Figure 11. Globalization by region, East Asia.

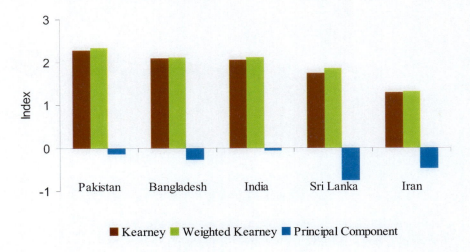

Figure 12. Globalization by region, South Asia.

7.4. Development of Globalization over Time

Despite short period of observation from 1995-2001 the estimates of various approaches of globalization are capable to provide satisfactory explanation of development of globalization over time. The idealistic situation should be to weight the indices by countries share of GDP or population to provide a satisfactory survey of the coverage of temporal changes in the globalization process. The components of globalization are able to provide break up indices over time. Both weighted and unweighted globalization are fluctuating between and the throughout the time period of the study. Between 1995 and 1997 the unweighted index rose steadily from 2.892 to 3.074, but declined in 1998 to 2.926, again increased thereafter for the rest of the period (3.003 to 3.184). Weighted globalization index shows the same pattern of movement during those periods while the PC index increased continuously from 1995-2001 (see Table 9).

In terms of the contribution of separate components on globalization index, political factor is the most important contributor over the entire time period. The shares of political and personal factors are fluctuating over time whereas economic factor is declining over the study period. Both weighted and unweighted economic integration increased in 1997 and thereafter remained low for the rest of the periods 1998-2001. The decline is a consequence of emerging markets with high level of protection and also the East Asian financial crisis accentuated the drop of the value. Also the protectionist trade measure by the developed countries for the primary items also contributed this fact. Only technological factor is seen in a rising tendency increased from 0.223 to 0.524.

Table 9. Development of Globalization Index and its Components Over Time

Year	Eco	Eco (w)	Persl.	Persl (w)	Tech	Tech (w)	Political	Gindex (k)	Ginde (kw)	PC
1995	0.744	1.162	0.546	0.710	0.223	0.320	1.380	2.892	3.572	-0.204
1996	0.725	1.101	0.605	0.771	0.316	0.451	1.372	3.018	3.694	-0.178
1997	0.810	1.226	0.560	0.714	0.349	0.493	1.355	3.074	3.787	-0.143
1998	0.577	0.825	0.566	0.737	0.402	0.586	1.381	2.926	3.529	-0.081
1999	0.557	0.796	0.637	0.821	0.438	0.659	1.371	3.003	3.647	0.024
2000	0.562	0.807	0.617	0.785	0.479	0.752	1.381	3.039	3.724	0.207
2001	0.516	0.685	0.602	0.771	0.524	0.824	1.541	3.184	3.821	0.373

As a most globalized country, Ireland witnessed rapid progress in globalization throughout the entire study period. In the initial year the value of the index was 6.040, continued up to 6.458 in 1997. Thereafter made a jump to 10.825 in 1998 and hold the momentum till the end. For Switzerland globalization followed a stable path through out the entire period where the index ranges between 7.442 and 8.699. For the remaining countries in the group their index value varies between 6.707 and 9.118 for Sweden, 6.718 and 7.419 for UK, 6.412 and 7.564 for Netherlands, 6.222 and 7.181 for Finland, 6.191 and 8.057 for Denmark, 5.697 and 7.808 for Norway, 5.757 and 6.500 for Austria, 4.572 and 5.772 for France, 4.057 and 5.627 for Germany, 3.670 and 5.635 for Portugal, 3.678 and 4.791 for Italy, 3.120 and 4.451 for Spain and 2.880 and 3.561 for Greece.

Almost all North American countries hold its globalization at a steady level. Excluding Canada all other countries in North America strengthen their position in globalization from the 1995 level. Globalization index of Canada dropped marginally from 7.289 in 1995 to 7.130 in 2001. For USA, the second ranked country in the group picked up the index value from 6.047 in 1995 to 7.192 in 2001. The index value varies between 4.658 and 5.269 for New Zealand and 4.202 and 5.173 for Australia.

The globalization process in South East Asian countries coincided with the economic crisis. Singapore is among the 'Asian Tigers' showed a fluctuating tendency in their globalization process. Starting from 9.184 in 1995 it reached 10.125 in 1996, dropped suddenly to 7.059 in the next year, reached as low as 6.827 in 2000. This downturn happened in the backdrop of financial crisis and the subsequent economic recession plagued in 1998.

Except Malaysia and Thailand all other countries witnessed a sharp drop and the wild fluctuations throughout the entire period in their level of globalization. Singapore saw a significant acceleration in globalization 9.184 to 10.193 over 1995-96, but dropped to 10.125 in 1997 and took a nosedive to 7.372 in 2001 before touching the bottom level of 6.847 in 2000. Malaysia and Thailand hold a steady level through the time period.

The Czech Republic is leading the group of East Europe with good overall performance in the index components, although the index value drops from 4.873 in 1995 to 4.658 in 2001. The story is being repeated for Hungary too where the index value started from 5.018 in 1995 dropped sharply to 3.858 in 2001. Croatia showed a marked improvement in their level of globalization increased from 1.957 in 1995 to 3.071 in 2001 although reached its peak at 3.096 in 1999. For other countries the index varies between 3.293 and 3.485 for Poland, 2.672 and 3.092 for Russian Federation, 2.201 and 3.658 for Slovenia, 2.103 and 3.028 for Slovak, 1.703 and 2.439 for Romania and lastly 1.520 and 2.361 for Ukraine.

Most Latin American countries began to open their economies in the late 1980s as part of their structural adjustment program. Panama topped the group with its strong impact in economic factor witnessed a sharp decline in level of globalization from 3.807 to 2.390 between 1995 and 2001. Chile, pioneer in the reform process got better advancement from 2.387 to its top at 3.187 in 2001. Chile unilaterally eliminated quantitative restrictions and reduced import tariff to a uniform level of 10 percent by the early 1990s which resulted in the improvement in index from 2.387 to 3.187 during the study period.

Nigeria, as a leading country in the Sub Saharan group started out well at 3.135 in 1995, but its index value consolidated within the range of 2.438 and 2.937 for the rest of the period. Botswana experienced a steady fall in the index value from 2.940 in 1995 to reach the bottom level at 2.118 in 2001. Interestingly, other low ranked countries in the region recorded an improvement in their globalization process. Their index value varies between 2.105 and 2.659 for Senegal, 2.064 and 2.479 for Kenya, between 1.640 and 2.980 in South Africa and between 1.639 and 1.938 for Uganda. Economic and political factor affected the process of globalization. Poor climatic factors continued to have a major impact on economic performance.

Table 10. Percentage Change In Globalization Index and its Components Over Time

Year	Economic	Personal	Technology	Political	Gindex(K)	Gindex(KW)	PC
1995-96	-2.59	10.77	41.96	-0.54	4.34	3.43	-12.62
1996-97	11.84	-7.34	10.32	-1.26	1.88	2.50	-19.79
1997-98	-28.82	1.00	15.40	1.94	-4.80	-6.81	-43.52
1998-99	-3.42	12.57	8.77	-0.73	2.61	3.36	-130.27
1999-00	0.86	-3.08	9.53	0.68	1.21	2.11	749.59
2000-01	-8.10	-2.43	9.37	11.65	4.78	2.59	79.93

In South Asia, where most countries experienced a steady progress in the globalization process, only Bangladesh experienced a marginal fall in the index value. In India, the increase in the index value was more pronounced. The index increased from 1.964 to 2.329 over between 1995 and 2001. For Pakistan, high and the low index value varies between 2.169 and 2.507, for Bangladesh varies between 1.962 and 2.205, for Sri Lanka varies between 1.649 and 2.073 and for Iran varies between 1.226 and 1.361. Declining economic integrations and very insignificant presence of technology transfers are among the prime factor responsible holding back their globalization process.

7.5. Changes in Globalization

The average changes in index components and composite indices are reported in Table 10. The changes are based on the mean value from previous period, neglecting the between-country variation. The level of globalization increases over time except in 1997-98 where the change is negative. As far as the components of globalization are concerned only technological component showed positive improvement over time. In 1997-98 economic component recorded a major decline.

8. INDIA AND GLOBALIZATION

Beginning from mid 80s, Government of India gradually undertook a series of adjustment in industrial policy for opening the door for foreign capital and simultaneously provided long term cover to foreign investment. In early 1991, India embarked into the integration with the world economy in a much bigger scale through the removal of various directives, regulations and controls. However, the necessity of reform had arisen out of the next to rescue the economic system from financial and external payment crisis. Other political factors also provided the motivation. It had to approach the IMF for fresh loans to clear its fallen debt due. Thus, on the behest of the IMF and the World Bank India sincerely followed structural adjust program, which contain loaded prescriptions like trade liberalization, lifting up restriction on foreign direct and portfolio investments, current account convertibility in phases and partial capital account liberalization, shifting towards market-determined exchange rate regime, beginning the privatization process and measures to pass on substantial portion of the domestic market to the trans national corporations (TNCs).

Thus, the ultimate objective of the above policy measures was to remove all irritants and stumbling blocks for opening up of the economy. Through these measures government attach greater importance on the strengthening of production and efficiency through the forces of modernization, technological change, cost reduction and quality upgrading. Despite the imminent threat of policy change the dynamics of economic reform after the reform was perceived as an immense opportunity to capture the global market. At the same time, with the removal of restrictions on the movement of factors of production, goods and services global standard come to control on the quality and prices. A noteworthy change is observed after the reform by the healthy transformation of Indian corporate sector with the new flow of foreign investment. India has emerged as a profitable production destination for the multinationals.

Since independence, India followed a mixed economy structure with major thrust on state owned public sector nurtured in a relatively closed or protected environment, with trade and foreign investment playing a limited role and a significant agrarian sector marked by low per capital income and income inequality. Still agricultural growth is the major force in stimulating domestic demand for industrial products. Organized manufacturing sector in India includes all public sector enterprises and all non agricultural establishments employing ten or more workers. The post-globalization phase of Indian manufacturing industries is facing three-pronged attacks. A segment of manufacturing is now getting linked with the global capital and technology. This has posed a significant challenge for the domestic industry, its self-reliant industrial development and the industrial growth.

Firstly, the domestic industry irrespective of size and class is encountering the problem of demand deficiency. It is to be noted here that unlike the industries in East and South-East Asia India's share in world industrial output and export is not commensurate with its size and potentiality. India accounts for less than 1 per cent share in world trade. Hence, the major demand for the industry stems from the domestic market. The decade of nineties characterize large volatile fluctuation in the market demand. Pent up demand for the consumer durables was absorbed with one time hike in wages and salaries in the public and organized sector in the mid-nineties. By that time the entry of the foreign firms and products in the Indian market as a result of increased openness eroded significantly the market share of the domestic industries.

Secondly, the domestic industry has been facing stiff competition in the domestic market from the foreign firms and products in terms of price, brand names and the attributes. With trade liberalization and implementation of rationalization of tariff and non-tariff barriers, Indian market is now infested with cheap imports of both consumer and intermediate products. They are now posing serious threat to the market share and profitability of the Indian industry.

Lastly and most importantly, domestic as well as global financial surplus is now no longer geared to the requirements of the Indian industry. Financial liberalization has de-linked the finance from industrial investment.

To cope with the emerging challenges in the domestic and global market as well as to create a level playing field for the Indian industry it is of utmost necessity that technological development takes place in industry. But that warrants huge investment in import of capital good embodied new technology, new product innovation, marketing strategy and production processes. Without assistance from the financial system of the country this is neither possible nor feasible. Finance *per se* has no meaning unless it is canalization to the real economy. Real economic growth takes a back seat unless financial resources are made available and accessible. In fact, the above mentioned second challenge can be easily overcome if finance does not become a major hurdle for industrial expansion. In the present situation, firms adopted their survival strategy in the form of reduced product range, outsourcing and intra-industry trade (IIT)[2]

In terms of contribution to GDP Indian manufacturing industries registered a steady growth rate since the beginning of economic reform, reached as high as 14 per cent in 1995-96. On an average the growth rate industrial production stayed above 6 per cent per annum throughout the reform period. However, there exists large heterogeneity in the growth rate across the different industrial sectors. As far as the sectoral sources of growth rate are concerned, consumer goods (62.84%) accounted for more than half of the overall growth. The contribution of capital goods declined from 13.28% in the pre reform period to 11.81% in the post reform period. However, the contribution of intermediate inputs increased from 23.87% to 35.65%.

---

[2] for detailed discussion on IIT see Veeramani (2003)

Table 11 reports the correlation coefficients of the different indices and their components for India. The numbers in the parentheses are respective correlation coefficients. The globalization process is increasing over time for each index, where principal component index recorded greater correlations followed by Kearney and weighted Kearney. The economic component is significantly decreasing over time (-0.745). The personal component also recorded a falling trend (-0.322), while technology (0.943) and political (0.947) components show an increasing trend. It is surprising to note that technological components and economic components are negatively (-0.116) correlated. This contradicts with the proposition that trade and foreign direct investment brings technology.

Table 12 gives information on the development of globalization index over time in India. It appear that despite its short period it can provide a partial picture of globalization covering the recent time periods. Both unweighted and weighted globalization index showed a fluctuating trend, increased from 1995-1997. It declined sharply in 1998 due to fall in overall components except technological change. The index bounces back in 1999 propelled largely by better personal and political components. Once again it declined in 2000 due to overall fall in each of the components.

Table 11. Correlations Coefficients of Globalization and its Components in India

	Time	Economic	Personal	Technology	Political	K	KW	PC
Time	1.000							
Year	-0.745 (0.055)	1.000						
Economic	-0.322 (0.481)	0.588 (0.165)	1.000					
Personal	0.943 (0.001)	-0.647 (0.116)	-0.388 (0.390)	1.000				
Technology	0.947 (0.001)	-0.647 (0.116)	-0.362 (0.425)	0.874 (0.010)	1.000			
Political	0.810 (0.027)	-0.287 (0.533)	0.067 (0.886)	0.733 (0.061)	0.888 (0.008)	1.000		
Gindex (K)	0.650 (0.114)	-0.042 (0.930)	0.251 (0.588)	0.597 (0.157)	0.750 (0.052)	0.968 (0.000)	1.000	
GIndex (KW)	0.921 (0.003)	-0.531 (0.220)	-0.354 (0.435)	0.952 (0.001)	0.947 (0.001)	0.865 (0.012)	0.758 (0.048)	1.000

Table 12. Development of Globalization Index in India over Time

Year	Eco	Eco (w)	Persl.	Persl (w)	Tech	Tech (w)	Political	GIndex	Ginde (w)	Prin 123
1995	0.127	0.212	0.176	0.177	0.002	0.004	1.571	1.876	1.965	-0.192
1996	0.153	0.257	0.281	0.282	0.003	0.006	1.549	1.986	2.094	-0.207
1997	0.128	0.203	0.269	0.270	0.002	0.005	1.725	2.124	2.202	-0.129
1998	0.070	0.096	0.169	0.170	0.004	0.008	1.731	1.974	2.005	-0.137
1999	0.053	0.071	0.215	0.216	0.005	0.011	1.829	2.103	2.127	-0.040
2000	0.050	0.065	0.201	0.203	0.008	0.017	1.813	2.073	2.098	0.041
2001	0.090	0.106	0.186	0.188	0.010	0.019	2.016	2.301	2.329	0.229
Mean	0.096	0.144	0.214	0.215	0.005	0.010	1.748	2.062	2.117	-0.062

In the present chapter we make an attempt to understand the implications of the globalization process on the labor market in organized manufacturing sectors.

The organized manufacturing sector covers only a narrow segment of India's massive workforce, providing about 10% employment as a whole. The justification for considering the organized manufacturing labor only stems from the following reasons. One justification for looking at the organized manufacturing labor stems from the fact that organized manufacturing sector in Indian is highly encircled by various rules and regulations compared to other sectors of the economy, which guaranteed organized their labor rights to job security. Organized manufacturing sector comprised only a small segment of India's total export. Small presence notwithstanding, organized manufacturing remain the core of manufacturing activity in India.

In order to estimate the impact of globalization on the labor market in manufacturing sector we have collected data from Annual Survey of Industries, published by Central Statistical Organization. In the Industry level analysis we used a balanced panel of 22 two digit industries for the years 1994-95 to 2000-2001. The summary statistics shows that the average size of employment in the manufacturing industries is 6.87 million, while on an average each firm employs 52 workers (See Table 13). Each worker receives 30.37 thousand rupees per annum. The average output produced during these periods is 80.95 million rupees. So far as labor productivity in manufacturing is concerned each worker produces the value of output of about 0.87 million rupees.[3]

Table 13. Summary Statistics of the Aggregate Data of Indian Manufacturing (1995-2001)

Variable definition	Mean
Total manufacturing employment in million	6.87
Employment per factory	51.67
Annual wage/ worker (in thousand rupees)	30.37
Aggregate output (in million rupees)	80.95
Annual growth rate of industrial production	7.71
Output per worker (in million rupees)	0.87

Source: Annual Survey of Industries, 2000-01

In order to shed lights on the nature of relationships between the composite globalization indices and a number of key indicators from Indian manufacturing we undertook a series of regression analysis.[4] The results suggest that the low level of wages in India does not promote Indian globalization when globalization computed using the 13 indicators selected by the Kearney. Neither the level of globalization, weighted or unweighted, in a significant way affect the level of any of the four key indicators from Indian manufacturing, namely: wages, employment, output or net value added. Thus, the direction of causality can not be established. Such a linkage can neither be found in relation with only the economic component of globalization.

---

[3] One Rupees was 0.022 US$ in March 2005
[4] These results are not reported here. These can be obtained upon request.

The entire variations in the four indicators are explained by industry specific effects. The adjusted R-squares are in the interval 0.92 to 0.97. The lack of relationship between globalization and these indicators might be explained by inadequate representation of globalization or the manufacturing lack of representation for the entire labor market in India. It should be noted that these four manufacturing indicators are both industry and time variant, while the globalization index is only variable over time. Wage is increasing, employment decreasing, output increasing, and net value added constant over time. The dominance of sector-specific changes over time-specific changes is confirmed in Galbraith et al. (2004) who studied pay inequality in the Indian manufacturing for the period 1979-1998. The results indicate that pay inequality has risen both across sectors and regions, though more across sectors in the period following the introduction of reforms and foremost in the electricity sector.

9. SUMMARY AND CONCLUSIONS

Despite its long historical background the process of globalization can be perceived as a modern phenomenon. The present study attempts to conceptualize and quantified the globalization process by means of empirical evidences available. Factors that have contributed to globalization include reduced transportation and communication costs, lower trade barrier, sophisticated communication, raising capital flows, increased competition, standardization and the movement of people. Hence, globalization is a complex phenomenon involving multidimensional components. The study has used the measurement of two indices of globalization - Kearney and principal component analysis. Depending on the data availability the Kearney is composed of four major components: economic integration, personal contact, technology and political engagements. The development of the index components has also been constructed over time and across countries. Alternatively both weighted and unweighted versions of the Kearney index are also computed.

There results show that the process of globalization is not witnessed a steady growth rather fluctuating throughout the time period. There is large heterogeneity in the degree of globalization across countries and regions. West European countries dominate the top ten positions of in the world with Ireland leading the group. They share good all-round performance of the various indicators. The bottom of the group is dominated by countries belongs to the region of Sub-Saharan Africa and south Asia. The position of low ranking countries is not only associated with internal and external conflicts but also sociopolitical environment holds back its growth and development, which seems to reduce the globalization prospects of the countries. The breakdown of the index into major components offers the possibility to identify the sources of globalization. Of all components, political engagement is the biggest contributor followed by economic integration, personal contacts and technology.

It is interesting to note that during the current phase of globalization former least globalized countries emerge as best performer. Right now both China and India are the fastest growing economy but they are way behind in globalization. They are integrating their economy at a faster pace, clearly holds a lesson for many other developing countries. In India high population growth coupled with complex cultural geography and continuing geopolitical tension jeopardize the equitable development of globalization.

In India the world wide movement towards globalization is coincided with the structural reform and economic liberalization that began in mid 1991. The rate growth of the economy picked up after the reform and sustained since then. The globalization process is increasing over time for each category of the index. Economic component is decreasing significantly, while personal, technology and political component show an increasing trend. In a regression analysis we investigated the relationship between the composite globalization indices and a number of key indicators from labor market in Indian manufacturing. The result shows that globalization did not affect labor market in Indian manufacturing in any significant ways.

Despite certain limitations attached to the indicators of globalization employed, we believe that they are capable to provide a valuable picture of the level of globalization of each country. The index is in its early stage of development but has identified several directions along which future advances can be made. There are important issue in understanding how globalization functions and learning to use the generated information in policy formulation and the evaluation of development.

APPENDIX

Appendix A. Mean Globalization (1995-2001) by Country Ranked by Weighted Kearney Globalization Index (KW)

Rank	Country	Economic	Personal	Technology	Political	K	KW	PC
1	Ireland	2.456	2.024	0.577	1.524	6.581	8.829	1.026
2	Singapore	2.503	1.597	0.974	0.765	5.838	8.321	0.082
3	Switzerland	1.450	1.975	1.015	1.717	6.158	8.238	1.021
4	Sweden	1.430	0.970	1.372	2.244	6.016	8.125	1.210
5	Canada	0.779	0.892	1.502	2.448	5.621	7.175	1.146
6	UK	1.397	0.937	0.912	2.240	5.486	7.064	1.092
7	Netherlands	1.742	1.019	0.840	1.570	5.172	7.032	0.754
8	Finland	0.909	0.804	1.756	1.831	5.299	6.919	0.797
9	Denmark	1.262	1.072	0.982	1.963	5.279	6.860	0.817
10	USA	0.439	0.345	2.323	2.571	5.678	6.844	1.409
11	Norway	0.778	0.781	1.645	1.708	4.912	6.645	0.604
12	Austria	0.849	1.271	0.820	2.096	5.036	6.316	0.787
13	France	0.655	0.814	0.347	2.550	4.367	5.227	0.971
14	New Zealand	0.573	0.736	1.265	1.139	3.713	4.868	0.136
15	Germany	0.664	0.648	0.588	1.956	3.855	4.837	0.610
16	Australia	0.511	0.363	1.385	1.417	3.677	4.617	0.302
17	Portugal	0.831	1.089	0.300	1.424	3.645	4.560	0.101
18	Czech	0.797	1.278	0.254	1.440	3.769	4.361	0.180
19	Italy	0.592	0.590	0.264	2.107	3.554	4.234	0.506
20	Malaysia	1.097	0.737	0.200	1.297	3.331	3.917	-0.237
21	Spain	0.589	0.684	0.304	1.574	3.151	3.847	0.249
22	Hungary	0.810	0.812	0.192	1.311	3.126	3.704	-0.008
23	Israel	0.516	1.078	0.541	0.771	2.905	3.670	-0.392
24	Panama	1.777	0.328	0.055	0.641	2.801	3.481	-0.533
25	Poland	0.356	0.633	0.145	1.896	3.030	3.385	0.177
26	Greece	0.302	0.903	0.180	1.330	2.714	3.209	-0.058
27	Japan	0.278	0.117	0.622	1.533	2.550	3.168	0.202
28	Argentina	0.412	0.103	0.078	1.999	2.592	2.974	0.250
29	Korean Republic	0.437	0.269	0.424	1.107	2.236	2.874	-0.299

Appendix. (Continued.)

Rank	Country	Economic	Personal	Technology	Political	K	KW	PC
30	Russian Federation	0.333	0.110	0.038	2.204	2.685	2.860	0.226
31	Slovenia	0.492	0.592	0.555	0.525	2.164	2.809	-0.684
32	Croatia	0.526	0.961	0.128	0.596	2.212	2.800	-0.660
33	Chile	0.674	0.199	0.152	1.130	2.155	2.768	-0.210
34	Nigeria	0.589	0.310	0.001	1.684	2.584	2.765	-0.122
35	Egypt	0.220	0.481	0.006	1.936	2.643	2.731	0.066
36	Slovakia	0.589	0.409	0.226	0.916	2.140	2.574	-0.557
37	Botswana	0.725	1.137	0.022	0.466	2.350	2.534	-0.871
38	Tunisian	0.379	0.532	0.014	1.282	2.206	2.365	-0.331
39	Senegal	0.350	0.549	0.005	1.318	2.221	2.344	-0.375
40	Pakistan	0.164	0.416	0.001	1.708	2.290	2.339	-0.133
41	Kenya	0.204	0.514	0.006	1.502	2.226	2.252	-0.351
42	China	0.337	0.047	0.014	1.617	2.015	2.245	-0.095
43	Mexico	0.433	0.250	0.048	1.140	1.872	2.189	-0.251
44	Indonesia	0.433	0.076	0.009	1.501	2.020	2.179	-0.222
45	South Africa	0.490	0.138	0.148	0.937	1.712	2.149	-0.434
46	Venezuela	0.398	0.103	0.050	1.316	1.868	2.138	-0.188
47	Thailand	0.614	0.143	0.046	1.056	1.859	2.126	-0.472
48	Romania	0.295	0.329	0.052	1.242	1.918	2.121	-0.326
49	India	0.096	0.214	0.005	1.748	2.062	2.117	-0.062
50	Taiwan	0.505	0.429	0.499	0.008	1.442	2.114	-1.163
51	Philippines	0.742	0.157	0.021	0.904	1.824	2.110	-0.526
52	Bangladesh	0.065	0.399	0.000	1.629	2.093	2.107	-0.270
53	Turkey	0.266	0.262	0.043	1.356	1.927	2.079	-0.228
54	Brazil	0.250	0.050	0.068	1.438	1.805	2.043	-0.120
55	Morocco	0.258	0.642	0.005	0.942	1.847	1.927	-0.589
56	Sri Lanka	0.370	0.614	0.007	0.747	1.737	1.856	-0.747
57	Ukraine	0.391	0.275	0.013	1.043	1.722	1.854	-0.629
58	Saudi Arabia	0.416	0.145	0.009	0.983	1.552	1.831	-0.445
59	Uganda	0.211	0.854	0.001	0.629	1.695	1.812	-0.824
60	Peru	0.312	0.165	0.091	0.934	1.502	1.790	-0.424
61	Colombia	0.315	0.169	0.036	0.970	1.491	1.759	-0.402
62	Iran	0.145	0.067	0.003	1.065	1.281	1.294	-0.481

Notes. Kearney unweighted (K), Kearney weighted (KW) and Principal Component (PC) globalization indices.

REFERENCES

Addison, T. and A. Heshmati (2004): "The New Global Determinants of FDI Flows to Developing Countries: The Impacts of ICT and Democratization", *Research in Banking and Finance* 4, 151-186.

Agénor, P. R. (2003): *"Does Globalization Hurt the Poor?"*. Washington, DC: World Bank, Unpublished manuscript.

Aghion, P. and J. G. Williamson (1998): *"Growth, Inequality and Globalization: Theory, History and Policy"*, Cambridge: Cambridge University Press.

Andersen, T. M., and T. T. Herbertsson (2003): "Measuring Globalization", *IZA Discussion Paper* 2003: 817.

Balakrishnan, P. (2003): "Globalisation, Growth and Justice", *Economic and Political Weekly*, June 26.

Baldwin, R. E. and P. Martin (1999): "Two Waves of Globalization: Superficial Similarities, Fundamental Differences" *NBER Working Pa*per 6904.

Bata, M. and A. J. Bergesen (2002a): "Global Inequality: An Introduction (to Special Issue on Global Economy – Part I)". *Journal of World-System Research*, 8 (1): 2-6.

Bata, M. and A. J. Bergesen (2002b): "Global Inequality: An Introduction (to Special Issue on Global Economy – Part II)", *Journal of World-System Research*, 8 (2): 146-48.

Baylis, J. and S. Smith (2001): *"The Globalization of World Politics – An Introduction to International Relations"*, Oxford University Press.

Besley, T. and R. Burgess (1998): "Land Reform. Poverty Reduction and Growth: Evidence from India", *Development Economics Discussion Paper Series*, 13, London School of Economics, The Suntory Centre.

Bevan, D. L. and A. K. Fosu (2003): "Globalization: An Overview". *Journal of African Economies*, 12 (1): 1-13.

Bhagwati, J. (2004): "Anti Globalization: Why?", *Journal of Policy Modeling*, Vol. 26, pp. 239-463.

Bolaky, B and C. Freund (2004): *"Trade, Regulations, and Growth"*, World Bank Working Papers.

Bordo, M. D., Eichengreen, B., and Irwin, D. A., (1999): "Is Globalization Today Really Different than Globalization a Hundred Years Ago?" *NBER Working Paper* 7195, June

Bowles, S. (2001): "A Future of Labour in the Global Economy", *TIPS Working Paper*, 4-2001.

Castells, M. (1996): *"The Information Age: Economy, Society and Culture"*, Vol. 1; The Rise of the Networked Society, Blackwell Publishers Inc, USA.

Collins, W. J. and Williamson J. G., (1999): "Capital Goods Prices, Global Capital Markets and Accumulation: 1870-1950" *NBER Working Paper* 7145.

Dollar, D and A. Kraay (2001): *"Trade, Growth and Poverty"*, World Bank, Mimeo.

Dollar, D. and A. Kraay, (2002): "Institutions, Trade and Growth" Paper prepared for the *Carnegie-Rochester Conference Series on Public Policy*.

Dollar, D., and P. Collier (2001): *Globalization, Growth and Poverty: Building an inclusive World Economy*. Oxford: Oxford University Press.

Eckel, C. (2003): "Labor Market Adjustments to Globalization: Unemployment versus Relative Wages". *North American Journal of Economics and Finance*, 14 (2): 173-88.

Finance and Development (2002): *"The Globalization of Finance"*, March 2002, Volume 39, Number 1.

Galbraith, J. K., D. R. Chowdhury and S. Shrivastava (2004): "Pay Inequality in the Indian Manufacturing, 1979-1998", *UTIP Working Paper* 2004:28.

Giffin, K. (2003): "Economic Globalization and Institutions of Global Governance", *Development and Change* 34(5): 789-807.

Gomory, R. E. and W. J. Baumol (2004): "Globalization: prospects, promise, and problems", *Journal of Policy Modeling*, Vol. 26, pp. 425-438.

Heshmati, A. (2003): "Measurement of a Multidimensional Globalization and its Impact on Inequality", *WIDER Discussion Paper* 2003/69, Helsinki 2003/69, Helsinki: UNU-WIDER.

Heshmati, A. (2006): "Measurement of a Multidimensional Index of Globalization", *Global Economy Journal* 6(2), Paper 1.

ILO (2004): *"Economic Security for Better World: ILO Socio-Economic Security Programme"*, Geneva.

Intriligator, M. D (2004): "Globalization of the world economy: potential benefits and costs and a net assessment", *Journal of Policy Modeling*, Vol. 26, Issue 4, pp. 485-498.

James, J. (2002): *"Technology, Globalization and Poverty"*, Cheltenham: Edward Elgar.

Kearney, A. T., Inc., and the Carnegie Endowment for International Peace (2002): "Globalization's Last Hurrah?" *Foreign Policy*, January/February: 38-51.

Kearney, A. T., Inc., and the Carnegie Endowment for International Peace (2003): "Measuring Globalization: Who's up, who's down?", *Foreign Policy*, January/February: 60-72.

Khan, A. R., and C. Riskin (2001): *"Inequality and Poverty in China in the Age of Globalization"*. Oxford: Oxford University Press.

Kindleberger, C., 1996, Manias, panics, and crashes, Wiley, New York.

Klein, L. (2004): "New Growth Centers in This Globalized Economy", *Journal of Policy Modeling*, Vol. 26.

Lindert, P. H. and J. F. Williamson (2001): "Does globalization makes the world more unequal?", *NBER Working Paper* 8228.

Lockwood, B. (2001): "How Robust if the Foreign Policy/Kearney Index of globalization?", *CSGR Working Paper* 79/01.

Maddison, A. (2001): "The World Economy: A Millennial Perspective". *OECD Development Centre Studies*. Paris: OECD.

Manning, S. (1999): "Introduction (to Special Issue on Globalization)". *Journal of World-Systems Research*, 5 (2): 137-41.

McCarthy, I and A. Anagnostou (2004): "The impact of outsourcing on the transaction costs and boundaries of manufacturing", *Int. J. Production Economics* 88 (2004) 61–71.

Miller, T. C. (2001): "Impact of Globalization on US Wage Inequality: Implications or Policy", *North American Journal of Economics and Finance*, 12 (3): 219-42.

Nagaraj, R. (2003): "Foreign direct investment in India 1990s: Trends and issues", *Economic and Political Weekly*, 26 April, pp. 1701-1702.

Nayyar D. and J. Court (2001): "Governing globalization: issues and institutions, *WIDER Policy Brief* 5, Helsinki: UNU/WIDER.

Nayyar, D. (2001): "Globalization: What does it mean?" in Jome K. S. and S. Nagaraj edited *"Globalization versus Development"*, Palgrave.

Nayyar, D. (2002): "Cross border movement of people" in D. Nayyar (eds.) *"Governing Globalization: Issues and Institutions"*, Oxford University Press.

O'Rourke, K. H. (2001): "Globalization and Inequality: Historical Trends". *NBER Working Paper* 8339. Cambridge, MA: National Bureau of Economic Research.

O'Rourke, K. H., and J. G. Williamson (2000): *"Globalization and History: The Evolution of a Nineteenth-Century Atlantic Economy"*. Cambridge, MA: MIT Press (see Review Essay by A. G. Frank (2002). *Journal of World-Systems Research*, 8 (2): 276-90).

Obstfeld, M., Taylor A. M., (1998): "The Great Depression as a Watershed: International Capital Mobility over the Long Run" Published in Bordo, M. D., Goldin, C., and N. White, E. N., Eds. *The Defining Moment: The Great Depression and the American*

Economy in the Twentieth Century. pp. 353-402 (Chicago: University of Chicago Press, 1998).

Rodrik D., A. Subramanian, and F. Trebbi (2002): *"Institutional Rule: The Primacy of Institutions over Geography and Integration in Economic Development"* Mimeo, IMF.

Rowntree, L *et al.* (2000): "*Diversity amid globalization: World religion, environment* and development", Prentice Hall.

Sarma, A. (2002): "Prospects of trade and investment in India and China", *International Studies*, 39, 1, pp. 25-43.

Stiglitz, J. (2004): "Globalization and growth in emerging markets", *Journal of Policy Modeling*, Vol. 26, Issue 4, pp. 465–484.

Stiglitz, Joseph. (2002): *"Globalization and its discontents"*, New York: W. W. Norton.

Tanzi (2004): "Globalization and the need for fiscal reform in developing countries", *Journal of Policy Modeling*, 26 (2004) 525–542.

Tausch, A., and P. Herrmann (2002): *"Globalization and European Integration"*. Huntington, NY: Nova Science.

Veeramani, C. (2003): "Liberalisation, Industry-Specific Factors and Intra-Industry Trade in India", *ICRIER Working Paper* No. 97.

Williamson, J. G. (2002): "Winners and Losers over Two Centuries of Globalization". *WIDER Annual Lecture* 6. Helsinki: UNU-WIDER.

Winters, L. A. (2002): "Trade Policies for Poverty Alleviation", in B. Hoekman, A. Matto and P. English (eds.), *Trade, Development and the WTO*, Washington, DC, World Bank.

Woods, N. (1998): "Editorial Introduction. Globalization: Definitions, Debates and Implications". *Oxford Development Studies*, 26 (1): 5-13.

World Bank (2002): *"Globalisation, Growth and Poverty: Building an Inclusive World Economy"*, Policy Research Report, Oxford University Press, New York.

World Development Report (2003): *"FDI Policies for Development: national and International Perspectives"*.

In: Roadmap to Bangalore?
Editors: A. Heshmati, A. Tausch, pp. 109-137

ISBN: 978-1-60021-478-3
© 2007 Nova Science Publishers, Inc.

Chapter 4

GROWTH, INEQUALITY AND POVERTY RELATIONSHIPS

Almas Heshmati[*]

Hawler Institute for Economic and Policy Research
and Department of Economics,
University of Kurdistan Hawler,
30m Street, Zaniary,
Hawler, Federal Region of Kurdistan, Iraq

ABSTRACT

This chapter examines the causal relationship between inequality and a number of macroeconomic variables frequently found in the inequality and growth literature. These include growth, openness, wages, and liberalization. We review the existing cross-country empirical evidence on the effects of inequality on growth and the extent to which the poorest in society benefit from economic growth. The linkage between growth, redistribution and poverty is also analyzed. In the review of literature mainly empirical examples from 1990s are taken. In addition we test the conditional and unconditional relationship between inequality and growth in the post World War II period using WIDER inequality database. Regression results suggest that income inequality is declining over time. Inequality is also declining with the growth of income. There is a significant regional heterogeneity in the levels and development over time. The Kuznets hypothesis represents a global U-shape relationship between inequality and growth.

Keywords: growth, openness, income inequality, wage inequality, poverty, indices.

---

[*] Tel: +964-750-4360862, E-mails: almas.heshmati@hiepr.org and almas.heshmati@ukh.ac

ABBREVIATIONS

BMP	Black Market (exchange rate) Premium
CPS	Current Population Survey
D	Regional dummy variables
EDU	Education
EU	European Union
FDI	Foreign Direct Investment
GDP	Gross Domestic Product
GINI	Gini coefficient
ICT	Information and Communication Technology
INC	Per capita income
INV	Investment
IT	Information technology
IZA	Institute for the Study of Labor
MENA	Middle East and North Africa
MTT	MTT Economic Research
OECD	Organization for Economic Cooperation and Development
PWT	Penn World Tables
R^2	R-square
R&D	Research and Development
S	Dummy variable for socialistic countries
TEPP	Techno-Economics and Policy Program
Y	Real per capita income
UK	United Kingdom
UNU	United Nations University
USA	United States of America
USSR	Union of Soviet Socialist Republics
WIDER	World Institute for Development Economics Research
WIID	World Income Inequality database
WWII	World War II

1. INTRODUCTION

The world economy grows constantly but the growth pattern differs over time and among countries. This growth is due to technological change, increased efficiency and capacity in the use of resources and the creation of material wealth. Economic downturn, crises and other factors from time to time results in negative growth in certain regions and countries. The East Asian financial crisis and the negative growth of sub-Saharan Africa are the few examples of such development. Large disparities and negative growth rates undermine the integration of economies and social stability hampering the long-run economic growth.

Several literatures are there investigating the relationship between different combinations of openness, growth, inequality and poverty (Sachs and Werner 1995; Dollar and Kraay 2001a; Person and Tabellini 1994; Deininger and Squire 1998; Goudie and Ladd 1999; van der Hoeven and Shorrocks 2003). In general they found a positive relationship between openness and growth but the differences between and within countries in the impacts of growth on the poor can be large. In recent years the research and debate has focused on the extent to benefit the poor from this economic growth (Ravallion 1998 and 2001; Ravallion and Chen 2003; Ravallion and Datt 2000; Quah 2001). One extreme of the debate argues that the potential benefits of economic growth to the poor are undermined or offset by the inadequate redistributive policies and by increases in inequality that accompany economic growth. The second extreme argues that despite increased inequality, the liberal economic policies and open markets raise incomes of everyone in the society inclusive the poor which proportionally reduce the incidence of poverty. The poor in developing countries is often defined as the bottom quintile of the income distribution.

This chapter discusses the causal relationship between inequality and the numbers of macroeconomic variables frequently found in the inequality and growth literature are also in relation to pro-poor growth issues. These include growth, openness, wages, liberalization, etc.[1] Here the existing cross-country empirical evidence on the inequality effects of growth and the extent to which the poorest in society benefit from economic growth is reviewed. In the review of literature mainly empirical examples from 1990s are taken. In addition we test the conditional and unconditional relationship between inequality and growth in the post World War II period based on the WIDER inequality database. The results from the literature will also be compared with those based on the WIID database. Empirical results suggest that the outcomes of policy measures are heterogeneous in their impacts. Economic growth benefits the poor but the absence of effective redistribution policies might affect negatively on the income distribution. Several country-specific factors play a significant role in targeting policies to make economic growth pro-poor. Ravallion (2001) expresses the need for deeper micro empirical work on the growth and distributional change to identify specific policies to complement growth-oriented policies, and the evaluation of aggregate impacts and their diversity of impacts.

Rest of the chapter is organized as follows. Section 2 reviews the growth and convergence. It follows by a discussion of empirical evidence suggesting convergence in growth accompanied by divergence in inequality in Section 3. Section 4 explores the linkage between openness and growth to inequality. Section 5 reviews the Kuznets hypothesis. The redistribution of growth is discussed in Section 6. The inequality effects of growth and development is discussed in Section 7 which is followed by the discussion of wage inequality in Section 8. The other contributing factors are discussed in Section 9. The relationship between growth and inequality based on WIID database is examined in Section 10. The final Section summarizes.

---

[1] The relationship between income inequality, poverty and globalization is discussed in Heshmati (2003, 2004a and 2006a).

2. GROWTH AND CONVERGENCE

Most of the work in the growth area uses econometric methods to test the hypothesis of the convergence of per capita income across countries.[2] Convergence can be absolute or conditional (Barro and Sala-i-Martin 1995; Quah 1996c; Barro 1997; Dowrick and DeLong 2001; and Jones 2002). When the absolute convergence holds a negative relationship between GDP levels and growth rates is observed, implying that the poorer economies are growing faster than the richer countries. Lichtenberg (1994) criticizes this practice of testing convergence and suggests the use of variance of productivity over time to test the convergence hypothesis. The use of variance neglects the level of differences and is probably more appropriate in pooling countries with different initial development.

Conditional convergence refers to the convergence after accounting for differences in the steady state across countries which are at the control. Here in addition to the GDP level (initial income) one controls for the other determinants of growth like population growth, education and investment (Mankiew, Romer and Weil 1992). The capital is further decomposed into physical, human and health components in Knowles and Owen (1997) and Heshmati (2000). Health capital is measured as health care expenditure in Heshmati, but Knowles and Owen used life expectancy for measuring it. The growth rate of real per capita GDP is positively related to initial human capital, political stability, and physical investment, and negatively related to the initial level of real per capita GDP, government consumption and pubic investment (Barro 1991). Benhabib and Rustichini (1996) observed that in reality poor countries have invested at lower rate and have not grown faster than rich countries. The investment rate and growth gaps are persistently increasing.

Despite the numerous bodies of literature and empirics there are still disagreements with the concepts, modeling, estimation of growth and convergence models. The proponents of conditional convergence (Mankiew, Romer and Weil 1992; Barro 1997) find evidences of convergence at an annual rate of 2-5 per cent. Bernard and Durlauf (1996) consider convergence as catching up and as equality of long-term forecasts at a fixed time. They show that the cross-section tests are developed to test for whether convergence taken place which has much weaker restrictions on the behavior of growth across countries than time series tests. Many convergence studies are based on the observation of first and the last year of a country, neglecting the year-to-year variations in its growth rates. Therefore, integration of the two series is commended.

To overcome the problems of losing the year-to-year variations in the growth rate and valuable information, Islam (1995) uses a dynamic panel data approach and different estimators for studying growth convergence, producing different results than those obtained in the cross-country data. Different forms of inconsistency related to correlated country effects and endogenous explanatory variables and the choice of estimation methods result in per capita convergence of income to their steady-state levels at a rate of up to 10 per cent per year (Caselli, Esquivel and Lefort 1996). Nerlove (2000) also found that the conditional convergence rate is sensitive to the choice of estimation techniques. Lee, Pesaran and Smith (1997) in their examination of the beta and sigma convergence in stochastic and linearized

---

[2] For an evolutionary growth theory and viewpoint about the process of development and the origin of sustained economic growth see Galor and Moav (2001).

solution to the deterministic Solow growth model observed substantial biases in the rate of convergence due to the ignorance of growth heterogeneity.

Empirical results on more homogenous data show evidences of convergence in income levels and catching up in the levels of productivity of OECD countries (Dowrick and Nguyen 1989). However, convergence in aggregate productivity is not necessarily occurred at disaggregate e.g. industry level. Bernard and Jones (1996) find convergence in some sectors such as services but not manufacturing in 14 OECD countries. Barro and Sala-i-Martin (1991) examines the growth and dispersion of personal income and relate the patterns for individual U.S. states to the behavior of regions focusing on the role of agriculture, manufacturing, transportation and regional concentration. Differences in the within country or between sector growth rates is the main source of within country inequality.

To avoid heterogeneity bias, Bernard and Durlauf (1996) examined homogenous group of OECD countries to reject convergence but found evidences of a common trend. Evidence against convergence is also found in Quah (1993) who predicts widening rich-poor income disparity. Quah (1996b) finds regional income distribution in Europe to differ across countries and also fluctuate over time. Geographical and national factors are both important for explaining inequality dynamics. Quah (1996c) characterize the features of cross-country income dynamics as persistence, immobility and polarization. Lichtenberg (1994) using variance of productivity rejected the convergence among 22 OECD countries. Carree and Klomp (1997) using simulation experiment shows that although countries are relatively homogenous and integrated, test procedure above lead to low probability of accepting convergence in the short period of time.

3. DIVERGENCE IN EQUALITY

The empirical finding of convergence in the growth literature is contrary to the evidences of global divergence in the inequality literature (see Quah 1996a). Solimano (2001) explains the puzzle by the conditional convergence requirement that all countries share similar values for the determinants of growth and the same steady state value of long-run income per capita. In his view the strong assumptions of equality of the determinant factors whose differences are the core of differential growth performance across countries and international inequality, which limits the usefulness of conditional convergence. Heterogeneous development has given rise to uneven and complex regional convergence and divergence in GDP per capita and the growth rates increases the world inequality which are driven by the international or between country inequalities. To narrow global inequality it is required that a sustained acceleration in the rate of economic growth of low and middle income regions combined with the decline in domestic or within country inequality to improve the welfare position of the world's poor. Based on the WIID data post 1950, applied measurement methods and data irregularities, Heshmati (2006b and 2006c) does not find convincing sign of a significantly increasing or decreasing global trends in income inequality over the last 50 years. It should be noted that the inequality here is based on only within-country inequality data but are pooled and weighted such that the level differences reflect international inequality.

It is pointed out by Solimano (2001) that income inequality exploded since the early 19th century. This evolution is essentially due to the increase in inequality among countries or regions of the world. The contribution from the between country components have more impacts on the world distribution of income inequality than the within country component. This is also confirmed by Bourguignon and Morrisson (2002) who find evidences of convergence process among European countries but also divergence among regions and an increasing concentration of world poverty in some regions of the world such as sub-Saharan Africa and South Asia. Recently Galbraith and Garcilazo (2005) measured pay inequality in the European Union during the convergence process to the Monetary Union for the years 1995-2000. Inequality is decomposed into between, within regions and aggregate for the European continent as a whole. Results show a declining pay inequality across Europe influenced by the position of UK and Germany. No support is found to the view that Europe's unemployment problem stems from excessive equality.

At the regional level the dynamics of inequality among eight European countries using LIS data is considered by Iacoviello (1998). He investigates whether inequality converges to a steady state level of income inequality during the process of economic growth and to identify the variables that influences the process of convergence. However, Iacoviello does not reach to a conclusion about the exact nature of the relationship between income and inequality movements. Earlier Quah (1996b) in analyzing the regional convergence clusters across Europe found that physical location and geographical spill-over matter more for the convergence than do macro factors and account for substantial amount of regional income distribution dynamics. Based on a larger sample of 66 countries recently Ravallion (2003) found that within-country income inequalities have been slowly converging since the 1980s. Inequality is tending to fall (rise) in countries with initially high (low) inequality. The speed of convergence was not sensitive to the measurement error in the measurement of initial inequality. In Epstein and Spiegel (2002) when divergence from acceptable (natural) level of inequality occurs, both lower or higher production levels and economic growth may be expected. However, the direction of changes is ambiguous.

In sum the empirical findings in the literature, based on large sample of countries and relatively long time period, in general indicate the presence of convergence in per capita income, at least among countries with more homogenous development or sharing same regional location, but also significant divergence in income inequality. There is evidence of strong convergence process among more homogenous and integrated European countries and a weak within-country (between-region) convergence among Indian states, divergence among Chinese regions but also divergence among countries or regions of the world. The between-country contribution is much higher than within-country contribution to the world inequality. Lack of convergence might be explained by various national and global factors such as the absence of regional price indices, infrastructure for development, economic reforms and redistributive policies which affects the regions differently.

4. Openness, Growth and Inequality Relationships

There are a number of cross-country empirical studies investigating the relationship between openness and growth (see e.g. Edwards 1992 and 1998; Sachs and Werner 1995; Rodriguez and Rodrik 1999; and Dollar and Kraay 2001a and 2001b). In general they find a positive correlation between openness and growth and find that the growth premium of openness tends to decline over time and less beneficial and weaker for the poor countries. On the other hand the results do not indicate the presence of systematic relationship between changes in trade and changes in national inequality. Growing integration of economies and societies around the world is not associated with a higher inequality within countries. Trade does not redistribute income among different income groups. Fast growth reduces poverty, but many people living in countries and regions not participating in the integration are falling farther behind and reducing their prospects of growing out of poverty. Researchers often face methodological difficulties in the measurement of openness and to control for the determinants of economic growth and in establishing the causal relationship from openness and integration to the growth, inequality and poverty.

There are a number of other studies analyzing the relationship between inequality and growth (see e.g. Person and Tabellini 1994; Alesia and Rodrik 1994; Ravallion 1995; and Peroti 1996). A negative relationship is found between initial inequality in income distribution and growth. However, the findings that more unequal economies grow much slower are not robust due to the reason of data quality and comparability. The negative relationship emerges through the investment in human capital and political channels due to credit rationing (Stiglitz and Weiss 1981) and median voter behavior (Person and Tabellini 1994). An illustration of the later mechanism on inequality, median voter and redistribution is given in Lee and Roemer (1999). They show that as inequality rises taxation can be less efficient in reducing public spending and redistribution to counteract various forms of inequality in a society.

As several researchers noted above, the reverse linkage between inequality and growth might be indirect. Sylwester (2000) searched to find a transmission mechanism to determine how the change in government policies can lower the negative impact of income inequality on economic growth. In doing so, he explores how income inequality affects spending on public education and how education affects growth. The public expenditure on education and the growth rate of GDP are jointly estimated by Sylwester. Results based on a cross section of 54 countries for 1970-1985 shows that current education expenditures have a negative impact upon contemporaneous growth, but previous expenditures have a positive impact on growth. The negative cost of inequality on growth is found to be only a short-run cost and offset by the long-run positive effects of education.

The effects of education on economic growth can be different. The dual role of human capital, stock of educated workers, as an important determinant of growth and inequality is analyzed in Eicher and Garcia-Penalosa (2001). The impact of education on economic growth is through changes in the relationship between skilled and unskilled labor, the rate of technical change, labor demand and supply and wages. The relative productivity of skilled to unskilled labor is changing with the rate of technical change. These two types of labor are imperfect substitutes. Their results identify parameters of the demand and supply of labor that are central to the evolution of inequality during the development process. Wolff (2001) using family income current population survey (CPS) data for 1947-1997 finds that the largest effects on income inequality come from equipment investment and unionization. Investments in equipment increased inequality, while unionization decreased inequality. Total factor productivity and labor productivity growth and R&D investment have no effect on inequality.

One major shortcoming of the literature on the link between growth, openness, inequality and poverty is that the causal relationship between these variables has often been neglected. Application of co-integration test and an establishment of linkage and direction of causality among the variables of interest will determine whether these relations must be estimated using single equation, recursive or as a system of interdependent equations. Unavailability of time series data, especially on inequality and poverty, for cross section of countries limits application of this approach. As few examples of such development, Addison and Heshmati (2004) and Gholami, Tom-Lee and Heshmati (2006) tests for causality between foreign direct investment (FDI), GDP growth, trade openness and information and communication technology (ICT). Empirical results based on large samples of industrialized, transition and developing countries suggest that ICT infrastructure and ICT investment increases the inflow of FDI to the developing countries with implications in their economic growth.

5. THE KUZNETS HYPOTHESIS

In addition to welfare, reduction in poverty makes growth strategy important for the developing countries. Deininger and Squire (1998), in a different way, examine interaction between growth and inequality and investigate how these two factors in turn affect the efforts to reduce poverty in the course of economic development which is measured as GDP. The robustness of the inequality-growth relationship is tested by the estimation of the following relation:

$$Growth_{it} = \beta_0 + \beta_1 GDP_{i0} + \beta_2 GINI_{i0} + \beta_3 INV_{it} + \beta_4 BMP_{it} + \beta_5 EDU_{it} \qquad (1)$$
$$+ \beta_6 LAND_{it} + D_R + u_{it}$$

where $GINI_0$ and GDP_0 are initial income inequality and GDP, $LAND$ is land Gini, INV is investment, BMP is black market exchange rate premium, D is regional dummy variables, and u random error term. They use data on Gini index for 108 countries, several of which are observed in a number of periods allowing for the construction of country-specific Kuznets curves on the relationship between income inequality and growth:

$$GINI_{it} = \alpha_i + \beta_i Y_{it} + \gamma_i (1/Y_{it}) + \zeta S + \varepsilon_{it} \qquad (2)$$

where $GINI$ is Gini coefficient, Y is real per capita income, S is a dummy variable for socialist countries, and ε random error term.

Three main results emerge from the study by Deininger and Squire. First, there is a strong negative relationship between initial inequality in asset (land) distribution and long-term growth. Second, inequality reduces income growth for the poor, but not for the rich. Third, available longitudinal data provide little support for the temporal relationship as summarized in the Kuznets inverted-U hypothesis.[3] Policies that influence the growth of income in selected population subgroups and measures that increase aggregate investment and facilitate

---

[3] The Kuznets (1955) hypothesis postulates an inverted-U relationship between income and inequality according to which the degree of inequality would increase first and than decrease with level of income or economic growth. See also Aghion, Carol and Garcia-Penalosa (1999) for a recent survey of new growth theories and Galor (2000) examination of the income distribution and the process of development.

acquisition of assets by the poor might thus be doubly beneficial for the increase in growth and the reduction in poverty. Creation and redistribution of new assets (investment) are found to have a greater impact on poverty reduction and growth than the redistribution of existing assets like land.

Most studies divide economies into developed and less developed groups in testing the Kuznets hypothesis. The heterogeneous relationship between income inequality and economic development is investigated by Savvides and Stegnos (2000). They employed a threshold regression model and perform tests for the existence of threshold levels and for the possibility of endogenous separation of the sample into two (or more) regimes distinguished by the country's level of development. Threshold regression models have the advantages that they allow for heterogeneity in both intercepts and slopes. In testing the inverted-U hypothesis two common alternative specifications of the threshold model as considered by Savvides and Stegnos:

$$GINI_{it} = \alpha_0 + \alpha_1 INC_{it} + \alpha_2 (1/INC_{it}) + \varepsilon_{it} \qquad (3)$$

$$GINI_{it} = \beta_0 + \beta_1 \ln INC_{it} + \beta_2 (\ln INC_{it})^2 + \varepsilon_{it} \qquad (4)$$

where $GINI$ is the income inequality measured as Gini coefficients and INC is the per capita income in the same year. The null hypothesis of a simple linear specification versus Kuznets is obtained from $H_0 : \alpha_2 = \beta_2 = 0$. Empirical results for 92 countries provide weak evidence on the existence of negative inequality-development relationship, but the relationship is described by the two-regime split of the sample based on per-capita income measure of development. Chen (2003) also found inverted-U relationship between income distribution and long-run economic growth using cross-country data but not in a short-run. The latter is important in cases like economics of transition. For instance, Keane and Prasad (2002), in their analysis of the evolution of inequality in Poland and based on evidence from other transition economies argued that the transfer mechanisms including pensions, played an important role in mitigating the increase in inequality and poverty during the country's transition to the market economy. This observation suggests that the redistribution measures that reduce poverty can enhance economic growth during transition.

6. REDISTRIBUTION OF GROWTH

An establishment of the link between economic growth, inequality and poverty is not the ultimate goal, but redistribution that follows. Acemgoglu and Robinson (2000) studied that during nineteenth century development process leads to increasing inequality. Inequality can induce political instability and forces a period of fundamental political reforms. Political and economic reforms lead to democratization and to institutional changes which encourage taxation and redistribution. The latter is expected to result not only in a reduced inequality but also poverty. The authors argue that reform in political redistribution can be viewed as strategic decisions made by the political elite to prevent social unrest and revolution. The theory offers an explanation to the fall in inequality following the redistribution of policies due to the democratization in many Western economies. Acemgoglu and Robinson analyzed the behavior of income inequality in Britain, France, Germany and Sweden. Results suggest that development not necessarily induce a Kuznets curve because of the lack of positive association between inequality and development or because of the low degree of political mobilization. The inequality-output relationship may also be associated with two types of non-democratic paths: an 'autocratic disaster' with high inequality and low output like sub-Saharan Africa, and an 'East Asian Miracle' with low inequality and high output.[4]

Goudie and Ladd (1999) in their review of the literature are concerned with the interlinkages between relative poverty and inequality, absolute poverty and economic growth and in the way development strategies and development policies are designed. Regarding the effect of economic growth on inequality there is no clear relationship and little evidence that growth alters distribution in a systematic way. Countries with initially severe inequality of consumption and land are worse at reducing poverty probably because they achieve significantly slower economic growth. Goudie and Ladd find that the changes in mean income play the main role in changes in poverty, while high rate of growth has large impact on the absolute poverty. As pointed out earlier these countries are characterized by having poor institutions and lack well functioning taxation and redistributive systems. Economic growth can reduce urban poverty through the generation of economic opportunities and employment where municipal government has a key role to play in the process (Amis and Grant 2001). In similarity with the sectoral level, a positive relationship between inequality and growth and between political competitiveness and growth was found by Balisacan and Fuma (2003) using Philippines provincial data. This confirms the importance of institutions and redistributive channels to the growth-inequality relationship at different levels within a country.

In respect with the above discussion of growth-inequality-poverty relationship, Ravallion (2001) assumes that initial inequality interacts with growth using the data from 47 developing countries in 1980s and 1990s to estimate the following non-linear relation:

$$\Delta \ln GINI_{it} / \tau = (\beta_0 + \beta_1 \ln GINI_{i,t-\tau}) \Delta \ln Y_{it} / \tau + \varepsilon_{it} \qquad (5)$$

where $GINI$ is Gini coefficient, Y is private consumption, Δ indicates year-to-year changes, τ is the time difference between two surveys, and ε error term. In studying the relationship between growth, inequality and poverty, Ravallion prefers the investigations based on micro-empirical work on growth and distributional change to identify the effective growth oriented policies. Outcomes of policy measure are heterogeneous in their impact on different income

---

[4] The working mechanism of how government policies were able to reduce poverty and inequality through economic growth in East Asia is discussed by Kakwani and Krongkaew (2000) in an introduction to a collection of studies on the relationship between rapid reduction in poverty and income disparities alongside with high economic growth in the region. For analysis of income distribution and growth in East Asia see also You (1998) and Warr (2000) who analysis of poverty incidence and economic growth and the impact of the 1997 economic crisis in South East Asia. It should be noted that the development has not been uniform. For example, in the case of China, regional and sectoral disparities in inequality have increased (Khan and Riskin

groups. Depending on the initial position of the poor and the diversity of the impacts on poor might gain more from redistribution, but also suffers more from economic contraction compared to the rich.

In regards with the heterogeneity in the impacts of earlier studies Ravallion (1998) shows that aggregation can bias conventional tests of negative relationship between inequality and growth. The household and country level regressions are illustrated with 6651 farm-households panel data for 1985-1990 from rural China. The results indicate that asset inequality in the area of residence affects negatively on the consumption growth. The effect is lost in an aggregate level like that of regional growth models. Bigsten, Kebede, Shimeles and Taddesse (2003) also in their analysis of growth and poverty reduction in Ethiopia during the period of economic recovery, covering 1994-97, identify several group-specific determinant factors of escaping from poverty. A decomposition of changes in poverty into growth and redistributive components indicates that potential reduction of poverty is due to the increase in real per capita income was to some extent counteracted by worsening income distribution.

In two recent collections of essays on the issues of growth, inequality and poverty (See van der Hoeven and Shorrocks 2003; and Shorrocks and van der Hoeven 2004) aggregate growth is seen as both necessary and sufficient conditions for reducing poverty, but the concern is that the benefits of growth is not evenly distributed at the national level across different population subgroups, sectors and regions. Thus, in the analysis of the consequences of growth on poverty, the level and distributional impacts of growth needs to be taken into account. The overall conclusion pointed out the need of diverse strategy towards growth-poverty-inequality. Initial conditions, institutions, specific country structures, and time horizons all play a specific role in the creation of national solutions to the problem of poverty and in their contributions to the achievement of globally adopted poverty reduction targets.

7. INEQUALITY EFFECTS ON GROWTH AND DEVELOPMENT

Bigsten and Levin (2000) in their review of the literature deals with the relationships between economic growth, income distribution, and poverty did not find any systematic patterns of changes in income distribution during the recent decades or any links from fast growth to increasing inequality. However, recent evidence tended to confirm the negative impact of inequality on growth. Recently Forbes (2000) challenges the current belief on the negative relationship between inequality and growth for 45 countries observed during 1966-1995. She uses panel data techniques and the control for time-invariant country-specific effects reduces the omitted variable bias. Results using various estimation methods show that in short and medium term, an increase in income inequality has a significant positive relationship with subsequent economic growth. Sensitivity analysis indicates that the positive relationship is robust across samples, variable definitions, and model specifications.

Quah (2001) addresses several questions in the study of economic growth and income inequality. How quantitatively important is the relation? Why should that relation matter? The findings indicate that only under conceivably high increases in inequality economic growth do not benefit the poor. Improvements in living standard overwhelm any deterioration due to

---

2001). Shari (2000) link the post 1990s increasing trends in income inequality in Malaysia to the government policy reversal towards liberalization, deregulation and privatization.

the increase in income inequality. Other forces through their impacts on aggregate growth affect the poor – independent of the effect of inequality effect on economic growth. Furthermore, the uses of Gini coefficient might not reflect the true nature of inequality. Quah (2002) focus on the growth and inequality in China and India. These two countries account for a third of the world's population. The growth and inequality variables are modeled as components of a joint stochastic process, where the impacts of each on different welfare indicators and personal income distribution across the joint population are calibrated. Results show that the two key issues: if inequality causes growth, and if growth is disadvantageous to the poor, neither is empirically testable. Economic growth benefits the poor and the mechanism where inequality causes growth is empirically irrelevant for determining the outcomes of individual income distributions. On particular importance are how growth is distributed and its impacts on poverty. In relation with human development and economic growth Ravallion (1997b) finds that the biggest problem facing the world's poor is not low-quality growth but too little growth. There is no sign of systematic effects of growth on inequality (Ravallion 1995). However, a higher initial inequality affects negatively in reducing poverty. Inequality can be sufficiently high to result in rising poverty despite good underlying growth prospects (Ravallion 1997a).

In examining the income distribution and the process of development Galor (2000) presents a model that encompasses the transition between income inequality and the process of development. The focus is on the conflicting viewpoint about the effects of inequality on growth in the classical and the modern approaches of physical and human capital accumulations. In the classical approach inequality stimulate capital accumulation and growth, while in the modern approach equality stimulates investment in human capital and economic growth. No empirical example is available to illustrate the performances of the model. Moav (2002) demonstrates that initial income inequality persists and, provided that initial average income is above some threshold, inequality negatively affects investment on human capital and output in the long run.

8. WAGE INEQUALITY

There are a number of studies focusing on the impact of globalization, economic openness, import competition from low-wage developing countries, and technical change biased to skilled labor on wage inequality in industrialized countries. The results indicate a widening of wage differentials in favor of skilled labor and high-income earners in USA and UK during the recent two decades. This suggests a positive association between openness and wage inequality in industrialized economies. Borjas (1994 and 1999) finds the immigration of unskilled labor to USA, import competition and unskilled labor-saving technical change to explain the widening wage differential for the unskilled workers in USA.

With regards to the above explanations of the wage differential to inequality Atkinson (1999) shows that the world is working in a more complex ways than the simple unemployment, technological and trade liberalization explanations of inequality and its trend. He refers to the changes in social norms away from redistributive pay norm to one where market forces dominate the generation of wage settings which in turn lead to wage inequality. Progressive income taxation and social transfers can offset rising income inequality arisen from the market place wage settings and unemployment across, for instance, OECD countries (Atkinson 2000). Social transfers may also change the size of dependent population through the withdrawal of labor force with increasing impact on inequality.

For the developing countries the increased demand for unskilled labor relative to the skilled labor following the increased openness to trade is expected to reduce wage inequality by narrowing the wage gap between skilled and unskilled workers. Empirical results (Wood 1997) show the validity of this view in the case of East Asia in 1970s and 1980s but the experience of Latin America points out the contrary in 1980s and early 1990s. The contradicting results are explained by the shift in more skilled-labor intensive production in Latin America as a result of the entrance of China in the world market and the advent of technological change which are biased against unskilled laborers. Differences between the two regions and the two periods may explain different experiences. The critics of globalization point to the fact that growth may have an anti-poor effect, emphasizing the role of policy and institutions to promote pro-poor distribution of growth (See van der Hoeven and Shorrocks 2003).

The pattern of wage inequality can differ among industrialized countries. Wage inequality has increased less in Europe than in USA and UK for the same period (Linder and Williamson 2001). The non-uniform increase in inequality among industrialized countries suggests that policy matter. Atkinson (1999) finds rising inequality not necessarily inevitable. This is in contrast to the widely held belief that it is an unavoidable consequence of the present revolution in information and communication technology or the globalization of trade and finance. Government redistributive policy measures counteract the rise in market income inequality. The two most popular explanations for these differential trends are that: the relative supply of skills increased faster in Europe, and that European labor market institutions prevented increasing inequality.

Aghion (2002) argue that Schumpeterian Growth Theory, in which growth is driven by a sequence of quality-improving innovations, can provide explanations to the observed increase in between and within educational groups wage inequality in developing countries. Concerning the between skill groups inequality, Gottschalk (1997) finds that the rise in the price of skill being a result of both an increase in the real wages paid to more skilled workers and also a decline in the absolute real wages paid to the less skilled workers leaving mean wages unchanged. In the case of Russia, Fan, Overland and Spagat (1999) find Russia, having both much human capital and an education system that produces the wrong skills for a market economy. They suggest educational restructuring in Russia's transition strategy to lay groundwork for the future prosperity, better return to education and reduced inequality. In the context of South Africa Khan (1999) found that sectoral growth and skill acquisition can alleviate poverty for the black African population. Shupp (2002) suggest redistributive taxes to offset limited capital mobility between high and low-income regions to promote income growth and income equality. Lusting, Arias and Rigolini (2002) emphasis public (economic and social) policies needed to achieve simultaneous increase in economic growth and reduce poverty in Latin America given its scarce fiscal resources. Ravallion and Datt (2000) uses state level data to derive a state-specific measure of how pro-poor economic growth[5] had been

---

[5] For measurement of the rate of pro-poor growth by the mean growth rate of the poor, defined as the rate of change in the Watts index of poverty normalized by the headcount index, and examples using data from China see Ravallion and Chen (2003).

in India 1960-1994. They argue that the inter-state differences in the impact of a given rate of non-farm economic growth on consumption poverty reflect systematic differences in initial conditions. The importance of initial conditions is emphasized in Van der Hoeven and Shorrocks (2003) collection of essays among others on the role of growth in poverty reduction.

Acemoglu (2002) finds two traditional explanations above for not providing an entirely satisfactory explanation. A third of the explanation is that the relative demand for skilled labor increased differently across countries. Creation of wage compression and the encouragement of more investment in technologies increased the productivity of less-skilled workers, implying less skilled biased technical change in Europe than in the US. An increase in the rate of (ability-biased) technological progress raises the returns to ability and generates an increase in wage inequality between and within skill groups, increase in education attainment, and possibly a transitory productivity slowdown (Galor and Moav 2000).

9. OTHER CONTRIBUTING FACTORS TO INEQUALITY

Several other factors than those discussed above like growth and openness for given policy affect the inequality both at the national and global levels. Acemoglu and Ventura (2002) offers an alternative framework to the new classical growth model for analyzing the world income distribution. They show that even in the absence of diminishing returns in production and technological spillovers, international trade based on specialization leads to a stable world income distribution. Specialization in trade reduces prices and marginal product of capital and introduces diminishing returns. The dispersion of the world income distribution is determined by the forces that shape the strength of the effects of terms of trade, namely the degree of openness to international trade and the extent of specialization. Empirical results using data from 79 countries for 1965-1985 suggests that the above mechanism could be important in understanding cross-country differences in income levels.

In an econometric approach, Calderon and Chong (2001) - using a panel of countries for the period 1960 to 1995 - show that the intensity of capital controls, the exchange rate, the type of exports, and the volume of trade affect the long-run distribution of income. The result is consistent with Heckscher-Ohlin hypothesis of the link between trade and wage inequality. The export of primary goods from developing countries increases their inequality, while manufacturing exports from developed countries decreases inequality. Regression results based on the data from 73 countries show that liberalization through its impacts on wages increases inequality (Cornia and Kiiski 2001). Al-Marhubi (1997) finds developing countries with greater inequality have higher mean inflation. Inflation is found to be lower and stable in countries that are more open to trade.

A number of studies show links from the impact of globalization, immigration, economic openness, import competition, labor-saving technical change biased to skilled labor and unemployment among the unskilled to wage inequality in industrialized countries. Wage differential has been in the favor of skilled labor. Inequality is found to be an unavoidable consequence of the information technology (IT) or globalization of trade and finance. However, wage inequality can be offset by government redistributive policies of progressive taxes and transfers. Micro data based studies show evidence of the presence of permanent and transitory wage inequality. They find a positive relationship between initial earnings and subsequent earnings growth indicating divergent in earnings over the working career. Education, gender, marital status and race are the main factors contributing to the earnings inequality.

10. THE RELATIONSHIP BETWEEN GROWTH AND INEQUALITY BASED ON THE WIID DATABASE

Model Specification

The aim in this section is twofold. First, we investigate the trends in inequality and the presence of the relationship between growth and inequality. Second, in testing the Kuznets inverted-U hypothesis we apply a modified version of the two alternative linear and reciprocal unconditional specifications (equations 3 and 4) of the inequality growth relationship which are frequently used in the literature written as:

$$GINI_{it} = \alpha_0 + \alpha_1 INC_{it} + \alpha_2 (1/INC_{it}) + \sum_j \alpha_j X_{jit} + \sum_m \alpha_m Z_{mit} \qquad (6)$$
$$+ \lambda_t + \mu_r + \varepsilon_{it}$$

$$GINI_{it} = \beta_0 + \beta_1 \ln INC_{it} + \beta_2 (\ln INC_{it})^2 + \sum_j \beta_j \ln X_{jit} + \sum_m \beta_m Z_{mit}$$
$$+ \lambda_t + \mu_r + \varepsilon_{it} \qquad (7)$$

where $GINI$ is the average (of multiple observations) income inequality represented by Gini coefficient. The specification here is conditional, where INC is the real per capita GDP, X_{jit} is a vector of j other determinant variables like education, openness and population associated with country i in period t, Z is m vector of data characteristics, and λ_t and μ_r are unobservable time-specific and regional-specific effects. The conditional versus unconditional versions of the model can jointly or individually be tested, $H_0 : \alpha_j = 0$ and $H_0 : \beta_j = 0$, using F-test based on residual sum of squares, by setting the coefficient of conditioning variables equal to zero.

Data Sources

The data used here are obtained from several sources. One main source is the WIDER World Income Inequality Database (WIID) which is an expanded version of the Deininger and Squire (1996) database. WIID contains information on income inequality, income shares, and a number of variables indicating the source of data, and quality classification for 146 existing industrialized, developing and transition countries observed on an irregular basis mainly covering the period of post 1950 until 1998[6]. In the regression analysis we control for several characteristic variables like income concept, data source, and reference units. The Gini coefficient is measured in percentage points. The income type indicates whether inequality is defined by using expenditure or income. A dummy variable indicates whether the data originates from Deininger and Squire data set or WIDER extension. The reference variable includes family, household or persons as reference unit.

Education as a measure of human capital is the major variable that we control for in the specification of the conditional growth inequality relationship. Most widely used of such data are obtained from Barro and Lee (1996) database. This second source of our data provides information on education only at the five years intervals for the years between 1960 and 1995. Education is measured as the average number of schooling years for population above the age of 15.

The Penn World Tables (PWT) is a third data source used in our growth and income inequality study. It is also known as the Summers and Heston (1991) data. PWT provides information on international trade, GDP growth and population. Openness is measured as the ratio import plus export to the GDP produced. GDP is measured as real GDP per capita and population is defined in millions.

The unobservable time-specific effects (λ_t) are represented by time dummies capturing the 10-years decennial period effects and alternatively by a time trend starting from the first year of observation, 1867, and its square. Since several countries are observed each only one period, instead of unobservable country-specific effects we estimate regional-specific (μ_r) effects. The later implies that we control for unobserved between regional heterogeneity in income inequality, but we do not account for the within regional unobserved variations. The model is aimed at estimating global trends but yet account for regional heterogeneity in the levels of income inequality.

A summary statistics of the data is presented on Table 1. The mean Gini coefficient is 38.1 per cent with a standard deviation of 10.6 per cent. The range varies in the interval of 15.9 (Bulgaria 1965) and 79.5 (Zambia 1970) per cent. The dispersion in real GDP per capita (0.77) and openness (0.79) relative to sample mean is much higher than that of income inequality (0.28). The numbers in the parentheses are the coefficient of variation, i.e. the ratio of standard deviation and mean values of respective variable. The highest concentration of the variables is in the period 1960-1998. About 30 per cent of the data observations are from the West European countries, while 20 per cent from Latin American countries. Only 11.9 per cent of observations are based on the consumption data, remaining part are based on income data. The reference unit is mainly household (42.3 per cent) or persons (33.7 per cent).

Correlation coefficients among the key determinants of inequality are given in Table 2. The simple correlation matrix shows that inequality is declining over time, but income, level of education and trade openness are increasing over time. Income inequality is negatively related with mean income, level of education and openness. Openness and education are increasing with mean income.

---

[6] The WIID data contains 151 countries. The number of countries in our analysis differs due to the disintegration of Russia, Czechoslovakia, Yugoslavia, and reunification of Germany.

Table 1. Summary Statistics of the Data Covering the Period 1867-1998

Variable	Mean	Std Deviation	Minimum	Maximum
Income inequality measure:				
GINI coefficient	38.065	10.517	15.900	79.500
Determinants of inequality variation:				
Population in 1000	70.676	178.889	0.063	1238.599
INC Real GDP / capita in 1000	8.418	6.479	0.539	33.703
(1/INC)	0.117	0.014	0.096	0.159
Schooling year	6.236	2.726	0.300	11.900
Openness	59.804	47.511	3.378	439.029
Trend	112.211	13.805	1.000	132.000
Period dummy variables:				
Period dummy 1867-1949	0.015	0.123	0.000	1.000
Period dummy 1950-1959	0.068	0.252	0.000	1.000
Period dummy 1960-1969	0.158	0.365	0.000	1.000
Period dummy 1970-1979	0.204	0.403	0.000	1.000
Period dummy 1980-1989	0.271	0.445	0.000	1.000
Period dummy 1990-1998	0.283	0.451	0.000	1.000
Regional dummy variables:				
Middle East and North Africa	0.035	0.184	0.000	1.000
East Asia	0.057	0.232	0.000	1.000
South East Asia	0.053	0.225	0.000	1.000
South Asia	0.065	0.247	0.000	1.000
Latin America	0.196	0.397	0.000	1.000
Sub-Saharan Africa	0.096	0.295	0.000	1.000
East Europe	0.117	0.322	0.000	1.000
Former USSR	0.077	0.266	0.000	1.000
West Europe	0.303	0.460	0.000	1.000
Income characteristic variables:				
Expenditure	0.119	0.303	0.000	1.000
Deininger and Squire	0.207	0.368	0.000	1.000
Reference Unit person	0.337	0.435	0.000	1.000
Reference Unit family	0.031	0.144	0.000	1.000
Reference Unit household	0.423	0.439	0.000	1.000
Sample size:				
Countries	146	146	146	146
Observations	1631	1631	1631	1631

Source: Author's calculations.

Estimation Results

Several models based on equations 6 and 7 are estimated assuming fixed effects model and the results are reported in Table 3. In Model A1, all slope coefficients are assumed to be zero. This specification choice was made for two reasons. One, to show that large share of variations in the Gini coefficient can be captured by introduction of time and regional dummies. Second, the three data sets are not fully overlapping as the macro variables are missing for several countries. The use of macro variables, many of which are missing, resulted in reducing the sample size from 1631 to 1108 observations. It is to be noted that Model A1 is not nested to the remaining five models as time is modeled as 10-years period dummies. In comparison with a trend the period dummy variables has the advantage that they capture decennial fluctuations in income inequality.[7]

Table 2. Correlation Matrix Based on 1266-1631 Observations

	Year	Gini	Population	GDP/Capita	Schooling	Openness
Year	1.0000					
Gini coefficient	-0.2174 (0.0001)	1.0000				
Population	0.0274 (0.3168)	-0.1526 (0.0001)	1.0000			
GDP/Capita	0.2209 (0.0001)	-0.3736 (0.0001)	-0.1701 (0.0001)	1.0000		
Schooling	0.3088 (0.0001)	-0.4512 (0.0001)	-0.1291 (0.0001)	0.8007 (0.0001)	1.0000	
Openness	0.2430 (0.0001)	-0.0714 (0.0009)	-0.2735 (0.0001)	0.1663 (0.0001)	0.1362 (0.0001)	1.0000

Note: p-values under the coefficient.
Source: Author's calculations.

The estimated results are reported in Table 3 shows that the relative explanatory power of the macro variables compared to the regional and time heterogeneity effects is small. Despite the small impacts, various tests indicate that the explanatory variables should be accounted for. Model A2 is the first alternative specification of the equation 7 where the period dummies are replaced by a time trend and its square and explanatory macro variables are added. The Model A3 is distinguished from Model A2 by adding a number of control variables for income definition, data source and reference units. Model A4 and A5 are reciprocal counterparts of quadratic Models A2 and A3 with the difference that (INC^2) in equation 7 is replaced by (1/INC) in equation 6. Model A6 is the logarithmic equivalence of Model A3, where instead of level of INC its logarithm (lnINC) is used.

---

[7] At what point of the time a time trend starts has major impact on the estimated time effect. It is very common that in the case of unbalanced cross-section of time-series data to allow the global trend to start at the first year a unit is observed. In the WIID case 1867 is assigned 1. Another alternative is to allow for individual trends where the starting point of the trend is the year a country enters the sample. This has the disadvantage that when countries are observed only one or few periods non-consecutively, the time trend behave like any other continuous variables. A third alternative is to use decennial dummy variables or specify regional specific time trends where individual countries' incomplete trends overlap each other to build a continuous trend.

[9] Estimation results covering all combinations of sets of income, other conditional macroeconomic, time effects and data characteristics variables is available. Due to limited spaces only few are reported here.

Table 3. Least Squares Parameter Estimates Based
on WIID Database for the Period 1867-1998

Variable	Model A1	Model A2	Model A3	Model A4	Model A5	Model A6
Intercept	44.0688 a	229.6681a	245.1354 a	252.2288 a	266.5116 a	114.5669 a
Population.	-	-0.0044 a	-0.0034 b	-0.0030 b	-0.0021 .	0.5243 a
INC Real GDP per capita	-	-0.5436 a	-0.7281 a	-0.1453 c	-0.3105 a	-
INC squared	-	0.0167 a	0.0173 a	-	-	-
Log INC	-	-	-	-	-	34.2651 a
Log INC squared	-	-	-	-	-	-2.0928 a
(1 / INC)	-	-	-	-6.1100 a	-5.7331 a	-
Schooling year	-	-0.0379 .	-0.1043 .	-0.2430 .	-0.3153 b	-0.1445 .
Openness	-	0.0002 .	0.0034 .	-0.0083 .	-0.0048 .	0.0117 c
Trend	-	-3.2454 a	-3.5640 a	-3.6340 a	-3.9324 a	-3.8646 a
Trend squared	-	0.0139 a	0.0158 a	0.0157 a	0.0174 a	0.0171 a
Period 1867-1949 (ref.)	-	-	-	-	-	-
Period 1950-1959	-2.5399 c	-	-	-	-	-
Period 1960-1969	-2.7946 c	-	-	-	-	-
Period 1970-1979	-5.8086 a	-	-	-	-	-
Period 1980-1989	-8.5811 a	-	-	-	-	-
Period 1990-1998	-5.3881 a	-	-	-	-	-
Middle East and NA (ref.)	-	-	-	-	-	-
East Asia	-4.5831 a	-5.3064 a	-8.0888 a	-4.3574 a	-7.0852 a	-9.3478 a
South East Asia	4.7841 a	3.6691 a	2.5844 b	5.4374 a	4.2761 a	2.7013 b
South Asia	-1.9537 c	-3.5111 b	-3.5108 a	-0.5655 .	-0.6958 .	-1..9240 .
Latin America	9.0524 a	9.0032 a	7.0798 a	8.8382 a	6.9065 a	6.8819 a
Sub-Saharan Africa	10.4370 a	9.9279 a	10.1091 a	13.9514 a	13.8762 a	14.1010 a
East Europe	-11.9413 a	-11.4039 a	-13.4341 a	-11.5202 a	-13.5994 a	-14.1916 a
Former USSR	-5.8159 a	-5.9334 b	-8.7905 a	-5.5244 b	-8.3842 a	-9.1869 a
West Europe	-3.8103 a	-3.4707 a	-3.6181 a	-3.8972 a	-4.0739 a	-3.5435 a
Expenditure	-	-	-7.5041 a	-	-7.3493 a	-7.8753 a
Deininger and Squire data	-	-	-1.1856 c	-	-1.1134 c	-0.8210 .
Reference Unit person	-	-	-	-	-	-
Reference Unit family	-	-	1.9374 .	-	2.4465 c	2.1556 .
Ref. Unit household	-	-	0.2575 .	-	0.0070 .	0.0634 .
Income and trend elasticities:						
Average trend effect	-	-1.6857 a	-1.7911 a	-1.8723 a	-1.9799 a	-1.9458 a
Average income effect	-	-0.4030 a	-0.5825 a	-0.8602 b	-0.9813 a	-2.0047 a

Table 3. (Continued.)

Variable	Model A1	Model A2	Model A3	Model A4	Model A5	Model A6
Model performance:						
Adjusted R square	0.5352	0.5583	0.5896	0.5641	0.5942	0.5992
F-value	145.350 a	94.3000 a	84.7100 a	96.5400 a	86.3200 a	88.0900 a
RMSE	7.1701	6.8294	6.5830	6.7841	6.5460	6.5061
Sample size:						
Countries	146	93	93	93	93	93
Periods	1-53	1-53	1-53	1-53	1-53	1-53
Observations	1631	1108	1108	1108	1108	1108

Note: Significant at the less than 1% (a), 1-5% (b), 5-10% (c) and above 10% (.) levels of significance.
Source: Author's calculations.

Model A1 and A2 are not nested, but Model A2 and A3 are nested. F-test based on the residual sums of squares (21.89) is in favor of A3 indicating that the control variables are related to the data which should be included in the specification of equation 7. In the same way another F-test (21.21) indicates that the set of control variables should be included in the specification of equation 6. Depending on the way the income variable is given (non-logarithmic, logarithmic or reciprocal) the six models build three groups, where A1, A2 and A3 belong to the first group, while A4 and A5 to the second group, and A6 to the third group. The sets of models (A2 versus A4 versus A6) and (A3 versus A5 versus A6) are not nested across the groups. The within group testing results indicate that Model A3, A5 and A6, i.e. models incorporating macro variables, data characteristic variables, and controlling for time and regional effects are the preferred model specifications.[9] Unfortunately due to nonnestedness of the three models, they can not easily be ranked based on some test statistics.

Performance of the models is good. The R^2 values vary in the interval 0.54 to 0.59. In all models openness is insignificant. Only in Model A5 a higher level of education reduces inequality. An inclusion of population to control for the size of countries did not change the results much. Income definition is a major source of differences in the inequality levels across countries. Inequality is on an average 7.5 per cent lower than when income is measured on the basis of consumption than income. The time dummy and time trend variables indicate that inequality is declining but at a decreasing rate (second order is positive). In comparison with the period before 1950 the 1980 decline in income inequality is most pronounced. Regional dummies show presence of significant regional heterogeneity. Sub-Saharan Africa and Latin America are identified as the highest and East Europe the lowest inequality rates.

The null hypothesis of a simple linear specification versus Kuznets (added square of income or alternatively reciprocal of income) is obtained from $H_0 : \alpha_2 = \beta_2 = 0$. Empirical results for 93 countries after having controlled for time effects, regional effects, human capital, population, openness and various data characteristics[10] provide evidences on the

---

[10] A separation of countries by measurement of income may result in biased estimates and non-representative, and non-comparable samples. A comparison of paired estimates for same country and same period has not been possible based on the WIID data. A third and typical way to deal with differences in income definitions across countries and over time is by introducing dummy variables additively or multiplicatively. Here we employ the additive dummy variable adjustment approach. Atkinson and Brandolini (2001) prefer the alternative approach of using a data-set where the observations are as fully consistent as possible but at the high cost of significant reduction in the sample size.

existence of negative and significant inequality-development relationship. The effect is stronger when development is defined as an inverse of real GDP per capita or transformed to logarithms. The Kuznets hypothesis represents a global U-shape relationship. All six models in Table 3 produce uniform indications. The weakness is however, the small sample of countries and the short time series each country observed with interruptions. Several developing countries are observed only one single period.

Some Sensitivity Analysis

The high and significant constant term is an indication of the inadequacy of the Models A2-A6 in describing the data. The simple Model A1 is best in describing the data. An exclusion of the regional and time effects, i.e. a specification based on only determinants of income inequality, resulted in similar sign and significance of the coefficient as those in Models A2 and A4 but somewhat higher intercept, 52.07 and 50.24 respectively. The R^2 values are about 0.26. The source of distortion is thus the time effects. Only 1.5 per cent or 25 observations of the data are observed during the period 1867-1949.

To avoid any time distortion we have estimated the same models as in Table 3 but by excluding the period before 1950. The results are presented in Table 4. As expected the source of distortion in the trend effects and intercepts is the few observations from the period before 1950. The new intercepts in Models B1 to B5 vary in the interval 41.7 and 61.30. The intercept in Model B6 is higher, 87.6. The sign and significance of the new trend is similar, but the coefficient of the first order is much lower reducing the negative time trend elasticity from 1.69-1.98 to 0.49-0.58. All other results in Models B2 to B6 remain the same, as the early period of the data is excluded from the estimation procedure due to missing income, education, openness and population variables. A decomposition of countries by income classes or regions is not meaningful due to small sample size. The Kuznets hypothesis is again represents a global U-shape relationship. All six models in Table 4 produce uniform indications with respect to Kuznets hypothesis.

Ram (1995) has criticized the empirical studies on the Kuznets hypothesis on the ground that they employ second degree polynomials in levels or logarithms of income. This approach allows for only one turning point in the underlying relationship and is seen as inadequate in the case of industrialized countries where inequality-growth curve has doubled back after an inverted U. A non-linear mixture of quadratic and exponential functional forms is proposed. Different versions of the function have been used by Wan (2002):

$$GINI_{it} = (1 - \exp(-\beta_1 INC_{it})) \exp(-\beta_2 INC_{it}) + \beta_3 INC_{it} + \beta_4 INC_{it}^2 + u_{it} \tag{8}$$

$$GINI_{it} = \beta_0 + (1 - \exp(-\beta_1 INC_{it})) \exp(-\beta_2 INC_{it}) + \beta_3 \ln INC_{it} \\ + \beta_4 (\ln INC_{it})^2 + u_{it} \tag{9}$$

$$GINI_{it} = \beta_0 + (1 - \exp(-\beta_1 INC_{it})) \exp(-\beta_2 INC_{it}) + \beta_3 INC_{it} + \beta_4 (1/ INC_{it}) + u_{it} \tag{10}$$

Table 4. Least Squares Parameter Estimates
Based on WIID Database for the Period 1950-1998

Variable	Model B1	Model B2	Model B3	Model B4	Model B5	Model B6
Intercept	41.7078 a	57.0564 a	58.9424 a	59.5472 a	61.2997 a	87.6331 a
Population.	-	-0.0044 a	-0.0034 b	-0.0030 b	-0.0021 .	0.5243 a
INC Real GDP per capita	-	-0.5436 a	-0.7281 a	-0.1453 c	-0.3105 a	-
INC squared	-	0.0167 a	0.0173 a	-	-	-
Log INC	-	-	-	-	-	34.2651 a
Log INC squared	-	-	-	-	-	-2.0928 a
(1 / INC)	-	-	-	-6.1100 a	-5.7331 a	-
Schooling year	-	-0.0379 .	-0.1043 .	-0.2430 .	-0.3153 b	-0.1445 .
Openness	-	0.0002 .	0.0034 .	-0.0083 .	-0.0048 .	0.0117 c
Trend	-	-0.9646 a	-0.9773 a	-1.0656 a	-1.0727 a	-1.0671 a
Trend squared	-	0.0139 a	0.0158 a	0.0157 a	0.0174 a	0.0171 a
Period 1950-1959 (ref.)	-	-	-	-	-	-
Period 1960-1969	-0.1445 .	-	-	-	-	-
Period 1970-1979	-3.1520 a	-	-	-	-	-
Period 1980-1989	-5.9254 a	-	-	-	-	-
Period 1990-1998	-2.7351 a	-	-	-	-	-
Middle East and NA (ref.)	-	-	-	-	-	-
East Asia	-4.8690 a	-5.3064 a	-8.0888 a	-4.3574 a	-7.0852 a	-9.3478 a
South East Asia	4.4972 a	3.6691 a	2.5844 b	5.4374 a	4.2761 a	2.7013 b
South Asia	-2.2336 c	-3.5111 b	-3.5108 a	-0.5655 .	-0.6958 .	-1.9240 .
Latin America	8.8006 a	9.0032 a	7.0798 a	8.8382 a	6.9065 a	6.8819 a
Sub-Saharan Africa	10.0981 a	9.9279 a	10.1091 a	13.9514 a	13.8762 a	14.1010 a
East Europe	-12.2307 a	-11.4039 a	-13.4341 a	-11.5202 a	-13.5994 a	-14.1916 a
Former USSR	-6.1091 a	-5.9334 b	-8.7905 a	-5.5244 b	-8.3842 a	-9.1869 a
West Europe	-4.1572 a	-3.4707 a	-3.6181 a	-3.8972 a	-4.0739 a	-3.5435 a
Expenditure	-	-	-7.5041 a	-	-7.3493 a	-7.8753 a
Deininger and Squire data	-	-	-1.1856 c	-	-1.1134 c	-0.8210 .
Reference Unit person	-	-	-	-	-	-
Reference Unit family	-	-	1.9374 .	-	2.4465 c	2.1566 .
Ref. Unit household	-	-	0.2575 .	-	0.0070 .	0.0634 .
Income and trend elasticities:						
Average trend effect	-	-0.5344 a	-0.4883 a	-0.5797 a	-0.5342 a	-0.5379 a
Average income effect	-	-0.4030 a	-0.5825 a	-0.8602 b	-0.9813 a	-2.0048 a
Model performance:						
Adjusted R square	0.5343	0.5583	0.5896	0.5641	0.5942	0.5992
F-value	154.4700 a	94.3000 a	84.7100 a	96.5400 a	86.3200 a	88.0900 a
RMSE	7.1687	6.8294	6.5830	6.7841	6.5460	6.5061
Sample size:						
Countries	146	93	93	93	93	93
Periods	1-49	1-49	1-49	1-49	1-49	1-49
Observations	1605	1108	1108	1108	1108	1108

Note: Significant at the less than 1% (a), 1-5% (b), 5-10% (c) and above 10% (.) levels of significance.
Source: Author's calculations.

Empirical results in Wan are based on 24 transition countries each observed between 1 to 24 years (202 observations in total). The data is obtained from the WIID database. Wan estimates unconditional inequality growth relationship and thereby do not control for non-income determinants of inequality, trend or data characteristics. The results do not support the proposed flexible non-linear functions 8 to 10. The Kuznets hypothesis is rejected by the data, but a first half of the U-pattern is found to be adequate for describing the growth-inequality relationship among the transition countries.

Cornia (1999) also using WIID data studied trends in income distribution in the post World War II among 77 developed, developing and transition countries. Cornia found evidence of rising inequality among 45 countries, 23 of which with U-shaped relationship, falling inequality in 16 countries, 3 with inverted U-shape, and 12 countries with no trends. The similar results but based on 73 countries are presented in Cornia and Kiiski (2001) and Cornia and Court (2001). Biancotti (2003) limited the sample to 67 countries observed during 1970 to 1996 to describe the evolution of the polarization of societies. The distribution of inequality appears to be slightly bimodal at the start of the period and polarized in 1980s and 1990s especially in less developed countries.

A possible and probably optimal solution to test the Kuznets hypothesis at the country level is based on WIID database. The data can be aggregated to the world level using population shares of the world population in a given year as weights in the aggregation procedure. The period would cover the post World War II without interruptions in the series.

However, one major problem affecting negatively the aggregation is that countries with large population like China and India are observed only a few periods. Their periodical exit and entry to the series will cause major fluctuations in the World Gini and world income series. For the issue of instability in the aggregated income and inequality series see Heshmati (2004b). This will have implications for inverted-U shape. Despite its limitations, the aggregate data would better shed light on the U-shape nature of the inequality-growth relationship.

11. SUMMARY AND CONCLUSIONS

There exists a comprehensive body of literature investigating the relationship between openness, growth, inequality and poverty. In general there exists a positive relationship between openness and growth. The effect is declining over time and different in its impact on distribution of income. However, there is no indication of a systematic relationship between trade and inequality. One major shortcoming of the literature on the link between growth, openness, inequality and poverty is that the simultaneous and direction of causal relationship between these key variables has been neglected. An establishment of linkage and direction of causality will have major impacts on the relevance of results and inferences made based on such result.

The empirical findings based on large sample of countries and relatively long time period indicates the presence of convergence in per capita income but divergence in income inequality. There is evidence of strong convergence among more homogenous and integrated advanced countries but also divergence among less developed countries or regions of countries and the world. The between country contribution is much higher then within country contribution to the world inequality. Democratization in Western countries has led to institutional changes and the changes in taxation and redistribution, too, reduce inequality. Other paths are East Asian Miracle with low inequality and high growth, while the Sub-Saharan Africa with high inequality and low growth. There is a conflicting viewpoint about the causal effects of inequality on growth.

Empirical results on the relationship between growth, inequality and poverty, show that outcomes of policy measures are heterogeneous. Depending on the initial position of the poor and diversity of impacts the poor might gain more from the redistribution, but also suffer more from economic contraction. Results based on micro data indicates that asset inequality affects negatively on the consumption growth and the effect usually vanishes in an aggregate level like that of the regional growth models. In general it is rather difficult to measure the effects of inequality and growth on the efforts to reduce poverty in the course of economic development in the developing countries. In sum economic growth benefits the poor but at the absence of effective redistribution policies it might deteriorate the income distribution. Initial conditions, institutions, specific country structures, and time horizons each play a significant role in targeting policies to make economic growth pro-poor.

Globalization, openness and technical change have been biased to skilled labor in industrialized countries widening the wage differentials suggesting positive association between openness and wage inequality. However, the pattern is seen more complex. For developing countries these changes reduce wage inequality by narrowing the wage gap between skilled and unskilled workers. The relative demand for skilled labor and wage inequality has been developed differently across countries.

Regression results based on the WIID database suggest that income inequality is declining over time. Inequality is also declining with the growth of income. There is significant regional heterogeneity in the levels and development over time. The Kuznets hypothesis is representing a global U-shape relationship between inequality and growth. Similar indications are found in other studies based on the data used here. A possible solution to the Kuznets hypothesis at the country level would be to aggregate the data to the world level using population shares as weights. However, entry and exit of countries with large population affects stability of the inequality and development series and regression results. The period should ideally cover the post World War II with less or no interruptions in the time series.

ACKNOWLEDGEMENT

An earlier version of this paper was completed while I was working at the World Institute for Development Economic Research, UNU/WIDER. Encouragements by Ms. Chiman Saeed Jafaar and comments and suggestion from Amit Kumar Bhandari is gratefully acknowledged.

REFERENCES

Acemoglu D. (2002), Cross-country inequality trends, *NBER Working Paper* No. 8832.

Acemoglu D. and J. A. Robinson (2000), Why did the west extended the franchise? Democracy, inequality, and growth in historical perspective, *The Quarterly Journal of Economics CXV*, 1167-1199.

Acemoglu D. and J. Ventura (2002), The world income distribution, *Quarterly Journal of Economics CXVII*(2), 659-694.

Addison T. and A. Heshmati (2004), The new global determinants of FDI to developing countries, *Research in Banking and Finance* 4, 151-186.

Aghion P. (2002), Schumpeterian growth theory and the dynamics of income inequality, *Econometrica* 70(3), 855-882.

Aghion P., E. Carol and C. Garcia-Penalosa (1999), Inequality and economic growth: the perspective of the new growth theories, *Journal of Economic Literature XXXVII*, 1615-1660.

Al-Marhubi F. (1997), A note on the link between income inequality and inflation, *Economics Letters* 55, 317-319.

Alesina A. and D. Rodrik (1994), Distributive politics and economic growth, *Quarterly Journal of Economics* 109, 465-490.

Amis P. and U. Grant (2001), Urban economic growth, civic management and poverty reduction, *Journal of International Development* 13, 997-1002.

Atkinson A. B. (1999), Is rising inequality inevitable? A critique of the transatlantic consensus, The United Nations University, *WIDER Annual Lectures* 3, Helsinki: UNU/WIDER.

Atkinson A. B. (2000), Increased income inequality in OECD countries and the redistributive impact of the Government budget, *WIDER Working Papers* 2000/202, Helsinki: UNU/WIDER.

Atkinson A. B. and A. Brandolini (2001), Promise and pitfalls in the use of "secondary" data-sets: income inequality in OECD countries as a case study, *Journal Economic Literature* 39, 771-799.

Balisacan A.M. and N. Fuwa (2003), Growth, inequality and politics revisited: a developing-country, *Economics Letters* 79, 53-58.

Barro R.J. (1991), Economic growth in a cross section of countries, *Quarterly Journal of Economics* 106, 406-443.

Barro R.J. (1997), *Determinants of economic growth: a cross-country empirical study*, MIT press, Cambridge, MA.

Barro R.J. and J-W Lee (1996), International measures of schooling years and schooling quality, *American Economic Review* 86(2), 218-223.

Barro R.J. and X. Sala-i-Martin (1991), Convergence across states and regions, *Brookings Papers on Economic Activity* 1, 107-182.

Barro R.J. and X. Sala-i-Martin (1995), *Economic Growth*, McGraw-Hill Inc.

Benhabib J. and A. Rustichini (1996), Social conflict and growth, *Journal of Economic Growth* 1, 125-142.

Bernard A. B. and S. N. Durlauf (1996), Interpreting tests of the convergence hypothesis, *Journal of Econometrics* 71, 161-173.

Bernard A. B. and C.I. Jones (1996), Productivity across industries and countries: time series theory and evidence, *Review of Economics and Statistics* 78(1), 135-146.

Biancotti C. (2003), A polarization of polarization? *The distribution of inequality* 1970-1996, Bank of Italy.

Bigsten A., B. Kebebe, A. Shimeles and M. Taddesse (2003), Growth and poverty reduction in Ethiopia: evidence from household panel surveys, *World Development* 31,1, 87-106.

Bigsten A. and J. Levin (2000), Growth, income distribution and poverty: a review, Department of Economics, Göteborg University, *Working Paper in Economics* No. 2000:32.

Borjas G. J. (1994), The economics of immigration, *Journal of Economic Literature* 31 December, 1667-1717.

Borjas G. J. (1999), Economic research on the determinants of immigration: lessons for the European Union, *World Bank Technical Paper* No. 438.

Bourguignon F. and C. Morrisson (2002), Inequality among world citizens: 1820-1992, *American Economic Reviews* 92(4), 727-747.

Calderon C. and A. Chong (2001), External sector and income inequality in interdependent economics using a dynamic panel data approach, *Economics Letters* 71, 225-231.

Carree M. and L. Klomp (1997), Testing the convergence hypothesis: a comment, *The Review of Economics and Statistics* LXXIX(4), 683-686.

Caselli F., G. Esquivel and F. Lefort (1996), Reopening the convergence debate: a new look at cross-country growth empirics, *Journal of Economic Growth* 1, 363-389.

Chen B-L. (2003), An inverted-U relationship between inequality and long-run growth, *Economics Letters* 78, 205-212.

Cornia G.A. (1999), Liberalization, globalization and income distribution, *WIDER Working Paper* 1999/157, Helsinki: UNU/WIDER.

Cornia G.A. and J. Court (2001), Inequality, growth and poverty in the era of liberalization and globalization, *Policy Brief* No. 4, Helsinki: UNU/WIDER.

Cornia G.A. and S. Kiiski (2001), Trends in income distribution in the post WWII period: evidence and interpretation, *WIDER Discussion Paper* 2001/89, Helsinki: UNU/WIDER.

Deininger K. and L. Squire (1996), A new data set measuring income inequality, *World Bank Economic Review* 10(3), 565-591.

Deininger K. and L. Squire (1998), New ways of looking at old issues: inequality and growth, *Journal of Development Economics* 57, 259-287.

Dollar D. and A. Kraay (2001a), Trade growth and poverty, *Development Research Group*, The World Bank.

Dollar D. and A. Kraay (2001b), Growth is good for the poor, Policy Research Working paper 2001:2199, *Development Research Group*, The World Bank.

Dowrick S. and J.B. DeLong (2001), Globalization and convergence, Paper for NBER Conference on Globalization in Historical Perspective, Santa Barbara, California, In: Williamson J. (ed.), *Globalization in historical perspective*, Chicago, University of Chicago Press, forthcoming.

Dowrick S. and D-T. Nguyen (1989), OECD comparative economic growth 1950-85: catch-up and convergence, *American Economic Review* 79(5), 1010-1030.

Edwards T.H. (1992), Trade orientation, distortions, and growth in developing countries, *Journal of Development Economics* 39(1), 31-57.

Edwards T.H. (1998), Openness, productivity and growth: what do we really know, *Economic Journal* 108, 383-398.

Eicher T.S. and C. Garcia-Penalosa (2001), Inequality and growth: the dual role of human capital in development, *Journal of Development Economics* 66, 173-197.

Epstein G.S. and U. Spiegel (2002), Natural inequality, production and economic growth, *Labor Economics* 8, 463-473.

Fan C.S., J. Overland and M. Spagat (1999), Human capital, growth and inequality in Russia, *Journal of Comparative Economics* 27(4), 618-643.

Forbes K.J. (2000), A reassessment of the relationship between inequality and growth, *American Economic Review* 90(4), 869-880.

Galbraith J. and E. Garcilazo (2005), Pay inequality in Europe 1995-2000: convergence between countries and stability inside, *UTIP Working Paper* 2005:30.

Galor O. (2000), Income distribution and the process of development, *European Economic Review* 44, 706-712.

Galor O. and O. Moav (2000), Ability-biased technological transition, wage inequality and economic growth, the *Quarterly Journal of Economics* 115(2), 469-497.

Galor O. and O. Moav (2001), Evolution of growth, *European Economic Review* 45, 718-729.

Gholami R., S-Y. To, Lee and A. Heshmati (2006), The causal relationship between information and communication technology and foreign direct investment, *The World Economy* 29(1), 43-62.

Gottschalk P. (1997), Inequality, income growth, and mobility: the basic facts, *Journal of Economic Perspectives* 11(2), 21-40.

Goudie A. and P. Ladd (1999), Economic growth, poverty and inequality, *Journal of International Development* 11, 177-195.

Heshmati A. (2000), On the causality between GDP and health care expenditure in the augmented Solow growth model, *SSE/EFI Working Paper Series in Economics and Finance* 2001:423.

Heshmati A. (2003), Measurement of a multidimentional index of globalization and its impact on income inequality, *WIDER Discussion Paper* 2003/69, Helsinki: UNU/WIDER.

Heshmati A. (2004a), The relationship between globalization, poverty and income inequality, *IZA Discussion Paper* 2004:1277.

Heshmati A. (2004b), Data issues and databases used in analysis of growth, poverty and economic inequality, *IZA Discussion Paper* 2004:1263.

Heshmati A. (2006a), Measurement of a Multidimensional Index of Globalization, *Global Economy Journal* 6(2), Paper 1.

Heshmati A. (2006b), *Global Trends in Income Inequality*, Nova Science Publishers.

Heshmati A. (2006c), The world distribution of income and income inequality: a review of the economic literature, *Journal of World System Research* 12(1), 60-107.

Iacoviello M. (1998), Inequality Dynamics: evidence from some European countries, *Working Paper* No. 191, Maxwell School of Citizenship and Public Affairs, Syracuse University.

Islam N. (1995), Growth empirics: a panel data approach, *The Quarterly Journal of Economics* 110, 1127-1170.

Jones C.I. (2002), *Introduction to economic growth*, Second Edition, W.W. Norton and Compacy.

Kakwani N. and M. Krongkaew (2000), Introduction: Economic growth, poverty and income inequality in the Asia-Pacific region, *Journal of the Asia Pacific Economy* 5(1/2), 9-13.

Keane M.P. and E.S Prasad (2002), Inequality, transfers and growth: new evidence from the economic transition in Poland, *The Review of Economics and Statistics* 84(2), 324-341.

Khan A. Haider (1999), Sectoral growth and poverty alleviation: a multiplier decomposition technique applied to South Africa, *World Development* 27(3), 521-530.

Khan A.R. and C. Riskin (2001), *Inequality and poverty in China in the age of globalization*, Oxford University Press.

Knowles S. and P.D. Owen (1997), Education and health in an effective-labor empirical growth model, *The Economic Record* 73(223), 314-328.

Kuznets S. (1955), Economic growth and income inequality, *American Economic Review* 45, 1-28.

Lee K., M.H. Pesaran and R. Smith (1997), Growth and convergence in a multi-country empirical stochastic Solow model, *Journal of Applied Econometrics* 12, 357-392.

Lee W. and J.E. Roemer (1999), Inequality and redistribution revisited, *Economics Letters* 65, 339-346.

Lichtenberg F.R. (1994), Testing the convergence hypothesis, *Review of Economics and Statistics* 76(3), 576-579.

Lindert P.H. and J.G. Williamson (2001), Does globalization make the World more unequal?, *NBER Working Paper* 2001:8228.

Lustig N., O. Arias and J. Rigolini (2002), *Poverty reduction and economic growth*: a two-way causality, Inter-American Development Bank, Washington D.C., Sustainable Development Department, Technical Papers Series.

Mankiew N.G., D. Romer and D.H. Weil (1992), A contribution to the empirics of economics growth, *The Quarterly Journal of Economics* 107, 407-438.

Moav O. (2002), Income distribution and macroeconomics: the persistence of inequality in a convex technology framework, *Economics Letters* 75, 187-192.

Nerlove M. (2000), Growth rate convergence, fact or artifact? An essay on panel data econometrics, in J. Krishnakumar and E. Ronchetti, eds., *Panel Data Econometrics: Future Directions*, pp. 3-34, Amsterdam: North Holland.

Perotti R. (1996), Growth, income distribution, and democracy: what the data say, *Journal of Economic Growth* 1(3), 149-187.

Persson T. and G. Tabellini (1994), Is inequality harmful for growth? *American economic Review* 84, 600-621.

Quah D. (1993), Galton's fallacy and tests of the convergence hypothesis, *Scandinavian Journal of Economics* 95, 427-443.

Quah D. (1996a), Twin Peaks: growth and convergence in models of distribution dynamics, *The Economic Journal* 106(437), 1045-1055.

Quah D. (1996b), Regional convergence clusters across Europe, *European Economic Review* 40, 951-958.

Quah D. (1996c), Empirics for economic growth and convergence, *European Economic Review* 40, 1353-1375.

Quah D. (2001), Some simple arithmetic on how income inequality and economic growth matter, *Paper presented at WIDER conference on Growth and Poverty*, 25-26 May 2001, Helsinki.

Quah D. (2002), One third of the world's growth and inequality, *Economics Department, CEPR Discussion Paper* 2002:3316.

Ravallion M. (1995), Growth and poverty: evidence for developing countries in the 1980s, *Economics Letters* 48, 411-417.

Ravallion M. (1997a), Can high-inequality developing countries escape absolute poverty?, *Economics Letters* 56, 51-57.

Ravallion M. (1997b), Good and bad growth: the human development reports, *World Development* 25(5), 631-638.

Ravallion M. (1998), Does aggregation hide the harmful effects of inequality on growth?, *Economics Letters* 61, 73-77.

Ravallion M. (2001), Growth, inequality and poverty: looking beyond averages, *World Development* 29(11), 1803-1815.

Ravallion M. (2003), Inequality convergence, Economics Letters 80, 351-356.

Ravallion M. and S. Chen (2003), Measuring pro-poor growth, *Economics Letters* 78, 93-99.

Ravallion M. and G. Datt (2000), When growth is pro-poor? Evidence from the diverse experience of Indian states, *World Bank Policy Research*, WP 2263.

Rodriguez F. and D. Rodrik (1999), Trade policy and economic growth: a skeptic's guide to the cross-national evidence, *NBER* 1999:7081.

Sacks J. and A. Warner (1995), Economic reform and the process of global integration, *Brookings Papers on Economic Activity* 1:95.

Savvides A. and T. Stegnos (2000), Income inequality and economic development: evidence from the threshold regression model, *Economics Letters* 69, 207-212.

Shari I. (2000), Economic growth and income inequality in Malaysia, 1971-95, *Journal of the Asia Pacific Economy* 5(1/2), 112-124.

Shorrocks A. and R. van der Hoeven (2004), Eds., Growth, inequality, and poverty: *Prospects for pro-poor economic development*, Oxford University Press.

Shupp F.R. (2002), Growth and income inequality in South Africa, *Journal of Economic Dynamics and Control* 26, 1699-1720.

Solimano A. (2001), The evolution of world income inequality: assessing the impact of globalization, Unpublished manuscript, *ECLAC, CEPAL – Serie Macroeconomica del desarrollo No. 11*, Santiago, Chile.

Stiglitz J.E. and Weiss (1981), Credit rationing in markets with imperfect information, *American Economic Review* 71(3), 393-410.

Summers R. and A. Heston (1991), The Penn World Table (Mark 5): an expanded set of international comparisons, 1950-1988, *Quarterly Journal of Economics* 106, 327-368.

Sylwester K. (2000), Income inequality, education expenditures, and growth, *Journal of Development Economics* 63, 379-398.

Van der Hoeven R. and A. Shorrocks (2003), Eds., *Perspectives on growth and poverty*, United Nations University Press, Tokyo, Japan.

Wan G.H. (2002), Income inequality and growth in transition economies: are nonlinear models needed?, *WIDER Discussion Paper* 2002/104, Helsinki: UNU/WIDER.

Warr P.G. (2000), Poverty incidence and economic growth in Southeast Asia, *Journal of Asian Economics* 11, 431-441.

Wolff E.N. (2001), The impact of IT investment on income and wealth inequality in the Postwar US economy, *Information Economics and Policy* 14, 233-251.

Wood A. (1997), Openness and wage inequality in developing countries: the Latin American challenge to East Asian continental wisdom, *World Bank Economic Review* 11(1), 33-57.

You I. (1998), Income distribution and growth in East Asia, *Journal of Development Studies* 34(6), 000-000.

In: Roadmap to Bangalore?
Editors: A. Heshmati, A. Tausch, pp. 139-150

ISBN: 978-1-60021-478-3
© 2007 Nova Science Publishers, Inc.

Chapter 5

CAN LISBON STRATEGY CREATE GROWTH AND JOBS?

Jože Mencinger

University of Ljubljana and EIPF, Prešernova 21, Ljubljana, Slovenia

ABSTRACT

Modern societies and governments are preoccupied with efficiency and growth; it is taken as limitless due to enhanced total factor productivity and prevalence of services over production of goods. EU which had condensed this passion in the Lisbon strategy 2000, admitted that it failed. In February 2005, the old strategy was replaced by a new one. The realization of new, less firmly defined goals, however does not seem to be assured; the strategy relies on empty talks and new institutions. The "scientific" pillar of the strategy is production function; growth is to be attained by increasing total factor productivity. However, reorganization of science and creation of a multitude of institutions, regardless of financial resources, do not guarantee scientific discoveries. Even if they did, discoveries do not guarantee growth and jobs. Technological changes are predominantly labor saving, they may but not need create new jobs in other sectors, predominantly in services. Also this path is in Europe threatened by the globalization which swiftly turns its activities with high value added jobs into activities with low value added jobs.

European countries have shifted a large part of globalization challenges from the national to the EU level, which is, however, even if it became knowledge based society, unable to compete with much more ruthless societies. The Achilles' heel of Lisbon strategy is the overall neglect of aggregate demand. Very high economic growth is not a lasting phenomenon, it is often based on country specific features, and co-determined by shifts in aggregate demand. Long run and uniform economic growth cannot be assured by reductions of budget deficits or public expenditures. Indeed, the new Lisbon Partnership for Growth and Jobs of 2005 is threatened by the old Stability and Growth Pact of 1997.

Key words: economic growth, production function, technological change, globalization, aggregate demand.

1. EMPTY TALKS OF LISBON STRATEGY

Modern societies and governments are preoccupied with efficiency and economic growth[1] which is taken as limitless due to enhanced total factor productivity and prevalence of services over production of goods. EU condensed this passion in the Lisbon strategy signed in March 2000. The strategy should ensure Europe to become the most efficient knowledge based society of full employment, which could compete in the globalization contest. After some years of mantras on strategy, actual development and the report of the Wim Kok committee at the end of 2004 brought soberness and admittance that EU was not only far from the Lisbon goals for 2010, but also heading in the opposite direction. Despite contrary assertions of EU representatives[2] European Commission reluctantly admitted that Lisbon strategy failed. The old strategy was therefore in February 2005 replaced by "Partnership for Growth and Jobs – New Beginning of the Lisbon Strategy". In it, the ending year 2010 was abandoned, number of goals was reduced, and responsibilities were turned to the governments of member states. The new strategy, ready for the spring 2005 meeting of the Council of Europe, was said to be simple, pragmatic, and tangible[3]. It should be based on the partnership between the Commission and member states, which should create their own "National Lisbons" and become responsible for efficiency, increase of productivity, and employment. The sum of "National Lisbons" should result in common "EU Lisbon". Economic growth and job creation are in the core of the Partnership and they should be attained by assistance of healthy macroeconomic policy supporting structural reforms. The "Lisbon Action Plan" should improve the management of the strategy, for example, by founding national ministries for its implementation (Mr. or Mrs. Lisbon).

While the goals of the "Partnership" (growth, jobs, and social security) are not questionable the new strategy does not appear to be more trustworthy than the old one, which was already in the very successful year 2000, when it had been accepted, equally utopian as it was in 2005. The new strategy does not assure that low economic growth accompanied by budget deficits, high unemployment, and moderate inflation will not continue. There are no provisions for the turning point of this development. Instead, the new strategy surprises with the abundance of words, empty talks, newly invented phraseology and concepts, action plans

---

[1] Contemporary economics is based on the relation : Selfishness →Profit →Growth; most textbooks start with the assertion that economic activity attempts to fulfill limitless needs. However, if needs are limitless, so must be economic growth. Can we therefore talk about limitless growth which would fulfill limitless needs? The logical answer is no. If the needs are limitless, they cannot be fulfilled, if we produce in a finite environment, growth cannot be limitless. Nevertheless, the idea that economic growth is not limitless has only a few supporters. Most economists believe in the old assertion that productivity of natural resources is growing exponentionally (R. Sollow, 1957) and that economic growth is based on services and limitless growth of knowledge. Thus, production of material goods is not very relevant which should assure that growth can be limitless (Ayres, 2004).

[2] See for example the lectures of commissioners: Peter Mendelson: Strengthening the Lisbon Strategy: the Contribution of External Trade to the Growth and Competitivnes in Europe, Stocholm, February 15, 2005; Janez Potočnik: The Future of EU Research – chances for the new Member States, Warsaw, Februarjy 4, 2005; Neelie Kroes: Building a Competitive Europe – Competition Policy and Relaunch of the Lisbon Strategy, Milan, February 7, 2005.

[3] Communication to the Spring European Council, Working together for Growth and Jobs, A new start for the Lisbon Strategy, COM (2005) 24, Brussels, 02.02.2005.

and programs, priorities, mobilizations, new institutions and similar claptraps[4]. For somebody from a former socialist country, Lisbon strategy easily competes with numerous declarations in former Yugoslavia (Mencinger, 1988). In short, if economic growth in EU depended on rhetoric, it would be high. Because it does not, it is most likely that the new Lisbon strategy will soon turn into a worthless political document.

2. THE SUPPLY SIDE

The "scientific" pillar of the strategy is production function. Let us consider, for simplicity, that it has a form of Cobb-Douglas production function $Y = A*K^a*L^b$. It simply says that one must work (L) and have machinery (K) to produce (Y) while a and b indicate how changes in K and L affect Y. Growth, which cannot be explained by the increases of K and L is attributed to technological change or total factor productivity, embodied in A. It is A which also provides room for empty talks and slogans about development, human capital, use of knowledge, entrepreneurship, efficient and inexpensive state administration etc.

Though production function can have many different forms and additions, the essence and the causality remain unchanged; output is the dependent while labor, capital, and technological change are the independent variables. A (total factor productivity) is the crucial element of Lisbon strategy; less attention is given to capital and labor, though shallowness of the capital market and inflexibility of the labor market are often blamed for low growth and higher unemployment in Europe compared to USA. The inflexibility of labor implies that workers in EU countries are not willing to work for 200 € a month while Rumanian workers are, and Chinese workers are even willing to work for many times lower wages.

Crucial for the lagging[5] of Europe is nevertheless supposed to be slow growth of total factor productivity; caused by modest investment expenditures for research and development, inappropriate education, and feeble spread of knowledge. Thus, research and development, innovations, and knowledge should, according to the strategy, assure competitiveness of EU in the world market in which other countries compete with cheap labor and abundance of raw materials. The importance of scientific inventions and organization of European research area were stressed already in the old Lisbon strategy. They remain the pillars of growth and jobs in the new strategy, as well.

3. PRODUCTION OF SCIENTIFIC INVENTIONS, GROWTH AND JOBS

Thus, to end the lagging of EU behind USA, EU member countries should increase their R&D expenditures from the existing 1.95 percent in 2003 of GDP to 3 percent; expenditures for R&D in USA reached 2.76 percent of GDP and they were 3.14 percent in Japan (2002).

---

[4] See for example: Delivering on Growth and Jobs: A New and Integrated Economic and Employment Co-ordination Cycle in the EU, Companion document to the Communication to the Spring European Council (COM (2005) 24) Brussels, February 3,.2005.

[5] Whether EU actually lags behind USA, depends on how one defines performance, which is a matter of value judgement.

European Commission itself proposed doubling the amount of money for R&D from 5 to 10 billions € in the EU budget for the 2007-2013 fiscal period which would create research friendly environment. This financial effort would be enhanced by creating numerous more or less bureaucratic institutions considered necessary such as Joint European Technology Initiative, 22 European Technology Platforms, European Research Council, European Strategy Forum for Research Infrastructures, and National Contact Points. Does European Commission believe that production of scientific discoveries can be assured by creation of institutions dealing with orderly arranged procedures for research proposals? Will bureaucratic procedures suffice for scientific discoveries in the 7th and consecutive research framework programs? Is science not rather unplanned, intuitive, and full of surprises? I do not know the answers, but I am certain that most of money will be spent for the functioning of the institutions engaged in its distribution.

There are no inevitable causal links between expenditures for R&D, growth, and jobs. For example, in the period 1995-2002, Ireland attained far the fastest average growth in EU, more than 8 percent per year, while its expenditures for R&D in the same period were among the lowest, slightly more than 1 percent of GDP, and decreasing. Two countries with the highest expenditures for R&D, Sweden and Finland, attained rather modest growth. While expenditures for R&D in Sweden and in most other European countries were constant or fluctuated in the observed period, Finland was together with Denmark in which the share of R&D expenditures in the observed period was unquestionably growing; it was accompanied by the declining growth of GDP.

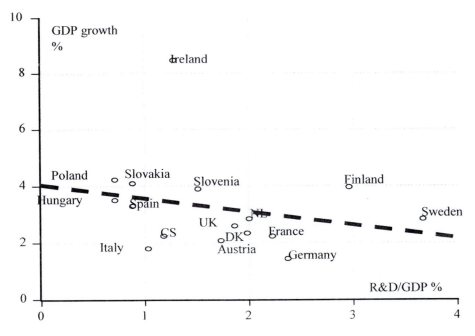

Source of data: Eurostat

Graph 1. Expenditures for R&D and Economic Growth averages, 1995-2003.

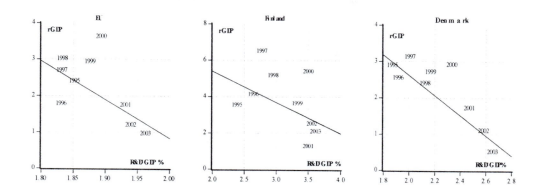

Graph 2. Expenditures for R&D and Economic Growth 1995-2003.

Negative relationship (cross- section) between expenditures for R&D and economic growth on Graph 1 or negative relationship (time series) between expenditures for R&D and economic growth in EU-25, Finland, and Denmark on Graph 2 can certainly not be considered a proposition that expenditures for R&D hinder economic growth. They only indicate that expenditures for R&D do not inevitably ensure growth.

Let us assume that reorganization, regulation, and institutionalization of science within EU will bring new technological inventions and growth. Technological changes in the past were indeed transformed into growth and tremendous increase in the standard of living. They should, according to the strategy and in combination with more flexible labor market, also bring more and better jobs, transfer of workers from jobs with low value added to jobs with high value added, and lower unemployment.

Technological changes undoubtedly increase productivity and create better jobs, they, however, at least directly, do not create more jobs or eliminate unemployment. Their aggregate effects on employment and unemployment are namely a combination of different processes; some reducing, others enhancing employment.

Technological changes are most often labor saving. New jobs created by technological change in a specific industry, in which the change takes place, are most likely fewer than jobs which are eliminated. Only some workers who lose jobs can find new jobs in the same industry or in other industries producing material goods with higher value added. Some of them move to the service sectors with the same, higher, or lower value added jobs, while some of them move to the activity with zero value added jobs, thus, among unemployed. Thus, technological changes, which directly reduce jobs, indirectly enable creation of new jobs in services, public or private, with the same, higher (public servants, lawyers. etc.) or lower (waitresses, garbage workers etc.) value added jobs. Let me repeat that this does not imply that R&D hinders job creation. I only say that R&D which increases output and standard of living does not inevitably create new jobs and does not inevitably reduce unemployment[6].

---

[6] Namely, average R&D expenditures in Finland in the 1995-2003 period were 3.61 percent of GDP, they were 2.19 percent in Denmark, and 1.45 percent in Slovenia, while standardized unemployment rates in 2003 were 9 percent in Finland, 5.6 percent in Denmark, and.6.5 percent in Slovenia. Though the data on age structures of unemployed are not fully comparable, they however indicate that high expenditures for R&D are not enough

In the last decade, practically all new jobs in EU-25 and EU-15 were created in services. In the period 1997-2005 13 millions jobs were created in EU-25, 16 millions jobs were created in services; 2 millions jobs were lost in industry and 1 million jobs were lost in agriculture. The share of employment in services therefore increased from 66 to 69.7 while the shares of industry lessened from 28.0 to 25.2, and agriculture from 6.0 to 5.1 percent. The central role in job creation in many countries has belonged to employment in the public sector; European Commission nevertheless assumes that liberalization of the labor market would create more jobs. This is a rather strange assumption; liberalization of the labor market is to increase its efficiency, which implies that the same amount of public services could be provided by fewer public servants[7]. Furthermore, value added in services, particularly public, is determined by monopolistic power of their suppliers and tendency of the state to make these services obligatory. If, for example, notaries - their number and their required services are regulated by the state - earn more than anybody else, their value added is by a definition the highest.

4. WILL GLOBALIZATION HELP EU?

Economic globalization "constitutes integration of national economies into the international economy through trade, direct foreign investment (by corporations and multinationals), short term capital flows, international flows of workers and humanity generally, and flows of technology" (Bhagwati, 2004, p 440). It is supposed to increase freedom of choice and opportunities, diminish transaction costs, enable efficiency in allocation, and enhance trade based on comparative advantages. The pressures of the world market are also considered more than proper alternatives to government interventions.

Admirers of globalization believe that it is a positive-sum game which would not only enable equalization of incomes within and among more and less developed countries, increase employment and wages, but which would also abolish provincialism, racism and ignorance, thus, and at least in the long run, enhance welfare of everybody. Theoretical pillars for these beliefs are to be found in neoclassical economics stressing perfect adaptability of economic units, and benefits of competition, or in institutional economics stressing the increase of freedom of choice and opportunities which are provided with globalization. Both schools therefore denounce any barriers to globalization. Critics and skeptics, on the other side, are warning of the "globalization trap", they are cautious regarding the increases in efficiency, and stress negative social features. For them, only a few individuals and countries enjoy fruits

---

to favorably affect age structure of unemployment. In Finland, unemployment in the age group 15-24 increased from 8.9 in 1990 to 21.6 percent in 2003, in the age group 25-54 from 2.1 to 7.3 percent, and the age group 55-64 from 2.7 to 7.7 percent. In Denmark, unemployment rate in the age group 15-24 decreased from 11.5 to 9.8 percent, in the age group 25-54 from 7.9 to 5 percent, and in the age group 55-64 from 6.1 to 3.9. In 2002, in Slovenia the unemployment rate in the age group 15-24 was 15 percent, in the age group 25-49 it was 5.2 percent and in the age group over 50 years 3.6 percent (CESifo DICE).

[7] The ability to constantly create new institutions and consequently new jobs appears to be an important pillar of EU stability. Namely, new institutions although excessive when they are created, soon become imperative and can not be dismantled. They thus strengthen the whole institution because they become essential part of it. Imagine how to dismantle Euro and keep EU alive! Furthermore, all new institutions are creating a few new well paid jobs in Brussels and many more corresponding jobs in EU member countries. It is therefore reasonable to expect that civil servants of EU will defend their jobs and EU.

of globalization, it increases income disparities among and within countries, creates unemployment in developed countries while keeping wages in developing countries meager. Workers are turned into "just in time workers" or a kind of raw materials. Merciless battles for the market shares enhanced by mergers and takeovers, end in a kind of economic cannibalism.

Indeed, the assertions that globalization increases welfare and economic growth, have recently become conditional; the assertions are to be true only for the countries which are "globalizers". However, most often countries with presently high economic growth are simply said to be open and those with presently low growth are considered to be closed. The claims that globalization reduces poverty have also become less affirmative. The proper answer is most likely that "globalization may bring enhanced growth, but need not, and it may lead to increased poverty, but need not" (Stiglitz, 2004, p 466).

Globalization occurred when American model of capitalism prevailed not only over socialism but also over other models of capitalism. The collapse of socialism was simply attributed to the advantages of the "western" world, which was most often reduced to the American institutional arrangements considered to be the only viable and therefore eternal. This belief was best expressed by the Francis Fukujama's "end of history". One can but hardly have faith in natural dominance of "better" over "worse" if the dominance is imposed by political pressures, economic sanctions, or in the worst case, even by military interventions. They all lead to the globalization of market fundamentalism[8]. One should also not neglect that linkages between national state on one side and globalization and internationalization on the other, have changed. While fast internationalizations in the past were linking national economies and preserving their national sovereignty, globalization is weakening it. It creates borderless world or world of corporations and multinationals in which nation states become redundant economic subjects.

By joining EU some of the globalization challenges of the member countries were shifted from the national to the EU level. It seems however that also EU is not able to successfully compete in the globalization contest and to preserve European social model, existing standard of living, and economic growth. A decrease of costs by further liberalization of labor market, reduction of social benefits, and disregard of environmental externalities large enough for the competition with much more ruthless societies, China in particular, would imply total abandoning the social market model which is politically impossible and socially unacceptable. Due to the vanishing of the traditional employer-employee relationship, predominance of "share holder value" maximand, and unbounded mobility of capital, multinational corporations simply move production to the countries with exceptionally low labor costs in which nobody cares for environmental and other externalities. Indeed, multinational corporations do not only relocate production of many traditional industries with low value added jobs (textiles) but also industries with presently high value added jobs. By their relocation to the countries with miserable wages, nil social security, and disregard of externalities, which all contribute to high initial profits, these industries also swiftly turn to industries with low value added jobs. The relocation of production, thus, also diminishes the ability of EU countries for creating more jobs in services. Therefore, EU will be forced, while

---

[8] Fundamentalism is not meant to be insulting. I simply want to express doubts in ideological constructions of reality which are often uttered by economists who consider themselves being liberals and overlook that American institutional arrangements are not the only ones that work.

repeating slogans of adherence to free trade, to gradually close its market for goods and services produced outside EU. This will be most likely done by imposing "ISO standards" requesting that imported goods and services are produced in accordance with the rules which exist in EU[9]. It is also true that by higher economic growth and increase in the standard of living in the rest of the world, new markets will emerge, but their emergence will lag behind the disappearance of jobs in EU due to production being shifted from EU.

5. WHAT ABOUT AGGREGATE DEMAND?

The Achilles' heel of Lisbon strategies, the old one and the new one, is total neglect of aggregate demand and full reliance on the premises of supply side economics (neoclassical and institutional versions), according to which demand equals supply because of perfect adaptation of economic subjects. This is also evident from implicit central position of production function in the strategy. Production function is, no doubt, a useful device for establishing potential growth but it is much less useful for establishing actual growth in a developed economy. Causality implied by the production function is namely not very relevant in an economy in which companies are much more concerned with how to sell products they produce rather than with how to produce them. Therefore, for a contemporary market economy, aggregate demand, aggregate investment function, and aggregate employment function are highly relevant for determining output, investments in fixed assets, and jobs. It is argued that increased production will decrease the costs of production, so that prices will fall which would increase demand, and, that additional supply in itself creates demand for other goods and services. This is all true in a frictionless and timeless world but far less true in reality.

The belief that price stability and growth can be assured by elimination of budget deficit and reduction of public expenditures has also acquired the status of conventional fact and seems to be undisputable certainty for official economic policy of EU if this policy is what is proclaimed. by The Stability and Growth Pact signed in 1997. Though fiscal policies, together with wage policies, formally belong to member countries, in reality, this is not entirely true. It was not only compulsory for the members to adopt VAT, the minimum tax rate of 15 percent as a standard rate and 5 percent as a reduced rate were also set[10]. The Stability and Growth Pact also created mechanisms for interventions, by which fiscal policies should support monetary policy of ECB[11].

Budget deficits of the EMU member countries, between 1993 and 2000, indeed declined and some of the countries had budget surpluses, while reported budget deficit in 2000 was in no country higher than 3 percent. Public debt in 2001 was lower than in 1993. The decline of budget deficits and public debts was however not surprising, taking into account high economic growth in the period. It was simply part of the economic mechanism of a normally

---

[9] European commissioner for trade Peter Mendelson already articulated this, op.cit. str.2)

[10] 6th Directive on the harmonisation of the laws of member states relating to turnover taxes, Dir 77/388, paragraph 12.

[11] Mechanism has three pillars – medium term notifying mehhansm, mechanism for shortterm control of the programs for stability and procedures which would start at too high deficit, and institutions responsible for the the implementation of the Program. These are European Commission (EC), Economic and financial committee (EFC) and Council of ministries for economy and finance (ECOFIN).

functioning European market economy. Therefore, one could expect that budget deficits will start increasing with declining growth, which happened after 2000.

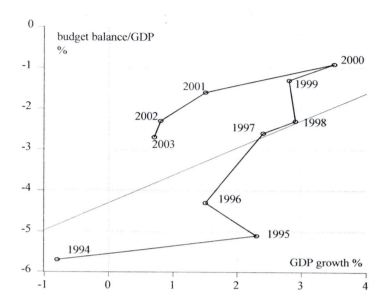

Source of data: Eurostat

Graph 3. Growth and budget balance in EMU countries, 1993-2003.

Stability and Growth Pact can thus be looked at as an attempt to modify the existing macro economic mechanism of the European social market model. Pact was functioning well (it was not harmful) in the period of high economic growth when the restrictions imposed by it were anyhow irrelevant. It became troublesome when growth dropped. Consequently, budget deficits began to rise in 2000 and soon also officially exceeded the "magic" 3 percent Maastricht level in Germany and France. Until 2005, other countries followed. Relatively high double deficits prevail in most new members with exception of Estonia which has enormous current account deficit accompanied by budget surplus, and Slovenia, with small current account surplus and not too large budget deficit. Strangely enough, while budget balances are considered important performance indicators, current account balances are not. EU also does not apply sanctions which are supposed to be applied against member countries (which was for large and powerful members predictable from the very beginning) or does not dissolve the Growth and Stability Pact which would be the only reasonable thing to do. Instead, EU is nervously looking for excuses for higher deficits and for new definitions of public deficit, which would lower it below the magic 3 percent and 60 percent level. The measures for the implementation of the Pact however add to lower economic growth and employment in EU, destabilize economy, and also threaten the implementation of the new Lisbon strategy. Indeed, the two strategies appear to exclude each other; it is most likely that both will end as political rhetoric which will have not much to do with economic reality.

Cutbacks of budget deficits in the 1994-2000 period were not inevitably accompanied by increases of gross fixed investments which enable long run economic growth. Ups and downs in budget deficits can be more or less considered movements back and forth between private and public spending as suggested by the data in Table 1. They indicate that decreases in budget deficits, thus increased savings of the government, were not accompanied by increased but rather by decreased savings of the population.

Table 1. Budget Deficit, Private Savings and Gross Fixed Investments

	budget deficit/GDP			savings/disposable income			gross fixed investments/GDP		
	1995	2000	2003	1995	2000	2004	1995	2000	2004
Austria	-5.2	-2.8	-1.0	11.7	8.3	7.8	23.3	23.8	21.9
Belgium	-3.6	-1.3	1.1	18.8	13.4	14.1	19.9	21.0	20.1
Denmark	-2.3	0.9	2.2	6.9	4.8	6.1	18.7	23.1	23.0
Finland	1.5	6.4	3.0	5.2	-0.9	1.3	18.0	19.9	19.1
France	-4.6	-1.7	-3.2	11.2	10.8	12.1	18.8	20.6	19.8
Ireland	-1.2	2.4	-1.0	8.8	7.9	Na	17.5	21.2	17.9
Italy	-7.1	-2.1	-1.6	22.5	14.5	15.9	18.3	20.6	21.1
Germany	-2.8	-1.6	-2.3	11.2	9.8	10.8	22.4	22.5	19.6
Netherlands	-4.3	-1.0	-1.7	14.9	6.7	10.8	20.3	22.3	20.7
Portugal	-4.8	-4.3	-1.5	13.6	9.5	12.1	22.8	28.1	22.9
Spain	-4.9	-1.5	0.5	14.4	10.6	10.2	22.0	24.7	25.0
Sweden	-5.1	3.6	0.7	8.3	2.4	6.8	16.0	17.6	16.8
United Kingdom	-4.7	0.9	-2.9	10.0	4.3	5.8	16.3	18.3	17.9

Source: CESifo Dice.

The importance of aggregate demand can be illustratively shown by comparing GDP growth of the three small European countries mentioned above: Finland, Denmark, and Slovenia. Finland and Denmark are both small highly developed successful economies and as such they have been for a decade a kind of bench mark economies for small countries of Central and Eastern Europe while Slovenia is the most developed among new EU member countries from Central and Eastern Europe. Denmark and Finland are also at the top of different rankings of economic freedom[12] while Slovenia is often at their bottom. However, the growth path of Finland resembles the growth path of Slovenia and not of Denmark, which can only be attributed to major shifts of aggregate demand. In Finland, depression in the early 1990s was caused by the collapse of Soviet Union and its market, and depression in Slovenia by the collapse of Yugoslavia and its market. The recovery of both countries was enabled by increased foreign demand.

Growth was accompanied by asymmetric development in unemployment, growing fast during depression and decreasing slowly during recovery. In Finland, unemployment increased from 3.2 percent in 1990 to 16.7 percent in 1994, and then slowly decreased to 9 percent in 2003. In Slovenia (the two rates are not fully comparable), unemployment grew from less than 1 percent in the eighties, to 9.1 percent in 1993, and then decreased slowly to 6 percent in 2003.

---

[12] By the average of the Heritage foundation index and Fraser institute index, Denmark on the third, Finland on the fifth, and Slovenia on the last place among 25 EU countries (Prokopijevich, op.cit, p 27).

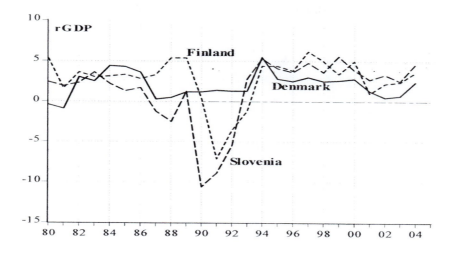

Graph 3. GDP Growth in Slovenia, Finland, and Denmark.

In Denmark, where there was no depression, unemployment rate grew from 7.2 in 1990 to 9.6 percent in 1993 followed by relatively rapid decrease to 4.3 percent in 2001, and a jump to 5.6 percent in 2003 (Economic Survey of Europe, 2004, No.2).

REFERENCES

Ayres, U.R, in Warr. B. (2004) Accounting for growth : the role of physical work, *Structural Change and Economic Dynamics*, Vol 16, 181-209.

Bhagawati J. (2004) Anti-globalization: why?, *Journal of Policy Modeling*, Vol.26, (2004) 439-463.

EU (2005): Communication to the Spring European Council, Working together for Growth and Jobs, *A Restart for the Lisbon Strategy, COM* (2005) 24, Brussels, 02.02.2005.

EU (2005): Delivering on Growth and Jobs: A New and Integrated Economic and Employment Co-ordination Cycle in the EU, *Companion document to the Communication to the Spring European Council (COM* (2005) 24) Brussels, 3.2.2005.

European Economists for an Alternative Economic Policy in Europe (2002): Better Rules, Tools and Institutions for Full Employment and Social Welfare in Europe, *Memorandum 2002*, 26, mimeo.

Kroes, N. (2005) : *Building a Competitive Europe – Competition Policy and Relaunch of the Lisbon Strategy*, Milan, February 7, 2005.Mencinger, Jože (1988) Ideološki preboj, teoretska zmeda in stvarne prepreke, (Ideological path through, theoretical confusion, and real barriers), *Gospodarska Gibanja*, 6/1988, 39-45.

Mendelson, P. (2005): *Strengthening the Lisbon Strategy: the Contribution of External Trade to the Growth and Competitiveness in Europe*, Stockholm, February 15, 2005.

Potočnik, J. (2005): *The Future of EU Research – chances for the new Member States*, Warsaw,. February 4, 2005.

Prokopijević, M.(2005): Alice is Not Missing Wonderland, The Eastward Enlargement of the European Union:. *Journal for the New Europe*, Vol. 2, 5-32.

Sollow R. (1957) : Technological Change and the Aggregate Production Function, *Review of Economics and Statistics,* 312-320.

Stiglitz, J. (2004) : Globalization and Growth in the Emerging Markets, *Journal of Policy Modeling*, June 2004. 465-484.

In: Roadmap to Bangalore?
Editors: A. Heshmati, A. Tausch, pp. 151-174

ISBN: 978-1-60021-478-3
© 2007 Nova Science Publishers, Inc.

Chapter 6

AN ECONOMIST'S MANIFESTO ON UNEMPLOYMENT IN THE EUROPEAN UNION

*Franco Modigliani, Jean-Paul Fitoussi, Beniamino Moro,
Dennis Snower, Robert Solow, Alfred Steinherr and
Paolo Sylos Labini**

1. FOREWORD

This *Manifesto* challenges a pernicious orthodoxy that has gripped Europe's policy makers. It is that demand and supply side policies must have different aims, that a limited number of supply side policies are to be devoted to fighting unemployment, and that demand management (and particularly monetary policy) is to be devoted solely to fighting inflation. The prevailing orthodoxy also claims that the choice of policy instruments for combating

---

* Massachussetts Institute of Technology, Cambridge, Mass. (USA);
 Observatoir Français de la Conjoncture Économique, Paris (France);
 Facolta' di Economia, Viale San Ignazio 17, 09123 Cagliari (Italy)
 Birkbeck College, London (Great Britain);
 Massachussetts Institute of Technology, Cambridge, Mass. (USA);
 European Investment Bank, Basle (Switzerland);
 Università degli Studi di Roma "La Sapienza", Roma (Italy).

* Economists who want to express their broad support for the arguments and policy recommendations of the *Manifesto*, without necessarily agreeing with every detail, are welcome. Communications of support can be sent to any Author, and will be made public. The following is a first group of economists who expressed their agreement (sometime with some reserves on single proposals) with a preceding version of the *Manifesto* (published in Italian in *Sviluppo economico ed occupazione*, a cura di B. Moro, Franco Angeli, Milano, 1998) whose main arguments are here reported: Francisco Alburquerque Llorenz (Consejo Superior de Investigaciones Científicas, Madrid), Rosario de Andrés Gómez de Barreda (Universidad de Madrid), Mario Baldassarri (Università degli Studi di Roma "La Sapienza"), Giacomo Becattini (Università degli Studi di Firenze), José Benítez Rochel (Universidad de Málaga), Oliver Blanchard (MIT, Cambridge, Mass.), Alan Blinder (Princeton University), Ascensión Calatrava Andrés (Consejo Superior de Investigaciones Científicas, Madrid), Maria Luisa Ceprini (MIT, Cambridge, Mass.), Carlo D'Adda (Università degli Studi di Bologna), Rudiger Dornbusch (MIT, Cambridge, Mass.), Hans Helmut Kotz (Deutsche Girozentrale, Frankfurt a.M.), Giorgio La Malfa (Università degli Studi di Catania), Assar Lindbeck (Stockholm University, Stockholm).

unemployment is a political decision, in which each instrument is evaluated on a case-by-case basis.

In what follows, we outline various practical proposals aimed at a prompt reduction of unemployment. We are confident that if the advice is given proper attention by governments and monetary authorities, unemployment can be reduced significantly in a matter of a few years.

We will divide the proposed actions into those bearing on the revival of aggregate demand (demand policies) and those addressed to the reform of the labour and product markets and the system of benefits for the unemployed (supply policies). But we stress from the very beginning that we regard our proposals as strictly complementary with one another. Each proposal, applied in isolation, may produce little or even perverse effects, while the simultaneous application can be counted upon to yield the desired outcome. This holds in particular with respect to the relation between demand and supply policies. The underlying idea is that it is much easier to encourage people to look for jobs if there are jobs to be found and it is much easier to encourage firms to offer more jobs if there are more people willing to accept them.

2. THE UNEMPLOYMENT PROBLEM

We share the view that at present time unemployment is the most serious and urgent problem facing the European Union (EU). Today (October 1998), the average rate of unemployment in these countries is 11% (19 million), with peaks of 15-20%, while in the 60s and early 70s it was almost universally well below 3% and nowhere over 5%. Such a huge rate of unemployment results in an immense waste of resources, through loss of output, that can be estimated at some 15% or more, and even larger loss of saving-investment potential. It is degrading and demeaning for the unemployed and with damaging long run consequences, especially for the young that represent, in most countries, the bulk of the unemployment. And it is also a source of dangerous social tensions.

We also share the view that the measures that have been proposed in numerous meetings of representatives of member governments at various levels, including the Amsterdam (June 1997) and Luxembourg (November 1997) meetings especially devoted to this problem, suggest that many of European leaders have not adequately confronted the nature of the problem. Consequently they have not succeeded in agreeing on politically feasible programs that have a chance of producing an appreciable decline in the current, high unemployment rate in the relevant near future.

Siro Lombardini (Università degli Studi di Torino), Carlos Machado (Universidade do Minho), Antonio Marzano (Università degli Studi di Roma "La Sapienza"), Ana Melero Guilló (Universidad de Madrid), Giangiacomo Nardozzi (Università degli Studi di Milano), Fiorella Padoa-Schioppa (Università degli Studi di Roma "La Sapienza"), Luigi Pasinetti (Università Cattolica del S. Cuore di Milano), George Perry (Brookings Institution, Washington), Manuel Rodríguez-Zúñiga (Consejo Superior de Investigaciones Científicas, Madrid), Alessandro Roncaglia (Università degli Studi di Roma "La Sapienza"), Gumersindo Ruiz Bravo de Mansilla (Universidad de Málaga), Antonio Ruiz Molina (Universidad de Málaga), Paul Anthony Samuelson (MIT, Cambridge, Mass.), Javier Sanz Cañada (Consejo Superior de Investigaciones Científicas, Madrid), Gustav Schachter (Northeastern University, Boston), James Tobin (Yale University, New Haven) and Elvira Urzainqui Miqueleiz (Universidad de Madrid). Jean-Paul Fitoussi has some reserves on the supply side policies.

3. FALSE AND MISLEADING EXPLANATIONS FOR EUROPEAN UNEMPLOYMENT

The widespread acceptance of the timid program agreed so far seems to reflect in part the view, by now common in Europe, that unemployment is a calamity due to causes beyond the capacity of governments to manage, except possibly by increasing profits and generally increasing income inequalities. And this conclusion has led to a convergence of both the right and the left on the view that the scourge must be bravely endured for fear that any remedy might make matters worse.

Many possible causes have been advanced to account for the high and persistent rate of unemployment in the EU. They vary some-what along the political spectrum. On the right, it has been argued that EU unemployment is primarily the outcome of i) the absence of the needed skills (there are jobs but the unemployed are not qualified to fill them), ii) the large share of long-term unemployed who lack motivation to seek jobs, and iii) the crushing burden of taxes. All these arguments contain grains of truth, but it is easy to be misled by them.

The first argument is supported by the observation that the rise in unemployment has fallen disproportionately on the less skilled and qualified segments of the labour force. But American experience over the past few decades suggests that when unskilled workers are not consigned to an 'unemployment trap' through misguided welfare entitlements, then the demand for unskilled labour fluctuates with the availability of jobs. When available jobs shrink, workers with higher qualifications displace those less qualified, and when demand and job opportunities improve, the unemployment rate of the less qualified declines.

The share of long-term unemployment varies substantially among EU member states; but there is good reason to believe that a large share of long-term unemployed is more the effect than the cause of a high and persisting unemployment.

As for taxes, it is estimated that in 1997 total government levies amounted to about 43% of GDP in the EU versus 31.6% in the US. But these figures fail to distinguish between taxes that pay for government services and social security levies, that represent contributions toward pension benefits – i.e. saving – even if compulsory. If one leaves out social security contributions, the tax burden (direct plus indirect taxes) drops to 27% in Europe, versus some 23% in the US. The difference in the untaxed share of income – 73% in Europe versus 77% in US – is by no means dramatic and certainly cannot account for the fact that European unemployment is 8% higher than before the early 70s, while that of the US is not higher. If unemployment were so sensitive to small differences in taxation, why is it that Germany – with a tax burden similar to that of the US (23.3%) – has unemployment similar to the rest of the European countries (11%), while the UK – with a tax burden 6 percentage points larger than Germany (29.5%) – has much smaller unemployment (5.6%)?

It is of course true that in Europe social security levies take a much larger bite from income (16% of GDP versus 9% in US). Of course the average rate of contribution for those workers actually covered by social security in many countries is much higher than 16%, and the fiscal pressure is well over 40% for countries like Italy (44%) and France (46.8), where the replacement rate (the rate of unemployment benefits to wages) is very high. These high levies, it is said, increase unemployment both by sapping the incentive to work and by raising the cost of labour to employers. But these assertions are fundamentally flawed. Firstly, the higher European levies do not, as is generally supposed, reflect the need to cover the higher costs of a more wasteful and intrusive government. They are instead the result of an explicit social choice of saving (in compulsory form) a larger portion of income in the working years in order to receive a larger pension in retirement (and to retire earlier), combined with the inefficiency of the pay-as-you-go public pension system. Secondly, social security levies generally have little influence on real labor costs in the long run because they are born primarily by labor, and not by profit earners, whether they are formally collected from the employee nominal compensation or from the employer.[1] A possible exception may arise for workers on a minimum wage, if that wage is fixed in terms of real take home pay. In that case higher social security levies cannot be shifted to the worker and will instead result in a higher real cost and price and thus higher unemployment.

As for the assertion that high social security levies reduce the incentive to find a job by reducing the difference between unemployment compensation and take-home pay, the conclusion is obviously valid only if the government pays the social insurance contributions of unemployed workers, or if pensions are independent of the workers' contributions, which is certainly not the general practice.

On the left side of the political spectrum, European unemployment has been portrayed as the outcome of iv) a crisis of capitalism, v) an excessively rapid rate of technological progress, and vi) competition with low-wage countries. All of these explanations are called into question by a very simple consideration: if they were valid, they should produce the same high rate of unemployment in all other developed countries. But in fact the sharp rise in unemployment since the 80s has no parallel among other advanced industrial countries. In fact, the unemployment rate of every OECD country nowadays is below the EU average and only two such countries have unemployment rates that are even close.

One further and very different line of thought that has supported tolerance toward the *status quo* is the argument that the demand and supply side factors above are an inevitable part of European political and social policy and reforms would be intrinsically undesirable. The restrictive demand side policies are commonly viewed as necessary prelude for the further economic and political integration of Europe; and the restrictive supply side measures are frequently seen as required to retain economic equality and social cohesion. It is held that governments must choose between two disagreeable options: a 'flexible' labor market bedeviled by wide income disparities and an 'inflexible' labor market crippled by unemployment. The 'flexible' market, where people's wages reflect their productivity, is allegedly achieved by reducing job security, restricting unemployment benefits and welfare entitlements, eliminating minimum wages, bashing the unions, and opting out of the social chapter. The 'inflexible' market, where people's earnings reflect politicians' judgements about fairness and social cohesion, is supposedly achieved by the opposite policies. This generates the conviction that the ultimate choice, then, is between inequality and unemployment. In this light, the high level of European unemployment is sometimes portrayed as a price that must be paid for the achievement of other important long-term objectives.

These presumptions are reflected in much of the European Union's policy approach to unemployment. The Luxembourg communiqué and those issued on earlier occasions restrict

---

[1] Social security levies may be directly deducted from the take-home pay. But even if they are not, say, because they are levied on the employer, they will tend to be added to nominal labor cost and passed on into higher

their purview to a very limited timid set of supply side policies and do not even mention the possible role of demand management policy, and monetary policy in particular, in affecting unemployment. Furthermore, they stress that unemployment is a problem that can and must be solved within each country, without explicit co-ordination of policies between EU countries even though, in joining the euro system, the member countries renounce the possibility of independent demand management policy, monetary or fiscal, and come into close competition on supply side policies.

By contrast, we believe that the bulk of European unemployment serves no useful purpose whatsoever. On the contrary, it is overtly harmful to the achievement of the objectives that have been used to rationalize the problem. Since work is the major avenue whereby people are able to claw their way out of poverty and overcome economic disadvantage, high levels of unemployment – particularly long-term unemployment – are deleterious to social cohesion and economic integration.

We call for rejecting the powerful pernicious myth, that blinds policy makers to unemployment policies that could reduce unemployment without widening the gap between the rich and poor. Thus it is important to expose the myth and get on with the urgent business of fundamental policy reform. The trick is to recognize that much of the current employment policy is responsible for the disagreeable choice between unemployment and inequality.

It is thus extremely important to differentiate carefully between the genuinely promising policy proposals and those that are unpromising in the sense that they may reasonably be expected to turn out ineffective or counter-productive. Making this distinction is not easy because many of the policies that influence unemployment are highly complementary with one another. This means that potentially enlightened policy initiatives are often ineffective when implemented in isolation from one another. Employment-promoting supply side policies frequently enhance the effectiveness of employment-promoting demand side policies, and vice versa. Furthermore, counter-productive policies often emasculate the influence of enlightened policy measures. In the domain of unemployment policy, bad measures drive out the good, and good measures reinforce one another.

In the next Section we review several of the major 'conventional' policies which have been implemented or proposed and show that they belong to the 'unpromising' set and are, in the end, an important source of European unemployment.

4. MISGUIDED POLICIES AS A CAUSE OF HIGH UNEMPLOYMENT

We hold the view that the European unemployment is, in important part, the result of policy errors. These errors involve both a mismanagement of aggregate demand (demand policies) and an unimaginative approach to the supply side of the economy. We are confident that these errors can be corrected promptly, putting an end to the unremitting longer-run growth of European unemployment.

---

price – much like an *ad valorem* tax – thereby reducing the real take-home pay by the extent of the levy, at least to a first approximation.

4.1. Errors in Demand Management

The words aggregate demand policy have become familiar to economists ever since Keynes used it to provide an understanding of the Great Depression and the role played in that episode by central banks. Yet at present the concept has become taboo among many European central bankers and political leaders, even though there is plenty of evidence that, in recent years, it plays a significant role in accounting for the rising unemployment.

A first suggestive piece of evidence is provided by the observation made earlier that double digit unemployment is common only in Europe – or more specifically among the countries that are in (or are candidates for) the euro. In fact, the European countries not in the euro have substantially lower unemployment rates: in Norway the rate is 4%, in Switzerland 5.5% and in the UK 5.6%.

This observation has some powerful implications. It suggests that in order to gain insight into the constellation of causes responsible for EU unemployment, it is important to identify factors that are shared by most EU member states but are not in evidence in non-euro countries.

On the demand side one experience that the euro countries have shared in common in the last few years, and generally not shared with others, has been the very restrictive aggregate demand policies, both fiscal and monetary. They have been forced to pursue these policies as a result of their common endeavour to join the euro. The common fiscal policy was the result of the Maastricht parameters and it was very restrictive in the light of the huge unemployment and resulting depressed government revenues, and of the tight monetary policy. One by-product of this policy has been the slowdown of public sector infrastructure that is complementary with private sector investment. Similarly, monetary policy was made uniform by the fact that exchange rates were to be kept narrowly fixed while all restrictions on the free movement of capital were eliminated. Under these conditions, interest rates had to be the same for all the candidate countries and there was no room for the national banks to pursue an independent monetary policy. And the common monetary policy appears to have been also much too tight, especially in the light of the tightening of fiscal policy, resulting in a long period of excessively high real interest rates that have discouraged investment and swollen unemployment.

The relation between unemployment and the demand for labour provides further evidence. Since the beginning of the oil crisis, in 1973, the rate of growth of demand has fallen considerably below that of capacity output – the sum of productivity and labor force growth. In fact the growth of demand has been roughly the same as that of productivity. Thus demand could be satisfied without a significant increase in jobs and the growth in the labor force of around 2% went to swell the ranks of the unemployed. This process of jobs falling relatively to the labor force is confirmed by direct information on the available jobs, the sum of employment and vacancies. In most EU countries, the number of jobs offered in each year as a percentage of the country's labor force has tended to fall.[2]

---

[2] For example in France in 1973 there were 101 jobs offered for every 100 persons in the labor force, but by 1993 the jobs available had shrunk to 89. As one would expect, unemployment moved inversely to job availability: as jobs kept shrinking well below the people seeking them, vacancies dwindled from 4% of the labor force in 1973 to a mere 1% in 1986; search time for an unemployed person grew longer and thus unemployment rose from 2.7 to 11.6%. There was only a short span of years, between 1986 and 1990, when demand rose

We believe that one reason for the drastic European decline in the demand for labor relative to its available supply – and the resulting rise in unemployment – has been a decline in investment relative to full-capacity output. In this connection it is interesting to observe that the difference between the growth of unemployment since the early 70s in Europe (8.5%) versus the US (0%) occurs mostly in two episodes since 1982. Up to that year joblessness had increased sharply on both continents as consequence of a restrictive monetary policy and resulting fall in investment, which was unavoidable to halt an inflationary spiral, ignited by the two oil crises. But after 1982 the shortfall and unemployment continued to rise in Europe till 1986, whereas in the US both fell promptly and significantly. The second episode begins in 1992 and extends to the present. In both these episodes, the investment rose relative to full capacity in the US but remained stagnant at peak levels in Europe.

4.2 Misguided Supply Policies

The measures to combat unemployment that have been suggested do not, in our opinion, reflect the best options available from the potential portfolio of feasible policy choices. One important source of the European unemployment problem are the misguided conventional policies that have been put into place to support the unemployed and protect the employed from job loss. The following provide three important examples.

Minimum Wage Legislation

Minimum wages are widespread in Europe and are potentially an important source of unemployment. The institute of the minimum wage (MW) is inspired by a lofty ideal, that any one who wishes to work should be able to secure a minimum decent living standard. The trouble is that the translation of this principle into practice typically takes a form which ignores basic economic laws and thus ends up creating great injustices and doing more harm than good. The form it takes consists in essence in forbidding firms to hire anybody for less than an imposed (fair) minimum wage or, equivalently, making it a 'crime' for anyone to accept a job for less than that fair wage. Clearly this system will 'work' for those that can in fact secure a job at the minimum wage. But if the number of people that would be willing to work at that wage or less exceeds the number of jobs that the system can offer at that wage, then it is obvious that the excess supply (if any) is condemned to unemployment, with all its negative economic and social implications. In practice these unemployed will largely consist of young people with no experience and little human capital.

It must be acknowledged that despite numerous studies attempting to measure the influence of minimum wage legislation on unemployment, to date there is little consensus about the precise nature of the impact. Although empirical studies have shown that relatively modest increases in the minimum wage may not raise unemployment, there is widespread agreement that large minimum wage hikes – wage increases sufficient to eliminate the major income inequalities between mainstream employees and workers marginally attached to the labour market – would have such an effect.

---

temporarily somewhat faster than productivity, jobs increased from 90.7 to 92.7%, and unemployment promptly fell from 10.9 to 8.1%. A similar story may be told of other EU member states.

One further negative impact of minimum wages comes from their interaction with high social security levies. In so far as the minimum wage aims at assuring a minimum real take-home pay, higher Social Security levies cannot be shifted to the employee: an increase in compulsory saving will be borne by the employer and raise the cost of the employee. This is one of the important factors that make a minimum wage so high in Europe, discouraging the employment of less skilled labour.

Job Security Legislation

Some commentators have maintained that job security legislation helps reduce unemployment. The underlying argument is that such legislation reduces both firing (by making it more costly for employers to dismiss their employees) and hiring (by discouraging employers from taking on new recruits who may have to be dismissed in the future). But at given real wages, the firing costs generated by job security legislation discourage firing more than they discourage hiring, since firms that fire must pay the firing costs now, whereas firms that hire may have to pay the firing costs at some point in the future.

However, this argument rests on tenuous foundations. In the first place, even though firms may initially find it economical to employ more people than would be optimal in the absence of constraint, they eventually will find it advantageous to shrink their labor force, at least through attrition and aging and also rely more on overtime. Second, and far more serious, the slowdown in the flow of hiring greatly reduces the chance of outsiders, and particularly new entrants in the labor force, to find a job and is a major cause for the high, in some cases almost unbelievably high, incidence of unemployment among young people. This high rate is particularly striking in countries where no unemployment benefits are provided for people that have never held a job. In addition, a rise in firing costs cannot be expected to leave real wages unchanged. On the contrary, the greater the firing costs, the greater will be the market power of the incumbent employees (insiders) and thus the higher the wages these workers can achieve. Taking further into account the fact that the high cost of firing will add to labor costs both directly and through redundancy, we can expect a lower demand for labor, at least in an open economy. On the whole, job security legislation must be regarded as a major negative influence on unemployment, especially youth unemployment, even if it might have desirable effects in other directions. Consequently, the lower will be the demand for labor. For these various reasons, increasing job security is far more likely to eventually decrease jobs and employment rather than the reverse.

Work-Sharing and Early Retirement

There can be no objection to people reducing their work week or retiring early if they are prepared to accept the corresponding reduction in weekly pay, but we hold that there is no justification for the government to provide incentives for people to work shorter hours or retire earlier.

The logic underlying work-sharing and early retirement is of course elementary. If there is a fixed amount of paid work to be done in the economy, and if this work falls very unequally across the population – with a majority of people enjoying full time employment while a minority is saddled with long periods of unemployment – then considerations of equity and social cohesion make it reasonable to seek policies that share the burden of unemployment more democratically. In short, if the pain and impoverishment of unemployment are inevitable, it may the best to spread the misery as evenly as possible.

The problem with this approach is that the underlying premise is false. We do not believe that the European unemployment problem is unavoidable. The amount of work to be done in the economy is not fixed. When the economy is in recession, an increase in production and employment – in response, for instance, to a rise in export demand or on private investment – will lead to a rise in purchasing power and thereby generate a further increase in production and employment. In this sense, unemployment is not inevitable. Policy makers who see it as such are being unduly defeatist; they should spend more thought on bringing unemployment down rather than on spreading it more thinly.

We therefore agree that those measures are not appropriate as the central pillar of a policy strategy to reduce unemployment. In fact, they pose some dangers of becoming counter-productive in the sense they might reduce the total number of hours worked in the economy even if they succeeded in increasing the number of people working. It has proved very difficult to implement them without raising non-wage labour costs (particularly costs of hiring and training) and thereby discouraging firms from creating more jobs. Furthermore, by diminishing the number of people competing for jobs, these measures may indirectly put upward pressure on wages and thereby on prices. Governments or monetary authorities may then feel called upon to dampen inflation through contractionary fiscal and monetary policies, thereby generating further unemployment.

The push for shorter work week as a device to reduce unemployment by work sharing has taken recently a dangerous turn when some of its sponsors, in an effort to gain popular support for the measure, have proposed that the reduction from 40 to 35 hours should be accompanied by an unchanged weekly pay. We regard this version as little more than demagogy. It would compound the difficulties already encountered in reducing individual hours while maintaining the hours worked by the firm, by imposing a rise in hourly wages by 5/35 or nearly 15%. The effect could not but be disruptive. The increase in labor costs could hardly be expected to come out of profits but could be expected, instead, to be passed along in higher output prices. This would result in a weekly real wage equivalent to 35 hours and/or in successful demands for higher nominal wages, initiating a wage-price spiral. But with fixed exchange rates or a single currency, the rising prices would also reduce the share of the country's foreign and domestic markets and prove a new source of unemployment. This effect might be mitigated if all countries undertook the measure simultaneously, but the inflationary spiral would be reinforced.

5. PROPOSED POLICIES FOR A TIMELY REDUCTION OF UNEMPLOYMENT

In what follows, we set forth a number of practical proposals aimed at a prompt reduction of unemployment. We are quite confident that if the advice is given proper attention by governments and monetary authorities, unemployment can be reduced by 4 or 5 percentage points in a matter of a few years and without compromising the recent gain in subduing inflation.

Our proposals cover both demand and supply side policies. We wish to emphasize that these policies are not to be assessed on a case-by-case basis. Our recommended policy package is not to be viewed as a portfolio of independent measures, from which policy makers can pick and choose. Rather, as noted at the beginning of the *Manifesto*, we regard the policies as complementary to one another, with the demand side policies creating a need for the new jobs that the supply side policies make available.

The failure to exploit policy complementarities may be an important reason why so many of the partial, piecemeal labour market reforms implemented in EU member states have done little to reduce Europe's unemployment problem. In Spain, for example, a labor market reform has been introduced in 1984, whose main aim was to achieve a greater flexibility in labor contracts. Among other things, this reform introduced fixed-term labor contracts with low firing costs. As a result, fixed-term labor contracts have grown quickly and Spanish firms have used them to buffer fluctuations in demand by changing the number of fixed-term employees. But, at the same time, this policy reduced the risk of unemployment for workers with permanent contracts, which reinforced the bargaining strength of the insiders. Since wage bargaining agreements mainly reflect the interests of the latter, this reform has turned out to cause more rigidity rather than more flexibility of the wage rate. To mitigate this unwanted effect, Spain has recently reintroduced some restrictions on fixed term contracts and has reduced firing costs for all workers.

In France, several acts have been passed aimed at introducing a greater flexibility in the labor market and at preventing the negative effects of both minimum wages and the highest payroll taxes among OECD countries. Moreover, restrictions on part time work have been eased, and work-sharing has been encouraged. But nothing has been done in this country to reduce the stringency of job protection legislation and the bargaining power of insiders.

In Italy, a reform of the labor market was first passed in 1991, which allowed small- and medium-size firms to dismiss redundant workers, but only with the agreement of the unions. The so-called 'mobilità lunga' (long mobility) was also introduced, which consists in the possibility to put the unwanted workers in the social security system (thus aggravating its operating costs) before giving these workers the right to definitely retire. A second reform has been recently introduced in 1997, which permits firms to hire workers temporarily from appropriate employment agencies.[3]

Also in Sweden, some reforms have been approved in order to increase labor market flexibility. In this country, unemployment benefits are of comparatively short duration, but the replacement ratios are high. Thus, jobless people can move from unemployment benefits to training programs and back, while generous welfare state entitlements encourage leisure relative to employment. In general, the welfare benefits in this country are so generous to render the condition of inactivity, especially for medium-aged people, more appealing than employment.

The United Kingdom and the Netherlands are the only two European countries that have witnessed appreciable reductions in unemployment from their labor market reforms over the last two decades. These successes may well be due to the broad-based nature of their reforms, enabling them to exploit significant policy complementarities. The UK, for instance, introduced legislation restricting strikes and secondary picketing, decentralizing wage bargaining, liberalizing hiring and firing restrictions, reducing the duration of unemployment benefits and tightening the associated eligibility criteria. Moreover, minimum wages have been abolished (soon to be reintroduced by the current Labour government) and

---

[3] However, in a typical display of Italian partisan economic obtuseness, it has been suggested that the people to be rented out on a part time basis, should be hired by the agency on a permanent basis!

unemployment benefits have been reduced, and, at the same time, new procedures have been implemented in order to facilitate the search for a job for the unemployed people. These reforms, together with the decision to opt out from the European Monetary Union, at least in the initial stage, have spared this country the need to adopt restrictive aggregate demand policies and have greatly contributed to the fall in the UK unemployment rate from 10.5% in the 1993 (approximately equal to the EU average) to 5.6% in 1998. This result, moreover, has been achieved without substantially changing other welfare state entitlements, such as housing benefits, or by a thoroughgoing drive to improve education and training systems.

The experience of the UK and the Netherlands also highlights the dangers of leaving particular policy complementarities unexploited. In both countries the tightening of the unemployment benefit system was not matched by a correspondingly fundamental reform of the sickness and incapacity benefit systems. Consequently budgetary pressures have shifted from unemployment benefits to sickness and incapacity benefits. Since the latter have a longer duration than unemployment benefits, the shift created more serious conditions of dependency from publicly-provided income support than unemployment insurance. Thus in the Netherlands, which has one of the most generous disability benefits systems among the OECD countries, the percentage of persons directly involved in social benefits reaches 17%.

In sum, European countries have not, on the whole, sought to reduce unemployment by implementing a coherent strategy of fundamental reforms across a broad range of complementary policies. In the main, these countries have adopted a number of *ad hoc* measures that attempt marginal corrections to the most egregious distortions stemming from existing labor market policies or regulations. We argue that, since only marginal, piecemeal changes have been implemented, existing restrictive institutions and regulations that are complementary to each other continue to interact, blocking the effectiveness of the recent reforms and prolonging unemployment.

Accordingly, our recommended policy strategy is *a*) to implement a broad spectrum of supply side policy reforms that give employers a greater incentive to create jobs in response to increases in demand and give employees a greater incentive to accept these jobs, and *b*) to implement demand side policies that enable the European economies to raise their growth rates of capital formation and productivity, and to use the productive potential that has been released through the supply side reforms.

5.1. Aggregate Demand Policies

We believe that the demand side strategy for reducing EU unemployment should involve policies that stimulate a broad revival of investment activity, taking care not to ignite inflationary pressures or increase the size of the national debt relative to national assets. The process of stimulating investment is, to a very considerable extent, self-reinforcing, because of a well-established mechanism, known as the accelerator effect. As investment rises, increasing employment and output, the initially existing excess productive capacity will become more fully utilized and there will soon be a need for additional capacity, which will require new investment.

It is generally agreed that labor and capital are often complementary in the production process, so that an increase in the capital stock usually leads to a rise in labour productivity. Provided that the economy is kept out of recession – so that the danger is avoided that firms employ as little labor as possible to meet a given, deficient product demand – and provided that there are sufficient supply incentives in place to encourage employers and potential employees to exploit profitable job opportunities, increases in labor productivity will generally lead to increases in labor demand and consequent reductions in unemployment.

The endeavour to expand the rate of investment need not, and should not, be limited to private investment. The constraints on public investment are currently felt with particular stringency because of the large public-sector debt existing in many European countries, and because of the consequent limitations on fiscal deficit imposed by the Maastricht parameters, together with the unfortunate circumstance that, in computing the deficit, all expenditures, whether on current account or for investment, are treated identically. Under these conditions, governments have frequently found it expedient to cut investments, even if highly desirable, rather than cut the budget for public employment (e.g., by reducing the number of employees). Given the prospective difficulties many EU member states face in satisfying the Maastricht criteria, this under-investment is likely to continue.

In order for an expansion of public investment to produce the same beneficial effects on unemployment as private investment, it is necessary that it should be financed neither by cutting other expenditure – except for transfer payments whenever it is possible – nor by raising taxes (which at present would be practically impossible anyway). This means that the additional investments must be financed, for most of the countries, in just the same way as private investments are typically financed, namely by raising the money in the capital markets in the form of debt or equity. Private-sector finance of public investment, along the lines currently being explored in some EU countries such as the UK, needs to be expanded as well.

In this context, it would be important to introduce a distinction, long overdue, between the current and the capital account deficit, and to redefine the budget deficit, for the purpose of the Maastricht agreement and the later stability pact, as consisting of the current account deficit only. The Current Account Budget should include all current expenditures and receipts (expenditures that benefit those present and receipts collected from them) and it is appropriate to require that this budget be balanced, as this places the cost of current expenditure on the current beneficiaries.

The amount of public capital expenditures, on the other hand, should be primarily limited by the requirement that each project should have a return over its life at least as competitive as market returns (with proper adjustment for taxes). However the difference, if any, between the cash receipts and the annual cost of providing the services, including the interest cost, and the depreciation, would be charged to the Current Account as a current expense (if negative) or treated as a current income (if positive).

Of course, deficit financing of government expenditure, when there is no room for an expansion of employment, tends to crowd out private investment, and thus burden future generations by depriving them of the return on crowded out capital. But we hold that the program of government investment we advocate will not harm and may even improve the lot of future generations. In the first place, when there is an enormous reserve of unemployed resources, investment will increase income and thus saving, at least to the extent of financing the investment without any crowding out. In the second place, infrastructural investment increases the marginal product of both capital and labor in the private sector, which will have expansionary effects. Finally, we agree that debt financing of capital expenditures satisfying the above criteria, unlike that financing a current account deficit, would not be harmful to future generations, even if it displaced an equal amount of private investment, because its return would at least compensate for the return lost on private investment.

We propose to concentrate public investment on specific infrastructures capable of giving returns in the short run. To finance these investments we propose that the existing European Structural Funds should be more used than in the past. Such funds, already considerable (153 billions of ecus for the period 1994-99), should be enlarged and their regulations should be re-negotiated, especially with regard to the procedure to spend them, since in the future they could become the main financial instrument of the European strategy to cure unemployment and promote growth. Today these funds can be spent only if the state using them provides simultaneously an equal amount of funds. This regulation is wise, but an interval should be granted when there is a proper guarantee. Moreover, to avoid delays, a particular care should be devoted to the organization of the structures in charge of the projects.

In any case, some public support for job creation is perfectly justified. The European Structural Funds were created for that purpose. Although important, their grant nature leads to inefficient uses and quarrels between providers and recipients. Therefore, there is little hope for a substantial increase of these funds in the EU. We propose to augment the grant of the Structural Funds with loans at interest rates at or below market rates. Such loans could be provided by the European Investment Bank (EIB), which has the resources and the experience in project evaluation to ensure that these funds finance sound and job-creating investments. The EIB already received the mandate of the Amsterdam and Luxembourg meetings to attach top priority to job creation. We argue that this mandate should be scaled up. For such a programme, interest rates below market rates are important otherwise the potential to stimulate investment and job creation remains limited. In countries like Italy, in which it is particularly important to keep at a low level the public deficit, recently achieved after a long and costly effort, it would be advisable to partly finance the infrastructural investments by also using a share of the receipts obtained from the privatization of public enterprises.

However, the success of the operation requires a revision of the principle that has emerged from the meetings in Amsterdam and Luxembourg, namely that the solution of the unemployment problem is not a collective responsibility but a task to be tackled by each country on its own. This approach is mistaken and will make a prompt solution very unlike. It springs from the view that unemployment is mainly due only to the malfunctioning of the labor market. But while we all concur that labour relations greatly contribute to the problem, we also share the view that demand plays a major role, relying on the evidence presented above as well as other evidence and reasoning. But the agreements of the two recent summits actually hamper the exercise of demand policy, because, after assigning to the individual states the task of reducing unemployment, they deprive them of all the classical tools of demand management: i) monetary policy, because individual central banks have already little control over interest rates and will have, gradually, even less; ii) fiscal policy, because of the rigid constraint on fiscal deficit; and iii) exchange rate policy. And the European Union, besides being exonerated of any responsibility, has no tools either: the Bruxelles Commission has no resources to spend, and the European Central Bank (ECB) is to concern itself exclusively with price stability.

The solution we are advocating, by contrast, requires co-ordination of policies of EU member states. Indeed, if any country were to engage in a demand side expansion alone, then, as is well known, its effect on unemployment would be much smaller than under a co-ordinated policy approach, because much of its beneficial impact would be lost to it and would spill over to others, through higher imports. The resulting deterioration of the current account could be so severe as to make the expansion inadvisable. But when the expansion is simultaneous and symmetric, then the increased imports will be offset by an increase in exports resulting from the increased imports of the other countries, and this will both help the current account balance and restore the potency of the expansion of investment. In short, in a simultaneous expansion, countries would be helping each other.

The Role of the European Central Bank

In addition to the supply side measures illustrated in Section 4.2 below, our proposed plan advocates a significant revival of aggregate demand and that revival in turn is expected to come from a strong and long lasting inversion of the persistently declining or stagnant trend of private investment activity. We expect that some of this inversion may come from the supply measures below; but most of it, especially in the early stages, must come from the long acknowledged, classical tool of investment control: monetary policy. But this policy is the prerogative of the central banks, which, hereafter, means essentially the new European Central Bank (ECB).

This has one very basic implication: if Europe really intends to achieve a rapid reduction in unemployment, it is necessary to give a broader and more constructive interpretation to the statutes that define the role of the ECB than that which is currently widely accepted. According to that interpretation, the Bank has but one target (one single front on which to do battle), namely preventing inflation. We urge a fundamental broadening of that interpretation – analogous to that of the US Federal Reserve – to include, on an equal footing, another target: keeping unemployment under control. And we are confident that it can do so without renouncing or sacrificing its commitment against inflation.

There are three major considerations that support this view of the proper role of the ECB on the path of return to high employment. In the first place, making price stability the overriding target at this time is much like using all your military budget to fight the last war, an enemy that is no longer there. Inflation has been a most serious problem because of, and during, the two oil crises and their aftermath (including German reunification). But since 1991 inflation has been falling steadily for the group as a whole, and within each country, with hardly any exception. It is now around 2%, clearly a small number especially when taking into account the unquestionable upward bias of all inflation indices.

In summary, the perils of inflation as a result of a revival of investments are negligible at the present time. And that danger will be further reduced by applying several of the supply measures advocated below, which will increase the incentives to accept jobs as they become available. We submit therefore that, under present conditions, assigning the ECB the single task of fighting inflation should not be acceptable. It leaves it far too much unnecessary leeway, e.g. given that wages are rigid, it can satisfy that target by a prudential policy of raising interest rates *ad libitum*, reducing investment and raising unemployment further.

A second reason why the ECB should not make price stability its single, overriding focus is that, realistically, it has very limited control over the price level, at least in the short run. Indeed, its policy instruments – the money supply or interest rate policy – do not directly affect prices when there is slack in the labor market. Given large-scale unemployment, they can affect prices only indirectly by affecting the rate of economic activity, and hence the rate of unemployment (and utilization of capacity) and thereby the growth of wages and finally prices. But unemployment is not a very potent instrument to control inflation when there is already plenty of slack while it has a major impact on society's welfare.

The third and crucial reason for the central role of the ECB in the program of investment expansion is that, as control over monetary policy shifts from the states to the ECB, the latter becomes the only institution that has substantial power to influence investments. The other possible approach to stimulate investments could be through fiscal measures (subsidies, tax rebates, tax credits), but such measures cannot play a significant role at this time in view of the severe fiscal squeeze resulting from the Maastricht parameters.

One can think of various objections to this reinterpretation of the role and responsibilities of the ECB. One is that the Bank lacks the power to stimulate investment. This objection is especially popular among central bankers. But this argument is disingenuous. How can a central bank claim that it can control prices if it cannot control demand and how can it control demand if it has no control at all over investment? Another objection is that the euro needs to establish itself as a prestigious, credible currency in the world capital markets. To satisfy this need what is required is a policy that will be viewed as continuation of the tough policies of the Bundesbank, involving high interest rates that will attract capital and help to support high exchange rates, especially with respect to the dollar, seen as the major competing world currency. We believe that it would be a deadly mistake for the ECB to focus on a competitive struggle with the dollar, fought through the escalation of interest rates, and at the expense of an economic revival. The high value of the dollar is the result of the strength of the American economy achieved through a policy of full employment pursued with 'benign neglect' of the international 'pecking order'. The ECB must adopt the same attitude of independence aiming at fostering an economy as vigorous and prosperous as the American economy.

The awesome responsibility of the ECB for maintaining high growth in Europe have become even more serious with tragic events of the last few weeks in Asia, and Russia and the sharp set back in the equity markets. It is up to the ECB and to Europe with its still sound fundamentals to engage in a policy of supporting domestic investment and demand offsetting the expected decline in net exports.

5.2. Supply Side Measures

We do not believe that a widespread liberalization of the labor market in Europe, along the lines of that existing in the American or Japanese labor markets, is advisable, even if it were feasible. It is important to keep in mind that the present European welfare systems spring from different cultures and from different ways to interpret the solidarity and equality principles. However, we think that, in order to fight unemployment, it is necessary and feasible to introduce a substantially higher degree of flexibility in the European labor and product markets including, where necessary, a relaxation of job security legislation, a reduction in the coverage of collective bargaining agreements, and a reduction of barriers to entry of firms and of barriers to geographic mobility of labor. We believe that if such measures are combined with the reform strategy outlined below, both the efficiency and equity of European labour markets can be improved. The economic instruments now available in many European countries to pursue these efficiency and equity goals are insufficient. The portfolio of policy instruments needs to be expanded, along the lines suggested hereafter.

The labor market flexibility policies, unlike the macroeconomic management, cannot be uniformly adopted by all the European countries; on the contrary, they should be adapted to the different situations of each country and region. We begin by recalling that an important aspect of European unemployment is found in the regional differences that characterize this phenomenon. We believe that one important source of differential unemployment within countries is the uniformity of wages imposed by unions or custom in national negotiations, disregarding the glaring fact of important regional differences in productivity. We are in agreement that to remedy this problem requires recognizing the need for regional differentiation in labor cost per hour reflecting regional differences in productivity. But in order for these reforms to obtain a large social consensus, it is necessary that they be accompanied by measures that compensate for their negative effects on income distribution. In fact, it is evident that fundamental labor market reforms are very difficult to implement because usually, while they have readily identifiable distributional consequences for specific groups of people, it is not always easy to readily see their advantages for everybody. For this reason, it is likely that the most radical components of the reform packages will probably face strong opposition from the groups most affected by such reforms. Compensating the prospective losers is important to mitigate this difficulty. With respect to the realignment of labor in line with productivity one basic approach is not to put all the emphasis on reducing wages but on reducing cost to the firm through appropriate subsidies. Some suggestions for accomplishing this task efficiently are suggested below (see e.g. the paragraph on the benefit transfer program).

There is also evidence that the lower productivity and higher unemployment in some regions, like the South of France, Italy and Spain, reflects a paucity of entrepreneurs. We share the opinion that in these less developed regions, more active policies are needed in order to encourage new firms and help small- and medium-size firms, whose growth can be accelerated by some appropriate measures. For example, Italy has had some success with industrial districts. By industrial districts we mean here some horizontal aggregations of small- and medium-size firms, where each firm operates in an autonomous way from the others, but whose production is in fact co-ordinated with others in the district, with resulting external economies.

A successful example of regional development pushed on by the diffusion of industrial districts is the functional integration of small- and medium-size firms that occurred in many Italian regions like Toscana, Marche, Veneto and Emilia Romagna. But, for the regional development to further proceed by the implementation of this model, we need to introduce some reforms of the industrial districts, so as to reinforce them and make them more effective and dynamic. Such measures should aim primarily at creating advisory institutions in the field of bureaucratic, fiscal, financial and technological matters. As for the new technologies, it is fitting to emphasize the importance of the re-organization and the expansion of institutions for labor training and of the relations between firms and universities and other research institutions.

Another characteristic common to many underdeveloped regions is the rationing and high cost of credit, which affects new and small firms in general, reflecting both the cost of processing small loans, their risk, as well as the monopolistic power (and sometime the inefficiency) of the local banks. In these regions the spread between lending and borrowing rates has been huge and nearly prohibitive, discouraging small firms and new initiative. In some countries like Italy a great improvement in the availability and cost of loans has been obtained through the formation of cooperative of borrowers. The members of the cooperative, in exchange for the availability and lower cost of credit, must be willing to assume some personal responsibility to guarantee the repayment of the overall obligation assumed by the cooperative, something they are willing to do because of personal knowledge and trust of those who are admitted to the cooperative. In addition local governments (regional or subregional) typically have provided a rotating fund which also serves to increase the guarantee offered to the banks.

We advocate, where necessary, a broad supply side reform package that includes the following well-known elements:

  — *job creation policies* and product market reform to reduce barriers to employment creation.

Examples of such policies include tax reform or relaxation of regulations restricting the entry of firms, restrictions on land use, regulations limiting product market competition, as well as measures to avoid penalizing flexible time schedules and part time work. Measures to encourage part time leasing of workers may help not only to provide currently unemployed workers with a stepping stone into the world of work, but also help firms restructure their organization of production and work in accordance with the new advances in information technology and flexible manufacturing.

The tight regulation of the atypical working contracts now existing in many European countries deserves special attention in formulating labor market reforms.

  — *Restructuring of the minimum wage institution.* We have indicated that the minimum wage tends to be harmful because it is a potential source of unemployment. Yet we cannot advocate the simplistic solution of abolishing that institution altogether because we share the view that its purpose to ensure a decent minimum standard of living to a full time worker is a worthy one. The trouble with the present structure is that a 'decent' wage may prove to be higher than what would be required to induce employers to absorb the excess supply. If so, the only way to reconcile the 'fairness' principle with high employment is to create a wedge between the remuneration received and the cost to the employer.

In reality such a wedge already exists in most economies, but in the direction opposite to the desired one: that is, the cost to the employer is typically substantially higher than what the worker actually receives in his pay-envelope. In many European countries this so called wedge may be close to 50%: the pay envelope may be not much more than half the cost to the employer.

This has led to simplistic solutions to the problem of lowering the cost without reducing the income – namely to abolish the wedge, misleadingly regarded as 'fiscal levies' on the firm. But this solution ignores the fact that in reality the wedge is part of the remuneration of the worker, even if it is not in the form of cash. It consists in the first place of the income tax, which is part of workers' income, even if it is withheld from this income. The rest consists mostly of social security contributions, or compulsory saving (amounting in much of Europe around to one third part of income), of which some one third may be formally taken out of wage, while the other and major part is paid by the employer, but on behalf of the worker. On top of this the employer may pay some insurance for the worker. It is obvious that these amounts are part of the worker's remuneration, as they provide him with personal benefits, such as a pension or insurance against unfavorable events, even though they may be mandated. If the wedge, or part of it, were abolished, the worker would in effect receive a smaller remuneration. In addition, the social security system, being generally on a pay-as-you-go basis, would run into deficit. This could be avoided if the cost of the wedge were taken over by the government, as has been done some time on a limited scale. But this would be expensive and inconsistent at present with the need to satisfy the Maastricht criteria, unless more taxes were raised, hardly conceivable at present. What we seek then is a way to reduce the cost to the employer, while maintaining the take-home pay and minimizing the negative effects on the budget and the social security system.

We suggest that this might be achieved along the following lines.[4] Let the employer continue to pay the same take-home pay, and some fraction, say one third, of the social security contributions. Suppose, in addition, the government agreed to forego the income tax levied on this income, say around 20%. Then labor cost per hour would be reduced by some 40-45%.

Let us next stipulate that this special kind of treatment would be reserved to those unemployed that are least employable, namely those who have never held a job and the long-term unemployed in the depressed areas.[5] We submit that in this case there would be no significant loss to the government because the recipients would likely have remained unemployed and paid no taxes anyway. For the same reason, the social security would not loose revenue but more likely gain, because of the payment of one third of the contribution. Would then any one bear any loss from our proposal? At first sight the answer may seem: the worker who has been deprived of the two thirds of the employers contribution toward his pension benefits. But on the close examination this answer does not hold. In the first place, if he remained unemployed, the contribution to his pension would be zero, compared with one third under our proposal. It remains true that he will have lost two thirds of the contribution compared with what he would have secured had he found a job at standard wage (which he could not). But that only means that his current compulsory saving is below standard. All this should be perfectly acceptable in a life cycle perspective where we expect people to save little, if any, when they are young and relatively poor. We should expect then to make up for the low saving by saving more when they can afford it better. We propose to use this lead by incorporating into our scheme the right of any one accepting our 'special' minimum wage (which is in any event not compulsory) to make up for say another third of this initially lost contribution. (The employer could be asked to match this contribution partly, as further inducement to a delayed contribution.)

The above is merely meant as an illustration of the appropriate strategy to deal with minimum wages: not abolishing them but finding appropriate acceptable ways of reducing the wedge.

– *An extension and generalization of fixed-term and part time jobs* could favor youngsters and women, whose possibility to work is often tied to these more flexible kinds of contracts. Usually, on the contrary, the existing laws favor only permanent or long-term labor contracts, which are much less flexible.

– *Reform of job security legislation policies* to reduce the ratio of firing costs to average wages.

We have criticized earlier the policies that have pushed job protection, to the point where firing of workers was a nearly impossible task. Although the situation has generally

---

[4] What follows is a broad description of the proposed approach, with the caveat that the details have to be elaborated taking into account the existing institutions.

[5] Note that e.g. in Italy the first of this two groups alone represents about half of total unemployment.

improved, there seems little question that the present institutions in many European countries still contribute to the unemployment problem by discouraging firms from hiring permanent employees even in the presence of a rising demand. We therefore share the view that the reforms needed to reduce unemployment must include substantial reforms of the job security provisions.

We do not believe that it would be possible or advisable to push reforms as far as the American system, where job security provisions are largely absent. But there must be a marked liberalization of the ability of firms to eliminate surplus labor, and some with respect to dismissal of individual workers for cause. This is particularly important in order to deal with youth unemployment, which is a serious problem in many European countries.

However we recommend that these reforms be postponed to a more suitable time. To carry them out now, when the demand is greatly depressed and there is plenty of unemployment, probably a good deal of redundant labor in many firms and few vacancies would have simply the effect of condemning many workers to join the rank of the unemployed, initially reducing instead of increasing employment. It would therefore meet with an understandably bitter opposition of union and workers who might well succeed in maintaining the *status quo*. In our view, therefore, the reforms should be postponed until, and made conditional upon, the realization of more favorable labor market conditions, which should hopefully not take very long if our program is pursued. But it would seem feasible and desirable to spell out promptly the conditions for proceeding with the reforms, e.g. when unemployment first reaches 7%. Furthermore, the content of these reforms should be agreed upon promptly. This two-stage approach should make the reforms far more palatable to labor while at the same time encouraging employers to assume more labour as the demand expands in the expectation that, if eventually the new employee assumed should prove redundant, they would be able to scale down their labor force.

— *Search promoting policies* to reduce labor market search costs, such as job counselling, information provision to unemployed workers and firms with vacancies. The UK experience with its Restart Programme and its counselling initiatives associated with the Welfare to Work policy indicates that such search promoting policies have an important role to play in enhancing the effectiveness of other employment creation measures, such as employment vouchers and training initiatives. These latter measures are likely to have a strong influence only if the currently unemployed workers are aware of them and help to make use of them as part of explicitly formulated strategies of gaining long-term employment in accordance with their idiosyncratic abilities.

— *Policies to stimulate worker mobility*, such as policies to increase the portability of housing subsidies, as well as the portability of health insurance and pensions between firms; and

— *unemployment benefit reforms*. Unemployment benefit systems should be reformed in such a way as to give unemployed people appropriate incentives to seek work when jobs are available for them and to support them when such jobs are absent. Accordingly, the size of unemployment benefits could be made to depend on the ratio of vacancies to unemployment. The greater the number of vacancies relative to unemployed (in specified skill categories), the lower the unemployment benefits would be (within these categories). This proposal would promote efficiency, since it would give the unemployed a greater incentive to search, the greater is the firms' demand for their services. It would also help fulfil governments' equity objectives, since unemployed people are in greatest need of support when they are unable to find work.

This policy would generate a favourable complementarity between demand side and supply side policies. A government stimulus to aggregate demand (and thereby vacancies) could then be financed, partially or wholly, through the associated drop in unemployment benefit payments.

The political economy of unemployment benefit design could be influenced through the device of charging the cost of unemployment compensation to the public in the form of a separate tax. At present, the cost of unemployment, both its social cost and the cash cost of the benefit systems is not well known, because, as has been frequently noted, it typically affects but a small fraction of the population, and the cash cost is not the very visible. This has the consequence that, on the one hand, the public does not put enough pressure on the government and the central bank to correct the situation, and on the other hand it makes voters frequently inclined to favor programs that grant excessive unemployment benefits through mechanisms that are economically wasteful. The above segregation would improve voters' information on this issue and permit them to make better informed policy choices.

Finally, we should like to stress that while the enforcement of specific micro-supply policies is primarily a matter for the individual member governments, all the member states share a common interest in the design of the unemployment policies and in making sure that these policies are forcefully pursued everywhere. This conclusion rests on the consideration that, because of the rising degree of factor mobility within the EU, as well as EU regulations concerning open market access and cross-border competition, the appropriate level of subsidiarity in unemployment policy making does not lie exclusively at the level of the EU member states. In addition, each member state has a very real and tangible interest in the reduction of unemployment in other countries as it contributes to reduce its own. Therefore the European Commission needs to take the lead in providing a legal and institutional framework within which necessary labor market reforms can take place and in making sure that the reforms are promptly carried through.

In addition, we believe that EU governments should also consider some more innovative supply side policy proposals that are designed to reform the incentives that employers and employees face. Currently EU governments spend massive sums of money on unemployment support, further education and training. We believe that the question that should be asked is whether these funds could be redirected to create more incentives for employers to generate jobs and workers to become employed. The following are some illustrative policy measures that take this tack.

Conditional Negative Income Taxes

This measure may be seen as an alternative to supporting jobless people through unemployment benefits. The conditions attached to the proposed negative income tax would be analogous to those attached to current unemployment benefits. For instance if, under the current unemployment benefit system, people must provide evidence of serious job search in order to qualify for unemployment benefits, then they must also be required to provide such evidence under the proposed conditional negative income tax system; if unemployment benefits decline with unemployment duration under the current benefit system, then so too must the negative income taxes.

The Earned Income Tax Credit (EITC) in US belongs to this family of initiatives. The socially desirable relation between the magnitude of the negative income tax and the individual level of income has yet to be analyzed rigorously. The EITC is hump-shaped (so that the magnitude of the negative income tax rises with income at low income levels and then falls toward zero at higher income levels), whereas many of the proposed negative income tax schemes involve a strictly inverse relation between the size of the tax and the income level.

The broad argument in favor of a switch from unemployment benefits to negative income taxes is that this policy could meet the equity and efficiency objectives of current unemployment benefit systems more effectively than the unemployment benefit systems themselves. Although conditional negative income taxes would generate the same type of policy inefficiencies as unemployment benefits, the former would tend to do so to a lesser degree than the latter. For example, negative income taxes may be expected to discourage job search, but by less than unemployment benefits, for when a worker finds a job, he loses all his unemployment benefits, but only a fraction of his negative income taxes.

It is worth noting that a major criticism of the traditional negative income tax schemes – namely, that they make people's material well-being less dependent on employment and thereby discourage employment – obviously does not apply to conditional negative income taxes, since these taxes are conditional on the same things as current unemployment benefits.

Furthermore, conditional negative income taxes also tend to be more effective than unemployment benefits in overcoming labor market inefficiencies generated by credit constraints (e.g. people being unable to take enough time to find an appropriate job match or unable to acquire the appropriate amount of training on account of credit constraints), since the presence of these constraints is more closely associated with low incomes than with unemployment.

The Benefit Transfer Program (BTP)

The aim of the Benefit Transfer Program is simply to redirect the funds that the government currently spends on the unemployed – in the form of unemployment benefits, temporary layoff pay, redundancy subsidies, poverty allowances, and more – so as to give firms an incentive to employ these people. The BTP gives the long-term unemployed people the opportunity to redirect some of the benefits to which he is entitled to a voucher that can be turned over to a firm that will hire him.

The magnitude of the vouchers is to be set by the government, and depends on the magnitude of individuals' unemployment benefits (the higher the benefits, the higher the vouchers) and unemployment duration (the longer the unemployment spells, the higher the vouchers). The size of the vouchers is set so as to be financed from the unemployment benefits and other welfare entitlements foregone when people move from unemployment into jobs. Once a person is hired, the voucher gradually declines as the duration of employment proceeds. The vouchers could be given either to the prospective employers or employees. When unemployed people find jobs, they give up their unemployment benefits in exchange for the wage they earn.

The vouchers come in two varieties: 'recruitment vouchers' and 'training vouchers'. The former are granted solely on the condition that a previously long-term unemployed person is recruited; the latter are conditional on the employer being able to prove that the voucher is spent entirely on training the new recruit at nationally accredited training schemes. The recruitment and training vouchers both are related in the same way to the duration of a person's previous unemployment and the duration of that person's subsequent employment, but the level of the training voucher (other things equal) is higher than that of the recruitment voucher.

Since the BTP is voluntary, it extends the range of choices open to the unemployed and their potential employers. The unemployed will join only if it is to their advantage, i.e. if the wages they would be offered are higher than their unemployment benefits. At the same time, employers will join only if they find it profitable. Once again, many could well do so, since the vouchers could reduce their labor costs. In short, employees may wind up receiving substantially more than their unemployment support, and many employers may find themselves paying substantially less than the prevailing wages. The BTP has the unique capability of making most participants in the labor market better off: the unemployed who earns more, the employer who secures a lower cost, and the government that reduces its expenses incurred for the unemployed. This 'free lunch' is possible since the BTP induces people who were previously unemployed to become productive, and the proceeds of the output they generate may be divided among the economic agents above.

The BTP has been implemented in various forms in the UK, the Netherlands and several other OECD countries. Empirical studies of the program indicate that there are three major obstacles to its effectiveness: i) displacement of current employees by the targeted groups of workers, ii) dead-weight (paying vouchers to unemployed people who would have found jobs anyway), and iii) substitution (the employment of the targeted group rather than unemployed workers outside the targeted group). The first obstacle can be mitigated by confining the vouchers to firms that increase their total employment relative to their industry average.[6]

The second and third obstacles can be reduced by targeting the employment vouchers at the long-term unemployed (since they have a relatively low probability of finding jobs anyway and are often imperfect substitutes for the short-term unemployed). However, these measures can only reduce, but never completely eliminate displacement, dead-weight and substitution. Nevertheless, evaluations of the program in the UK and the Netherlands have shown that, when the program is appropriately designed, it is able to create significant additional employment without putting upward pressure on wages. Moreover, even if the vouchers lead some firms to substitute their current employees for subsidized workers to retain the subsidized workers only so long as their vouchers last, the program will still succeed in substituting short-term for long-term unemployment. This would still lead to a fall in aggregate unemployment, since the short-term unemployed have higher chances of employment than the long-term unemployed.

Beyond that, the BTP is not inflationary, since it reduces firms' labor costs and since the long-term unemployed have no noticeable effect on wage inflation. If designed properly, it costs the government nothing, since the money for the employment vouchers would have been spent on unemployment support anyway.

By offering higher vouchers for training, the Program could become the basis for an effective national training initiative. Clearly, firms will spend the vouchers on training only if they intend to retain their recruits after the subsidies have run out. Thus the training for the unemployed would automatically come with the prospect of long-term employment. This is

---

[6] The condition must be formulated relative to the industry average, for otherwise the scheme would be less effective in economic downturns – when the need for employment creation is greatest – than in upturns.

something that the existing government training schemes do not offer. Many existing schemes also run the risk of being ill-suited to people's diverse potential job opportunities, whereas under the BTP firms would naturally provide the training most appropriate to the available jobs. And whereas the existing training schemes are costly to run, the BTP is free.

Finally, the BTP could play a vital role in tackling regional unemployment problems. Regions of high unemployment would become areas containing a high proportion of workers with training vouchers, thereby providing an incentive for companies to move there and provide the appropriate training.

Auctioning off Unemployment Benefits and Employment Vouchers

Existing unemployment benefit systems could be radically reformed to improve the incentives for job creation and job search without exacerbating disparities in incomes. Auctioning employment vouchers and auctioning unemployment benefits may be useful in this regard.

Regarding the former proposal, the government could auction employment vouchers to the firms. Firms would qualify for a number of vouchers equal to a) the number of previously unemployed people they intend to hire minus b) the number of employees they fire (or separate from).[7] Firms' entitlement would also be withdrawn if they used the vouchers to displace current employees. To make this provision credible, employees who believe they have been displaced would have the right of complaint, to be investigated by an independent body. If the complaint is found to have been justified, the firm in question would be fined.[8]

To prevent the short-term unemployed driving the long-term unemployed out of the market, there would be separate options for workers belonging to broad groups with different unemployment durations. Another possibility is for the government to auction employment vouchers to unemployed people.

The aim of the supply side proposals here presented, then, is to transform unemployment benefits and other social security grants in incentives to firms to create more jobs and to workers to accept them.

6. CONCLUSION

In sum, we believe that the EU unemployment problem needs to be attacked on two fronts: through a broad spectrum of supply side policies and the demand management policy. The expansion of aggregate demand is necessary to increase both investment and employment. However, unless supply side measures are also taken, demand expansion can result in more inflation instead of more employment, because of the mismatch between the demand and supply of labor. What is important to stress is that both demand and supply side policies must be adopted together by all European countries, in order both to avoid beggar-

---

[7] This difference may be adjusted for average changes in employment within that sector. Specifically, if sectoral employment is shrinking (expanding), then firms receive a number of vouchers greater (less) than the difference between the number of unemployed people hired and the number of employees fired. The reason for this adjustment is to avoid the possibility that the effectiveness of the voucher policy may diminish as the sector falls into a recession.

[8] This anti-displacement provision has been successfully tried in Australia.

my-neighbor problems, and, at the same time, to catch all the possible complementary effects of these policies.

In: Roadmap to Bangalore?
Editors: A. Heshmati, A. Tausch, pp. 175-251

ISBN: 978-1-60021-478-3
© 2007 Nova Science Publishers, Inc.

Chapter 7

GLOBALIZATION AND THE FUTURE OF THE "EUROPEAN SOCIAL MODEL"

Arno Tausch[1]

Department of Political Science, A-6020 Innsbruck University,
Innrain 52/III; Austria

ABSTRACT

Starting from the current debate about the European social model, a radical new assessment of the deficits of the European social model is presented in this article. Our approach underlines the up to now neglected effects of the lack of industrial policy and structural dependence on economic growth and social development in Europe. Much of the re-ascent of Europe and Japan after 1945 was due to import substitution. When that ended, Europe and Japan began to slide back again vis-à-vis the United States, thus re-affirming the old wisdom of development history research in contrast to "pure" free trade economic theory (Senghaas, 1985). Senghaas' analysis of the development history of European states today finds its confirmation in global development statistics summarized by the United Nations (2002). Re-analyzing the existing data for the 1990s clearly shows that the winners and losers of globalization were indeed distributed very unevenly around the globe. In a significant portion of the countries of the globe, inequality and globalization – the inflow of foreign direct investments per host country GDP - are on the increase since 1980, as we confirm here, based on the data series of the ILO, the UTIP project at the University of Texas, and the World Bank . These analyses of the dynamics in the world system calculated the time series correlations of globalization, economic growth (Global Development Network Growth Database, William Easterly and Mirvat Sewadeh, World Bank), unemployment (Laborsta ILO), and inequality (UTIP, University of Texas Inequality Project, Theil indices of inequality, based on wages in 21 economic sectors). Within this framework the author then analyzes falling relative price levels (Eurostat, Lisbon indicators) or unequal exchange. A lowering of the price level will, according to the underlying Commission logic, mean "price reform", while a

---

[1] Arno Tausch: Adjunct Professor (Universitaetsdozent) of Political Science at Innsbruck University, (Founder: Professor Anton Pelinka). Available book publications: http://www.campusi.com. E-mail address: Arno.Tausch@bmsg.gv.at

hypothetical movement upwards on the indicator will mean a "setback". With the UNDP Human Development Indicators, 2000 we show that a high price level (in the terminology of Eurostat) is exceptionally highly and positively correlated with positive indicators of the development performance of a nation, and very highly negatively correlated with indicators of human misery. Contrary to the Commission's assumptions, it would have to be expected that movements in the direction of a "lower price level" lead indeed to social imbalances and crises. Pushing Europe towards even more "price reform" will mean a Yotopoulos cycle of backwardness and stagnation. Our analyses show the dramatic world shifts in price levels relative to the United States in recent years. Contrary to what European policy makers expected with their Eurostat politically binding price level indicator, which is, after all, one of their 14 main Lisbon targets, the United States as the Lisbon competition target country was a high price region throughout much of the late 1990s and the early 2000s. By and large, it is shown that the member countries of the "old" EU-15 are on the losing side in that transnational equation. No "old" European country improved its position; on the contrary, "old Europe" becomes a region that is itself a victim of price reform (unequal exchange, low international price level). Starting with the writings of Perroux, Prebisch and Rothschild in the 1930s, we then show that there is no empirical support for the thesis that globalization is good for the poor. By using latest (United Nations and other data) and multivariate techniques, investigating the determination of 14 indicators of development in 109 countries with complete data by 12 determinants of development, we show that a reliance on the "Washington Consensus" alone will not "fix" the performance of the EU-25. The most consistent consequence of the "dependency" analysis of this essay is the realization that a reliance on foreign capital in the short term might bring about positive consequences for employment – especially female employment – but that the long-term negative consequences of dependence in the social sphere, but also for sustainable development, outweigh the immediate, positive effects. Our three-fold empirical understanding of the process of globalization – reliance on foreign savings, MNC penetration and unequal transfer/price reform (ERDI), - goes beyond the average analysis of the workings of dependency structures and shows how different aspects of dependency negatively affect development performance. EU membership, by contrast, fails to have sufficiently enough dynamic effects and its democratic deficits become ever more clear. What is more, the unweighted average dependency rates of the EU-25 are much higher than in India, the US and China. Among the EU countries, only Turkey, Italy, Greece had a lower MNC penetration rate than the US, and Slovenia (see Mencinger in this volume) is the country with the lowest MNC penetration rate among the countries of the "new Europe" and at the same time the most successful one in social policies. Indeed, one could say that we are confronted with "Dependencia y desarrollo en Europa "

THE "EUROPEAN SOCIAL MODEL" IN CRISIS?

In his speech outlining the British Presidency in the European Union, the British Prime Minister, the Rt. Honorable Anthony Blair M. P. said before the European Parliament on June 23rd 2005:

What would a different policy agenda for Europe look like?

First, it would modernise our social model. Again some have suggested I want to abandon Europe's social model. But tell me: what type of social model is it that has 20m unemployed in Europe, productivity rates falling behind those of the USA; that is allowing more science graduates to be produced by India than by Europe; and that, on any relative index of a modern economy - skills, RandD, patents, IT, is going down not up. India will expand its biotechnology sector fivefold in the next five years. China has trebled its spending on RandD in the last five.

Of the top 20 universities in the world today, only two are now in Europe. (...)

The purpose of our social model should be to enhance our ability to compete, to help our people cope with globalization, to let them embrace its opportunities and avoid its dangers. Of course we need a social Europe. But it must be a social Europe that works. (:..)

And we've been told how to do it. The Kok report in 2004 shows the way. Investment in knowledge, in skills, in active labor market policies, in science parks and innovation, in higher education, in urban regeneration, in help for small businesses. This is modern social policy, not regulation and job protection that may save some jobs for a time at the expense of many jobs in the future. (...)

And since this is a day for demolishing caricatures, let me demolish one other: the idea that Britain is in the grip of some extreme Anglo-Saxon market philosophy that tramples on the poor and disadvantaged. (British Prime Minister Tony Blair, available at: http://www.number10.gov.uk/output/Page7714.asp)

From the viewpoint of international social policy, it is noteworthy that it has become commonplace to speak of a "social Europe" and an "economically efficient America". However, several major errors are hidden here. These errors go back in a way to "official" European Union policy. The German Irish sociologist Peter Herrmann remarks:

"Strangely the document that can be found here had been circulated as confidential paper during the Social Affairs Council on March 29th, 1996. The European Social Model is again and again discussed but rarely explored in concrete terms. Here, the French government tabled a more detailed presentation of the idea of that model, which usually is diffusely just distinguished from the US American model. So it is not clear why a concretising attempt remains confidential." (Peter Herrmann, available at http://socialpolicy.ucc.ie/EU_Social_policy_general.htm)

The mentioned document does not always distinguish between what the free online standard *"Stanford Encyclopedia of Philosophy"*[2] calls modal logic ("it is necessary that", "it is possible that"), deontic logic ("it is permitted that", "it is forbidden that"), temporal logic (it will be always be the case that", "it will be the case that", "it has always been the case that" and "it was the case that") and doxastic logic ("x believes that"), somewhat bombastically stating:

"Over the course of their history the countries of Europe have laid the foundations for a social model that distinguishes Europe from the other continents. Throughout Europe, the men and women enjoy protection against the hazards of existence and a guaranteed income after they retire.

---

[2] http://plato.stanford.edu/contents.html

Throughout Europe, the role of the social partners in economic and social life is acknowledged. Nowadays, the social dialogue enables the most practical and solid progress to be made in the fight against unemployment, by promoting linked work and training, creating new ways of organizing work, and encouraging a sharing of productivity that is more favourable to employment.

Throughout Europe, the State lays down the basic rule concerning employment relationships and guarantees national cohesion.

Throughout Europe, social protection systems are deeply rooted in the identity and culture of the people.

Contrary to what some believe, these social achievements are an asset to Europe. They have been a factor for economic growth because they have ensured social cohesion. In the future they will enable countries of Europe to adjust to a new society where work will take different and more diversified forms, and to the new economy that is emerging before our eyes. (French Memorandum to the Social Affairs Council on March 29th, 1996, as quoted by Peter Herrmann, available at: *http://socialpolicy.ucc.ie/EU_Social_policy_general.htm*)

Popular, as such sentences may be, the usual explanations of the growth differentials between Europe and the US do not hold. First, we have to distinguish between gross and net expenditures for social protection. Each year, the average European works until May just for the tax collectors, while in America you've finished working for the federal tax system by around mid-March. European federal welfare states on average spend 29% their Gross Domestic Product on social policies, while this gross spending ratio for the US Federal Government is only 16.4% GDP. But net of taxes, and including public and private social spending, even in the "old Europe" of the richer, Western 15 EU states, net total social spending is only 24% of GDP, while in the USA this portion is 23.40%.

Table 1. Gross and Net Social Spending in Europe and America

	gross and net social expenditures (in% of the GDP)			
	public social expenditures		total social expenditures	
	Gross	Net	Gross	Net
Sweden	35.7	28.5	39.1	30.6
Netherlands	27.1	20.3	32.6	24.0
Germany	29.2	27.2	31.6	28.8
Austria	28.5	23.4	30.3	24.6
Italy	29.4	24.1	30.1	25.3
France	(no data)	–	–	–
UK	23.8	21.6	28.0	24.6
USA	15.8	16.4	24.6	23.4

Source.   Streissler   based   on   OECD   2002,   available   at: http://www.arbeit-wirtschaft.at/aw_10_2004/art6.htm.

Serious comparisons of the *inequality of personal incomes in Europe* and in the *United States* always maintained that even for the EU-15, the level of income inequality is quite high, when we take the huge income differences between the European states and intra-country or inequality between the regions into account at the same time. Summing up the results of the *"Sapir Report"* that for a time was available from the website of the European Commission under http://europa.eu.int/comm/lisbon_strategy/pdf/sapir_report_en.pdf. we arrive at the following inequality rates:

	1985		1995	
	GINI before Taxation	GINI after Taxation	GINI before Taxation	GINI after Taxation
EU-15	0.381	0.279	0.408	0.294
USA	0.415	0.337	0.421	0.342
EU-27[3]				0.404

Source. our own calculations from „Sapir Report" on behalf of the European Commission.

The *regional concentration* (GINI-coefficient) of value added in the EU-15 in mid 1990s was, according to Aiginger and Leitner, 0.5106 and 0.5374 in the US, with very a slight decrease of regional inequality taking place between 1987 and 1995 in both systems. The same holds true for employment, where the GINI coefficient was 0.4762 in Europe and 0.5232 in the United States. No such calculations exist for the EU-25 as yet.

Such perspectives contribute towards a better understanding of the European and American political economy. Arguably, the United States experienced over the last years under the Bush Presidency a very concerted effort at neo-liberalism and *"Robin Hood in reverse"* – i.e. the famous *"dooh nibor"* principle[4]. But it is misleading for us Europeans to negate the positive aspects that the US social system offered over the years – a heavy involvement of the state and the private sector in human capital formation, proper life and work chances for women, and heavy expenditures in the social sphere at the state and at the municipal level, combined with low federal taxes and a socially active corporate structure and a great number of volunteers in the social sector, not to forget the "real existing socialism" and the "welfare state" of the United States Armed Forces and their hundreds of thousands of employees and the household members dependent on them.

Another aspect that will fundamentally change the stereotype of "welfare Europe" versus the "anti-social US" is the effect of EU-enlargement on the overall picture of poverty and inequality in the new Europe. Several critics of United States social structures maintained that poverty and inequality couldn't be separated from the history of the unequal integration of the American South as a raw material exporter and a Slave economy in the evolving system of world capitalism[5]. But center-periphery structures also exist in East Central Europe, and

---

[3] „Sapir-Report", page 102: The Report calculates only a Theil Index for the entire EU-27, duly considering inequality between and within countries, an open-ended inequality index which is 33 % bigger (0.220) than for the EU-15, assuming Italian inequality rates for the new member states. Unfortunately, no GINI Index was calculated; but we can roughly guess that the GINI for the EU-27 is also about a 1/3 bigger than the GINI Index for the EU-15.

[4] Paul Krugman in http://www.commondreams.org/views04/0601-07.htm

[5] see „Rassenbeziehungen in den USA" by Bernd Rüster, Darmstadt, Luchterhand, 1973, 314 pages, Sammlung Luchterhand; Vol. 95.

especially in the Balkan region. The plight of 8 million Roma present an additional European social problem of the 21st Century that is, by its very dimensions, comparable to the "race problem" in the US.

Table 2. Poverty Rates in Europe and America (Eurostat-concept)

poverty poverty rates in % of the total population: poverty defined by threshold 50% of median income		
	mid 1980s	mid 1990s	long-term unemployment
Sweden	5.3	6.4	1.1
Netherlands	3.4	6.3	0.8
Germany	6.4	9.4	1.8
Austria	6.1	7.4	–
Italy	10.3	14.2	–
France	8.0	7.5	–
UK	6.9	10.9	6.1
USA	18.3	17.0	4.6

Source: Streissler   based   on   OECD   2002,   available   at: http://www.arbeit-wirtschaft.at/aw_10_2004/art6.htm

So, after enlargement Europe confronts its own *"Myrdalian"* poverty problem and a *"European Dilemma"*, only that this process takes place not in the 19th and the early 20th Century, but in the 21st Century[6]. Furthermore it is a common place in the US "critical" literature to maintain that US history involved massive violence against the indigenous population, and that racial discrimination is a constant feature of US society from the very beginning to the present day[7]. The present author, in a series of recent publications[8], tried to re-evaluate these comparative theses by showing that Europe itself is not free from massive colonial expansion and violence from the 10th Century onwards against religiously dissenting minorities on the Continent and that the contemporary map of the sometimes catastrophic European regional unemployment in the East and South of the Continent very well corresponds to the history of religious and ethnic cleansing from the year 1000 onwards – especially also against the *Dar al Islam* (house of Islam) in the European *"mezzogiorno"* in Italy, Spain, and Portugal and against minorities in the first half of the 20th Century in the European East. Systematic comparisons of the US and European states reveal the following poverty tendencies.

---

[6] Myrdal, Gunnar, (1996) *,An American dilemma : the Negro problem and modern democracy'*. Gunnar Myrdal; with a new introduction by Sissela Bok. New Brunswick, NJ: Transaction Publishers

[7] „Schwarzbuch USA" by Eric Frey, Frankfurt a.M., Eichborn Verlag, 2004, 496 pages, Price: 24,90 Euros.

[8] (2004) *'Die EU-Erweiterung und die soziale Konvergenz. Ein „Working Paper" zur Globalisierung und wachsenden Ungleichheit im neuen und alten Europa'* Studien von Zeitfragen, ISSN-1619-8417, 38(2): 1 – 185, available at http://druckversion.studien-von-zeitfragen.net/Soziale%20Konvergenz%20EU-Erweiterung.pdf and (2004) *,Soziale und regionale Ungleichgewichte, politische Instabilität und die Notwendigkeit von Pensionsreformen im neuen Europa'* Schriftenreihe des Zentrums für europäische Studien, Universität Trier, Band 56, ISSN 0948-1141, available at http://www.uni-trier.de/zes/schriftenreihe/056.pdf

Table 3. UNDP Poverty Indicators for the EU-25 in Comparison to the US

Poverty situation in 2002, as measured by United Nations indicators	*EU 25: nation with a worse performance than the US*
Percent of population surviving beyond age 60	Slovakia, Poland, Lithuania. Hungary, Latvia
Avoiding long-term unemployment	Luxembourg; Netherlands; Austria; Denmark; Sweden; United Kingdom; Ireland; Portugal; Finland; Hungary; France; Belgium; Czech Republic; Germany; Spain; Greece; Italy; Poland; Slovakia
Avoiding functional analphabetism	United Kingdom; Ireland; Hungary; Slovenia; Poland; Portugal
Avoiding a high percentage of people below the 11 $ per capita and day poverty line	United Kingdom
Real purchasing power of the poorest 20%	Latvia; Estonia; Poland; Lithuania; Hungary; Portugal; Slovakia; Greece; United Kingdom; Spain; Czech Republic; Slovenia; Italy
Probability at birth of not surviving to age 40 (% of cohort), 1995-2000	Latvia; Estonia; Lithuania; Hungary; Portugal; Poland
Human development index	Latvia; Lithuania; Estonia; Poland; Hungary; Slovakia; Czech Republic; Malta; Slovenia; Portugal; Cyprus; Greece; Spain; Italy; Ireland; Luxembourg; Germany; Denmark; Austria; United Kingdom; France; Finland; Netherlands
Infants with low birth-weight	Hungary
Life expectancy	Latvia; Estonia; Hungary; Lithuania; Slovakia; Poland; Czech Republic; Slovenia; Portugal; Denmark; Ireland

Summarizing recent comparisons of real poverty rates[9], we arrive at the following results that show that the current *median-based relative measures of poverty are by far inferior to measures, based on real living standards.*

In trying to answer at least partially to these unsatisfactory developments, the Commission launched its new Social Agenda for modernizing Europe's social model under the revamped Lisbon Strategy for growth and jobs at the beginning of February 2005[10]. The new, very modest agenda focuses on providing jobs and equal opportunities for all and ensuring that the benefits of the EU's growth and jobs drive reach everyone in society. By modernizing labor markets and social protection systems, it will *"help people seize the opportunities created by international competition, technological advances and changing population patterns while protecting the most vulnerable in society."*

---

[9] compiled from UNDP (2004) and Sharpe (2001), based on OECD, EU Commission, and World Bank

[10] http://europa.eu.int/rapid/pressReleasesAction.do?reference=IP/05/152&format=HTML&aged=0&language=EN&guiLanguage=en

Table 4. Real Poverty Measures, EU-25 and the US Compared

Poverty situation in mid 1990s to 2002, as measured by OECD, World Bank and United Nations indicators	*EU 25: nation with a worse performance than the US*
% of the population with a daily per capita income of less than 2 $ per day (mid 1990s)	Netherlands (no data available from the new member states)
% of the population with a daily per capita income of less than 4 $ per day (mid 1990s)	Netherlands; Slovakia; Poland; Lithuania; Estonia; Latvia
% of the population with a daily per capita income of less than 14.40 $ per day (mid 1990s)	Netherlands; Spain; Ireland (no data available from the new member states)
social strata with a real income that is lower than the real income of the poorest 20% in the United States of America (21.6 $ per capita and day) (2002)	Lithuania middle 60%; Poland middle 60%; Italy bottom 20%; Slovenia bottom 20%; Czech Republic bottom 20%; Spain bottom 20%; Latvia middle 60%; United Kingdom bottom 20%; Greece bottom 20%; Slovakia bottom 20%; Portugal bottom 20%; Hungary bottom 20%; Lithuania bottom 20%; Poland bottom 20%; Estonia bottom 20%; Latvia bottom 20%

Source. our own compilations from UNDP (2004) and Sharpe (2001).

Vladimír Špidla, Commissioner for Employment, Social Affairs and Equal Opportunities, said at this occasion: *"This dynamic new agenda will help to provide what citizens most want: decent jobs and social justice. It is about equipping everyone to manage the changes facing our society and about looking after the neediest. It is designed to preserve and modernize our valued social model as the essential tool underpinning Europe's drive to boost growth and jobs. It maps the route for reforming labor markets in order to make work a real option for everyone. At the same time, it provides pathways for modernizing welfare systems and combating poverty."*

Under employment, the Agenda will focus on:

-   Creating a European labor market, through enabling workers to take pension and social security entitlements with them when they work in a different Member States and by establishing an optional framework for collective bargaining across frontiers; the Commission will also examine transition periods for workers from new Member States;
-   Getting more people into better jobs, particularly through the European Youth Initiative and supporting women in (re-)entering the labor market;
-   Updating labor law to address needs created by new forms of work, i.e. particular short term contracts; a new health and safety strategy;
-   Managing the process of restructuring through the social dialogue.

Under poverty and equal opportunities, the Agenda will focus on:

- Analyzing the impact of ageing populations and the future of relations between the different generations, by launching a Green Paper on demography;
- Supporting the Member States in reforming pensions and health care and tackling poverty;
- Tackling discrimination and inequality; the Commission will examine minimum income schemes in the Member States and set out a policy approach for tackling discrimination, particularly against ethnic minorities such as the Roma;
- Fostering equal opportunities between women and men, for example by setting up a gender institute;
- Clarifying the role and characteristics of social services of general interest;

A further governmental debate on the *"European Social Model"* will take place at the informal heads of government summit during the British Presidency in October 2005 *(EUObserver.com,* August 5th 2005).

EUROPE — A CONTINENT CHARACTERIZED BY THE FAILURES OF GLOBALIZATION

Drawing on the condensed results of a comparison, published in Tausch, 2005e, we start by the certainly provocative assertion that a thorough analysis of existing data suggests that development by free trade is a myth. Much of the re-ascent of Europe and Japan after 1945 was due to import substitution. When that ended, Europe and Japan began to slide back again vis-à-vis the United States, thus re-affirming the old wisdom of development history research in contrast to "pure" free trade economic theory (Senghaas, 1985). Senghaas' analysis of the development history of European states today finds its confirmation in global development statistics summarized by the United Nations (2002).

Much of the free trade 19th Century and the first half of the 20th Century witnessed a European decline *vis-à-vis* the US, and only the import substituting and regulated postwar period after 1945 saw a relative closing of the gap, that began to widen again after 1973.

The late Andre Gunder Frank has implied for a long time that Europe's quest to catch up with the US by 2010 has to be seen in the larger perspective of Asia's re-ascent in the world system. The United Nations Economic Commission for Latin America, ECLAC/CEPAL, in its essay *"Globalización y desarrollo"* (2002)[12] provided estimates that support such a view that stresses the simultaneousness of the ascent of Asia from the 1950s onwards with the decline of Europe after 1973 in the world system.

Usually, world systems theories maintain that the present ongoing era of globalization already has its parallel in the 19th Century. The UN CEPAL/ECLAC data neatly demonstrate that these epochs of globalization in the 19th Century and after 1973 shifted incomes relatively away from Western Europe, Eastern Europe and Japan and in favor of the United States and the "dominions", while the era of regulation after 1945 (Arrighi, 1995) clearly re-

---

[12] http://www.eclac.cl/cgi-bin/getProd.asp?xml=/publicaciones/xml/6/10026/P10026.xml&xsl=/tpl/p9f.xsl&base=

allocated relative incomes to the West Europeans, to the East Europeans and the Japanese. Latin America also gained during the era of import substitution from around 1930 to around 1973.

Table 5. The Evolution of the Gap between Europe and the US Since 1820
(Real GDP Per Capita, United States = 100 for each Year Since 1820)

GDP per capita in …	1820	1870	1913	1950	1973	1990	1998
Western Europe (in % of the US, AUS, NZ, CND)	102.60	81.20	66.10	49.50	71.30	71.50	68.50
United States, Australia, NZ, CND	100.00	100.00	100.00	100.00	100.00	100.00	100.00
Japan (in % of the US, AUS, NZ, CND)	55.70	30.30	26.40	20.70	70.70	84.00	78.10
Asia (excl. Japan) (in % of the US, AUS, NZ, CND)	47.90	26.50	12.20	6.80	7.60	9.50	11.20
Latin Amer and Car. (in % of the US, AUS, NZ, CND)	55.40	28.70	28.70	27.50	28.00	22.60	22.20
Eastern Europe + former USSR (in % of the US, AUS, NZ, CND)	55.50	37.70	28.60	28.00	35.40	28.80	16.70
Africa (in % of the US, AUS, NZ, CND)	34.80	18.30	11.10	9.20	8.40	6.20	5.20

Source. our own calculations from CEPAL/ECLAC.

On the basis of another analysis, presented in Tausch (2005a, and 2005c), based on ILO data, it is to be expected that Western and Eastern Europe, Latin America, and also Japan that all owed their relative ascent in global society after 1945 to their import substitution strategies, will be the main losers during the ongoing globalized decades. Re-analyzing the existing data for the 1990s clearly shows that the winners and losers of globalization were indeed distributed very unevenly around the globe.

Thus, the final balance of globalization since 1990 was the income impoverishment of Eastern Europe and the Muslim world in the Middle East and North Africa.

Table 6. The Social Effects of Globalization, 1990 – 1999

absolute and relative values	Millions of people < 1 $ a day 1990	% pop < 1 $ a day 1990	Millions of people < 1 $ a day 1999	% pop < 1 $ a day 1999
East Asia and Pacific	486	30.5	279	15.6
Eastern Europe and Central Asia	6	1.4	24	5.1
South Asia	506	45	488	36.6
Latin America and Caribbean	48	11	57	11.1
Middle East and North Africa	5	2.1	6	2.2
Sub-Saharan Africa	241	47.4	315	49
Total	1292	29.6	1169	23.2

/MDG/tpl/top-bottom.xsl

Table 7. Changes in the Social Structure of the World System, 1990 - 1999

changes since 1990	increases/decreases in the percentages of population with < 2 $ a day
Eastern Europe and Central Asia	13.5
Middle East and North Africa	2.3
Sub-Saharan Africa	-1.3
Latin America and Caribbean	-1.6
South Asia	-5
East Asia and Pacific	-19.6
Total	-6.5

Source: our own calculations from ILO sources, 2003 (Report of the Director-General: *"Working out of Poverty"*. International Labor Conference 91st Session 2003, ILO, Geneva).

The wave of global politics and economics in the 1990s negatively affected the social balances in many countries. In a significant portion of the countries of the globe, inequality and globalization – the inflow of foreign direct investments per host country GDP - are on the increase since 1980, as the present author could confirm in his recent works based on the data series of the ILO, the UTIP project at the University of Texas, and the World Bank. These analyses of the dynamics in the world system calculated the time series correlations of globalization, economic growth (Global Development Network Growth Database, William Easterly and Mirvat Sewadeh, World Bank), unemployment (Laborsta ILO), and inequality (UTIP, University of Texas Inequality Project, Theil indices of inequality, based on wages in 21 economic sectors).

Table 8. The Success and Failure of Globalization since 1980

World Society

globalization and its effects – world sample with complete data	states that fulfilled the criterion	states that did not fulfill the criterion	total number of states with complete data	% of states meeting the promises of globalization
rising foreign direct investment inflows (time series correlation > 0.0)	78	10	88	88.6
sinking comparative price levels	66	25	91	72.5
accelerating economic growth	60	28	88	68.2
sinking unemployment	38	53	91	41.8
sinking inequality	19	69	88	21.6

Table 8. (Continued.)

EU-25

globalization and its effects – EU-25 sample with complete data	states that fulfilled the criterion	states that did not fulfill the criterion	total number of EU-25 states with complete data	% of states meeting the promises of globalization
sinking comparative price levels	21	2	23	91.3
rising foreign direct investment inflows (time series correlation > 0.0)	21	2	23	91.3
accelerating economic growth	19	4	23	82.6
sinking unemployment	10	13	23	43.5
sinking inequality	5	18	23	21.7

In all, 118 nations of the world were compared.

We briefly explain our methodology with the random example of Tunisia: sharply rising inequality, but no noteworthy linear increase in economic growth or globalization.

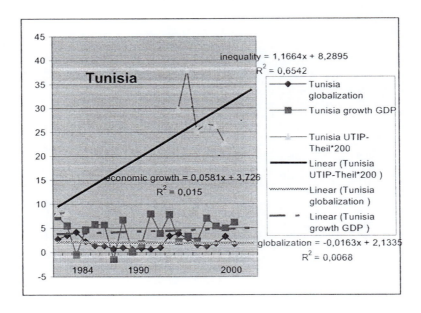

Graph 1. The methodology used to study the time series patterns of globalization, economic growth, and inequality in 118 nations of the world with fairly complete data since 1980.

The correlations of our globalization and economic and social performance indicators corresponded to the following patterns on the level of the world system and the EU-25 countries. The cutting points are defined as follows: Strong tendency towards globalization (>0.5), tendency towards slow growth (<0.0), tendency towards rising inequality (>0.0) etc.

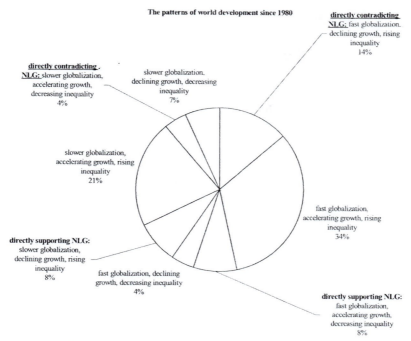

NLG: neo-liberal globalization

Graph 2. The development paths in the world system since 1980.

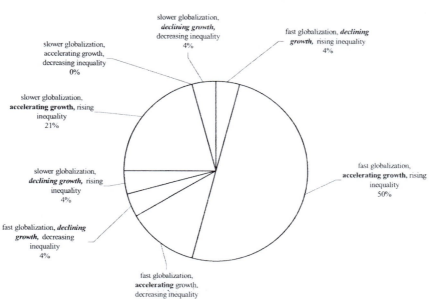

Graph 3. The European Union (EU-25) in the world system since 1980.

In our following Table, EU-25 member countries are underlined. And globalization indeed was omnipresent in Europe, and the only exceptions were.

Table 9. EU-25 – Global Best Practice in Globalization, Global Worst Practice Rates of Decreasing Social Well-Being?

"Best practice" *globalizers:* **European among the world's top 30 globalizers (correlation over time of the rates of inflows of foreign direct investment per GDP; see appendix)**
Poland; France; Portugal; *Costa Rica;* **Croatia;** *Pakistan; China; Israel;* Latvia; *Uganda;* **Moldova; Russian Federation;** Slovak Republic; **Romania;** Lithuania; *Mongolia; India; Chile; Azerbaijan; Honduras; Mexico; Nicaragua;* Austria; Belgium; Denmark; **Turkey;** *Armenia;* Hungary; *Venezuela; RB; Nepal;* Germany

"Best practice" *reduction of the comparative price level* **(US=100): Europeans among the world's top 30 reducers of the price level (see Chapter below)**
Luxembourg; *Equatorial Guinea; Argentina; Singapore; Brazil;* **Switzerland;** Denmark; Germany; Austria; France; *Uzbekistan; Hong Kong; China (SAR); Uruguay;* Belgium; *Japan;* Netherlands; Sweden; Finland; Italy; *Croatia; Paraguay; Australia; Lesotho; Rwanda;* Greece; **Norway;** *New Zealand; South Africa; Tajikistan; Peru; Chile*

But *worst practice* **rises in inequality: European among the world's top 30** *increases in inequality* **(see appendix)**
China; Slovak Republic; *Nigeria;* Czech Republic; *Bangladesh; Gambia; The;* Spain; Hungary; *Panama; Australia;* Latvia; **Romania;** *Egypt; Arab Rep.; Gabon; Mexico; Venezuela; RB; Philippines;* **Moldova; Bulgaria;** *Pakistan; New Zealand;* Netherlands; *Japan;* Slovenia; *Tunisia;* **Turkey;** *Azerbaijan;* Ireland; Portugal; Poland; *Malawi*

Worst practice **long-term tendency towards** *stagnation:* **Europeans among the world's top 30 in slow long-term economic recovery; measured by the time series correlation of economic growth rate over time (see appendix)**
Pakistan; Burundi; Japan; **Moldova; Russian Federation;** Bulgaria; *Egypt; Arab Rep.;* **Romania;** *Indonesia; Mongolia; Zimbabwe; Kenya; Thailand; Jordan;* Italy; **Cyprus;** *Colombia;* Latvia; *Malaysia; Algeria; South Africa; Gambia; The; Kyrgyz Republic; Singapore; Brazil; Zambia;* Lithuania; **Turkey;** *New Zealand;* **Norway;** Czech Republic

Worst practice *tendency towards unemployment:* **Europeans among the world's top 30 with unemployment is rising over time (time series correlation of ILO Laborsta unemployment rates over time; see appendix)**
Mauritius; Haiti; South Africa; Tajikistan; Azerbaijan; Estonia; **Croatia;** *Indonesia; Namibia; Algeria; Argentina;* Greece; Czech Republic; **Ukraine;** *Saudi Arabia; Brazil;* Luxembourg; *Philippines; Bangladesh; Pakistan; Japan; Uzbekistan;* Slovakia; **Albania;** *Uruguay; Egypt; Ecuador; Nicaragua;* **Russian Federation;** Finland; *Israel*

Using the University of Texas Inequality Project data series on inequality in the world system since the 1960s, based on solid pay data, we arrive at the following world map of time series correlations with inequality. The real explosion of pay inequality in the European East has to be noted. Still, the share of the poorest 20% in total incomes in the US is lower than in most European countries (except in the former USSR, see our data based on UNDP sources). *Eastern Europe* was the region which *most rapidly globalized* and which had the most *rapid tendency towards inequality at the same time.*

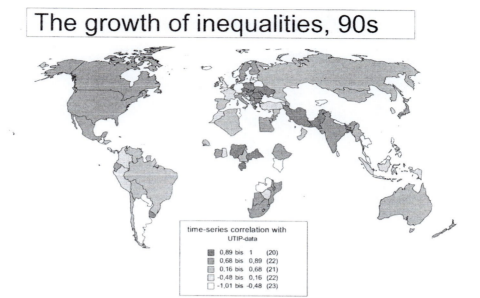

Source: our own calculations from UTIP[13]. In this and in all other maps in this work, *"bis"* is the shorthand for *"ranging from ... to"*. Countries painted in green color: missing data.

Map 1. The growth of inequalities in the 1990s in the world system and in the wider Europe.

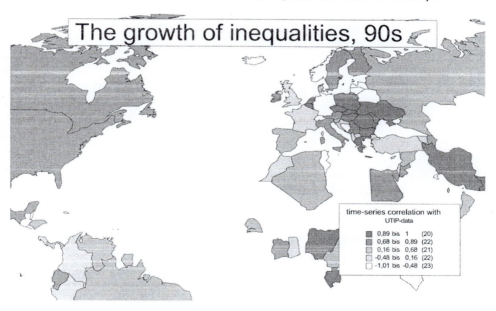

Map 2. The growth of inequalities in the 1990s in the world system and in the wider Europe.

---

[13] http://utip.gov.utexas.edu/

Source: our own compilations, based on UNDP electronical statistics system, available at:
http://hdr.undp.org/statistics/

Map 3. Inequalities in the wider Europe and in the US at the turn of the 21st Century (UNDP data).

EUROPE IN THE 21ST CENTURY – SHRINKING SAVINGS RATES, FALTERING MASS DEMAND

The following inferences about rising income inequality and reduced mass demand in Europe under the constraints of globalization are based on the political economy of Franco Modigliani. In the post-WWII-world in which the often neglected great political Italian American economist Franco Modigliani (1918 – 2003) – who won the Nobel Prize in Economics in 1985 - wrote his path-breaking essays on the life cycle, savings and the wealth of nations, the division between the centers, the peripheries and the semi-peripheries was relatively stable. Modigliani above all shows to us what happens with the saving rate as the main expression of past economic growth and past "mass demand".

The analysis of long-run saving trends suggest that the centers of gravity in the world economy are dramatically shifting towards the Asia-Pacific region, and he days of "Eurocentrism" are really outnumbered.

World system and dependency scholars have always maintained that conditions of economic and social "injustice" drain the societal savings rates and block productive investments in the periphery and the semi-periphery. On the other hand, conditions of mass demand, economic justice and economic growth provide a powerful impetus for the savings rate. It is more than symbolic that the highest negative correlation of the savings rate is with the variable: food consumption as % of total household consumption, while the highest positive correlation of the saving rate is with the UNDP human development index. *"Social justice"* enhances savings.

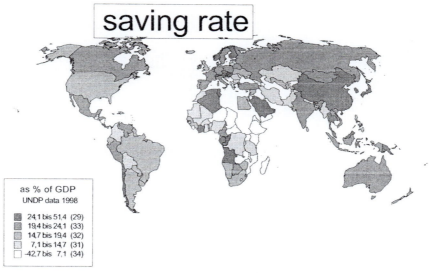

Note: Missing values for Greenland, Antarctica, and several countries in the Balkan region, Africa and West Asia.

Map 4. The political economic geography of saving rates today.

Modigliani was right in assuming – to put in the language of world system theory - that the dynamics of saving rates reflect the underlying dynamic of the world capitalist system. Our following map clearly shows this:

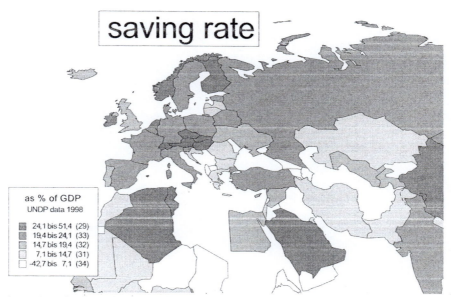

Note: Missing values for Greenland, Antarctica, and several countries in the Balkan region, Africa and West Asia.

Legend: missing values for Antarctica, some African and Balkan countries

Map 5. The dynamics of saving rates in the 1990s – correlation of saving rates with the time axis since 1990.

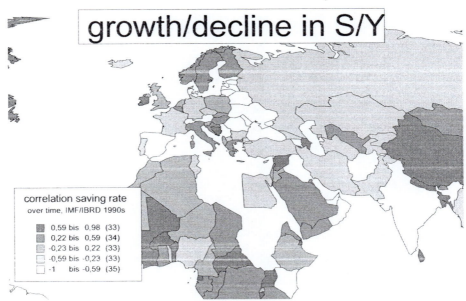

Legend: missing values for Antarctica, some African and Balkan countries

In the countries of the European Union, the following time series correlations of the saving rate could be observed in the 1990s.

Table 10. Time Series Correlations Of Saving Rates in the
European Union from 1990 to 1999

	correlations
Romania	-0.8470339
Latvia	-0.8438029
Austria	-0.7707177
Malta	-0.7231613
Spain	-0.7194430
Lithuania	-0.6727442
Denmark	-0.6606365
Estonia	-0.6419052
Portugal	-0.5890469
Germany	-0.3910182
Czech Republic	-0.3250650
France	-0.2843949
Slovenia	-0.1932458
Poland	-0.1690530
Netherlands	-0.1399943
Cyprus	-0.0770066
United Kingdom	0.1658408
Slovak Republic	0.2209186
Sweden	0.2478183
Greece	0.3735193
Hungary	0.4617506
Belgium	0.5296027
Finland	0.5844432
Italy	0.5845099
Luxembourg	0.8992010
Ireland	0.9432118

Our maps again show the relevance of the "Re-Orient" hypothesis by Professor Andre Gunder Frank and the dramatic decline and growing impoverishment of the Euro-Atlantic region. The future of the world system lies in the Pacific.

THE PERIPHERIZATION PROCESS AND THE TECTONIC SHIFTS IN THE INTERNATIONAL SYSTEM TO WHICH IMPLEMENTATION OF PRICE REFORM (EUROSTAT "COMPARATIVE PRICE LEVEL" INDICATOR) CONTRIBUTES

Comparative "price levels" are, the Eurostat definition goes, the ratio between GDP at purchasing power parities (PPPs) and GDP at market exchange rates for each country. To quote Eurostat:

"Comparative price levels are the ratio between Purchasing power parities (PPPs) and market exchange rate for each country. PPPs are currency conversion rates that convert economic indicators expressed in national currencies to a common currency, called Purchasing Power Standard (PPS), which equalises the purchasing power of different national currencies and thus allows meaningful comparison. The ratio is shown in relation to the EU average (EU-25 = 100). If the index of the comparative price levels shown for a country is higher/ lower than 100, the country concerned is relatively expensive/cheap as compared with the EU average." (Quotation from Eurostat website, April 6, 2005, at: *http://epp.eurostat.cec.eu.int/portal/page?_pageid=1133,1406352,1133_140637 3and_dad=portaland_schema=PORTAL*

The Commission and its statistical apparatus Eurostat, as well as the member governments who all sanctioned that, oddly enough, contribute and contributed to the peripherization process in Europe by the politically binding "price level indicator" in the Eurostat main structural Lisbon indicator series. The necessary debate about the peripherization of Europe is just at the beginning. *"Comparative price levels"*, measure nothing else than the reciprocal value of our variable "unequal exchange" (ERDI). A country, following the Commission's price reform strategy, is a country with a low international price level and a high ERDI.

As is well known, the EU-25 member governments to monitor their progress towards reaching the famous Lisbon agenda use the „structural indicators". Eurostat says on its website that the

"shortlist allows for a more concise presentation and a better assessment of achievements over time vis-à-vis the Lisbon agenda. In keeping with the recent streamlining of procedures in the wider context of the Lisbon strategy, it is foreseen to keep this list stable for three years".

The short-listed indicators are:

- GDP per capita in PPS
- Labor productivity
- Employment rate
- Employment rate of older workers
- Educational attainment (20-24)
- Research and Development expenditure
- Comparative price levels
- Business investment
- At risk-of-poverty rate
- Long-term unemployment rate
- Dispersion of regional employment rates
- Greenhouse gas emissions
- Energy intensity of the economy
- Volume of freight transport

A number of European economists, among them Dr. Ewald Walterskirchen[14] from the Austrian Institute for Economic Research (WIFO) have criticized the "price level" index used by Eurostat.

In the literature, we find a clarification for this price level concept. One important source would be of course the work by the eminent Turkish economist Prof. Cem Somel from Middle East Technical University in Ankara, published under the title "Estimating the surplus in the periphery: an application to Turkey" in *Cambridge Journal of Economics* 27:919-933 (2003). We have to assume that the Eurostat numerical values for the index were calculated by GDP exchange rates divided by GDP purchasing power parity in line with the logic described, inter alia, by Rao, who supports such reasoning in a background paper for the UNDP in 1998 by saying:

> "The Exchange Rate Deviation Index or ERD is measured as the ratio of GDP at international prices relative to GDP at national prices. Since both are measured in terms of the US $ numeraire, the ratio is the (weighted average) international price level relative to the respective country's national price level (P^{IP}/P_i^{NP}). Following the ICP (i.e. International Comparison Programme (ICP) of the United Nations Kravis et al.) results, this ratio is greater than one for the LDCs and negatively related to income levels. (...) Price levels have risen faster than world price levels for the rich countries while the reverse has been the case for the poor countries. (...) Evidence over several decades thus fails to sustain the expectation of growing price convergence from growing globalization. (...) These findings call for a reassessment of the theoretical basis for favoring liberal, free trade policies, i.e. the mechanisms that are routinely adduced to assert a connection between free trade and growth" (Rao J. M., 1998: 14-15).

But the theoretical problems connected with this concept are, as Professor Cem Somel has shown in his referred *"Cambridge Journal of Economics"* article, manifold, and open a veritable Pandora's box of debates in social and economic theory. The usual explanation for the phenomenon is the different weight of tradables and non-tradables in the GDP of poorer and richer nations[15]. Falling relative price levels in countries like Germany over the last years would suggest in the neo-classical argument that the weight of the non-tradables in the German economy increased dramatically over time.

The argument made by Yotopoulos and Sawada however is worthwhile remembering here:

> "Currency substitution represents an asymmetric demand from Mexicans to hold dollars as a store of value, a demand that is not reciprocated by Americans holding pesos as a hedge against the devaluation of the dollar!"

Yotopoulos and Sawada then establish in their 1999 paper, refined in their 2005 analysis, the so-called Y-Proposition:

---

[14] http://www.iv-mitgliederservice.at/iv-all/dokumente/doc_2063.pdf

[15] For a heterodox view the recent papers by Stanford emeritus Professor Pan Yotopoulos and Professor Yasuyuki Sawada from the University of Tokyo at http://www.e.u-tokyo.ac.jp/cirje/research/dp/2005/2005cf318.pdf as well as http://siepr.stanford.edu/papers/pdf/99-4.pdf and http://www.esri.go.jp/en/archive/e_dis/abstract/e_dis007-e.html should be consulted.

"in free currency markets hard currencies fluctuate, while soft currencies depriciate systematically (...) The alternative scenario deprives devaluation of any of its remedial properties that in the conventional view lead to a process of stable interactions and equilibrium...."

They go on to show that the basic problem of international currency markets is *asymmetric reputation.*

This process of asymmetric reputation of the periphery deepens the cycle of underdevelopment:

"Mexico cannot service its foreign debt from the proceeds of producing nontradables. These are traded in pesos. It has instead to shift resources away from the nontradable sector to produce tradable output in order to procure the dollars for servicing the debt (...) The process (...) can create a negative feedback loop that leads to resource misallocation in soft-currency countries (...) This shift of resources represents misallocation and produces inefficiency and output losses (...) Distortions inherent in free currency markets lead to a systematic devaluation of soft currencies – to „high" nominal exchange rates. Devaluation of the exchange rate means increasing prices of tradables and leads to increased exports. But not all exports are a bargain to produce compared to the alternative of producing nontradables (...) Countries graduate from being exporters of sugar and copra to exporting their teak forests, and on to systematically exporting nurses and doctors, while they remain underdeveloped all the same. If this happens, it may represent competitive devaluation trade as opposed to comparative advantage trade."

The authors further explain their ideas by an econometric analysis of economic growth rates in 62 countries from 1970 onwards that shows how this process of competitive devaluation trade leads to stagnation. They also present an economic model in the tradition of Paul Krugman that shows how currency substitution triggers financial crises. In their 2005 paper, the authors show the relevance of their theories with time series data from 153 countries. Thus, if they are correct, a high ratio between purchasing power and GDP at exchange rates, i.e. an under-valued currency, will lead to stagnation. The countries with the strongest currencies, like Denmark, the UK, Sweden, are typical centers of the capitalist world economy with a favorable ratio of tradables to non-tradables, while the countries with a Eurostat "good" low price level, like Turkey, are countries with an unfavorable relation between tradables and non-tradables, suffering from what neo-Marxists like to call "unequal transfer" or "unequal exchange" (price reform (low international price level).

A good world system proxy for the "comparative price level" proposed by Eurostat could be simply to calculate internationally, for each country of the world, GDP per capita exchange rates/GDP per capita PPP, and then fix the value for the United States of America as 1. High numerical values, under any specification, using the Eurostat method or proxy methods, will correspond, as in the Eurostat statistic, to countries like Norway, and low values will correspond to countries like Romania. A lowering of the indicator will, according to the underlying Eurostat logic, mean "price reform", while a hypothetical movement upwards on the indicator (in our Table for Turkey from, say, 55 to 110) will mean a "setback". However, a closer look at the underlying logic immediately tells us that such a "setback" could be brought about the appreciation of the Turkish Lira over time, while Turkey under this logic, for all purposes, "wonderfully performed" during the disastrous currency crisis of 1994 and 2001 which impoverished large strata of the population.

The relationship between GDP per capita at PPP and undervalued/overvalued exchange rates was introduced, among others in the classic article by Kravis, Heston and Summers, available freely online at: http://www.roiw.org/1981/339.pdf

Ever since the famous Kravis, Heston and Summers study, the relationship between the real GDP per capita income level and the ratio GDP PPP/GDP per capita has been thought to be an inverse one. Kravis, Heston and Summers say on page 344 of their famous article:

> "That is, the exchange-rate-converted estimates of GDP tend to understate the real GDPs of poor countries relative to the GDPs of the US and Europe. The systematic relationship between the ICP estimates and the exchange-rate-derived figures may be clearly seen by arranging the countries in order of increasing real GDP per capita; it can then be seen clearly that the ratio of real GDP per capita to exchange-rate converted GDP per capita – the "exchange rate-deviation index" – falls as per capita real GDP rises (..). A systematic association between the exchange-rate-deviation index and the level of real GDP per capita is a basic structural feature of the world economy" (Kravis, Heston and Summers, op. cit. p. 344)

The richer you are, the lesser you are confronted with the factor GDP PPP divided by GDP exchange rates.

A movement of countries over time on the "price reform" front could be brought about (with other things being equal), by a sharp decline in the external value of the currency or by an increase in the purchasing power at home. The pessimism, regarding the asymmetric reputation of currencies in the world system, proposed by Yotopoulos, is again re-vindicated in our graphs about the rise of "asymmetric reputation over time" or "price reform" and unemployment and our evidence about the effects of the absence of "asymmetric reputation" or "price reform" on the income of the poor in the world system. Assuming the logic, described by Rao (1998), and comparing the movements of the ERD over time (DYN GDP PPP/DYN GDP exchange rate[16]) with the country to country time series correlation of unemployment rates on the time axis, calculated from the ILO Laborsta data set[17], we arrive at the following relationship between the *dynamics* of implied *"asymmetric reputation"* (or the dynamics of "price reform" in the sense of Rao/Eurostat) and the *dynamics* of unemployment in the world system.

Yotopoulos is also right in assuming that a numerically high relationship between GDP per capita exchange rate divided by GDP PPP has – contrary to much of the current debate – a developmentally positive effect on most of the basic human needs indicators. The price level (GDP exchange rate/GDP PPP) neatly determines the buying power of the poorest 20% in the nations of the world system. With the UNDP Human Development Indicators, 2000 we also show that a *high price level* (in the terminology of Eurostat) is exceptionally highly and positively correlated with positive indicators of the development performance of a nation, and very highly negatively correlated with indicators of human misery.

---

[16] calculated from UNDP Human Development Reports, 2000 - 2004

[17] http://laborsta.ilo.org/

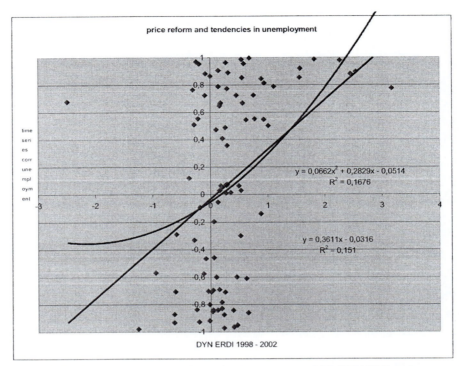

Legend: ERDI is defined according to Kravis, Heston, Summers as = GDP PPP/GDP exchange rate

Graph 4. The rising rates of price reform (low international price level) and rising unemployment in the world system.

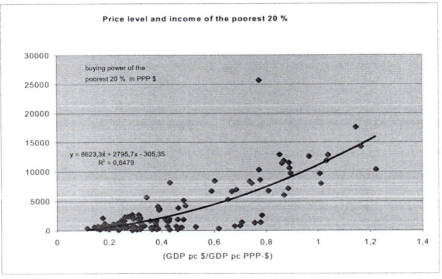

Source: Our own calculations from UNDP sources.

Graph 5. Price levels and the buying power of the poorest 20% in the countries of the world system.

Table 11. "Price Level", Eurostat Concept, and Social Well-Being
(UNDP HDR Data, 2000)

	correlation with price level
GNP per capita	0.93
women's GDP per capita	0.88
GDP per capita PPP	0.88
main telephone lines per 1000 people	0.84
GDP output per kg energy use	0.80
gender empowerment	0.75
Televisions per 1000 people	0.72
human development index	0.69
internet hosts per 1000 people	0.62
daily supply of calories, 1998	0.62
% population, aged >65y, 1998	0.61
life expectancy, 1995-2000	0.58
male life expectancy	0.57
female life expectancy	0.56
contraceptive prevalence rate	0.54
injuries and deaths from road accidents per 100.000 inhabitants and year	0.54
public health expenditure per GDP	0.52
female literacy	0.51
male literacy	0.49
% parliamentary seats held by women	0.45
gross domestic savings rate	0.42
doctors per 100.000 people	0.38
central government expenditures as % of GDP	0.36
% immunization against measles	0.33
% women in government, ministerial level	0.32
economic growth, 1975-98	0.30
female tertiary students as % of males	0.26
growth of female economic activity (1975=100)	0.23
GNP per capita annual growth rate, 1990-98	0.23
public education expenditure per GNP	0.22
overall budget surplus/deficit as % of GDP	0.22
% women in government, all levels	0.20
% women in government, sub ministerial level	0.12
female unemployment rate	-0.16
youth female unemployment rate	-0.17
juvenile convictions as % of all convictions	-0.18
HIV rate	-0.21
share of income/consumption richest 20% to poorest 20%	-0.23
male unemployment rate	-0.24
food imports as % of merchandise imports	-0.29
youth male unemployment rate	-0.29
TBC cases per 100.000 inhabitants	-0.31
% infants with low birth-weight	-0.41
maternal mortality ratio	-0.44
% people not expected to survive age 60	-0.53
teen-age mothers as % of all mothers	-0.53
infant mortality rate	-0.55
food consumption as % of total household consumption	-0.67

It would have to be expected that movements in the direction of a "lower price level" lead indeed to social imbalances and crises. The misery that Latin America is facing is in stark contrast to the relative well being of countries that did not significantly lower their internationally comparable price levels, including the Lisbon target country United States of America.

Our following maps show the dramatic world shifts in price levels relative to the United States in recent years. Contrary to what European policy makers expected with their Eurostat *politically binding price level indicator*, which is, after all, *one of their 14 main Lisbon targets*, the United States as the Lisbon competition country was a high price region throughout much of the late 1990s and the early 2000s, as is evident from our own maps 11 – 15 and also the graph drawn with the Eurostat numbers:

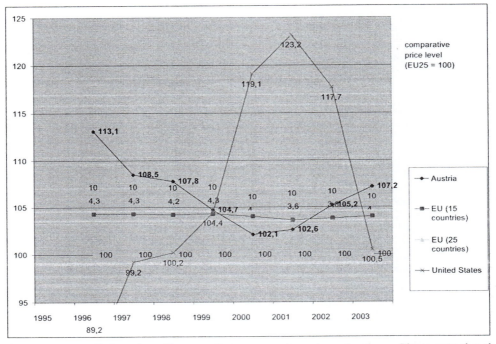

Legend: our own compilations from Eurostat. See our remarks and graphs above. Please note that the "high price level" in the US between 1998 and 2003 is a function of the high value of the US Dollar on international currency markets, which coincides with the Eurostat price level curve for the US which has the shape of an inverted U.

Graph 6. Relative prices in the United States and in Europe.

In 1998, and in comparison to the US, Canada and Australia, much of Europe was still a high-price region.

It is important to grasp the *"tectonic shifts"* that underlie this process. The net result that brought about the time period of the Euro experiment (however much we might disagree on the causal processes behind it) was a Europe that shifted much more towards becoming a *low-price region* than the United States. Thus the warnings of many observers about "Euro-monetarist fundamentalism" are in our view correct.

comp. price levels, 1998

US = 100

148 bis 159	(1)
133 bis 148	(3)
118 bis 133	(5)
103 bis 118	(7)
88 bis 103	(7)
73 bis 88	(7)
58 bis 73	(19)
43 bis 58	(27)
28 bis 43	(47)
13 bis 28	(38)

Legend: "bis" is the shorthand for "ranging from" "to". Countries marked in green color: missing values.

Map 6. Comparative price levels (US=100) in the world system, 1998.

In 2002 however, important European countries had a lower relative price level than the United States.

comp. price levels, 2002

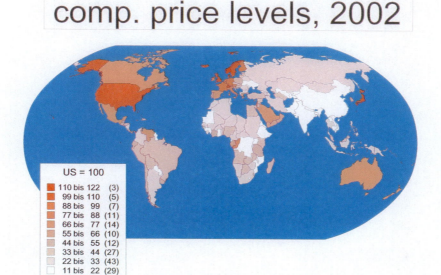

US = 100

110 bis 122	(3)
99 bis 110	(5)
88 bis 99	(7)
77 bis 88	(11)
66 bis 77	(14)
55 bis 66	(10)
44 bis 55	(12)
33 bis 44	(27)
22 bis 33	(43)
11 bis 22	(29)

Legend: "bis" is the shorthand for "ranging from" "to". Countries marked in green color: missing values.

Map 7. Comparative price levels, 2002 (US=100). The United States became a global high-price country, while several European countries lost their relative position.

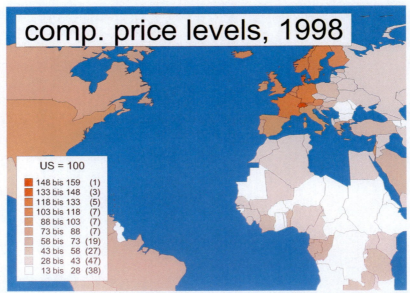

Legend: "bis" is the shorthand for "ranging from" "to". Countries marked in green color: missing values.

Map 8. Comparisons of the shifts, 1998 – 2002 in the "Atlantic arena".

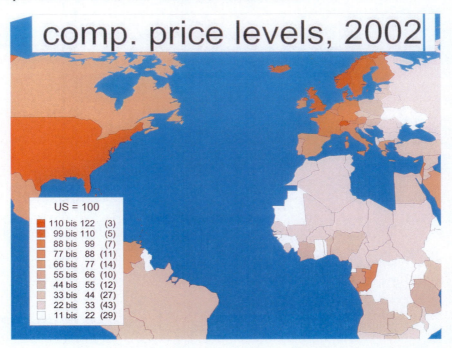

Legend: "bis" is the shorthand for "ranging from" "to". Countries marked in green color: missing values.

Our following map shows the radical character of the neo-liberal transformation that many European nations had undergone in what Rao called *"the growing price convergence from growing globalization."* Europe pushed liberal, free trade policies, pushing down its price level in a much more radical fashion than the United States of America.

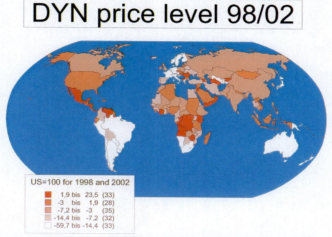

Legend: "bis" is the shorthand for "ranging from" "to". Countries marked in green color: missing
      values.
DYN price level = (100/ERD 2002*0,9927670) – (100/ERD 1998*1,01248497).
ERD US 2002 = 0,9927670; ERD US 1998 = 1,01248497.

Map 9. The shifts 1998 – 2002 in a systematic perspective. (note that the value for the US is 0, because it is the standard for the calculation.

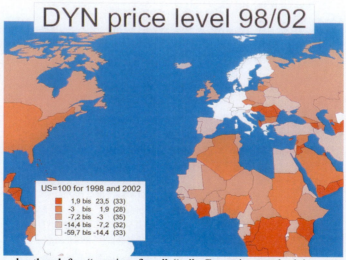

Legend: "bis" is the shorthand for "ranging from" "to". Countries marked in green color: missing
      values.
DYN price level = (100/ERD 2002*0,9927670) – (100/ERD 1998*1,01248497).
ERD US 2002 = 0,9927670; ERD US 1998 = 1,01248497.

Our prediction is that dissatisfaction with European Monetary Union and Maastricht will rise in the wake of the 2 failed referenda on the European Constitution in France and in the Netherlands.

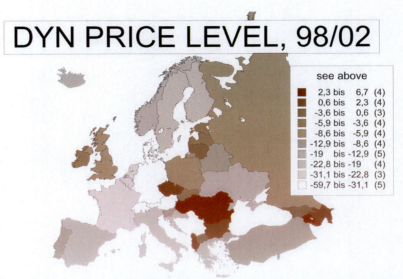

Legend: "bis" is the shorthand for "ranging from" "to". Countries marked in green color: missing values.

Map 10. Comparative price level shifts in Europe (US=100).

By and large, it is shown that the member countries of the "old" EU-15, and especially the Euro zone countries, are on the losing side in that transnational equation. No "old" European country improved its position; on the contrary, "old Europe" becomes a region that is itself a victim of unequal transfer. It also emerges that *ceteris paribus* the Muslim world indeed became the main loser of these tectonic shifts. A positive sign of a regression coefficient in our equation below must be interpreted as an increase of the negative phenomenon in the structures of price reform (low international price level).

Table 12. The Determinants of a Rising Rate of Price Reform (Low International Price Level), 1998 – 2002

	changes in (un)equal transfer 1998 – 2002: explaining movements in the direction of price reform (low international price level), 1998 – 2002 left column: un-standardized regression coefficients second column: standard error of the estimate				t-test[18]
% population, aged >65y, 1998	0.097	0.273	r^2=0.145	F = 1.2416	0.354
% women in government, ministerial level	0.103	0.095		df = 95	1.085

---

[18] (p<.10; two-tailed test)

Table 12. (Continued)

	changes in (un)equal transfer 1998 – 2002: explaining movements in the direction of price reform (low international price level), 1998 – 2002 left column: un-standardized regression coefficients second column: standard error of the estimate				t-test
(I-S)/GNP	-1.835	1.490			-1.231
Absence of economic freedom	-0.158	0.231			-0.683
military expenditure as % of GDP	-0.001	0.009			-0.064
MNC PEN 1995	-0.162	0.110			-1.479
public education expenditure per GNP	0.003	0.052			0.065
initial low level of prices (ERDI, 1998)	0.007	0.005			1.266
EU-membership years by 2004	-0.009	0.050			-0.177
Islamic conference	0.418	0.220			1.902
ln(GDP PPP pc)	-0.001	0.008			-0.176
ln (GDP PPP pc)^2	0.015	0.013			1.167
pension reform	-0.034	0.036			-0.959
Constant	7.644	5.710			1.339

Legend: the error probability for the entire equation is rather unsatisfactory ($p = 0,264$); the error probabilities for the predictors are:

% population, aged >65y, 1998	0.7241
% women in government, ministerial level	0.2807
(IS)/GNP	0.2214
Absence of economic freedom	0.4963
military expenditure as % of GDP	0.9491
MNC PEN 1995	0.1424
public education expenditure per GNP	0.9483
ERDI, 1998	0.2086
EU membership years by 2004	0.8599
Islamic conference	*0.0602*
ln(GDP PPP pc)	0.8607
ln (GDP PPP pc)^2	0.2461
pension reform	0.3400

It is entirely conceivable that these pressures – as Gernot Kohler has shown and as we already hinted at above – also explain a good part of the negative trends on the labor markets in the Muslim countries and in Europe. Graph 7 and the following maps about changing unemployment in the global system provide the tentative answer.

DYN unemployment 1980-2001

correlation over time
unemployment (ILO)

- 0,87 bis 1,01 (17)
- 0,55 bis 0,87 (20)
- -0,09 bis 0,55 (20)
- -0,7 bis -0,09 (16)
- -1 bis -0,7 (23)

Legend: "bis" is the shorthand for "ranging from" "to". Countries marked in green color: missing values. Our own compilations from Laborsta (ILO). No data for wide parts of Africa and West Asia.

Map 11. The changing structure of unemployment in the world system.

Unemployment 2000

ILO Laborsta unemployment
rate

- 12,5 bis 30,5 (19)
- 9,2 bis 12,5 (15)
- 6,8 bis 9,2 (16)
- 4,1 bis 6,8 (16)
- 1,3 bis 4,1 (18)

Legend: "bis" is the shorthand for "ranging from" "to". Countries marked in green color: missing values. Our own compilations from Laborsta (ILO). No data for wide parts of Africa and West Asia.

Map 12. Unemployment in the world system.

Globalization and Social Performance – Our Own Macro-Quantitative Results for the 1980s, 1990s and beyond

We will now analyze the consequences of "price reform" on the international level, compared to the effects of other dependency variables, state interventions in the economy versus economic freedom, the aging process, institutionalized feminism, and world political determinants of economic growth and social well-being, like military expenditures, EU-membership or membership in the Islamic Conference. We do this by drawing reference to a 109 country cross-national analysis of the determinants of economic, social and political development, presented in Tausch (2005c).

The choice of the 109 countries was determined by the availability of a complete data series for the independent variables (if not mentioned otherwise, UNDP data):

% population, aged >65y, 1998
% women in government, ministerial level
(I-S)/GDP (calculated from UNDP)
state interventionism (absence of economic freedom; Heritage Foundation and Wall Street Journal website for economic freedom[19], 2000)
EU-membership by 2000
Islamic conference membership (OIC website[20])
ln (GDP PPP pc)^2
ln(GDP PPP pc)
military expenditure as % of GDP
MNC PEN 1995 (UNCTAD)
public education expenditure per GDP
price reform (low international price level) (calculated from UNDP, concept: ERDI)

The following dependent variables were used; with list wise deletion of missing values each time determining the number of countries entering into the 14 final regression equations:

% people not expected to survive age 60
CO_2 emissions per capita
development stability (year with highest real income minus year with lowest real income) since 1975 (calculated from UNDP)
ESI-Index (Yale/Columbia environment sustainability index project website[21])

---

[19] http://www.freetheworld.com/; also: http://www.heritage.org/research/features/index/. We used the latter website as the source of our data. It has to be kept in mind, that the "worst" countries on the economic freedom scale have the numerically highest values, while the best countries have the numerically lowest values. Lao People's Dem. Rep. – the economically "unfreest" country in our sample, has the numerical value 4.6, while the economically freest country, Singapore, scores 1.45. We thus decided to call our indicator "state interventionism"

[20] http://www.oic-oci.org/ there the icon "members"

[21] http://www.ciesin.org/indicators/ESI/ We have chosen the 2001 data series at http://www.ciesin.org/indicators/ESI/archive.html. The general description of this indicator says that the

Factor Social Development (Tausch, 2001b, calculated from 35 UNDP social indicators, SPSS factor analysis[22])

female economic activity rate as % of male economic activity rate

female share in total life years (calculated from UNDP – share of female life expectancy in the sum of male and female life expectancy)

GDP output per kg energy use *("eco-social market economy"[23])*

GDP per capita annual growth rate, 1990-98

human development index

life expectancy, 1995-2000

Political rights violations (Freedom House, 2000[24])

share of income/consumption richest 20% to poorest 20%

unemployment (UN social indicators website)

The following countries featured in the analysis: Albania; Algeria; Argentina; Armenia; Australia; Austria; Azerbaijan; Bahrain; Bangladesh; Belarus; Belgium; Belize; Bolivia; Botswana; Brazil; Bulgaria; Burkina Faso; Burundi; Cambodia; Chad; Chile; China; Colombia; Costa Rica; Côte d'Ivoire; Croatia; Cyprus; Czech Republic; Denmark; Egypt; El Salvador; Estonia; Ethiopia; Fiji; Finland; France; Gabon; Gambia; Georgia; Germany; Ghana; Greece; Guatemala; Guyana; Honduras; Hungary; India; Indonesia; Iran, Islamic Rep. of; Ireland; Israel; Italy; Japan; Jordan; Kazakhstan; Kenya; Kyrgyzstan; Lao People's Dem. Rep.; Latvia; Lebanon; Lesotho; Lithuania; Luxembourg; Madagascar; Malawi; Malaysia; Mali; Malta; Mauritania; Mexico; Moldova, Rep. of; Mongolia; Namibia; Nepal; Netherlands; New Zealand; Nicaragua; Nigeria; Norway; Pakistan; Panama; Philippines; Poland; Portugal; Romania; Russian Federation; Saudi Arabia; Senegal; Singapore; Slovakia; Slovenia; South Africa; Spain; Sri Lanka; Sweden; Switzerland; Syrian Arab Republic;

'Environmental Sustainability Index (ESI) is a measure of overall progress towards environmental sustainability, developed for 142 countries. The ESI scores are based upon a set of 20 core "indicators," each of which combines two to eight variables for a total of 68 underlying variables. The ESI permits cross-national comparisons of environmental progress in a systematic and quantitative fashion. It represents a first step towards a more analytically driven approach to environmental decision making.'

[22] Female life expectancy; life expectancy, 1995-2000; life expectancy, 1970-75; male life expectancy; human development index; female literacy; male literacy; contraceptive prevalence; daily supply of calories; immunization against measles; public health expenditure; doctors per inhabitants; average cigarette consumption; female tertiary students as % of male tertiary students; parliamentary seats held by women; gender empowerment; women's GDP per capita in purchasing power; growth of female economic activity; public education expenditure; women in government, ministerial level; women in government, all levels; female share in professional and technical workforce; women in government, sub-ministerial level; female share in administrative and managerial workforce; female economic activity rate as % of male economic activity rate; teen-age mothers; food import dependence; share of top 20% compared to bottom 20% in income distribution; female economic activity rate; TBC cases per 100,000 inhabitants; HIV rate; infants with low birth-weight; maternal mortality rate; infant mortality rate; % of people not expected to survive age 60.

[23] This term is most probably an Austrian invention. The governing Conservative People's Party – to be precise, its former Chairman Dr. Josef Riegler – seems to have invented this term in the late 1980s. For more on that debate: http://www.nachhaltigkeit.at/bibliothek/pdf/Factsheet11OekosozMarktw.pdf; and Michael Rösch, Tubingen University at http://tiss.zdv.uni-tuebingen.de/webroot/sp/spsba01_W98_1/germany1b.htm. As an indicator of the reconciliation between the price mechanism and the environment we propose the indicator GDP output per kg energy use; the term 'eco-social market economy' neatly grasps all the aspects of this empirical formulation

[24] Taken here from Stiftung Entwicklung und Frieden, edition 2002. The political freedom data referring to the year 2000 can also be downloaded at: http://www.freedomhouse.org/ratings/index.htm

Tajikistan; Thailand; Tunisia; Turkey; Uganda; United Kingdom; United States; Uzbekistan; Venezuela; Yemen; Zambia; Zimbabwe.

Summarizing the main theoretical expectations, we could present the following diagram. The variables for the *"Washington Consensus"* are:

State interventionism (absence of economic freedom; Heritage Foundation and Wall Street Journal website for economic freedom, 2000). Effect on development: MNC PEN 1995 (UNCTAD). Effect on development: +price reform (calculated from UNDP, concept: ERDI). Effect on development: +We have to start here from the assumption that the basic tools of multivariate macro-quantitative analysis in political science and sociology are known to the audience of this article (for further literature on the subject, see Achen; Clauss and Ebner; Huang; Jackman; Kriz; Krzysztofiak. and Luszniewicz; Lewis - Beck; Microsoft Excel; Opp and Schmidt).

A sophisticated re-analysis of the tendencies of world development in the 1990s should start from the assumption that the development level has a decisive, non-linear trade-off with subsequent development performance: poor countries increase rapidly their average life expectancy or economic growth and they quickly reduce their income inequality etc.

Social scientists interpreted this effect mainly in view of an acceleration of economic growth in middle-income countries *vis-à-vis* the poor countries and in view of the still widening gap between the poorest periphery nations *('have-nots')* and the *'haves'* among the former Second and Third World (Tausch/Herrmann, 2002):

(Equation 1) development performance = a1 + b1* $\ln (PCI_m)$ - b2* $(\ln (PCI_m))2$

The same function is also applied to income inequality and the rest of our 14 indicators, following a famous essay published by S. Kuznets in 1955. Growth and development accelerate with redistribution, and then stagnate. In general terms, we explain development performance by the following standard multiple cross-national development research equation:

(Equation 2) development performance $_{1990 - end\ 1990s}$ = a_1 +- b_1*first part curvilinear function of development level +- b_2*second part curvilinear function of development level +- b_3 **transnational investment per GDP* (UNCTAD) $_{mid\ 1990s}$ +- b_4 **price reform (low international price level)* (ERDI) +- b_5 * *foreign saving* +- b_6 * *military expenditures per GDP* +- b_7 * *aging* +- b_8 * *public education expenditures per GDP* +-b_9 * *membership in the Islamic Conference* +- b_{10} * *European Union membership* +- b_{11} * *absence of economic freedom (state interventionism)*

In the following, we will present our results about the effects of globalization in a multivariate perspective.

The Final Results for 109 Countries

In general terms, several but not all aspects of the presented theories are confirmed, while other central assumptions of both the *"Washington Consensus"* and of its dependency theory counterpart are rejected. Also, theories about aging; feminist theories; human resource theories; military Keynesian theories/peace theories (i.e. theories maintaining that militarism has a very bad effect on long-run development); globalization critique and international economic integration theories have to tally with both positive and negative effects of their key indicators on different measurements of social, environmental and economic welfare, indicating that the time of the "quick fixes" has definitely gone and that contemporary development realities are very complex indeed. It should be noted that in this and in the following presentations, we already considered duly that "good effects" are "good effects" and that "bad effects" are "bad effects" when presenting our results; i.e. a development strategy that *increases*, say, under 60 *mortality* rates, is a *bad* strategy and thus has *negative* effects.

Our results can now be summarized briefly as follows:

Aging is part and parcel of the structure of industrialized societies, East and West. Aging contributes to a generalized scarcity of labor, which in turn leads to improved distributive relationships between the rich and the poor. However, several negative effects must also be considered properly – especially the negative effects of an aging population structure on the process of human development, which is basically the dire consequence of unreformed pension systems (Tausch, 2003).

	aging: % population, aged >65y, 1998
GDP output per kg energy use (eco-social market economy)	positive
female economic activity rate as % of male economic activity rate	positive
share of income/consumption richest 20% to poorest 20% (income redistribution)	positive
unemployment (UN) (employment)	positive
CO_2 emissions per capita (Kyoto)	negative
female share in total life years	negative
% people not expected to survive age 60 (survival)	negative
life expectancy, 1995-2000	negative
Factor Social Development	negative
human development index	negative

Political feminism has an aggregate positive effect on many phenomena of human and ecological development, but it fails to transform political power into improved employment and distribution structures. This is due mainly to the process of distribution coalition formation, featuring so prominently in neo-liberal theories of economic growth (see especially, the writings of Weede).

	political feminism % women in government, ministerial level
CO2 emissions per capita (Kyoto)	positive
female share in total life years	positive
% people not expected to survive age 60 (survival)	positive
life expectancy, 1995-2000	positive
Factor Social Development	positive
human development index	positive
GDP output per kg energy use (eco-social market economy)	negative
female economic activity rate as % of male economic activity rate	negative
share of income/consumption richest 20% to poorest 20% (income redistribution)	negative
unemployment (UN) (employment)	negative

As one of the three main indicators of dependency, the reliance on *foreign savings* eases the distribution burden against the poorer segments of society during the accumulation process, but it has several negative effects on a variety of other development processes, including the environment and political democracy.

	foreign saving (I-S)/GDP
share of income/consumption richest 20% to poorest 20% (income redistribution)	positive
CO2 emissions per capita (Kyoto)	negative
human development index	negative
ESI-Index (sustainability)	negative
Political rights	negative

Absence of economic freedom (state interventionism), paradoxically enough, increases the rationality of the societal resource allocation and leads towards an improved development stability but it fails to resolve two basic issues: overall environmental stress and societal sexism in the employment sphere. State interventionism has negative consequences for women as the more vulnerable group in society.

	absence of economic freedom (state interventionism)
CO2 emissions per capita (Kyoto)	positive
GDP output per kg energy use (eco-social market economy)	positive
development stability (year with highest real income minus year with lowest real income) since 1975	positive
ESI-Index (sustainability)	negative
female share in total life years	negative
female economic activity rate as % of male economic activity rate	negative

Military expenditures have a certain Keynesian effect but they contribute towards a worse environmental balance. Military expenditures lead towards a drying up of what Marxists term "the reserve army of labor", which, in turn, leads to a certain better social cohesion and employment gender balance. But militarized structures consume large amounts of fossil fuel, with advanced air forces especially contributing to that process.

female economic activity rate as % of male economic activity rate	positive
share of income/consumption richest 20% to poorest 20% (income redistribution)	positive
CO2 emissions per capita (Kyoto)	negative
GDP output per kg energy use (eco-social market economy)	negative

MNC penetration contributes to an improved ESI Index and towards better female employment, but it has negative consequences for human survival and life expectancy. In addition, an interesting phenomenon worthy of further research is the interconnection between decaying public services, decaying public transport and decaying public health services in the host countries of transnational investment on the one hand and the strategic policies of transnational corporations on the other hand, concentrated on the private sector, private transport, private medical services and the private automobile. The strengthening triple alliance between the MNCs, local capital and the state is a net result of the globalization process, and it still has dire social consequences as well.

	dependency on foreign capital MNC PEN 1995
female economic activity rate as % of male economic activity rate	positive
ESI-Index (sustainability)	positive
% people not expected to survive age 60 (survival)	negative
life expectancy, 1995-2000	negative

Human resources and human development investments ever since the publication of the first United Nations Human Development Reports in the early 1990s are regarded as the key towards a socially equitable and sustainable development. However, as often happens in development theory, the early optimism regarding the effects of one variable has soon to be qualified. There are very surprising clear-cut negative interactions between *public education expenditure* and an eco-social market economy and political democracy. Positive effects exist as well, but they are not statistically significant. A plausible intervening variable, which we did not as yet consider in our investigation, could be the years of experience of a country as a centrally planned economy.

	public education expenditure per GDP
GDP output per kg energy use (eco-social market economy)	negative
Political rights	negative

Price reform (low international price level) has the most clear-cut negative results of all dependency indicators on the process of development, as understood in this investigation; especially on democracy, the environment, gender justice and employment. The positive effect on income redistribution has to be seen in the context of the siphoning-off of the surplus value from periphery countries that reduces the share of the richest 20% in total income distribution.

	price reform (low international price level)
share of income/consumption richest 20% to poorest 20% (income redistribution)	positive
GDP output per kg energy use (eco-social market economy)	negative
Political rights	negative
female economic activity rate as % of male economic activity rate	negative
ESI-Index (sustainability)	negative
CO_2 emissions per capita (Kyoto)	negative
female share in total life years	negative
unemployment (UN) (employment)	negative

There are very diverse views nowadays on the *European Union*. As an interesting paper, published in the journal *"Parameters"* of the US Army, maintains (Wilkie, 2003):

> "Still, there are those on both sides of the Atlantic who believe that the European Union, as an old-fashioned socialist bureaucracy, is "fundamentally unreformable" and also culturally hostile to the United States" (Wilkie, 2003: 46)[25]

There is a wide range of literature now available that highlights the negative effects of European integration in a globalized world economy (for a survey of the literature and politometric evidence, see Tausch and Herrmann, 2001). In the present research design, the most considerable effect is the negative trade-off between EU membership and political democracy, once you control for the other intervening variables that together explain jointly 66.1 % of political rights violations.

	EU-membership
Political rights	negative

The "real existing" Union will have a lot to do to fulfill the Lisbon agenda to become by 2010 *"...the most competitive and dynamic, knowledge-based economy in the world, capable of sustainable economic growth, creating more and better jobs and greater social cohesion"*[26]. The race between the Euro and the Dollar on the world currency markets has added to the sense of competition between the two systems that years ago were still considered to be the "Atlantic West". But even a first brief look at the EU's statistical

---

[25] http://carlisle-www.army.mil/usawc/Parameters/02winter/wilkie.htm

[26] http://www.bmaa.gv.at/view.php3?f_id=51&LNG=en&version=

website, Eurostat[27] shows how far "old Europe" (quotation from Donald Rumsfeld; in Brussels "newspeak" simply "the EU-15") or for that matter also "the old and the new Europe" (the "EU-25" now comprising 25 European states, including 8 former Communist states in East Central Europe, Cyprus and Malta after the enlargement of May 1st 2004) are still away from this goal of becoming the most competitive and dynamic economy in the world.

Our results about the European Union might be considered more provocative still, when we also consider that – contrary to popular assumptions – membership in the *Islamic Conference* is not an impediment to political democracy. Our results clearly contradict many of the expectations inherent in the writings of Professor Samuel Huntington. 4 development indicators – 2 for the environment, 1 on human development, and 1 on democracy – are positively and significantly determined by membership in the Islamic Conference, once you properly control the effects of the other influencing variables. However, gender justice and redistribution remain the "Achilles heel" of today's members in the Islamic Conference, strengthening the cause of those who advocate – like in the *United Nations Arab Human Development Report* – more social inclusion and more gender justice in the region.

	Islamic conference membership
Political rights	positive
GDP output per kg energy use (eco-social market economy)	positive
CO2 emissions per capita (Kyoto)	positive
life expectancy, 1995-2000	positive
share of income/consumption richest 20% to poorest 20% (income redistribution)	negative
female economic activity rate as % of male economic activity rate	negative

The well-known *acceleration* and *maturity* effects of development have to be qualified in an important way. Ever since the days of Simon *Kuznets*, development researchers have applied curve-linear formulations in order to capture these effects. However, the results for equation 1 above are not as clear-cut as one might have expected; and – in addition – the direction of the influence does hardly correspond with the equation. The curve-linear function of *growth*, being regressed on the natural logarithm of development level and its square, is sometimes called the 'Matthew's effect' following Matthew's (13, 12):

'For whosoever hath, to him shall be given, and he shall have more abundance: but whosoever hath not, for him shall be taken away even that he hath'

Social scientists interpreted this effect mainly in view of an acceleration of economic growth in middle-income countries vis-à-vis the poor countries and in view of the still widening gap between the poorest periphery nations ('have-nots') and the 'haves' among the semi-periphery countries (Jackman, 1982). Their hypothesis is only partially confirmed here –

---

[27] http://europa.eu.int/comm/eurostat/newcronos/reference/display.do?screen=detailref&language=de&product =EU_strind&root=EU_strind/strind/ecobac/eb011

there is no significant acceleration at low levels of development, but a significant economic growth stagnation/saturation effect. The first expression - + b1* ln (PCI*tn*) – yields the following results:

	acceleration effects development ln (GDP PPP pc)
female economic activity rate as % of male economic activity rate	positive

The second part of the "Kuznets-curve" - b2* (ln (PCI*tn*))2 - has today the following results:

	maturity effects development ln (GDP PPP pc)^2
female economic activity rate as % of male economic activity rate	positive
life expectancy, 1995-2000	positive
share of income/consumption richest 20% to poorest 20% (income redistribution)	positive
ESI-Index (sustainability)	positive
female share in total life years	positive
human development index	positive
Factor Social Development	positive
GNP per capita annual growth rate, 1990-98	negative

By far the *most negative influence* on development is wielded by *price* reform (low international price level), followed by the *aging process* (especially without *pension reform*) and certain negative aspects of *feminist distribution coalitions* in society:

	% negative effects	% positive effects	% insignificant effects
price reform (low international price level)	50.0	7.1	42.9
aging: % population, aged >65y, 1998	42.9	28.6	35.7
political feminism % women in government, ministerial level	28.6	42.9	28.6
foreign saving (I-S)/GDP	28.6	7.1	64.3
absence of economic freedom (state interventionism)	21.4	21.4	57.1
military expenditure as % of GDP	14.3	14.3	71.4
dependency on foreign capital MNC PEN 1995	14.3	14.3	71.4
public education expenditure per GDP	14.3	0.0	85.7
Islamic conference membership	14.3	28.6	57.1
EU-membership	7.1	0.0	92.9
maturity effects development ln (GDP PPP pc)^2	7.1	50.0	42.9
acceleration effects development ln(GDP PPP pc)	0.0	7.1	92.9

By far the most *positive effects* on social, ecological and economic development come about by the *maturity effects* of development, followed by *the positive aspects of feminism, the aging process* and membership in the *Islamic Conference*:

	% negative effects	% positive effects	% insignificant effects
maturity effects development ln (GDP PPP pc)^2	7.1	50.0	42.9
political feminism % women in government, ministerial level	28.6	42.9	28.6
aging: % population, aged >65y, 1998	42.9	28.6	35.7
Islamic conference membership	14.3	28.6	57.1
absence of economic freedom (state interventionism)	21.4	21.4	57.1
military expenditure as % of GDP	14.3	14.3	71.4
dependency on foreign capital MNC PEN 1995	14.3	14.3	71.4
price reform (low international price level)	50.0	7.1	42.9
foreign saving (I-S)/GDP	28.6	7.1	64.3
acceleration effects development ln(GDP PPP pc)	0.0	7.1	92.9
public education expenditure per GDP	14.3	0.0	85.7
EU-membership	7.1	0.0	92.9

The results for the *dependency explanation* of world development are the following. Relationships contradicting the theory are printed in bold letters:

	foreign saving (I-S)/GDP	dependency on foreign capital MNC PEN 1995	price reform (low international price level)
% people not expected to survive age 60 (survival)	..	negative	..
CO2 emissions per capita (Kyoto)	negative	..	negative
development stability (year with highest real income minus year with lowest real income) since 1975	..	..	..
ESI-Index (sustainability)	negative	positive	negative
Factor Social Development	..	..	..
female economic activity rate as % of male economic activity rate	..	positive	negative
female share in total life years	..	..	negative
GDP output per kg energy use (eco-social market economy)	..	..	negative
GNP per capita annual growth rate, 1990-98	..	..	..
human development index	negative	..	..
life expectancy, 1995-2000	..	negative	..
Political rights	negative	..	negative
share of income/consumption richest 20% to poorest 20% (income redistribution)	positive	..	positive
unemployment (UN) (employment)	..	..	negative

BY WAY OF COMPARISON

This volume compares patterns of globalization and patterns of development in the world system. In contrast to Heshmati and Bhandari/Heshmati (in this volume), we do not rely on the 62 countries of the Kearney Index, but on a much larger sample of 109 countries with complete, mostly UNDP and UNCTAD data (see above).

Table 13. Conditions of Dependency and Knowledge Creation at the Turn of the 21st Century

Country code	MNC PEN 2000	DYN MNC PEN 1995-2000	changes in un-equal transfer 1998 – 2002	price reform (low international price level) 2002	public education expenditure per GNP
India	4.10	2.50	0.77	5.49	3.20
Turkey	4.70	1.70	0.39	2.42	2.20
Italy	10.50	4.70	0.26	1.29	4.90
Greece	11.10	-0.10	0.31	1.50	3.10
United States	12.40	5.10	-0.02	0.99	5.40
Slovenia	15.50	6.10	0.19	1.65	5.70
Austria	16.10	8.60	0.29	1.15	5.40
Romania	17.70	14.50	-0.95	3.20	3.60
France	19.90	7.60	0.27	1.12	6.00
Finland	20.00	13.50	0.18	1.03	7.50
Lithuania	20.60	14.80	0.06	2.59	5.50
Poland	21.30	15.10	0.21	2.16	7.50
Cyprus	23.70	5.90	-0.10	1.37	4.50
Germany	24.10	16.30	0.29	1.13	4.80
Slovakia	24.20	19.80	0.29	2.91	5.00
Spain	25.80	7.10	0.19	1.34	5.00
Bulgaria	26.40	23.00	-0.28	3.66	3.20
Portugal	26.50	9.40	0.15	1.53	5.80
Latvia	29.10	16.60	0.19	2.56	6.30
United Kingdom	30.50	12.90	0.04	0.99	5.30
China	32.30	12.70	0.49	4.63	2.30
Sweden	36.10	23.20	0.16	0.97	8.30
Denmark	39.60	26.40	0.23	0.96	8.10
Czech Republic	42.60	28.50	-0.08	2.32	5.10
Hungary	43.40	16.70	-0.20	2.07	4.60
average, EU-25	44.02	28.26	0.18	1.59	5.56
Estonia	53.20	39.10	0.27	2.55	7.20
Netherlands	65.90	37.90	0.23	1.12	5.10
Ireland	68.20	53.80	0.03	1.17	6.00
Malta	84.70	56.30	0.17	1.79	5.10
Belgium	174.00	133.20	0.25	1.16	3.10
Luxembourg	174.00	133.20	0.55	1.30	4.00

The systematic comparison between the dependency indicators yields the following interesting results for Europe and its main economic rivals in the 21st Century, India, the US and China.

The unweighted average dependency rates of the EU-25 are much higher than in India, the US and China. Among the EU countries, only Turkey, Italy, Greece had a lower MNC penetration rate than the US, and Slovenia (see Mencinger in this volume) is the country with the lowest MNC penetration rate among the countries of the "new Europe" (© Donald Rumsfeld) and at the same time the most successful one in social policies

Results for the EU are dismal indeed: *Belgium* and *Greece* have a *lower public education spending rate than India,* and in addition, *Belgium, Greece, Luxembourg; Cyprus; Hungary; Germany; Italy; Slovakia; Spain; the Czech Republic; Netherlands; Malta; United Kingdom* have a *smaller share of public expenditures devoted to education than the US* (the US Federal system channels enormous amounts of public and private system into education, not covered by these central government public education expenditure rates). Only Austria; Lithuania; Slovenia; Portugal; France; Ireland; Latvia; Estonia; Finland; Poland; Denmark; and Sweden have higher public education expenditure rates than the US Federal Government.

Our comparisons with the data series Global Development Network Growth Database (William Easterly and Mirvat Sewadeh, World Bank, yearly inflows of FDI per GDP and real per capita economic growth rates [28]), Laborsta ILO[29] and UTIP (University of Texas Inequality Project)[30] reveals furthermore:

1) in both "fiery dragons", India and China, globalization flow rates decreased over time, while in the EU globalization increased at staggering proportions since the early 1990s, only to be followed by the US (at much lower levels than the EU)

2) although economic growth arguably could pick up in Europe again, the US definitely overtook the EU in 1988, and the "fiery dragons" India and China[31] had

---

[28] http://www.worldbank.org/research/growth/GDNdata.htm

[29] http://laborsta.ilo.org/.

[30] http://utip.gov.utexas.edu/

[31] It is necessary also to compare here the average level of customs by groups of trade partner countries and traded goods which shows how radical Europe's drive towards globalization – except for agriculture – really has become. The *CEPII* Institute in Paris collects such data in their *MacMap* data collection, which is freely available on the Internet at: http://www.cepii.fr/anglaisgraph/bdd/macmap/A5.xls. Let the numbers, presented by CEPII, speak for themselves. It should be remembered that the data refer to the year 2001.

	Partner:	Developed Countries			Developing countries			LDC		
	Importer:	Agric.	Manuf.	Textile	Agric.	Manuf.	Textile	Agric.	Manuf.	Textile
alb	Albania	9.7	7.6	11.2	9.4	8.6	12.5	8.4	9.1	10.4
arg	Argentina	12.4	13.1	19.2	11.3	9.4	18.3	8.8	5.6	19.1
aus	Australia	2.3	4.7	14.8	1.3	3.4	17.7	0.4	3.0	17.4
bgd	Bangladesh	20.5	12.3	30.4	21.1	18.9	28.6	15.2	18.7	17.9
bwa	Botswana	17.7	6.3	25.5	24.7	5.0	27.5	9.0	1.3	26.5
bra	Brazil	11.7	12.6	18.1	9.6	8.4	18.1	9.5	1.1	15.0
bgr	Bulgaria	20.1	4.7	14.5	18.4	4.5	14.3	7.2	3.6	10.4
can	Canada	17.3	2.0	11.6	5.7	0.6	13.3	0.4	0.0	16.2
xca	Central America	13.6	4.1	9.3	17.0	3.9	10.1	10.2	2.4	10.0
chl	Chile	7.0	6.9	7.0	6.9	6.7	6.9	7.0	6.9	7.0
chn	*China*	*23.7*	*13.7*	*20.2*	*25.8*	*9.9*	*18.4*	*10.7*	*2.6*	*9.6*
col	Colombia	15.1	9.4	17.7	15.3	9.1	17.3	12.7	9.2	15.2
hrv	Croatia	23.4	2.4	7.0	20.5	2.4	10.2	11.1	1.4	11.1
cyp	Cyprus	51.2	1.5	3.3	51.4	2.3	10.2	23.6	1.1	11.3
cze	Czech Republic	15.1	4.3	7.4	7.5	2.6	7.9	0.0	0.0	0.0
est	Estonia	12.6	0.0	0.0	7.0	0.0	0.0	1.8	0.0	0.0
eur	European Union (15)	17.0	2.5	6.6	13.7	0.8	6.5	2.7	0.0	1.0

(continued...)

much higher growth rates than Europe (with India arguably becoming the superstar of economic growth in the early 21st Century)

3) India (1981) and China (1987) halted the trend towards inequality in primary incomes (income inequality between 21 sectors, based on wages – UNIDO/UTIP data), while in the US and in Europe, inequality explodes from initial low levels at around 1996

4) among the reform countries of East Central Europe, little *Slovenia* provides an interesting paradigmatic case, worthwhile of much further research (see also Mencinger in this volume). In fact it is the *only country* in the *region* that *combined relatively higher economic growth* after the transformation crisis with a *relatively stable inequality* (after the expected prior rises in inequality rates due to the transformation process until around 1994), and a *falling rate of globalization* at the end of the 1990s.

hkg	Hong Kong	0.0	0.0	0.0	0.0	0.0	0.0	0.0	0.0	0.0
hun	Hungary	26.4	4.0	3.3	20.2	4.2	7.9	17.4	1.0	5.9
ind	*India*	*53.7*	*31.1*	*30.3*	*64.8*	*29.2*	*30.5*	*34.1*	*26.5*	*23.0*
idn	Indonesia	9.4	5.5	9.3	7.4	4.5	9.5	3.5	1.1	5.8
jpn	Japan	33.1	0.6	10.1	26.7	0.3	10.1	9.1	0.1	0.1
kor	Korea	45.3	5.5	10.7	46.7	4.7	11.4	33.2	3.4	9.3
lva	Latvia	14.8	0.6	6.9	8.6	0.6	9.4	5.1	0.5	14.0
ltu	Lithuania	10.9	0.2	2.9	11.0	0.9	11.9	3.7	0.2	16.2
mwi	Malawi	12.1	9.8	23.0	14.7	10.6	22.2	7.9	6.7	15.8
mys	Malaysia	11.2	12.2	14.4	24.9	9.5	13.7	45.2	2.6	13.9
mlt	Malta	4.6	5.2	10.2	5.4	4.1	11.5	5.4	0.7	12.6
mex	Mexico	25.3	7.3	12.8	33.4	12.8	26.9	20.6	11.8	28.1
mar	Morocco	40.8	16.4	37.1	41.7	20.5	38.9	28.1	15.6	34.8
moz	Mozambique	14.3	7.4	21.6	13.4	8.5	22.8	14.8	6.8	10.3
nzl	New Zealand	2.5	2.5	6.7	1.0	1.5	9.2	0.1	0.0	9.6
per	Peru	16.7	12.1	17.5	15.8	11.7	16.7	13.5	12.0	15.2
phl	Philippines	9.6	3.9	7.3	12.8	4.3	8.0	7.0	2.7	7.1
pol	Poland	44.8	3.6	4.5	27.6	6.9	16.8	18.8	2.4	25.6
rom	Romania	24.0	7.6	15.3	21.2	8.5	20.6	9.8	2.2	12.1
rus	Russian Federation	13.2	10.0	14.4	12.4	8.2	16.1	6.6	7.6	15.5
sgp	Singapore	1.4	0.0	0.0	1.6	0.0	0.0	0.0	0.0	0.0
svk	Slovakia	15.2	4.3	7.3	7.2	2.6	7.9	0.0	0.0	0.0
zaf	South Africa	16.3	6.3	25.5	24.3	5.1	27.8	9.0	1.3	26.5
lka	Sri Lanka	18.7	6.3	4.2	23.6	5.9	6.3	15.8	3.5	4.2
che	Switzerland	42.7	1.2	1.9	26.1	1.4	4.5	4.0	0.0	0.0
twn	Taiwan	18.5	10.2	9.2	25.1	6.0	10.4	29.3	3.0	11.4
tza	Tanzania	20.5	10.7	21.9	21.9	14.3	22.7	22.3	11.1	15.5
tha	Thailand	29.2	11.0	20.3	30.1	8.5	23.4	27.6	1.2	15.8
tur	Turkey	38.7	2.0	7.8	39.8	3.4	12.2	24.2	0.7	4.6
uga	Uganda	11.4	6.7	12.8	11.5	7.9	12.3	12.6	7.7	9.8
usa	*United States*	*4.3*	*1.6*	*9.7*	*2.7*	*0.7*	*10.9*	*2.2*	*0.1*	*13.1*
ury	Uruguay	12.5	10.9	19.1	10.0	7.6	18.0	8.8	5.0	19.0

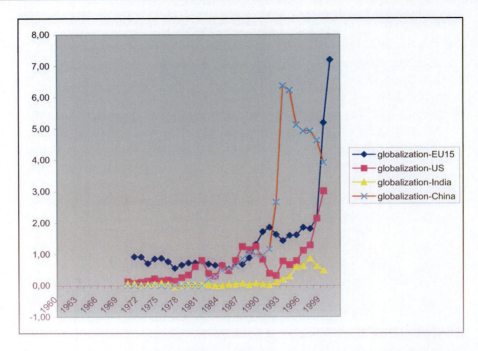

Graph 7. Patterns of globalization, growth and inequality in the EU-15, the US, India, China and Slovenia.

The evidence provided in this comparison and in this paper strengthens the belief of those who like the United Nations Commission for Latin America and the Caribbean long held a critical view of the globalization process. Indeed, one could say that we are confronted with *"Dependencia y desarrollo en Europa[32]"*

The short-term comparison of the development patterns of the EU-15 and the US reveals that globalization, measured by the recent wave of FDI inflows as a% of GDP, really began to rise in the US by around 1992 and in the EU-15 by around 1998, while inequality, as measured by the University of Texas Inequality Project data series (UTIP), based on wage differences between the 21 UNIDO categories of economic sectors, really began to rise in Europe by around 1995 and in the US by around 1996. European unemployment, reaching its first peak by 1988, its second peak by 1995 and now seriously rising again, started by around 1982 to be higher than in the US. There is an approximate three-year time lag in the business cycle between Europe and America, reflecting Europe's weaker position in terms of leading sector industries, research and development, and technology. Our figures are again based on the *University of Texas Inequality Project[33]*, the *"Global Development Network Growth Database"* (William Easterly and Mirvat Sewadeh, World Bank[34]) and the *Laborsta-Data series* by the ILO[35].

---

[32] See also the rightly famous book Cardoso Fernando Henrique and Enzo Faletto (1973) *"Dependencia y desarrollo en America Latina"* Mexico D.F.: Editorial Siglo XXI.

[33] http://utip.gov.utexas.edu/

[34] http://www.worldbank.org/research/growth/GDNdata.htm

[35] http://laborsta.ilo.org/

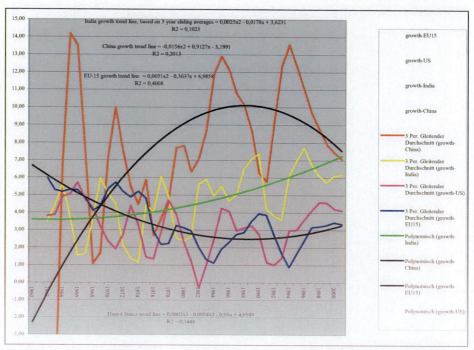

Legend: "Polynomisch" means "polynomial expression"; "3 Per. Gleitender Durchschnitt" means 3 period sliding average.

Graph 8. Patterns of globalization, growth and inequality in the EU-15, the US, India, China and Slovenia.

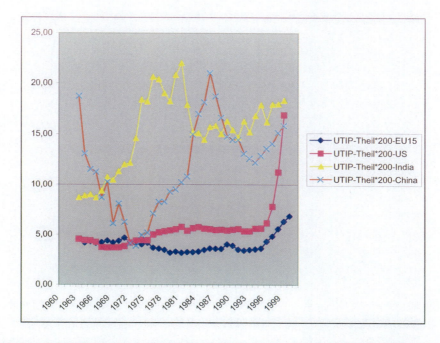

Graph 9. Patterns of globalization, growth and inequality in the EU-15, the US, India, China and Slovenia.

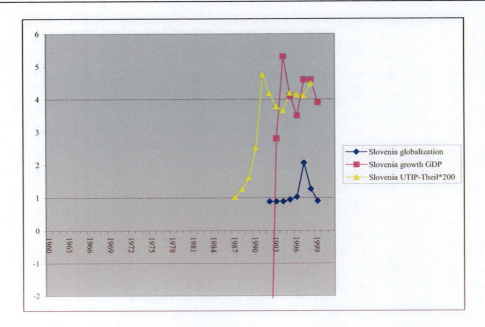

Graph 10. Patterns of globalization, growth and inequality in the EU-15, the US, India, China and Slovenia .

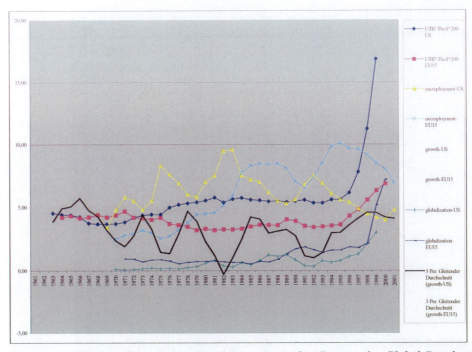

Source: our own compilations from *University of Texas Inequality Project,* the *Global Development Network Growth Database* (William Easterly and Mirvat Sewadeh, World Bank) and the *Laborsta-Data series* by the ILO.

Graph 11. Globalization, inequality, unemployment and growth in the US and in the EU since 1960.

If the explanation of the European malaise (high unemployment, low growth) by the neo-liberal school were right (over-regulation causing the crisis) then there is no way to explain how in a period of still larger European regulation during the 1950s, 1960s and early 1970s European growth was higher and European unemployment was lower than in the United States, which always was less regulated than the EU! With more and more deregulation, the gap between Europe and America does not close!

CONCLUSION

It is shown in this article that transnational integration is and remains to be a contradictory process that does not lead 1:1 to a greater amount of social cohesion and sustainable development in the host countries of transnational penetration. So, in the words of Osvaldo Sunkel:

> 'The advancement of modernization introduces, so to speak, a wedge along the area dividing the integrated from the segregated segments (…) The effects of the disintegration of each social class has important consequences for social mobility. (...) Finally, it is very probable that an international mobility will correspond to the internal mobility, particularly between the internationalized sectors (...) The process of social disintegration which has been outlined here probably also affects the social institutions which provide the bases of the different social groups and through which they express themselves. Similar tendencies to the ones described for the global society are, therefore, probably also to be found within the state, church, armed forces, political parties with a relatively wide popular base, the universities etc.' (Sunkel, 1972: 18-42).

This picture, drawn more than 3 decades ago, will – in the light of this empirical analysis – correspond much more to the trajectory of countries in the "new Europe" and beyond over the next decades than optimistic analyses, which are shared by the majority of decision makers on a European level.

APPENDIX

The two-tailed t-Test for 30 degrees of freedom or more at the 10% error probability level[36]) yields the following results:

---

[36] These calculations were performed with the T-VERT and F-VERT routines in the EXCEL program.

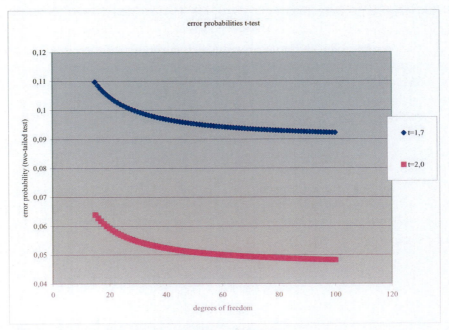

Original data for the analysis of the dynamics in the world system.

Based on:

Global Development Network Growth Database (William Easterly and Mirvat Sewadeh, World Bank[37])

Laborsta ILO[38].

UTIP (University of Texas Inequality Project)[39]

Time Series Correlations with Globalization, Growth and Inequality

	globalization – correlation with time axis 1980 - 2001	growth – correlation with time axis 1980 – 2001	inequality – correlation with time axis 1980 - 2001
Albania	0.6202	0.0407	0.3412
Algeria	-0.309	-0.1550	0.4945
Argentina	0.6686	0.2758	0.4621
Armenia	0.7608	0.6811	0.0338
Australia	0.2031	0.1635	0.9271
Austria	0.7848	0.1916	0.5785
Azerbaijan	0.7959	0.4095	0.7991
Bangladesh	0.6644	0.0346	0.9462
Belgium	0.7835	0.0982	-0.743
Bolivia	0.7429	0.7673	0.5254
Brazil	0.5559	-0.0580	0.6779
Bulgaria	0.7215	-0.4140	0.8482
Burundi	-0.4000	-0.4990	0.7678
Chile	0.8015	0.2271	0.0647

[37] http://www.worldbank.org/research/growth/GDNdata.htm

[38] http://laborsta.ilo.org/.

[39] http://utip.gov.utexas.edu/

Time Series Correlations with Globalization, Growth and Inequality (Continued)

China	0.8514	0.0339	0.9629
Colombia	0.4957	-0.2410	0.7491
Costa Rica	0.9056	0.4592	-0.5280
Cote d'Ivoire	0.5822	0.6210	0.6387
Croatia	0.9047	0.8229	-0.1000
Cyprus	-0.9090	-0.2470	-0.5910
Czech Republic	0.7051	0.0053	0.9490
Denmark	0.7825	0.2374	0.7026
Egypt, Arab Rep.	-0.5630	-0.3680	0.9194
El Salvador	0.4015	0.7133	0.6950
Ethiopia	0.6858	0.2333	0.7431
Fiji	-0.0060	0.0433	0.0379
Finland	0.5877	0.0061	0.3943
France	0.9233	0.1083	-0.0750
Gabon	0.0583	0.1150	0.9170
Gambia, The	0.7225	-0.1240	0.9451
Germany	0.7496	0.2414	-0.875
Ghana	0.4646	0.4915	0.3791
Greece	-0.4690	0.3127	0.7617
Guatemala	0.0147	0.6817	0.6115
Honduras	0.7945	0.1149	0.7648
Hungary	0.7605	0.0948	0.9323
India	0.8065	0.0987	-0.1180
Indonesia	0.2286	-0.3540	-0.7580
Iran, Islamic Rep.	0.3010	0.1712	0.5300
Ireland	0.6234	0.7690	0.7770
Israel	0.8512	0.0171	0.6332
Italy	0.2579	-0.2620	0.4941
Japan	0.4288	-0.4640	0.8147
Jordan	0.1792	-0.2630	-0.3590
Kenya	-0.4550	-0.3040	-0.7030
Kyrgyz Republic	0.7427	-0.1230	-0.3980
Latvia	0.8504	-0.2120	0.9258
Lesotho	0.7341	0.1742	0.5112
Lithuania	0.8195	-0.0360	-0.7780
Madagascar	0.6333	0.4645	0.4297
Malawi	0.662	0.2620	0.7718
Malaysia	0.2089	-0.1860	-0.0540
Malta	0.2020	0.3153	0.7544
Mexico	0.7941	0.0238	0.9023
Moldova	0.8460	-0.4510	0.8806
Mongolia	0.8103	-0.3280	0.3015
Nepal	0.7519	0.1214	-0.5630
Netherlands	0.7234	0.5226	0.8167
New Zealand	0.4086	0.0023	0.8273
Nicaragua	0.7882	0.2836	-0.0670
Nigeria	0.6278	0.2947	0.9545

Time Series Correlations with Globalization, Growth and Inequality (Continued)

Norway	0.5893	0.0034	0.1200
Pakistan	0.8626	-0.7370	0.8276
Panama	0.6544	0.1293	0.9285
Philippines	0.7089	0.1701	0.8873
Poland	0.9762	0.4554	0.7744
Portugal	0.9207	0.2228	0.7769
Romania	0.8285	-0.3560	0.9220
Russian Federation	0.8337	-0.4390	0.5970
Senegal	0.3988	0.1891	0.5737
Singapore	-0.1620	-0.0840	-0.9580
Slovak Republic	0.8306	0.1888	0.9617
Slovenia	0.4035	0.7438	0.8119
South Africa	0.5166	-0.1340	0.7189
Spain	0.4415	0.2187	0.9428
Sri Lanka	0.3462	0.1164	-0.6260
Sweden	0.6254	0.1067	0.6772
Syrian Arab Republic	0.4855	0.0602	0.1503
Thailand	0.6762	-0.2830	-0.2660
Tunisia	-0.0820	0.1226	0.8089
Turkey	0.7793	-0.0160	0.8074
Uganda	0.8504	0.5893	-0.3090
United Kingdom	0.5940	0.1656	0.7432
United States	0.6005	0.4465	0.5563
Venezuela, RB	0.7574	0.1213	0.8909
Yemen, Rep.	-0.5210	0.4346	0.1253
Zambia	0.6696	-0.0440	0.6846
Zimbabwe	0.5739	-0.3100	0.4364

Time Series Correlations with Unemployment over Time;
Changes in Unequal Exchange 1998 - 2002

Country code	changes in price reform (low international price level) 1998 – 2002 (simple differences)	correlation of unemployment over time
Albania	-0.300	0.766
Algeria	0.140	0.907
Argentina	2.550	0.898
Australia	0.270	0.070
Austria	0.290	0.358
Azerbaijan	-0.240	0.971
Bahamas	-0.120	-0.574
Bangladesh	0.940	0.814
Barbados	-0.180	-0.093
Belarus	0.930	0.548
Belgium	0.250	-0.708

Time Series Correlations with Unemployment over Time (Continued)

Belize	0.160	0.030
Bolivia	0.520	-0.298
Botswana	0.650	-0.860
Brazil	1.560	0.855
Bulgaria	-0.280	-0.329
Canada	0.060	-0.458
Chile	0.620	-0.608
China	0.490	0.064
Colombia	1.010	0.503
Costa Rica	-0.080	-0.465
Croatia	0.580	0.956
Czech Republic	-0.080	0.883
Denmark	0.230	-0.971
Dominican Re-public	0.040	-0.840
Ecuador	-0.090	0.725
Egypt	0.450	0.725
El Salvador	0.010	-0.707
Estonia	0.270	0.964
Fiji	0.450	-0.597
Finland	0.180	0.669
France	0.270	0.012
Georgia	-0.020	-0.917
Germany	0.290	0.075
Greece	0.310	0.891
Guatemala	-0.040	-0.701
Haiti	0.540	0.988
Honduras	-0.610	-0.705
Hungary	-0.200	-0.926
Iceland	0.100	-0.598
India	0.770	0.553
Indonesia	-0.190	0.954
Ireland	0.030	-0.851
Israel	0.170	0.662
Italy	0.260	0.489
Jamaica	-0.630	-0.933
Japan	0.140	0.789
Korea. Rep. of	0.130	-0.055
Latvia	0.190	-0.783
Lithuania	0.060	-0.195
Luxembourg	0.550	0.854

Time Series Correlations with Unemployment over Time (Continued)

Malaysia	0.120	-0.840
Mauritius	0.680	0.997
Mexico	-0.590	-0.288
Moldova. Rep. of	-1.250	-0.978
Mongolia	-0.240	-0.836
Morocco	0.460	-0.950
Namibia	1.570	0.921
Netherlands	0.230	-0.874
New Zealand	0.280	0.067
Nicaragua	-2.490	0.680
Norway	0.100	0.473
Pakistan	1.110	0.789
Panama	-0.280	0.511
Peru	0.620	0.545
Philippines	0.890	0.847
Poland	0.210	0.409
Portugal	0.150	-0.690
Romania	-0.950	-0.567
Russian Federation	0.560	0.669
Saudi Arabia	0.000	0.866
Singapore	0.350	0.016
Slovakia	0.290	0.774
Slovenia	0.190	-0.829
South Africa	1.820	0.987
Spain	0.190	0.060
Sri Lanka	0.400	-0.964
Sweden	0.160	0.648
Switzerland	0.180	0.065
Tajikistan	2.270	0.979
Thailand	0.880	-0.139
Trinidad and Tobago	-0.370	0.120
Tunisia	0.530	0.030
Turkey	0.390	-0.841
Ukraine	2.460	0.882
United Kingdom	0.040	-0.694
United States	-0.020	-0.800
Uruguay	0.750	0.725
Uzbekistan	3.170	0.775
Venezuela	-0.210	0.555
Zimbabwe	-0.630	-0.872

Globalization, Inequality, Growth and Unemployment – The Time Series Evidence

	correlation with unemployment over time, 1980 - 2002	correlation with globalization over time, 1980 - 2002	correlation with economic growth over time 1980 – 2002	correlation with inequality over time, 1980 - 2002
Albania	0.77	0.62	0.04	0.34
Algeria	0.91	-0.31	-0.15	0.49
Argentina	0.90	0.67	0.28	0.46
Australia	0.07	0.20	0.16	0.93
Austria	0.36	0.78	0.19	0.58
Azerbaijan	0.97	0.80	0.41	0.80
Bangladesh	0.81	0.66	0.03	0.95
Belgium	-0.71	0.78	0.10	-0.74
Bolivia	-0.30	0.74	0.77	0.53
Brazil	0.85	0.56	-0.06	0.68
Bulgaria	-0.33	0.72	-0.41	0.85
Chile	-0.61	0.80	0.23	0.06
China	0.06	0.85	0.03	0.96
Colombia	0.50	0.50	-0.24	0.75
Costa Rica	-0.46	0.91	0.46	-0.53
Croatia	0.96	0.90	0.82	-0.10
Cyprus	-1.00	-0.91	-0.25	-0.59
Czech Republic	0.88	0.71	0.01	0.95
Denmark	-0.97	0.78	0.24	0.70
Egypt. Arab Rep.	0.72	-0.56	-0.37	0.92
El Salvador	-0.71	0.40	0.71	0.70
Fiji	-0.60	-0.01	0.04	0.04
Finland	0.67	0.59	0.01	0.39
France	0.01	0.92	0.11	-0.07
Germany	0.08	0.75	0.24	-0.87
Greece	0.89	-0.47	0.31	0.76
Guatemala	-0.70	0.01	0.68	0.61
Honduras	-0.70	0.79	0.11	0.76
Hungary	-0.93	0.76	0.09	0.93
India	0.55	0.81	0.10	-0.12
Indonesia	0.95	0.23	-0.35	-0.76
Ireland	-0.85	0.62	0.77	0.78
Israel	0.66	0.85	0.02	0.63
Italy	0.49	0.26	-0.26	0.49

Globalization, Inequality, Growth and Unemployment (Continued)

Japan	0.79	0.43	-0.46	0.81
Latvia	-0.78	0.85	-0.21	0.93
Lithuania	-0.20	0.82	-0.04	-0.78
Malaysia	-0.84	0.21	-0.19	-0.05
Mexico	-0.29	0.79	0.02	0.90
Moldova	-0.98	0.85	-0.45	0.88
Mongolia	-0.84	0.81	-0.33	0.30
Netherlands	-0.87	0.72	0.52	0.82
New Zealand	0.07	0.41	0.00	0.83
Nicaragua	0.68	0.79	0.28	-0.07
Norway	0.47	0.59	0.00	0.12
Pakistan	0.79	0.86	-0.74	0.83
Panama	0.51	0.65	0.13	0.93
Philippines	0.85	0.71	0.17	0.89
Poland	0.41	0.98	0.46	0.77
Portugal	-0.69	0.43	0.10	0.92
Romania	-0.57	0.83	-0.36	0.92
Russian Federation	0.67	0.83	-0.44	0.60
Singapore	0.02	-0.16	-0.08	-0.96
Slovak Republic	0.77	0.83	0.19	0.96
Slovenia	-0.83	0.40	0.74	0.81
South Africa	0.99	0.52	-0.13	0.72
Spain	0.06	0.44	0.22	0.94
Sri Lanka	-0.96	0.35	0.12	-0.63
Sweden	0.65	0.63	0.11	0.68
Thailand	-0.14	0.68	-0.28	-0.27
Tunisia	0.03	-0.08	0.12	0.81
Turkey	-0.84	0.78	-0.02	0.81
United Kingdom	-0.69	0.59	0.17	0.74
United States	-0.80	0.60	0.45	0.56
Venezuela. RB	0.55	0.76	0.12	0.89
Zimbabwe	-0.87	0.57	-0.31	0.44

globalization – yearly inflow of foreign direct investments per GDP (World Bank)[40]

growth –real GDP per capita income growth rates, per annum, based on World Bank

unemployment – unemployment rate (ILO[41])

UTIP – Theil-Index inequality of wages [42] in 21 economic sectors, based on UNIDO (Inequality Project, University of Texas)

---

[40] http://www.worldbank.org/research/growth/GDNdata.htm

[41] http://laborsta.ilo.org

[42] http://utip.gov.utexas.edu/

Changes in the Price Level (US = 100 each), 1998 - 2002

Country code	DYN Price level 1998-2002
Luxembourg	-59.6390
Equatorial Guinea	-46.9609
Argentina	-43.1413
Singapore	-39.8905
Brazil	-37.6171
Switzerland	-37.3371
Denmark	-34.9158
Germany	-33.2479
Austria	-31.1132
France	-30.3282
Uzbekistan	-28,2247
Hong Kong, China (SAR)	-27.5693
Uruguay	-25.5971
Belgium	-25.1388
Japan	-25.0829
Netherlands	-24.8452
Sweden	-22.7561
Finland	-21.9988
Italy	-21.7011
Croatia	-20.6471
Paraguay	-20.0640
Australia	-19.9385

Changes in the Price Level (US = 100 each), 1998 – 2002 (Continued)

Lesotho	-19.3247
Rwanda	-19.0557
Greece	-18.9990
Norway	-18.0145
New Zealand	-17.5449
South Africa	-16.8380
Tajikistan	-16.4591
Peru	-15.8719
Chile	-15.8678
Papua New Guinea	-15.4112
Namibia	-14.5402
Israel	-14.3819
Spain	-14.2100
Ukraine	-13.7023
Botswana	-13.3475
Cameroon	-13.2148
Iceland	-12.9379
Dominica	-12.8732
Swaziland	-12.8356
Colombia	-12.8140
Uganda	-12.3356
Cape Verde	-11.6873
Mauritius	-11.3322
Solomon Islands	-11.2996
Fiji	-10.9661
Thailand	-10.9180
Mauritania	-10.5465
Guinea	-10.4983
Malawi	-10.2067
Burundi	-9.44030
Gabon	-9.4038
Slovenia	-9.2763
Bolivia	-9.2145
Belarus	-9.0225
Senegal	-8.8806
Turkey	-8.8207
Mozambique	-8.6546
Eritrea	-8.6355
Portugal	-8.6164
Ghana	-8.4820
Iran. Islamic Rep. of	-8.1153
Vanuatu	-7.7948

Changes in the Price Level (US = 100 each), 1998 – 2002 (Continued)

Egypt	-7.6243
Gambia	-7.1537
Tunisia	-7.1034
Pakistan	-6.8930
Malta	-6.8648
Philippines	-6.6828
Guinea-Bissau	-6.4554
Russian Federation	-6.4071
Morocco	-6.2442
United Kingdom	-6.2150
Ethiopia	-6.1343
Benin	-6.0713
Belize	-6.0418
Korea. Rep. of	-5.9844
Poland	-5.9351
Canada	-5.6176
Cambodia	-5.4911
Bangladesh	-5.4859
Estonia	-5.4090
Antigua and Barbuda	-5.3590
Central African Republic	-5.1120
Mali	-5.0076
Haiti	-4.6314
Slovakia	-4.5269
Togo	-4.4936
Burkina Faso	-4.2637
Latvia	-3.9866
Chad	-3.8324
Zambia	-3.7296
Ireland	-3.6057
Niger	-3.3960
India	-3.3582
Sri Lanka	-3.1877
Malaysia	-3.1673
Kazakhstan	-3.0438
China	-3.0074
Viet Nam	-2.1905
Guyana	-2.1488
Syrian Arab Republic	-2.1386
Macedonia. TFYR	-2.1247
Algeria	-1.9862
Nepal	-1.8788

Changes in the Price Level (US = 100 each), 1998 – 2002 (Continued)

Lithuania	-1.6900
Sierra Leone	-1.5327
Dominican Republic	-1.3171
Saudi Arabia	-1.2917
El Salvador	-1.1979
Lao People's Dem. Rep.	-0.9195
Tanzania. U. Rep. of	-0.6478
Georgia	-0.4441
Nigeria	-0.2003
Guatemala	-0.0684
United States	0.0000
Grenada	0.3681
Czech Republic	0.6489
Indonesia	0.6955
Azerbaijan	0.7660
Costa Rica	0.9420
Madagascar	0.9755
Mongolia	1.0319
Ecuador	1.3180
Bulgaria	1.4049
Sudan	1.4577
Samoa (Western)	1.5101
Côte d'Ivoire	1.9325
Kenya	2.1060
Albania	2.1068
Armenia	2.3449
Comoros	2.9852
Kyrgyzstan	3.0027
Congo. Dem. Rep. of the	3.2483
Hungary	3.3706
Zimbabwe	3.4989
Cyprus	3.6251
Bahrain	4.7021
Barbados	4.7682
Lebanon	5.2178
Moldova. Rep. of	5.8546
Honduras	6.2205
Romania	6.6516
Saint Kitts and Nevis	7.4601
Bahamas	7.5280
Jordan	7.5675
Venezuela	7.7614

Changes in the Price Level (US = 100 each), 1998 – 2002 (Continued)

Oman	9.4072
Panama	9.7914
Saint Vincent and the Grenadines	10.9425
Kuwait	12.1794
Turkmenistan	12.2241
Nicaragua	12.5976
Congo	13.5217
Saint Lucia	15.3699
Trinidad and Tobago	16.3422
Angola	18.5866
Mexico	19.4633
Yemen	21.8686
Jamaica	23.4267

The Main Winners and Losers at the Turn of the 21st Century in the Structures of Price Reform (Low International Price Level)

Country code	changes in price reform (low international price level) 1998 – 2002: increases (+) or decreases (-) in price reform (low international price level) (ERDI)	price reform (low international price level) 2002	price reform (low international price level) 1998
Nicaragua	-2.49	3.30	5.79
Angola	-2.29	2.50	4.79
Congo. Dem. Rep. of the	-1.56	5.91	7.48
Turkmenistan	-1.31	2.61	3.92
Moldova. Rep. of	-1.25	3.88	5.12
Kyrgyzstan	-1.03	5.06	6.10
Romania	*-0.95*	*3.20*	*4.15*
Yemen	-0.95	1.62	2.57
Jamaica	-0.63	1.32	1.95
Zimbabwe	-0.63	3.67	4.31
Honduras	-0.61	2.68	3.29
Mexico	-0.59	1.42	2.01
Jordan	-0.57	2.34	2.91
Armenia	-0.51	4.00	4.51
Comoros	-0.44	3.33	3.78
Sudan	-0.40	4.41	4.81
Trinidad and Tobago	-0.37	1.28	1.66
Oman	-0.35	1.67	2.02

The Main Winners and Losers at the Turn of the 21st Century in the Structures of Price Reform (Low International Price Level) (Continued)

Saint Vincent and the Grenadines	-0.33	1.50	1.83
Albania	-0.30	3.17	3.46
Panama	-0.28	1.47	1.76
Bulgaria	-0.28	3.66	3.94
Saint Lucia	-0.27	1.14	1.42
Congo	-0.26	1.20	1.46
Samoa (Western)	-0.25	3.33	3.58
Mongolia	-0.24	3.82	4.05
Azerbaijan	-0.24	4.30	4.53
Saint Kitts and Nevis	-0.22	1.50	1.72
Venezuela	-0.21	1.43	1.65
Kenya	-0.21	2.59	2.80
Hungary	*-0.20*	*2.07*	*2.27*
Indonesia	-0.19	3.95	4.14
Kuwait	-0.19	1.07	1.25
Barbados	-0.18	1.64	1.82
Bahrain	-0.16	1.56	1.72
Côte d'Ivoire	-0.14	2.15	2.28
Madagascar	-0.13	2.77	2.91
Bahamas	-0.12	1.06	1.18
Cyprus	*-0.10*	*1.37*	*1.47*
Lebanon	-0.09	1.12	1.22
Ecuador	-0.09	1.89	1.98
Costa Rica	-0.08	2.08	2.16
Czech Republic	*-0.08*	*2.32*	*2.40*
Grenada	-0.05	1.75	1.80
Guatemala	-0.04	2.10	2.14
Nigeria	-0.04	2.61	2.65
United States	-0.02	0.99	1.01
Georgia	-0.02	3.44	3.46
Tanzania. U. Rep. of	-0.01	2.17	2.18
Saudi Arabia	0.00	1.47	1.47
El Salvador	0.01	2.20	2.18
Ireland	0.03	1.17	1.15
Dominican Republic	0.04	2.64	2.60
United Kingdom	0.04	0.99	0.95

The Main Winners and Losers at the Turn of the 21ˢᵗ Century in the Structures of Price Reform (Low International Price Level) (Continued)

Antigua and Barbuda	0.05	1.14	1.10
Lithuania	*0.06*	*2.59*	*2.53*
Canada	0.06	1.29	1.23
Iceland	0.10	1.00	0.90
Sierra Leone	0.10	3.38	3.27
Norway	0.10	0.87	0.77
Malaysia	0.12	2.34	2.22
Syrian Arab Republic	0.12	2.96	2.83
Korea. Rep. of	0.13	1.69	1.57
Algeria	0.14	3.23	3.09
Japan	0.14	0.86	0.72
Zambia	0.14	2.32	2.18
Portugal	0.15	1.53	1.38
Belize	0.16	1.88	1.72
Sweden	0.16	0.97	0.81
Malta	*0.17*	*1.79*	*1.63*
Israel	0.17	1.24	1.07
Lao People's Dem. Rep.	0.17	5.59	5.42
Macedonia. TFYR	0.18	3.47	3.30
Finland	0.18	1.03	0.86
Switzerland	0.18	0.82	0.64
Latvia	*0.19*	*2.56*	*2.37*
Slovenia	0.19	1.65	1.46
Spain	0.19	1.34	1.15
Poland	*0.21*	*2.16*	*1.95*
Gabon	0.22	1.74	1.52
Denmark	0.23	0.96	0.73
Netherlands	0.23	1.12	0.89
Belgium	0.25	1.16	0.92
Hong Kong. China (SAR)	0.25	1.13	0.88
Italy	0.26	1.29	1.02
Estonia	*0.27*	*2.55*	*2.29*
France	0.27	1.12	0.85
Australia	0.27	1.36	1.09
New Zealand	0.28	1.46	1.18
Kazakhstan	0.29	3.55	3.27

The Main Winners and Losers at the Turn of the 21st Century in the Structures of Price Reform (Low International Price Level) (Continued)

Austria	0.29	1.15	0.86
Slovakia	*0.29*	*2.91*	*2.62*
Germany	0.29	1.13	0.83
Benin	0.31	2.59	2.28
Greece	0.31	1.50	1.19
Singapore	0.35	1.15	0.80
Guyana	0.35	4.71	4.36
Mali	0.36	3.09	2.73
Dominica	0.38	2.00	1.62
Turkey	0.39	2.42	2.03
Sri Lanka	0.40	4.08	3.68
Niger	0.44	4.14	3.70
Egypt	0.45	2.81	2.36
Fiji	0.45	2.37	1.91
Viet Nam	0.46	5.28	4.82
Morocco	0.46	3.13	2.67
China	*0.49*	*4.63*	*4.14*
Nepal	0.51	6.02	5.51
Bolivia	0.52	2.77	2.25
Vanuatu	0.52	3.00	2.48
Chad	0.53	4.25	3.72
Tunisia	0.53	3.15	2.62
Haiti	0.54	3.91	3.37
Luxembourg	0.55	1.30	0.74
Russian Federation	0.56	3.42	2.86
Burkina Faso	0.57	4.19	3.62
Croatia	0.58	2.04	1.46
Peru	0.62	2.37	1.75
Chile	0.62	2.38	1.76
Senegal	0.65	3.16	2.51
Botswana	0.65	2.64	1.99
Mauritius	0.68	2.91	2.23
Uruguay	0.75	2.17	1.42
India	*0.77*	*5.49*	*4.72*
Malawi	0.77	3.26	2.49
Central African Republic	0.77	4.50	3.73

The Main Winners and Losers at the Turn of the 21st Century in the Structures of Price Reform (Low International Price Level) (Continued)

Togo	0.84	5.00	4.16
Thailand	0.88	3.40	2.53
Philippines	0.89	4.28	3.39
Belarus	0.93	3.83	2.90
Bangladesh	0.94	4.83	3.89
Iran. Islamic Rep. of	0.95	4.05	3.10
Solomon Islands	0.95	3.50	2.55
Colombia	1.01	3.44	2.43
Cameroon	1.04	3.46	2.42
Pakistan	1.11	4.76	3.65
Cape Verde	1.14	3.83	2.69
Guinea-Bissau	1.15	5.00	3.85
Swaziland	1.36	4.08	2.73
Brazil	1.56	3.00	1.43
Namibia	1.57	4.24	2.67
Cambodia	1.59	6.43	4.83
Mozambique	1.63	5.36	3.73
Guinea	1.70	5.06	3.36
Papua New Guinea	1.71	4.36	2.65
Gambia	1.73	6.00	4.27
South Africa	1.82	4.38	2.56
Eritrea	2.17	6.33	4.16
Paraguay	2.18	4.62	2.44
Tajikistan	2.27	5.08	2.81
Burundi	2.36	6.43	4.07
Mauritania	2.39	6.20	3.81
Uganda	2.41	5.88	3.46
Ukraine	2.46	5.72	3.26
Ghana	2.50	6.95	4.45
Argentina	2.55	4.05	1.50
Ethiopia	2.89	8.62	5.74
Uzbekistan	3.17	5.33	2.16
Rwanda	3.25	6.12	2.87
Lesotho	3.29	6.14	2.85
Equatorial Guinea	5.03	6.67	1.64

Poverty in World Society According to OECD and UNDP

	% pop. < 2 $ per day	% pop. < $4 per day (OECD, UNDP)	% pop. < $14.40 per day (OECD, UNDP)	% pop. < $18 per day	% pop. < 50% median	Year OECD Survey	UNDP < 50% median (mid 1990s)
Norway	0.5	0.6	2.6	7.0	9.9	1991	6.4
Japan	0.3	0.5	3.7		11.8	1992	11.8
Finland	0.1	0.2	3.8	8.3	6.2	1991	5.4
Luxembourg	0.2	0.2	4.3	10.8	5.4	1985	6
Sweden	0.4	0.8	4.6	7.5	6.7	1992	6.5
Canada	0.4	0.7	5.9	10.2	11.7	1991	12.8
Denmark	1	1.4	7.6	17.0	7.5	1992	9.2
Australia	0.9	1.3	7.8	14.9	12.9	1989	14.3
Germany	0.8	1.8	11.5	21.6	7.6	1989	8.3
France	0.9	1.3	12.0	25.5	7.5	1984	8.0
Belgium	0.9	1.1	12.0	26.9	5.5	1992	8.0
United Kingdom	0.6	0.9	13.1	23.1	14.6	1991	12.5
United States	1.5	2.3	14.1	20.3	19.1	1994	17.0
Netherlands	1.9	2.4	14.4	29.3	6.7	1991	7.3
Spain	0.5	1.0	21.1	34.3	10.4	1990	10.1
Ireland	1.3	2.2	36.5	51.0	11.1	1987	12.3
Uruguay	3.9						
Guyana	6.1						
Tunisia	6.6						
Iran. Islamic Rep. of	7.3						
Jordan	7.4						
Malaysia	9.3						
Costa Rica	9.5						
Chile	9.6						
Turkey	10.3						
Jamaica	13.3						
Argentina	14.3						
Morocco	14.3						
Algeria	15.1						
Panama	17.6						
Brazil	22.4						
Colombia	22.6						
South Africa	23.8						
Mexico	26.3						
Paraguay	30.3						

Poverty in World Society According to OECD and UNDP (Continued)

Venezuela	32.0							
Thailand	32.5							
Bolivia	34.3							
Guatemala	37.4							
Peru	37.7							
Trinidad and Tobago	39.0							
Ecuador	40.8							
Egypt	43.9							
Honduras	44.4							
Yemen	45.2							
Sri Lanka	45.4							
Philippines	46.4							
China	46.7							
Mongolia	50.0							
Botswana	50.1							
Côte d'Ivoire	50.4							
Cameroon	50.6							
Indonesia	52.4							
Namibia	55.8							
Lesotho	56.1							
El Salvador	58.0							
Kenya	58.6							
Tanzania. U. Rep. of	59.7							
Mauritania	63.1							
Vietnam	63.7							
Zimbabwe	64.2							
Pakistan	65.6							
Senegal	67.8							
Lao People's Dem. Rep	73.2							
Sierra Leone	74.5							
Malawi	76.1							
Cambodia	77.7							
Mozambique	78.4							
Ghana	78.5							
India	79.9							
Nicaragua	79.9							
Ethiopia	80.7							
Burkina Faso	81.0							

Poverty in World Society According to OECD and UNDP (Continued)

Nepal	82.5						
Bangladesh	82.8						
Gambia	82.9						
Madagascar	83.3						
Central African Republic	84.0						
Rwanda	84.6						
Niger	85.3						
Zambia	87.4						
Burundi	89.2						
Mali	90.6						
Nigeria	90.8						
Slovakia		8.0					7.0
Poland		10.0					8.6
Lithuania		17.0					
Estonia		18.0					12.4
Bulgaria		22.0					
Romania		23.0					8.1
Ukraine		25.0					
Latvia		28.0					
Russian Federation		53.0					18.8
Kazakhstan		62.0					
Moldova. Rep. of		82.0					
Kyrgyzstan		88.0					
Austria							8.0
Czech Republic							4.9
Hungary							6.7
Israel							13.5
Italy							12.7
Slovenia							8.2
Switzerland							9.3

Percentage of Population with Less than $2 Per Capita and Day

	% pop. < $2 per day
Finland	0.1
Luxembourg	0.2
Japan	0.3
Sweden	0.4
Canada	0.4
Norway	0.5
Spain	0.5
United Kingdom	0.6
Germany	0.8
Belgium	0.9
France	0.9
Australia	0.9
Denmark	1.0
Ireland	1.3
United States	1.5
Netherlands	*1.9*
Uruguay	3.9
Guyana	6.1
Tunisia	6.6
Iran, Islamic Rep. of	7.3
Jordan	7.4
Malaysia	9.3
Costa Rica	9.5
Chile	9.6
Turkey	10.3
Jamaica	13.3
Argentina	14.3
Morocco	14.3
Algeria	15.1
Panama	17.6
Brazil	22.4
Colombia	22.6
South Africa	23.8
Mexico	26.3
Paraguay	30.3
Venezuela	32.0
Thailand	32.5
Bolivia	34.3
Guatemala	37.4
Peru	37.7
Trinidad and Tobago	39.0
Ecuador	40.8
Egypt	43.9
Honduras	44.4
Yemen	45.2

Percentage of Population with Less than $2 Per Capita and Day (Continued)

Sri Lanka	45.4
Philippines	46.4
China	46.7
Mongolia	50.0
Botswana	50.1
Côte d'Ivoire	50.4
Cameroon	50.6
Indonesia	52.4
Namibia	55.8
Lesotho	56.1
El Salvador	58.0
Kenya	58.6
Tanzania, U. Rep. of	59.7
Mauritania	63.1
Vietnam	63.7
Zimbabwe	64.2
Pakistan	65.6
Senegal	67.8
Lao People's Dem. Rep	73.2
Sierra Leone	74.5
Malawi	76.1
Cambodia	77.7
Mozambique	78.4
Ghana	78.5
India	79.9
Nicaragua	79.9
Ethiopia	80.7
Burkina Faso	81.0
Nepal	82.5
Bangladesh	82.8
Gambia	82.9
Madagascar	83.3
Central African Republic	84.0
Rwanda	84.6
Niger	85.3
Zambia	87.4
Burundi	89.2
Mali	90.6
Nigeria	90.8

Percentage of Population with Less than $4 Per Capita and Day

	% pop. < $4 per day
Finland	0.2
Luxembourg	0.2
Japan	0.5

Percentage of Population with Less than $4 Per Capita and Day (Continued)

Norway	0.6
Canada	0.7
Sweden	0.8
United Kingdom	0.9
Spain	1.0
Belgium	1.1
Australia	1.3
France	1.3
Denmark	1.4
Germany	1.8
Ireland	2.2
United States	2.3
Netherlands	2.4
Slovakia	8.0
Poland	10
Lithuania	17
Estonia	18
Bulgaria	22
Romania	23
Ukraine	25
Latvia	28
Russian Federation	53
Kazakhstan	62
Moldova, Rep, of	82
Kyrgyzstan	88

Percentage of Population with Less than $14.40 Per Capita and Day

	% pop. < $14.40 per day
Norway	2.6
Japan	3.7
Finland	3.8
Luxembourg	4.3
Sweden	4.6
Canada	5.9
Denmark	7.6
Australia	7.8
Germany	11.5
France	12.0
Belgium	12.0
United Kingdom	13.1
United States	14.1
Netherlands	14.4
Spain	21.1
Ireland	36.5

Percentage of Population with Less than 50% of the Median Income of Society Per Capita and Day, Regardless of Average Incomes

	UNDP < 50% median (mid 1990s)
Czech Republic	4.9
Finland	5.4
Luxembourg	6.0
Norway	6.4
Sweden	6.5
Hungary	6.7
Slovakia	7.0
Netherlands	7.3
Belgium	8.0
France	8.0
Austria	8.0
Romania	8.1
Slovenia	8.2
Germany	8.3
Poland	8.6
Denmark	9.2
Switzerland	9.3
Spain	10.1
Japan	11.8
Ireland·	12.3
Estonia	12.4
United Kingdom	12.5
Italy	12.7
Canada	12.8
Israel	13.5
Australia	14.3
United States	17.0
Russian Federation	18.8

Real Poverty and the Lisbon Process – The Absolute Incomes in Real Purchasing Power of the Poorest 20%, the Middle 60% and the Richest 20%

Income group	Income per capita and year (Euro PPS)	Income per capita and month (PPP$)	Income per capita and day (PPP $)	World rank (126 nations, 3 income groups (upper 20%, middle 60%, poorest 20%), i.e. 378 ranks
Luxembourg upper 20%	97330	8110.9	266.7	1
United States upper 20%	66951	5579.3	183.4	2
Ireland upper 20%	64377	5364.8	176.4	3
Norway upper 20%	55673	4639.4	152.5	5
Switzerland upper 20%	49452	4121.1	135.5	6
Netherlands upper 20%	47715	3976.2	130.8	10
United Kingdom upper 20%	47048	3920.7	128.9	11

**Real Poverty and the Lisbon Process – The Absolute Incomes in Real Purchasing Power
of the Poorest 20%, the Middle 60% and the Richest 20% (Continued)**

Austria upper 20%	46000	3833.4	126.0	12
Italy upper 20%	45390	3782.6	124.4	13
Denmark upper 20%	45292	3774.3	124.1	14
France upper 20%	44251	3687.5	121.2	15
Luxembourg middle 60%	43953	3662.8	120.4	16
Belgium upper 20%	42050	3504.1	115.2	17
Germany upper 20%	40890	3407.4	112.0	18
Finland upper 20%	39302	3275.2	107.7	20
Sweden upper 20%	38986	3248.8	106.8	21
Spain upper 20%	35363	2946.9	96.9	24
Portugal upper 20%	34309	2859.1	94.0	25
Greece upper 20%	33374	2781.2	91.4	26
Slovenia upper 20%	27064	2255.3	74.2	28
Norway middle 60%	26539	2211.6	72.7	29
Ireland middle 60%	24581	2048.4	67.3	33
United States middle 60%	23779	1981.6	65.2	34
Denmark middle 60%	23574	1964.4	64.6	35
Czech Republic upper 20%	23164	1930.3	63.5	37
Estonia upper 20%	22058	1838.2	60.4	38
Switzerland middle 60%	21597	1799.7	59.2	40
Austria middle 60%	21268	1772.3	58.2	41
Luxembourg bottom 20%	*21017*	*1751.5*	*57.6*	*43*
Netherlands middle 60%	20863	1738.6	57.2	44
Hungary upper 20%	20547	1712.3	56.3	45
Belgium middle 60%	20442	1703.6	56.0	47
Germany middle 60%	20168	1680.7	55.3	50
France middle 60%	19300	1608.4	52.9	53
Sweden middle 60%	19280	1606.6	52.8	54
Finland middle 60%	19169	1597.4	52.5	55
Italy middle 60%	18552	1546.1	50.9	57
Poland upper 20%	18351	1529.3	50.3	58
Slovakia upper 20%	18271	1522.6	50.0	59
United Kingdom middle 60%	17786	1482.1	48.7	60
Lithuania upper 20%	16879	1406.6	46.2	63
Spain middle 60%	15268	1272.4	41.9	68
Latvia upper 20%	15177	1264.7	41.5	70
Norway bottom 20%	14367	1197.3	39.3	74
Slovenia middle 60%	13949	1162.4	38.2	76
Greece middle 60%	12579	1048.3	34.4	81

**Real Poverty and the Lisbon Process – The Absolute Incomes in Real Purchasing Power
of the Poorest 20%, the Middle 60% and the Richest 20% (Continued)**

Turkey upper 20%	12202	1016.9	33.4	82
Portugal middle 60%	12034	1002.9	33.0	83
Czech Republic middle 60%	11571	964.3	31.7	87
Bulgaria upper 20%	11341	945.1	31.1	90
Ireland bottom 20%	*10556*	*879.7*	*29.0*	*93*
Denmark bottom 20%	10501	875.0	28.8	94
Romania upper 20%	10300	858.4	28.2	96
Finland bottom 20%	10281	856.7	28.1	97
Hungary middle 60%	10009	834.1	27.4	99
Slovakia middle 60%	9871	822.5	27.1	100
Sweden bottom 20%	9693	807.7	26.6	102
Austria bottom 20%	9678	806.5	26.5	103
Germany bottom 20%	9419	784.9	25.8	105
Belgium bottom 20%	9357	779.8	25.6	107
Netherlands bottom 20%	8686	723.8	23.8	110
Switzerland bottom 20%	8467	705.6	23.2	113
Estonia middle 60%	8338	694.9	22.8	115
France bottom 20%	7925	660.5	21.8	117
United States bottom 20%	7894	657.8	21.6	118
Lithuania middle 60%	7328	610.7	20.1	123
Poland middle 60%	7225	602.1	19.8	126
Italy bottom 20%	7025	585.4	19.2	127
Slovenia bottom 20%	6899	574.9	18.9	128
Czech Republic bottom 20%	6646	553.8	18.2	131
Spain bottom 20%	6581	548.4	18.0	132
Latvia middle 60%	6540	545.0	17.9	134
United Kingdom bottom 20%	6523	543.5	17.9	135
Greece bottom 20%	5435	452.9	14.9	148
Bulgaria middle 60%	5287	440.5	14.5	151
Romania middle 60%	4775	397.9	13.1	159
Slovakia bottom 20%	4620	385.0	12.7	161
Portugal bottom 20%	4335	361.3	11.9	164
Hungary bottom 20%	4219	351.6	11.5	167
Turkey middle 60%	4111	342.6	11.3	173
Lithuania bottom 20%	3334	277.8	9.2	190
Poland bottom 20%	3152	262.7	8.7	194
Estonia bottom 20%	3058	254.8	8.3	200
Latvia bottom 20%	2862	238.6	7.9	203

Real Poverty and the Lisbon Process – The Absolute Incomes in Real Purchasing Power of the Poorest 20%, the Middle 60% and the Richest 20% (Continued)

Romania bottom 20%	2200	183.3	6.1	222
Bulgaria bottom 20%	1953	162.7	5.3	234
Turkey bottom 20%	1594	132.8	4.3	251

Source. our own compilations from UNDP Human Development Indicators, 2004.

BIBLIOGRAPHY

Only a very limited bibliography can be printed here. Readers are referred to the full bibliographies available from the following recent main publications by the same author:

Senghaas D. (1985), *'The European Experience: A Historical Critique of Development Theory'* Leamington Spa, Dover: Berg.

Sharpe A. (2001), '*Estimates of Relative and Absolute Poverty Rates for the Working Population in Developed Countries'* Ottawa, Ontario, Canada: Centre for the Study of Living Standards, available at: http://www.csls.ca/events/cea01/sharpeilo.pdf

Sunkel O. (1966), 'The Structural Background of Development Problems in Latin America' *Weltwirtschaftliches Archiv*, 97, 1: pp. 22 ff.

Sunkel O. (1972/3), 'Transnationale kapitalistische Integration und nationale Desintegration: der Fall Lateinamerika' in 'Imperialismus und strukturelle Gewalt. Analysen ueber abhaengige Reproduktion' (Senghaas D. (Ed.)), pp. 258 - 315, Frankfurt a.M.: suhrkamp. English version: 'Transnational capitalism and national disintegration in Latin America' *Social and Economic Studies*, 22, 1, March: 132 - 76.

Sunkel O. (1973), '*El subdesarrollo latinoamericano y la teoria del desarrollo'* Mexico: Siglo Veintiuno Editores, 6a edicion.

Sunkel O. (1978a), 'The Development of Development Thinking' in 'Transnational Capitalism and National Development. *New Perspectives on Dependence'* (Villamil J.J. (Ed.)), pp. 19 - 30, Hassocks, Sussex: Harvester Press.

Sunkel O. (1978b), 'Transnationalization and its National Consequences' in 'Transnational Capitalism and National Development. *New Perspectives on Dependence'* (Villamil J.J. (Ed.)), pp. 67 - 94, Hassocks, Sussex: Harvester Press.

Sunkel O. (1980), '*Transnacionalizacion y dependencia*' Madrid: Ediciones Cultura Hispanica del Instituto de Cooperacion Iberoamericana.

Sunkel O. (1984), '*Capitalismo transnacional y desintegracion nacional en America Latina'* Buenos Aires, Rep. Argentina: Ediciones Nueva Vision.

Sunkel O. (1990), '*Dimension ambiental en la planificacion del desarrollo. English The environmental dimension in development planning* ' 1st ed. Santiago, Chile: United Nations, Economic Commission for Latin America and the Caribbean.

Sunkel O. (1991), '*El Desarrollo desde dentro: un enfoque neoestructuralista para la America Latina*' 1. ed. Mexico: Fondo de Cultura Economica.

Sunkel O. (1994), '*Rebuilding capitalism: alternative roads after socialism and dirigisme'* Ann Arbor, Mich.: University of Michigan Press.

Tausch A. (1998) 'Globalization and European Integration' Electronic book publication at the World Systems Archive (Coordinator: Christopher K. Chase-Dunn, University of California, Riverside) http://wsarch.ucr.edu/archive/books/tausch/spartoc.htm

Tausch A. (1999) Global Capitalism, Liberation Theology and the Social Sciences (edited volume, together with Andreas Müller OFM and Paul Zulehner; with contributions by Samir Amin et. al) Huntington, New York: Nova Science

Tausch A. (2001, together with Peter Herrmann) Globalization and European Integration. Huntington NY, Nova Science. ISBN: 1-560729295.

Tausch A. (2002a) 'Evropeiskii Sojus i budushaja mirovaja sistema" in Evropa, 2(3), 2002: 23 – 62, Warsaw, Polish Institute for International Affairs (in Russian language)

Tausch A. (2002b) 'The European Union and the World System'. In: 'The European Union in the World System Perspective' (The Polish Institute for International Affairs, Ryszard Stemplowski (Ed.)), Warsaw: Collections PISM (Polish Institute for International Affairs): 45 – 93.

Tausch A. (2002, together with Gernot Köhler) Global Keynesianism: Unequal exchange and global exploitation. Huntington NY, Nova Science. ISBN 1-59033-002-1.

Tausch A. (2003a) (Ed.) 'The Three Pillars of Wisdom? A Reader on Globalization, World Bank Pension Models and Welfare Society'. Nova Science Hauppauge, New York, 2003

Tausch A. (2003b) 'The European Union: Global Challenge or Global Governance? 14 World System Hypotheses and Two Scenarios on the Future of the Union' in 'Globalization: Critical Perspectives' (Gernot Kohler and Emilio José Chaves (Editors)), pp. 93 – 197, Hauppauge, New York: Nova Science Publishers

Tausch A. (2003c) 'Jevropejskaja perspektiva: po puti k sosdaniju "obshtshevo srjedisemnomorskovo doma" i integrirovaniju polozytelnovo potencjala obshestvjennovo razvitija islamskich stram' Evropa, 4 (9), 2003: 87 – 109, Warsaw, Polish Institute for International Affairs (in Russian language), also available at http://www.pism.pl/pdf/Europa%209%20Tausch.pdf

Tausch A. (2003d) „Social Cohesion, Sustainable Development and Turkey's Accession to the European Union". Alternatives: Turkish Journal of International Relations, 2, 1, Spring http://www.alternativesjournal.net/ and http://www.alternativesjournal.net/volume2/number1/tausch.htm

Tausch A. (2004) 'Towards a European Perspective for the Common Mediterranean House and the Positive Development Capability of Islamic Countries' In , European Neighbourhood Policy: Political, Economic and Social Issues' (Fulvio Attina and Rosa Rossi (Eds.) Università degli Studi di Catania Facoltà di Scienze Politiche: 145 – 168, available at: http://www.fscpo.unict.it/EuroMed/cjmEBOOKSengl.htm

Tausch A. (2005a) 'Europe, the Muslim Mediterranean and the End of the era of Global Confrontation'. Alternatives. Turkish Journal of International Relations, Volume 3, Number 4, Winter 2004, 1-29; available at: http://www.alternativesjournal.net/volume3/number4/arno3.pdf

Tausch A. (2005b) 'World Bank Pension reforms and development patterns in the world system and in the "Wider Europe". A 109 country investigation based on 33 indicators of economic growth, and human, social and ecological well-being, and a European regional case study'. A slightly re-worked version of a paper, originally presented to the Conference on "Reforming European pension systems. In memory of Professor Franco Modigliani. 24 and 25 September 2004", Castle of Schengen, Luxembourg Institute for

European and International Studies. Available from the Luxembourg Institute for European and International Studies (LIEIS), at http://www.ieis.lu/Reports/long_final_schengen_tausch.pdf

Tausch A. (2005c) 'Is Islam really a development blockade? 12 predictors of development, including membership in the Organization of Islamic Conference, and their influence on 14 indicators of development in 109 countries of the world with completely available data'. *Ankara Center for Turkish Policy Studies*, ANKAM, Insight Turkey, 7, 1, 2005: 124 - 135. Full PDF version available at http://www.insightturkey.com/tausch2005_multivariate_analysis_world_dev.pdf

Tausch A. (2005d, Ed., with Peter Herrmann) 'Dar al Islam. The Mediterranean, the World System and the Wider Europe. Vol. 1: *The "Cultural Enlargement" of the EU and Europe's Identity;* Vol. 2: The Chain of Peripheries and the New Wider Europe'. Hauppauge, New York: Nova Science Publishers

Tausch A.. (2005e) '*The "Evropeiskii Sojus", the "City on the Hill" and the "Lisbon Gap"*. Electronic Book Publication, Series: Reports, Luxembourg Institute for European and International Studies (Luxembourg), available at http://www.ieis.lu/Documents/PUB_LONG_TAUSCH_KIRCHBERG.pdf

Tausch A.. (2005f) ,Did recent trends in world society make multinational corporations penetration irrelevant? Looking back on Volker Bornschier's development theory in the light of recent evidence'. *Historia Actual On-Line*, 6 (2005), [revista en línea] Disponible desde Internet en: http://www.hapress.com/abst.php?a=n06a05

United Nations Conference on Trade and Development (current issues), '*World Investment Report.*' New York and Geneva: United Nations.

United Nations Development Programme (2004), '*Reducing Disaster Risk. A Challenge for Development. A Global Report*'. UNDP Brueau for Crisis Prevention and Recovery, available at: http://www.undp.org/bcpr/disred/documents/publications/rdr/english/rdr_english.pdf

United Nations Development Programme (current issues), '*Human Development Report'* New York and Oxford: Oxford University Press.

United Nations Human Development Programme (2004), '*Data from Human Development Report 2004*'. available from: http://hdr.undp.org/statistics/data/

In: Roadmap to Bangalore?
Editors: A. Heshmati, A. Tausch, pp. 253-283

ISBN: 978-1-60021-478-3
© 2007 Nova Science Publishers, Inc.

Chapter 8

Demographic Alternatives for Aging Industrial Countries: Increased Total Fertility Rate, Labor Force Participation, or Immigration

*Robert Holzmann**

World Bank, 1818 H-Street, Washington, N.W., 20433, USA

Abstract

The paper investigates the demographic alternatives for dealing with the projected population aging and low or negative growth of the population and labor force in the North. Without further immigration, the total labor force in Europe and Russia, the high-income countries of East Asia and the Pacific, China, and, to a lesser extent, North America is projected to be reduced by 29 million by 2025 and by 244 million by 2050. In contrast, the labor force in the South is projected to add some 1.55 billion, predominantly in South and Central Asia and in Sub-Saharan Africa. The demographic policy scenarios to deal with the projected shrinking of the labor forth in the North include moving the total fertility rate back to replacement levels, increasing labor force participation of the existing population through a variety of measures, and filling the demographic gaps through enhanced immigration. The estimations indicate that each of these policy scenarios may partially or even fully compensate for the projected labor force gap by 2050. But a review of the policy measures to make these demographic scenarios happen also suggests that governments may not be able to initiate or accommodate the required change.

---

* The author is director of the Social Protection Department, Human Development Network, World Bank. The findings, interpretations, and conclusions expressed herein are those of the author and do not necessarily reflect the views of the World Bank and its affiliated organizations or those of the executive directors of the World Bank or the governments they represent. The paper has profited from very able research support by Johannes Koettl (Washington, D.C.), very valuable comments by the participants of the G20 seminar on migration in Sydney and of an internal Bank seminar in DC, by Rainer Münz (Vienna), and great support by Thomas Buettner and Patrick Gerland from the United Nations Population Division (New York).

[1] See Chesnais (1990) for a good didactic presentation on the impact of demographic transition on population dynamics and age structure.

Key words: Demographic policy, aging, fertility rate, labor force, migration.

1. INTRODUCTION

Demographic developments—in particular, population aging and migration—are gaining increasing importance in the domestic and international policy debate. While essentially all countries in the world are aging, the demographic transition—rising life expectancy followed by falling fertility rates—is most advanced in the countries of the North. In these rich and developed economies, this process will lead to low or even negative population growth, a declining labor force, and a rising share of elderly in the population. In the countries of the South, the demographic momentum will, for some time, lead to rising numbers of births even as the fertility rate declines rapidly. In these poorer and developing economies, this will lead to a further rise in population and labor force, with the strongest ever youth cohorts entering the labor market.[1] Table 1 summarizes key demographic characteristics of world regions that have been selected for the aging of their population, projected change in population size, and current income level. China fits in this group with regard to demographic development, but not (yet) with regard to income level.

These discrepancies in demographic, economic, and, often, political development have already contributed to rising migration from the South to the North. Although most of the migration continues to be domestic and most of the 145 million official international migrants (175 million including refugees) migrated within regions in early 2000, the trend toward international and cross-regional migration is expected to continue and, perhaps, even accelerate (see table 2). The size and direction of international migration flows are driven by demographic, economic, and political gaps between countries and regions. The rising demographic gap between North and South, however, can also be seen as an opportunity for welfare-improving demographic arbitrage and a win-win-win solution (for migrant-sending and migrant-receiving countries and for the migrants themselves; see Holzmann and Münz 2004). The World Bank has started to investigate the role of migration as a development instrument for its client countries, with an initial emphasis on the role of remittances (see Maimbo and Ratha 2005, Caglar und Schiff 2005, and the 2006 issue of Global Economic Prospects: World Bank 2005).

Increased migration to the North over the last decades—and the economic and political fallout for some groups in the population—has made migration a politically charged topic in many countries. The recent terrorist events in the United States and Europe have quite likely strengthened the reservations that citizens in these countries have about further, more massive immigration. But in the absence of strong (managed) migration, low or even negative labor force growth, together with an ever higher share of elderly in the population, comes at a price for a country and her individuals.

Table 1. Key Demographic Indicators in Select World Regions

Region[a]	Total population (millions) 2003	Percent of total population in age group, 2003				Total population (millions)		Life expectancy at birth (years) 2000–05[b]	Crude birth rate (per 1,000 population), 2000–05	Crude death rate (per 1,000 population), 2000–05	GDP per capita (U.S. dollars), 2003	GDP, purchasing power parity per capita (international dollars), 2003
		0–14	15–34	35–64	65+	2025	2050					
China	1,300	22.7	33.9	36.1	7.3	1,441	1,392	71.5	14.0	7.0	1,090	4,958
Europe and Russia	745	16.6	28.4	39.7	15.4	724	669	74.1	10.1	11.4	16,394	18,247
High-income East Asia and Pacific	210	16.3	28.1	40.4	15.3	217	204	80.5	9.7	7.3	27,413	25,707
North America	324	20.8	27.7	39.2	12.3	388	438	77.6	13.7	7.9	36,257	36,608
Latin America and Caribbean	546	30.7	35.2	28.2	5.9	696	782	71.8	21.9	6.1	3,168	7,160
Low- and middle-income East Asia and Pacific	570	30.5	36.1	28.3	5.1	713	790	67.0	21.5	7.1	1,045	3,605
Middle East, North Africa, and Turkey	407	33.7	37.3	24.7	4.3	576	715	69.2	24.6	6.0	2,855	5,509
South and Central Asia	1,492	34.1	34.7	26.4	4.8	2,010	2,393	62.9	26.2	8.9	546	2,634
Sub-Saharan Africa	718	43.8	34.1	19.0	3.1	1,139	1,691	46.6	40.4	17.2	599	1,788
World[c]	6,314	28.9	33.5	30.4	7.2	7,905	9,076	65.4	21.0	9.0	5,775	8,207

Source: United Nations (2005):

a. Regional data are calculated by aggregating country data. Some data for small countries are not available.

b. Population-weighted average for region.

c. Numbers do not necessarily coincide with regionally aggregated data. See note a.

Table 2. Global Estimates of Official Migrant Stocks, by Region, in 2000 (in Thousands)

Receiving region	Sending region							
	Africa	Asia	Europe	Latin America	North America	Oceania	Not allocated	World
Africa	11,534	382	231	9	6	4	—	12,165
Asia	1,980	34,895	3,229	351	288	58	331	41,131
Europe	2,291	4,073	34,919	350	441	69	5,788	47,931
Latin America	1	144	1,685	2,930	426	0	621	5,807
North America	701	8,330	6,193	14,710	959	147	1,587	32,626
Oceania	323	1,463	2,656	—	220	685	143	5,490
World	16,830	49,286	48,914	18,349	2,340	963	8,470	145,150

Source: Holzmann, Koettl, and Chernetsky (2005), based on Harrison (2004).— Not available.

This is most visible with regard to retirement income and health care provisions, which rely on both labor force growth and a sufficiently high ratio of active population to beneficiaries. But the potential impact goes well beyond mere fiscal considerations and concerns issues of economic growth, national security, and international status.

This paper investigates the two main alternatives to continued or enhanced migration in order to compensate changes in the demographic shifts in the North: increased labor force participation and increased fertility rates of the domestic population. A scenario-like presentation of the main policy directions, the potential demographic quantities involved, and key policy requirements and implications is intended to distill the tradeoffs between these main alternatives to demographic policy. In order to do so, the paper progresses in three main sections. The first presents briefly the most recent demographic projection – medium variant - of the United Nations (UN 2005), outlines some conceptual considerations why one should, or should not, worry about demographic disequilibria, and presents the main alternatives for dealing with them. A key message of this section is that the sources of aging matter, while efforts to stabilize the demographic old-age dependency ratio, compared to growth of the labor force, may not. The second section presents three main scenarios for compensating low and negative labor force growth in the North: an instant move to total fertility replacement, enhanced labor force participation policies, and compensating immigration. A key message from these scenarios is that none of these policies alone may be able to compensate for the projected demographic changes. The third section reviews the policy implications for the demographic adjustment of instruments to increase the fertility rate, increase labor force participation, or accommodate higher migration flows. The key message from this section is that governments may lack the policy instruments to initiate or accommodate the required change. A summing-up and a few concluding remarks stand at the end. Summary tables are used in the text, while the annex contains more details.

2. WHAT ARE THE DEMOGRAPHIC PROSPECTS? SHOULD WE WORRY ABOUT DEMOGRAPHIC DISEQUILIBRIA? WHAT ARE THE POSSIBLE CORRECTING POLICES?

What are the projected demographic changes and emerging demographic disequilibria? Should they give rise to worries and for what reasons? And what are the potential correcting policies countries have? This section sketches the projected demographic developments according to the most recent medium variant projection of the United Nations' 2005 projection and a classification of world regions (and countries) according to their projected demographic development. This is followed by a brief clarification of some conceptual issues regarding the implication of these projected shifts for the financing of public programs, in particular, pensions and health care. The section ends with a short presentation of the main corrective policies.

2.1. The Medium Variant of the UN 2005 Projection

The most recent demographic projections by the United Nations and underlying assumptions for all the main variants confirm that a demographic transition is taking place worldwide (UN 2005). The expected increase in life expectancy in most countries (except those severely hit by HIV/AIDS), combined with falling fertility rates in countries with a total fertility rate above the replacement rate and continuing low rates in countries with a total fertility rate below the replacement rate, during the next 45 years—that is, until 2050—will substantially shift the demographic structure among countries and regions. The main common and distinct demographic changes are the following:

- All countries in the world are aging, and the change is sometimes most pronounced in middle-income countries (such as China). This projection applies to all definitions of aging, such as the level and change in average population age, old-age dependency ratio (typically defined as the ratio of persons ages 65 and older to persons ages 15 to 64), and share of elderly (ages 65 and older) in the total population.
- Due to the demographic momentum (that is, the path dependency of projected demographic developments in the near future as a result of current demographic structures), the total population in much of the developing world will continue to expand, as the strongest youth cohort ever enters the labor market. While the old-age dependency ratio will increase in low- to middle-income regions of Latin America, East Asia and the Pacific, Middle East, North Africa, and Turkey, South and East Asia, and Sub-Saharan Africa from as low as 0.06 (Sub-Saharan Africa in 2005) to as high as 0.29 (Latin America and the Caribbean in 2050), the total dependency ratio in these regions will either remain essentially unchanged or decline significantly (such as for Sub-Saharan Africa); see annex table A1.
- In the developed world in the "North" i.e. Europe plus Russia, the high-income countries of East Asia and the Pacific (Australia, Hong Kong, Japan, New Zealand, Republic of Korea, and Singapore), North America (United States and Canada), but also in China, the demographic projections under the medium variant foresee low or even negative demographic growth until 2050 and a substantial deterioration in both the old-age and the total dependency ratio within the next 45 years (annex table A1). For high-income countries in East Asia and the Pacific, the old-age dependency ratio is projected to reach 0.63 in 2050, and the total dependency ratio is projected to be 0.88.
- The effects of these demographic shifts are even more pronounced when considering the impact on the labor force (derived from projected population structure multiplied by the age and gender-specific labor force participation rate projections for 2010). For the medium variant, the labor force is projected to decrease until 2025 in Europe plus Russia and in high-income East Asia and the Pacific by 38 million and 6 million people, respectively. The decrease is projected to treble by 2050, including China, with a decrease of 89 million. And this projected change includes (moderate) migration assumptions. In a zero-migration scenario, the fall in labor force would be more pronounced for Europe and high-income East Asia

and the Pacific (but not China, which is assumed to remain a net exporter of migrants); North America also would see its labor force decline by some 9 million people by 2050 (see annex table A2). Under the zero-migration variant, the labor force in the North is projected to lose some 244 million persons, while the labor force in the South is projected to add some 1.55 billion, predominantly in South and Central Asia and in Sub-Saharan Africa.

2.2. Some Conceptual Clarifications and Implications of Demographic Disequilibria

These projected demographic shifts—in particular, the dramatic aging of the population, together with low or even negative growth of the population and labor force, in many countries in the North—are giving rise to many speculations and pronouncements. They include issues of national and international security, shifts in economic power, and more down-to-earth consequences for the financing of national social programs, in particular, pensions and health care. Such public programs cater to the elderly in the population but are financed by the contributions and non-consumed income of the working population (whether they are pay-as-you-go financed or pre-funded). They already consume a major share of the general budget and national output in the richer (and less rich) countries in the North. Some estimated 15 percent of GDP, on average, goes to public pensions and health care in the Organisation for Economic Co-operation and Development (OECD) countries, and an additional 5 or more percentage points of GDP are needed for privately financed pension income and health outlays. The projected demographic shifts (in North and South) are rightly expected to put further pressure on these already stressed social programs and public budgets.

This subsection attempts to clarify some critical conceptual issues linked with population shifts and pension and health care programs in order to inform the following discussion of corrective demographic policy actions and general policy requirements. The issues addressed concern (a) the essential irrelevance of the type of funding when faced with demographic shifts; (b) the dependence of both pension and health care benefits on the explicit and implicit rates of return; (c) the dependence of the implicit (and explicit) rate of return on the demographic structure and dynamics of a country; and (d) the importance of the causes of aging (reduced fertility or longer life expectancy) for policy reaction.

For the financing of pensions and health care commitments, the *form of financing (pay-as-you-go or pre-funded) matters much less than often assumed,* if at all (see, for example, Holzmann, Hinz, and Bank team 2005). In the end, all of these outlays need to be financed out of current GNP, whether unfunded or pre-funded, and each generation of retirees and heavy consumers of health care needs the next generation to pay contributions or to buy the accumulated assets. The form of financing matters with regard to the quality of collateral at the microeconomic and macroeconomic level: Do the contributions and insurance premiums create property rights? And do they contribute to enhanced national savings and thus capital stock (domestically or internationally)? As a result, policies that affect the number of individuals as payers of contributions or buyers of assets matter for the financial sustainability of these schemes.

While the notional (pay-as-you-go) or actual pre-funding of pension benefits is easily understood, the pre-funding of health care benefits is often not. Health care benefits—

whether public or private—typically do not work as a spot insurance market in which the premium is determined by the current-period risk profile of the insured which is typically related to age. This would make health insurance unaffordable for most elderly, especially as preexisting conditions become more evident with each insurance year. As a result, the typical health insurance premium is above the current-period actuarial expenditure level at a younger age and includes a component of savings to finance future expected health care expenditures above current contribution revenues. This explicit or implicit intergenerational component makes both health care and pension benefits dependent on the explicit or implicit rate of return of these social programs. And these rates of return are closely linked to the demographic structure.

It is increasingly understood that *the explicit or financial rates of return are also dependent on the demographic structure and dynamics of a country*. The savers of assets for retirement income or health care benefits need the buyers of these very assets once they want or need to sell them. International diversification of these assets in view of asymmetric aging across countries helps at the margin, but it does not constitute a solution (Holzmann 2002). And the interconnectedness of capital markets makes national interest rates also dependent on global demographic trends (see McKibbin 2005). The implicit rate of return of unfunded systems is closely linked to the growth of the base of contributions (which depends on productivity growth/the growth of real wages per capita, and the labor force/the growth in the number of contributors). This standing result, based on Samuelson (1958) for two-generation OLG models, needs to be adjusted in three- and more-generation models and include an adjustment factor that takes into account changes in the numbers of years between when contributions are paid and benefits are received (see Settergren and Mikula 2005, and footnote 1). Hence projected demographic shifts will influence the internal (and external) rate of return and thus the capacity to deliver pension and health care benefits through three channels.

First is the change in labor force. For some countries and regions, the impact of the projected fall in the labor force during the next 45 years is quite substantial (table 3). In Europe plus Russia, the impact would amount to a reduction in the (implicit) rate of return in the range of 0.7 to 0.9 percent annually. For North America, the assumed migration will add almost 0.6 percent annually to the rate of return during the next 45 years.

Second is the impact of aging on productivity growth. There are a number of reasons why an aging labor force may exhibit lower productivity growth per worker, taking into consideration knowledge creation and entrepreneurial spirit. Cross-country econometric evidence for 115 countries suggests that the share of the elderly population has a statistically significant impact on growth of real GDP per capita (IMF 2004: table 3.1). Using the coefficient from this research and the demographic forecast for advanced economies suggests a reduction in the annual real growth rate of GDP per capita of 0.5 percent, on average, by 2050—that is, per capita growth would be 0.5 percent lower than it would have been if the demographic structure had remained unchanged. Simulations with a general equilibrium model provide similar magnitudes of growth reduction per capita and per annum for OECD countries (Martins et al. 2005).

Third is the impact of population aging on the ratio of assets to liabilities of unfunded pension systems. While aging increases the liability position, it also increases the asset position by increasing the average number of years between contribution payments and benefit disbursement.[1] In a non-financial (or notional) defined-contribution system, the liability position can potentially be isolated from population aging, while the asset position is improved, leading to a potential (small) gain in the rate of return to the system of some 0.1 percent a year. Hence, the more quasi-actuarial the structure of an unfunded pension system, the less detrimental the impact on the rate of return provided.

Table 3. Annual Growth Rates of the Labor Force, 2005–50 Percent

Country	Medium variant	Zero migration	Difference
China	−0.28	−0.25	0.03
Europe and Russia	−0.68	−0.85	−0.17
High Income East Asia and Pacific	−0.56	−0.75	−0.19
North America	0.44	−0.12	−0.56
Latin America and Caribbean	0.83	0.95	0.12
Low and Middle Income East Asia and Pacific	0.79	0.86	0.07
Middle East, North Africa, and Turkey	1.36	1.38	0.02
South and Central Asia	1.25	1.29	0.04
Sub-Saharan Africa	2.32	2.34	0.02
Total	0.77	0.77	0.00

Sources: United Nations (2005); author's calculations.

Population aging can occur as the *result of a reduction in the total fertility rate or an increase in life expectancy*. In the real world, both effects occur at the same time and have been of roughly similar magnitude in many countries in recent years. But the effects on social programs and hence the policy conclusions are not identical.

With a total fertility rate at the replacement level (which in highly developed economies is in the range of 2.05 to 2.1 children per woman, but can be as high as 2.64 in countries such as Namibia if mortality rates are high throughout the fertility period), population aging occurs through a fall in the age-specific mortality rate, which raises life expectancy at all ages. In developing countries, recent gains in life expectancy have occurred at young ages; in highly developed economies, the gains have occurred at older ages (60 and beyond), as the mortality rates at younger ages are already low. A gain in life expectancy of some 10 years at age 60—from 80 to 90—and deterioration in the (demographic) old-age dependency ratio from, say,

---

[1]. In a notional defined-contribution system, the financial balance requires that the present value (PV) of assets (**A**) is greater or equal to liabilities (L) in each period. Liabilities consist of the accumulated notional accounts (K) and pension payments; the assets consist of the value of the reserve fund plus the value of contributions times the turnover density (TD)—that is, the product of the earnings-weighted average number of years participants have worked based on the age-earnings profile in period t and the payment-weighted average number of years payments have to be made in year t based on the payment profile in period t. See Settergren and Mikul (2005) and Palmer (2005). Annual deviations between assets and liabilities affect the (implicit or notional) rate of return (i) that can be granted to plan participants. This return consists of the normal growth of productivity (g) and the growth in the number of contributors (n) plus the adjustment factor (a).

(1) $PV(Lt) = PV(At)$

(2) $PV(Lt) = \Sigma\,Ki,t + \Sigma\,Pj,\tau,t$

(3) $PV(A_t) = TD * \sum c\,w_{i,t} + Fund_t$

(4) $a = [PV(At)/PV(Lt)] - 1$

(5) $i = g+n+a.$

2:1 to 3:1 can be easily addressed by raising the retirement age by 6.6 years (and using only the remainder for an extended retirement period of 3.3 years). This would reestablish financial balance in the old-age income system and leave the internal rate of returned largely unchanged.[2]

With a given life expectancy, population aging is driven by a fall in the total fertility rate. This also occurs when total fertility rates are falling and rates are above the replacement rate. If left constant, this situation leads to a constant population structure and a permanently growing population. At constant total fertility rates below the replacement level, the population structure also moves to a steady state, but the population is permanently shrinking. While the deterioration in the population structure and the resulting increase in the old-age dependency ratio can be corrected by an increase in the retirement age (as under rising life expectancy), the fall in both population and size of the labor force needs an additional correction to deal with the otherwise lower benefit level due to lower implicit rates of return.

The above estimates suggest that some countries and regions have an aging-induced deterioration in the internal rate of return for pension income of 1.3 percent a year (0.8 percent due to the smaller labor force and 0.5 percent due to lower productivity growth). Such calculations do not include the price effects for retirees of higher personal health care costs, which are likely to reduce income by a similar magnitude. Nor do they include the effects of lower rates of return on notional or actual pre-saving in health care insurance. Yet such a reduction in the annual rates of return over a whole life cycle has important implications for benefit levels. In a life-cycle setting, a 1 percentage point (100 basis point) lower rate of return translates broadly into a 20 percent lower pension benefit. The actual magnitude of a deteriorated rate of return may require compensation in a reduced replacement rate which exceeds 30 percent or more.

2.3. The Set of Corrective Demographic Policy Options

This subsection sketches the set of corrective demographic policy options, which is quite limited and includes essentially a higher total fertility rate (that is, more children per family) and higher labor force participation of the existing population, and increased immigration. There is, of course, a much larger set of potential non-demographic corrective policy options, such as enhanced productivity growth per employee or international diversification of investments. Although such policies may prove important, they are beyond the scope of this paper and are conjectured not to be full substitutes for the demographic policy options addressed here.

Higher total fertility rate. Fertility rates at the beginning of the new millennium reached a new low in many countries and regions: Russia, 1.2; Europe and Japan, around 1.4; China, 1.7; and North America, almost 2.0. The medium demographic variant assumes some recovery in the total fertility rate for Russia, Europe, Japan, and China toward 1.85 and a slight fall for North America by the end of the projection period. In all cases, the replacement level would not be reached by 2050.

---

[2]. The impact on the disability scheme should be small, as most individuals at age 60 have a health status equal to that of people aged 45–50 some 50 years ago. If people anticipate a later retirement, their lifelong investment in human capital should be higher and the age impact on productivity growth should be smaller.

One potential policy option is to attempt to reach a replacement-level total fertility rate as soon as possible and keep it there. This would stabilize the labor force in the long term and, eventually, create long-term population growth, but solely through an increase in life expectancy (or immigration). The short- and medium-term effects, however, would be limited. The past decline in the total fertility rate has already reduced the number of women of child-bearing age, so the increase in crude birth rates would be limited. And any increases in the number of births would need some time before they have an effect on the labor market—that is, some 15, 20, and more years. Furthermore, this option would contribute to an immediate deterioration in the total (demographic) dependency ratio—that is, the sum of the youth dependency ratio (the ratio of ages 0–14 to ages 15–64) and the old-age dependency ratio (the ratio of ages 65+ to ages 15–64).

Section 3 investigates the quantitative effects of this policy option, and section 4 sketches potential policy measures to make it happen.

Increased labor force participation. A second option to correct for population aging with regard to the system dependency ratio (that is, the ratio of beneficiaries to contributors in the pension system) consists of increasing labor force participation—that is, increase the share of population participating in the labor market, including the elderly. The labor force participation rate differs substantially across regions, countries, and gender, which gives rise to the potential policy options of an increase beyond current levels. While such an increase in labor force participation can expand the total labor force and hence may compensate for a fall in population in potentially active age brackets, it requires more: If the active population continues to decrease, even a partial compensation will require a continuous increase in the labor force participation rate. And increased labor force participation cannot be allowed to translate 1:1 into increased social benefits as such an approach would postpone, but not solve, the underlying financing needs of such programs.

Increased immigration. A simple mechanism in quantitative terms to compensate for low or negative population growth is to import population from other countries. Such an approach promises a number of direct advantages for the migrant-receiving countries. First, most of the migration typically takes place among person's ages 25 to 35. Hence immigration immediately enhances the labor force, while only gradually contributing to a higher dependency ratio—first through their children and only much later through their receipt of pension benefits. Second, given an assumed elastic supply of migration-willing individuals in developing countries, this policy may, in principle, compensate extremely well for any population gap in quantitative terms and, with an appropriate filtering mechanism, may also compensate for a gap in skills and other characteristics. Last but not least, with appropriate policies and incentives, part of the migrant population may be induced to return to the sending country, if this is deemed important and useful. The experience with such gap-filling immigration approaches, however, has met its limits, to which we return in section 4.

3. Scenarios of Demographic Options to Compensate Gaps in Labor Force

This section presents broad estimates of the extent to which, and the assumptions under which, the demographic gap in the North can be compensated for by the corrective policy options just outlined. To this end, the section relies on special scenario projections produced by the demographic division of the United Nations in New York. The reliance on these scenarios ensures consistency with the other projections used in this paper and by other authors internationally. However, it also limits the alternative policy scenarios that can be investigated.

3.1. Instant Move to Replacement-Level Total Fertility Rate

The first demographic option investigates the effect of an instant move to a total fertility rate at the replacement level. The possibility of such a move is clearly unrealistic, but it serves as a useful benchmark for less drastic policy options and provides highly interesting scenario projections. Table 3 presents the change in total population by main age groups for the two periods under investigation (2005–25 and 2005–50), calculated as the difference between the instant-replacement-level variant and the medium variant. Table 4 presents the effects, translated into changes in labor force, between these two scenarios and for 2025 and 2050. Both tables also include information about the regions in the South for reasons of completeness and interest.

Table 4 indicates the time-lagged effect on population growth of an instant move toward a replacement-level total fertility rate. For all regions, the impact on the young age group is proportionate to the distance to replacement level during the prior 20 years. The population surplus is moderate for North America, as actual fertility rate is close to replacement level, but is substantial for all other deficit regions. The population deficit is high for Sub-Saharan Africa, with a total fertility rate well above replacement, but is more moderate for other surplus regions in 2025. The impact on the active population group by 2025 is still small in both deficit and surplus regions.

By 2050 the impact on the young age group is, in aggregate, mitigated by the past total fertility rate in the medium variant. However, for fertility-deficit regions, the accumulated lagged effects of a higher total fertility rate under the baseline scenario become visible in the active population group: the projected population gain for this age group is more than 230 million. For the world as a whole, the overall population effect is mitigated by the dominant effect of reduced population for Sub-Saharan Africa under a replacement-level total fertility rate.

Table 5 translates changes in the size of population in 2025 and 2050 (for projected constant labor force participation rates as of 2010) into changes in total labor force numbers induced by the replacement-level total fertility rate compared to the medium variant. As expected, the impact on both projected initial-surplus and -deficit countries in 2025 is small. By this year, a higher or lower fertility rate during the previous 20 years has a limited impact. By 2050, the accumulated effect over 45 years is already well pronounced. For the initial-deficit regions, this amounts to a gain in total labor force of almost 200 million. For the initial-surplus regions, this amounts to a reduction in labor force of more than 380 million, a potentially welcome development in view of existing pressures on the labor market.

Table 4. Difference in Population between Instant-Replacement and Medium-Variant Projections, 2025 and 2050

Millions

Period and region	Age 0–14	Age 15–64	Age 65+	Total
Difference by 2025				
China	49.5	22.7	0.0	72.2
Europe and Russia	39.3	17.5	0.0	56.7
High-income East Asia and Pacific	11.0	5.2	0.0	16.3
North America	7.4	1.1	0.0	8.6
Latin America and Caribbean	−3.9	−5.9	0.0	-9.8
Low- and middle-income East Asia and Pacific	7.9	−3.2	0.0	4.6
Middle East, North Africa, and Turkey	−22.3	−11.4	0.0	−33.7
South and Central Asia	−49.3	−32.6	0.0	−81.9
Sub-Saharan Africa	−172.2	−55.3	0.0	−227.5
Total	−132.4	−61.9	0.0	−194.4
Difference by 2050				
China	83.6	114.3	0.0	197.9
Europe and Russia	53.7	80.4	0.0	134.1
High-income East Asia and Pacific	15.0	22.8	0.0	37.8
North America	14.6	15.3	0.0	29.9
Latin America and Caribbean	12.2	-6.1	0.0	6.1
Low- and middle-income East Asia and Pacific	21.7	14.6	0.0	36.3
Middle East, North Africa, and Turkey	−16.7	−44.3	0.0	−61.0
South and Central Asia	−10.6	−94.0	0.0	−104.6
Sub-Saharan Africa	−243.7	−337.2	0.0	−580.9
Total	−70.0	−234.1	0.0	−304.1

Sources: United Nations (2005); authors' calculations.

Table 5. Difference in Labor Force between Instant-Replacement and Medium-Variant Projections, 2025 and 2050

Millions

Region	Difference by 2025	Difference by 2050
China	11.4	96.8
Europe and Russia	4.1	61.9
High-income East Asia and Pacific	0.8	16.7
North America	0.4	11.3
Latin America and Caribbean	−2.6	-5.2
Low- and middle-income East Asia and Pacific	−1.2	10.0
Middle East, North Africa, and Turkey	−3.3	−27.6
South and Central Asia	−16.4	−72.6
Sub-Saharan Africa	−47.5	−283.6
Total	−54.2	−192.4

Sources: United Nations (2005); author's calculations.

3.2. Alternative and Combined Policies of Increased Labor Force Participation

The investigated policy options have as a starting point the demographic projections without any (net) migration. This baseline is used to obtain an unbiased estimate of the effects of three policy scenarios with regard to labor force participation. The investigated and estimated scenarios are the following:

(1)   *Benchmarking.* What would be the labor force effects if the countries and regions in the North would gradually increase their labor force participation rates to match those of countries with the highest rates in 2005? Three European countries (Denmark, Iceland, and Sweden) have rates well above those of other countries, including the United States, which comes close. Most countries are well below, in particular at higher age groups.

(2)   *Gender gap.* What would be the labor force effects if the labor force participation rate of women would approach that of men by 2050?[3] In some countries, there is hardly any difference between women and men with regard to labor force participation, especially in the younger and middle age groups. In quite a number of other countries, the labor force participation of women remains low, much lower than that of men.

(3)   *Retirement age.* What would be the labor force effects of a major increase in actual retirement age by 2050? The estimated effects assume an increase of five years by 2025 and of 10 years by 2050. Currently, the difference in actual retirement across countries and regions is substantial, which suggests a highly differentiated impact.

(4)   *Combined effects.* What would be the effect of all three policy measures combined: that is, gradually but jointly matching the highest labor force participation rates, eliminating gender gaps, and substantially increasing the actual retirement age?

The effects of these policy scenarios are detailed for each region investigated in annex tables A3–A6. This section summarizes the main results and key observations. Table 6 in the text presents the results by comparing the zero-migration benchmark and the four policy scenarios for the changes in the labor force between 2005–25 and 2005–50. Table 6, supported by the annex tables, suggests the following key observations:

- Overall, there are strong regional differences in the impact of the policy options, the options selected, and the time frame.
- A combination of all measures is able to keep the change in labor force positive in all regions by 2025, but even continued joint implementation of increased labor force participation is not able to compensate fully for the drop in active population in Europe plus Russia and the high-income countries of East Asia and the Pacific, once the projection horizon is extended to 2050. At least in these two regions, other policy measures would have to be added in order to stabilize the labor force. In the other two regions (China and North America), the combined measure would be sufficient to increase the labor force by 2050. But the drastic policies required to

achieve this may warrant the partial substitution of other measures (that is, an increase in the total fertility rate and migration).

- The results signal quite different starting positions among the regions, leading to quite differentiated impacts on the labor force under the same policy scenario. For example, benchmarking of labor force participation rates has little effect on China in both periods, indicating a high level of participation for the main age groups. In contrast, this measure is highly effective in reducing the expected fall in the labor force in Europe plus Russia, indicating that labor force participation in countries that are not benchmarked in the region is quite low. However, eliminating the gender gap has large effects in China and the high-income countries of East Asia and the Pacific, but moderate effects in Europe plus Russia and in North America, confirming the traditionally low rate of female labor force participation in countries like Japan and Korea. Raising the actual retirement age is, in most but not all cases, the most effective policy measure to compensate (partially) for low or negative population growth.

- The aggregate effect of the combined measures on the labor force is impressive. In the regions with a potential deficit, it amounts to a projected gain in labor force of 175 million by 2025 and 335 million by 2050. This compares quite favorably with the estimated effects of an instant move to the replacement-level total fertility rate, which is only 17 million by 2025 and 187 million by 2050.

3.3. Migration Needs to Keep the Labor Force Constant at the 2005 Level: The Magnitudes of Net and Gross Migration

At current labor force participation rates and in the absence of migration (the zero-migration variant), the labor force in Europe plus Russia will decline by 46 million during the period 2005–25 and by 118 million during the whole period analyzed, 2005–50 (tables 6 and 7). Labor migration might compensate for the whole "gap." But, in this case, between 2005 and 2025, Europe plus Russia will have to add a net amount of 2.3 million migrants annually to its work force. And between 2025 and 2050, this number will have to increase to 2.9 million migrants annually.[4] Assuming that, at best, 70 percent of newly arriving immigrants join the work force,[5] the annual net gain from migration will have to be on the order of 3.3 million annually until 2025 and 4.1 million between 2025 and 2050. Under these assumptions, between 2005 and 2050, a net migration gain of 169 million people aged 15 to 64 will be required to add 118 million economically active migrants to the labor force of Europe plus Russia. This does not account for children below the age of 15 and elderly aged

---

[3]. Assuming steady incremental change: 50 percent between 2005 and 2025 and 50 percent between 2025 and 2050.

[4]. The annual migration needs for EU25 alone are 1.3 million and 1.6 million, respectively.

[5]. This conclusion can be drawn from an analysis of the European Labor Force Survey showing labor force participation rates above 65 percent (ages 15–65) for West European immigrants living in another European Union member state as well as for Australian, Canadian, Japanese, and U.S. immigrants in the European Union (Münz and Fassmann 2004).

65 or older, which would add another 15 to 35 percent.[6] This would lead to net migration well above European levels in the recent decades.

Table 6. Change in the Labor Force, by Policy Variant, 2005–25 and 2005–50

Millions

Period and region	Zero-migration variant (baseline)	Scenario I (benchmarking)	Scenario II (gender gap)	Scenario III (retirement age)	Combined scenario I+II+III	Difference between I+II+III and baseline
2005–25						
China	24	29	63	65	93	69
Europe and Russia	−46	−16	−28	−20	21	67
High-income East Asia and Pacific	−9	−5	−2	−3	5	14
North America	1	9	6	13	26	25
Total	*−29*	*16*	*38*	*55*	*145*	*175*
2005–50						
China	−85	−77	−14	4	62	146
Europe and Russia	−118	−69	−91	−72	−2	117
High-income East Asia and Pacific	−32	−28	−22	−21	−8	24
North America	−9	6	1	15	39	48
Total	*−244*	*−168*	*−126*	*−75*	*91*	*335*

Source: United Nations (2005); author's calculations.

Table 7. Required Net and Gross Migration to Hold the Labor Force Constant, 2005–25 and 2005–50

Millions

Period and Region	Net requirement of labor force	Non-active migrants aged 15-64	Dependents aged 0-14 and over 65		Returning and circulating migrants aged 15-64		Gross requirement of migrants	
			Low	High	Low	High	Low	High
2005-25								
China	—	—	—	—	—	—	—	—
Europe and Russia	46	+20	+10	+23	+33	+131	108	219
High Income East Asia and Pacific	9	+4	+2	+4	+6	+26	21	43
North America	—	—	—	—	—	—	—	—
Total	*55*	*+23*	*+12*	*+27*	*+39*	*+156*	*129*	*262*
2005-50								
China	85	+36	+18	+42	+61	+242	200	406
Europe and Russia	118	+51	+25	+59	+84	+338	279	566
High Income East Asia and Pacific	32	+14	+7	+16	+23	+92	76	154
North America	9	+4	+2	+4	+6	+25	21	42
Total	*159*	*+68*	*+34*	*+80*	*+114*	*+455*	*375*	*762*

Source: United Nations (2005); author's calculations.

Notes: Net requirements based on zero-migration variant. Non-active migrants calculated assuming a labor force participation rate of migrants of 70 percent, as estimated in Münz and Fassmann

---

[6] This is the range suggested by migration data for European countries. See Migration Policy Institute (2005).

(2004). Dependent migrants calculated assuming to amount to 15 to 35 percent of migrants aged 15-64. Returning migrants calculated assuming return migration rate of migrants aged 15-64 between one third and two thirds, as estimated in Holzmann, Koettl, and Chernetsky (2005).
— No migration requirement during this period.

The corresponding magnitude for other regions with a potential deficit is less dramatic but, in aggregate, is still half that of Europe plus Russia. In the high-income countries of East Asia and the Pacific, they amount to 9 million and 32 million in 2005–25 and 2025–50, respectively. While China is projected to have a labor force surplus during the period 2005–25, to compensate the gap of 85 million by 2050 may require a total net migration of 121 million in the period 2025–50, or more than 4.8 million migrants annually. The equivalent values of total net migration remain small for North America, at 13 million, but are sizable for the high-income countries of East Asia and the Pacific, at 46 million.

When taking these dimensions into account, one might conclude that net immigration on the order of some 200 million people (compared to the starting population of 745 million in 2005) is beyond Europe's integration capacity, even if immigration of such a large number is distributed over a period of 45 years. The same conclusion may be reached for the high-income countries of East Asia and the Pacific, which may need to absorb a total net immigration of some 60 million (compared to a starting population of 212 million in 2005). But in this context, net migration is not the only factor. Both for recruitment and for an assessment of integration capacities, we also have to take into account the absolute number of migrants. For this it is important to note that in the past many people migrating to Europe or other parts of the North did not stay for good; instead, they eventually returned to their country of origin. For example, during the 1990s, 88 percent of Polish nationals migrating to Western Europe returned to Poland (see annex table A7). During the same period, 63 percent of Turkish nationals migrating to Western Europe returned to Turkey (see annex table A8). These rates, however, tend to overestimate the total number of persons involved as available statistics on migration flows include circular migrants, who are represented several times.

We have to assume that circular movements and returns to the country of origin will remain an important element of future migration patterns. Under this assumption, admitting or recruiting a net amount of some 200 million migrants (as discussed for Europe plus Russia) may require a pool of some 280 million to 570 million of total migrants, depending on the rate of circularity and return. Such calculations suggest that admitting or recruiting labor migrants (and dependent family members) can only be one part of a policy mix addressing the medium- and long-term labor market problems of countries and regions with fertility deficits.

4. POLICY IMPLICATIONS OF AND REQUIREMENTS FOR A REALIZATION OF DEMOGRAPHIC SCENARIOS

The demographic scenarios presented in section 3 investigate the magnitude of a potential measure to compensate for population aging and negative labor force growth in the North. While each of the broad policy approaches—higher fertility rate, higher labor force participation, and larger migratory inflows—may partially or even fully help to stabilize the labor force (or other objective variables) in the North, the actual policy measures with which to achieve such changes may not be available, effective or efficient, or may create problems of their own. This section sketches some of the key policy issues, including the identification of some important questions for future policy research.[7]

4.1. What Can Governments Do to Increase the Fertility Rate of a Country?

While there seems to be some empirical understanding of the determinants of the fertility decisions of women (less of couples), there seems to be less grasp of what governments can do to influence such a decision in a cost-effective manner. Two sets of public instruments are typically evoked to foster a fertility decision: offer direct monetary or real transfers and reduce the opportunity costs of female labor force participation. A third set of measures seems to be the pet of only a few academics and politicians: reduce the negative fertility effects of existing social programs, in particular, pension schemes.

Provide transfers in cash or kind. A number of countries provide monetary transfers to families with children for reasons of income support, pro-natal considerations, or both. Such transfers include birth premiums, parental leave, family allowances that are sometimes differentiated by the number of children (for example, high for third and fourth child, but low or zero for any further child), and housing allowances or preferential access to housing (a measure that was widespread in Central and Eastern Europe under communist rule). The empirical evidence of such transfers indicates a low to moderate degree of effectiveness, if any.[8] There seems to be broad agreement that such transfers—in particular, if they are assumed to be only temporary and are introduced during periods of sluggish labor markets—may influence the timing and spacing of children. But the long-run effects on the total fertility rate of mere transfers on their own seem to be very small. Such a result should come as no surprise because the present value of such transfers is dwarfed by the direct costs of raising children and, perhaps more important for women in developed economies, by the opportunity costs of raising children if they negatively affect labor force participation and career opportunities.

Reduce the opportunity costs of female labor force participation. The limited effectiveness of traditional pro-natal instruments and the wish of many well-educated women to manage both a professional career and a family have focused attention on appropriate policy actions. A first set of measures concerns the access of families with children to day care centers (crèches, kindergarten, full-day schools)[9] or simply the availability of nannies or live-in maids at reasonable prices and non-intrusive administrative procedures. Here government actions can be very supportive and apparently equally effective if done via budget expenditures (Sweden) or market mechanisms (the United States), as both countries have a total fertility rate of similar magnitude. A second set of measures may be equally important, but more difficult for government policy to influence, at least in the short run. It concerns the link between the level of partnership in family decisions and child rearing and in the marriage and fertility decisions of women. Influencing such behavior through government

---

[7] For broader issues of population policy, and the claim of its continued relevance for the developed and developing world, see May (2005).

[8] . Reviews of cross-country and case studies of the link between fertility and social policy include Bjoerklund (2002); Drago, Scutella, and Verner (2002); Neyer (2003).

[9] For a global survey on the limited effectiveness of such measures which echoes the findings in many other studies, see Caldwell, Caldwell and McDonald (2005).

action is much more difficult and controversial, and information about good and best practices is just beginning to emerge.[10]

Reduce distortions in the fertility decision. There is a long-standing fear that a pay-as-you-go pension system introduces distortions in the fertility decisions of families. Indeed, there are good reasons to believe the pay-as-you-go system induces a moral hazard effect and reduces individual incentives to invest in human capital (see, for example, Sinn 2004 and Meier and Wrede 2005). The basic source of such an effect is claimed to be an externality inherent in a pay-as-you-go system. The old-age benefit is fixed at the individual level, often scarcely linked to one's own financial contribution and certainly independent of the contribution of one's children or whether one has any children at all. Therefore, individuals have little incentive to take such contributions into account when making fertility decisions and the incentive to form a family is affected by the implicit subsidy that defined benefits provide to single (childless) households. The empirical evidence seems to support the conjecture that public pension schemes have a negative impact on fertility rates. But while the effects seem to be statistically significant, the magnitude is small. For example, reducing the contribution rate in pay-as-you-go schemes by 25 percent would increase the worldwide (and U.S.) fertility rate by 0.1 percentage point, say, from 2.2 to 2.3 percent (see Ehrlich and Kim 2003).

4.2. How Can Governments Support an Increase in the Labor Force Participation Rate?

In our scenario calculations, an increase in labor force participation can be affected at three levels: raising the labor force participation of women closer to that of men, raising labor force participation for all workers and genders at all ages, and raising the labor force participation of elderly workers.

Increase female labor force participation. Reconciling work and family by increasing female labor force participation is closely linked to the policy measures discussed above. More basically, female labor force participation is closely linked to the education level and the incentives and aspirations of women to use their educational achievements. A successful inclusion in the labor market, however, contributes to a delay in the age of first birth. In many OECD countries, a substantial and increasing share of women (20 percent and more) are having their first child at the age of 40 and older. While this contributes to higher female labor force participation, having the first child at an older age risks also reduce the total number of children per woman.

Increase the labor force participation rate overall. The overall increase in the labor force participation rate is linked to the performance of the labor market and its capacity to handle the challenges and opportunities of globalization. Worldwide and also in OECD economies, there is a fear that globalization leads to job losses and lower wages. Unemployment remains stubbornly high in many countries in Europe plus Russia, job creation is high on the agenda of China (with some 200 million to 300 million internal migrant workers), and essentially all countries are concerned about the level of and increase in youth unemployment. As a result,

---

[10]. For a review of OECD country experiences with reconciling work and family life, see OECD (2002, 2003, 2004a, 2005).

the possibility of a general increase in labor force participation across all ages is linked closely to the capacity of a country to adjust to a globalizing world and to create jobs.

Increase the labor force participation of the elderly. Increasing the labor force participation of the elderly is high on the agenda of all countries as a means to deal with the issue of how to finance the pension scheme. As a necessary condition, this requires reforms of the pension system to make a postponement of retirement more attractive or simply to increase the minimum retirement age. In addition, however, employers must have an incentive to keep or hire elderly workers. This requires changes in the wage profile for the elderly and measures to keep their productivity high and rising. For the latter, the factual implementation of lifelong learning seems important, which in turn calls for rethinking the contractual arrangements between trade unions and employers, such moving the negotiations beyond salaries and working time to training and life-long learning.[11]

4.3. What Can Governments Do to Accommodate Immigration Flows to Mutual Advantage?

Filling labor force gaps in rich countries through migration seems to be an easy task in view of the excess supply of willing migrants from the developing world. Yet sentiments against migrants, especially in countries that have not traditionally received a large number of immigrants, and the discussion about the best approaches to integration indicate that the absorption of migrants into society is not easy, in particular if attempted on a large scale. Is it possible to call for workers alone, or is it necessary to call for and prepare future citizens? Is a short-term guest-worker concept feasible in view of the gross number of immigrants required, and is it sustainable in view of the experiences of Germany and elsewhere? Good answers to these and related questions are crucial if this demographic option is to be implemented successfully. In addition, many other policy areas need to be addressed. The three addressed here often receive insufficient attention.

Adjust the economic environment. Large-scale immigration over a long period of time is like a sequence of supply shocks to which the economy needs to adjust. As with other shocks, it is best absorbed in an economy with sufficient flexibility, including flexibility in the markets for goods, services, and factors of production. Public management and support of migration flows are needed and important, but they cannot substitute for private initiative. Such an approach seems to be successfully applied in the traditional recipients of immigration, such as the United States, Canada, and Australia.[12] If correct, this would call for a fundamental review and adjustment of the economic environment in many nontraditional recipients of immigration (in Europe and elsewhere) before further large-scale immigration is envisaged.

---

[11] Over the last 2 years OECD has produce many studies on member countries which investigate employment policies in an aging society. See for example OECD (2004c).

[12] For example the workshop paper by David Card (2005) suggests that immigrants do not harm the labor market opportunities of native workers. This more positive assessment about the impact of migration is in line with other more recent as well as older research results and contrast with divers and more negative findings of Borjas (e.g. 2003). Boeri and Brueckler (2005) claim that the resistance of EU countries against migration is the result distorted labor markets. Under such settings their argument goes migration may entail significant direct and indirect costs.

Manage the skill mix. Economic considerations suggest that the (net) benefits of migration and their distributive effects between and within countries depend on the skill composition of migrants as well as of the labor force in the sending and receiving countries.[13] Selecting migrants with appropriate skills creates benefits for the receiving country but risks hurting the sending country. While the discussion about brain drain has given rise to more positive views of brain gain and brain circulation, the skill composition of migrants and potential collaboration between sending and receiving countries are gaining importance. Such collaboration may extend to the formation of skills, co-financing of education, certification of skill levels, and acquisition of better information about skill levels (Holzmann and Munez, 2005). The experience in migrant-receiving countries suggests that they substantially underutilize the skill level of their migrants due to information problems and uncertainties about the value of skills, including academic training, received abroad (for the Canadian experience, see, for example, Reitz 2005).

Improve the portability of social benefits. For a variety of reasons, a substantial share of migrants returns to their home country after years of work abroad. And governments of host and source countries may wish to encourage return migration for various reasons. For example, governments of migrant-sending countries may see return migration as highly beneficial for their development, essentially through remittances of production factors, including investment capital, return of human capital, and transfer of knowledge and skills. Governments of migrant-receiving countries may support return migration to stress the temporary nature of immigration for political reasons. Currently such decisions by migrants are very much distorted by lacking or incomplete portability of social benefits, in particular pensions and health care (see Holzmann, Koettl, and Chernetsky 2005). As a result, many migrants do not return to their home country because they do not want to lose their access to social programs, or they prefer to work in the informal sector in order to avoid contributing to these programs, payments that become, in essence, a mere tax.

5. SUMMARY AND CONCLUDING REMARKS

There is broad agreement that population aging linked with low or negative population growth creates a major challenge for many countries and regions in the North, especially for Europe plus Russia, the high-income countries of East Asia and the Pacific, China, and, to a lesser extent, North America. Without further immigration, the total labor force in these countries is projected to decline by 29 million between 2005 and 2025 and by 244 million between 2005 and 2050. At the same time, population aging will accelerate, and the old-age dependency ratio will deteriorate further.

Although the full economic and social implications of such a dramatic shift in age structure are not yet clear, simple financial considerations suggest that a declining labor force and a deteriorating age structure will put further pressure on the financing of pension and health care programs. In addition, economic considerations suggest that a reduction in the implicit and explicit rate of return of pension and health programs could reach 1.5 percent and more annually.

---

[13] For recent surveys of this topic, see Drinkwater and others (2003); Commander, Kangasniemi, and Winters (2003), Borjas (1999).

To compensate for negative population and, in particular, labor force growth, countries have three main demographic policy options: move the total fertility rate back to replacement levels, increase the labor force participation of the existing population, and fill the demographic gaps through enhanced immigration.

Scenario calculations for the four potential-deficit regions suggest that each of these three options may assist in compensating for the demographic gap. Moving immediately toward a replacement-level fertility rate in 2005 would create an additional labor force of some 17 million by 2025 and 187 million by 2050. Increasing labor force participation rates through three combined measures (moving toward benchmark countries, closing the gender gap, and raising the effective retirement age by 10 years) would add an additional labor force of 175 million by 2025 and 335 million by 2050 in aggregate (but would not fully compensate Europe plus Russia and the high-income countries in Asia). And enhancing net migration by 244 million people by 2050 to compensate for gaps in the labor force seems easy to achieve in quantitative terms but is only part of the story. One needs to consider "migration overhead," which includes inactive migrant workers and family members in the range of some 50 percent—that is, think about total net migration on the order of more than 350 million (170 million in Europe plus Russia alone). The gross flows that take into account return and circular migration may more than double these already staggering magnitudes.

While the magnitudes involved are high and the underlying policy decisions drastic, even more limited numbers question the capacity of governments to create or accommodate the envisaged effects. Empirical evidence suggests that governments have limited policy instruments with which to increase the fertility rate. Increasing labor force participation for all implies more successful labor market policies at a moment when many countries are struggling with the implications of a more globalized world. And accommodating a substantially larger number of migrants every year requires a major review of domestic policies and a rethinking of integration policies—an area where good practices have been little analyzed or broadly discussed.

This sobering assessment suggests that no single policy approach will, on its own, contribute significantly to covering the population gap, especially in high-deficit countries. It suggests that more knowledge is needed about the effectiveness and efficiency of policy measures to influence fertility and labor force participation and to better accommodate migratory flows. It also suggests the need to investigate measures beyond demography or simply prepare for a shrinking population in a number of countries, which some claim has advantages on its own.

ANNEX TABLES

Table A1. Dependency Ratios, by Region, 2005–50

Ratio	2005	2015	2025	2050
Old-age dependency ratio[a]				
China	0.11	0.13	0.20	0.39
Europe and Russia	0.23	0.26	0.32	0.48
High-income East Asia and Pacific	0.24	0.32	0.41	0.63
North America	0.18	0.22	0.28	0.34
Latin America and Caribbean	0.10	0.11	0.15	0.29
Low- and middle-income East Asia and Pacific	0.08	0.09	0.13	0.26
Middle East, North Africa, and Turkey	0.07	0.08	0.10	0.22
South and Central Asia	0.08	0.09	0.11	0.20
Sub-Saharan Africa	0.06	0.06	0.06	0.08
Total dependency ratio[b]				
China	0.41	0.39	0.46	0.65
Europe and Russia	0.47	0.48	0.55	0.74
High-income East Asia and Pacific	0.47	0.54	0.62	0.88
North America	0.49	0.51	0.57	0.62
Latin America and Caribbean	0.56	0.52	0.50	0.57
Low- and middle-income East Asia and Pacific	0.54	0.47	0.45	0.54
Middle East, North Africa, and Turkey	0.59	0.53	0.50	0.53
South and Central Asia	0.62	0.54	0.50	0.50
Sub-Saharan Africa	0.87	0.82	0.74	0.55

Sources: United Nations (2005); author's calculations.

a. Ratio of age group 65+ to age group 15–64.

b. Ratio of age group 0–14 plus 65+ to age group 15–64.

Table A2. Changes in Labor Force, 2005–25 and 2005–50

Millions

Variant	2005–25	2005–50
Medium variant		
China	19.1	−95.8
Europe and Russia	−37.5	−98.4
High-income East Asia and Pacific	−5.7	−25.0
North America	19.3	37.8
Latin America and Caribbean	77.6	110.3
Low- and Middle-income East Asia and Pacific	93.7	128.1
Middle East, North Africa, and Turkey	82.0	141.3
South and Central Asia	292.2	514.3
Sub-Saharan Africa	211.3	591.7
Total	751.8	1,304.3

Table A2. (Continued)

Variant	2005–25	2005–50
Zero-migration variant		
China	24.4	−84.8
Europe and Russia	−45.7	−118.2
High-income East Asia and Pacific	−9.0	−32.3
North America	0.9	−8.8
Latin America and Caribbean	85.4	130.0
Low- and middle-income East Asia and Pacific	99.5	141.3
Middle East, North Africa, and Turkey	83.3	143.9
South and Central Asia	303.2	536.2
Sub-Saharan Africa	213.5	598.2
Total	755.6	1,305.5

Sources: United Nations (2005); authors' calculations.

Table A3. Policy Scenarios: Total Labor Force in China, 2005, 2025, and 2050

Millions

Scenario	2005	2025	2050
Base scenario			
Total labor force (millions)	798.7	823.2	713.9
Index	100	103	89
Absolute change (millions, base = 2005)	n.a.	24.4	−84.8
Average age of labor force	37.2	40.8	41.2
Participation rate of 55–74 age group (percent)	42.7	41.7	39.2
Scenario I			
Total labor force (millions)	798.7	828.0	721.6
Index	100	104	90
Absolute change (millions, base = 2005)	n.a.	29.2	−77.1
Average age of labor force	37.2	41.5	42.8
Participation rate of 55–74 age group (percent)	42.7	46.3	47.2
Scenario II			
Total labor force (millions)	798.7	861.6	784.5
Index	100	108	98
Absolute change (millions, base = 2005)	n.a.	62.9	−14.2
Average age of labor force	37.2	41.5	42.8
Participation rate of 55–74 age group (percent)	42.7	48.8	52.8
Scenario III			
Total labor force (millions)	798.7	863.8	802.5
Index	100	108	100
Absolute change (millions, base = 2005)	n.a.	65.0	3.8
Average age of labor force	37.2	41.9	43.9
Participation rate of 55–74 age group (percent)	42.7	53.6	64.3

Scenario I+II+III			
Total labor force (millions)	798.7	891.7	860.4
Index	100	112	108
Absolute change (millions, base = 2005)	n.a.	93.0	61.6
Average age of labor force	37.2	43.1	46.1
Participation rate of 55–74 age group (percent)	42.7	62.4	82.3

Sources: United Nations (2005); authors' calculations
n.a. Not applicable.

Table A4. Policy Scenarios: Total Labor Force in Europe and Russia, 2005, 2025, and 2050

Millions

Scenario	2005	2025	2050
Base scenario			
Total labor force (millions)	371.8	326.1	253.6
Index	100	88	68
Absolute change (millions, base = 2005)	n.a.	−45.7	−118.2
Average age of labor force	39.2	41.1	41.0
Participation rate of 55–74 age group (percent)	25.6	24.4	23.6
Scenario I			
Total labor force (millions)	371.8	355.7	302.8
Index	100	96	81
Absolute change (millions, base = 2005)	n.a.	−16.1	−69.0
Average age of labor force	39.2	42.2	43.3
Participation rate of 55–74 age group (percent)	25.6	35.3	44.5
Scenario II			
Total labor force (millions)	371.8	343.3	280.6
Index	100	92	75
Absolute change (millions, base = 2005)	n.a.	−28.5	−91.1
Average age of labor force	39.2	41.6	42.0
Participation rate of 55–74 age group (percent)	25.6	28.6	31.3
Scenario III			
Total labor force (millions)	371.8	351.5	299.6
Index	100	95	81
Absolute change (millions, base = 2005)	n.a.	−20.3	−72.2
Average age of labor force	39.2	42.8	44.7
Participation rate of 55–74 age group (percent)	25.6	38.2	51.4
Scenario I+II+III			
Total labor force (millions)	371.8	392.8	370.2
Index	100	106	100
Absolute change (millions, base = 2005)	n.a.	21.0	−1.6
Average age of labor force	39.2	44.2	47.1
Participation rate of 55–74 age group (percent)	25.6	53.3	81.4

Sources: United Nations (2005); author's calculations.
n.a. Not applicable.

Table A5. Policy Scenarios: Total Labor Force in High-Income Countries in East Asia and the Pacific, 2005, 2025, and 2050

Millions

Scenario	2005	2025	2050
Base scenario			
Total labor force (millions)	43.8	43.4	33.9
Index	100	99	78
Absolute change (millions, base = 2005)	n.a.	−0.4	−9.8
Average age of labor force	39.8	43.0	43.7
Participation rate of 55–74 age group (percent)	40.9	38.7	38.2
Scenario I			
Total labor force (millions)	43.8	46.0	37.8
Index	100	105	86
Absolute change (millions, base = 2005)	n.a.	2.3	−5.9
Average age of labor force	39.8	43.2	43.9
Participation rate of 55–74 age group (percent)	40.9	43.0	45.0
Scenario II			
Total labor force (millions)	43.8	46.2	38.3
Index	100	106	88
Absolute change (millions, base = 2005)	n.a.	2.5	−5.5
Average age of labor force	39.8	43.5	44.6
Participation rate of 55–74 age group (percent)	40.9	44.0	47.8
Scenario III			
Total labor force (millions)	43.8	46.1	39.0
Index	100	105	89
Absolute change (millions, base = 2005)	n.a.	2.4	−4.8
Average age of labor force	39.8	44.4	46.6
Participation rate of 55–74 age group (percent)	40.9	50.4	61.5
Scenario I+II+III			
Total labor force (millions)	43.8	50.8	46.5
Index	100	116	106
Absolute change (millions, base = 2005)	n.a.	7.0	2.7
Average age of labor force	39.8	45.1	47.7
Participation rate of 55–74 age group (percent)	40.9	60.7	81.3

Sources: United Nations (2005); author's calculations.

Table A6. Policy Scenarios: Total Labor Force in North America, 2005, 2025, and 2050

Millions

Scenario	2005	2025	2050
Base scenario			
Total labor force (millions)	171.1	171.9	162.2
Index	100	100	95
Absolute change (millions, base = 2005)	n.a.	0.9	−8.8
Average age of labor force	39.8	40.9	41.4
Participation rate of 55–74 age group (percent)	40.8	35.4	36.0
Scenario I			
Total labor force (millions)	171.1	179.7	177.0
Index	100	105	103
Absolute change (millions, base = 2005)	n.a.	8.6	5.9
Average age of labor force	39.8	41.4	42.3
Participation rate of 55–74 age group (percent)	40.8	40.6	46.5
Scenario II			
Total labor force (millions)	171.1	177.3	172.2
Index	100	104	101
Absolute change (millions, base = 2005)	n.a.	6.2	1.2
Average age of labor force	39.8	41.2	41.8
Participation rate of 55–74 age group (percent)	40.8	38.1	41.3
Scenario III			
Total labor force (millions)	171.1	184.5	186.0
Index	100	108	109
Absolute change (millions, base = 2005)	n.a.	13.4	14.9
Average age of labor force	39.8	42.6	44.5
Participation rate of 55–74 age group (percent)	40.8	50.1	65.0
Scenario I+II+III			
Total labor force (millions)	171.1	197.1	209.8
Index	100	115	123
Absolute change (millions, base = 2005)	n.a.	26.0	38.7
Average age of labor force	39.8	43.3	45.6
Participation rate of 55–74 age group (percent)	40.8	58.7	81.9

Sources: United Nations (2005); author's calculations.

n.a. Not applicable.

Table A7. Ratio of Official Outflows to Inflows of Polish Nationals for Select Host Countries, 1992–2001

Percent

Country	1992	1993	1994	1995	1996	1997	1998	1999	2000	2001	Average
Austria							95.5	95.3	87.2	91.5	92.9
Belgium	33.3	42.9	25.0	37.5	33.3	45.5	45.5	33.3	45.5	6.9	30.4
Denmark	16.2	19.5	23.6	23.6	19.1	18.6	15.4	32.7	15.0	13.3	19.2
Germany	83.1	135.4	83.7	81.0	92.5	98.4	91.6	80.9	81.3	81.7	90.2
Netherlands		92.3	25.0	0.0	20.0	27.1	23.8	25.7	16.0	18.3	26.4
Norway	33.3	66.7	33.3	50.0	50.0	50.0	50.0	38.5	41.7	22.7	41.7
Total	82.5	132.8	82.1	79.1	89.9	95.5	88.9	79.8	78.9	77.2	87.9

Source: OECD (2004b).

Table A8. Ratio of Official Outflows to Inflows of Turkish Nationals for Select Host Countries, 1992–2001

Percent

Country	1992	1993	1994	1995	1996	1997	1998	1999	2000	2001	Average
Austria							64.4	51.4	51.4	45.5	52.5
Belgium	22.2	24.0	22.2	24.0	20.0	35.7	25.0	27.3	14.3	10.0	21.5
Denmark	18.2	28.6	33.3	25.0	8.3	20.0	16.7	18.2	22.2	22.2	20.0
Germany	50.0	67.1	72.6	58.7	59.4	82.1	94.0	86.8	79.4	65.8	69.4
Netherlands	19.8	21.8	37.2	33.3	23.4	16.9	17.6	16.7	13.3		21.8
Switzerland	54.7	62.5	78.9	71.1	73.5	79.3	88.5	50.0	46.4	35.5	63.7
Total	46.4	61.0	68.2	56.5	55.5	73.9	81.1	73.5	67.2	59.2	63.0

Source: OECD (2004b).

REFERENCES

Bjoerklund, Anders. 2002. *"Does Family Policy Affect Fertility? Lessons from Swedish Policy Experiment."* Mimeo. Stockholm University.

Boeri Tito and Herbert Brücker. 2005. "Why are Europeans so tough on migrants?" *Economic Policy* 44 (October): 631-703.

Borjas, George. 1999. "The Economic Analysis of Migration." In Orley Ashenfelter and David Card, eds., *Handbook of Labor Economics*, Vol. 3A. Amsterdam: North Holland: 69–133.

————. 2003. "The labor demand curve is downward sloping: Reexamining the impacts of immigration on the labor market". *Quarterly Journal of Economics* 118 (November): 1335-74.

Caglar Ozden and Maurice Schiff (eds.). 2005. *International Migration, Remittances and Development*. Palgrave McMillan: New York.

Caldwell, John, Pat Caldwell, and Peter McDondald. 2002. "Policy responses to low fertility and its consequences: A global survey". *Journal of Population Research 19(1):* 1-24.

Card, David. 2005. "Is the new immigration really so bad?" *NBER Working Papers Series – Working Paper No. 11547.* Cambridge, Mass.: National Bureau of Economic Research.

Chenais, Jean-Claude. 1990. "Demographic transition patterns and their impact on the age structure". *Population and Development Review* 16 (2): 327-336.

Commander, Simon, Mari Kangasniemi, and L. Alan Winters. 2003. *"The Brain Drain: Curse or Boon?"* IZA Discussion Paper 809. Bonn: Institute for the Study of Labor, June.

Drago, Robert, Rosanna Scutella, and Amy Varner. 2002. "Fertility and Work/Family Policies." *Paper presented at the conference on "Opportunity and Prosperity,"* University of Melbourne, April.

Drinkwater, Stephen, Paul Levine, Emanuela Lotti, and Joseph Pearlman. 2003. "The Economic Impact of Migration: A Survey." *FLOWENLA Discussion Paper 9.* Hamburg : Hamburg Institute of International Economics.

Ehrlich, Isaac, and Jinyoung Kim. 2003. *"Social Security, Demographic Trends, and Economic Growth: Theory and Evidence from International Experience."* Mimeo. State University of New York at Buffalo.

Harrison, Anne. 2004. *"Working Abroad: The Benefits Flowing from Nationals Working in Other Economies."* Paper presented to the Roundtable on Sustainable Development, OECD, Paris.

Holzmann, Robert. 2002. "Can Investments in Emerging Markets Help to Solve the Aging Problem?" *Journal of Emerging Market Finance* 1 (2): 215–41.

Holzmann, Robert, Richard Hinz, and Bank team. 2005. *Old-Age Income Support in the 21st Century: An International Perspective on Pension Systems and Reform*. Washington, D.C.: World Bank.

Holzman, Robert, Johannes Koettl, and Taras Chernetsky. 2005. "Portability Regimes of Pension and Health Care Benefits for International Migrants: An Analysis of Issues and Good Practices." *Global Migration Perspectives.* Geneva: Global Commission on International Migration. Forthcoming.

Holzmann, Robert, and Rainer Münz. 2004. *Challenges and Opportunities of International Migration for the EU, Its Member States, Neighboring Countries, and Regions.* Stockholm: Institute for Futures Studies.

————. 2005. *"Europe, North Africa, and the Middle East: Diverging Trends, Overlapping Interests, Possible Arbitrage through Migration."* Paper prepared for the joint workshop on "The Future of Demography, Labour Markets, and the Formation of Skills in Europe, and Its Mediterranean Neighbourhood," European Commission, World Bank, King Baudoin Foundation, and European Policy Centre, Brussels, July 4–5, 2005.

IMF (International Monetary Fund). 2004. *World Economic Outlook: The Global Demographic Transition* (September). Washington, D.C.: IMF.

Martins, Joaquim Oliveira, Frederic Gonand, Pablo Antolin, Christine de la Maisonneuve, and Kwang Yeol Yoo. 2005. The Impact of Ageing on Demand, Factor Markets and Growth. *Economic Working Papers No. 420.* Paris: OECD.

May, John F. 2005. "Population Policy". In D. Poston and M. Micklin, eds. *The Handbook of Population.* New York: Kluwer Academic/Plenium Publishers: 827-825.

Meier, Volker, and Matthias Wrede. 2005. „Pension, Fertility, and Education". *CESifo Working Paper No. 1521.* Munich: CESifo.

Migration Policy Institute. 2005. Global Data Center, Available at *http://www.migrationinformation.org/index.cfm.* Last accessed on October 3, 2005.

McKibbin, Warwick J. 2005. The Global Macroeconomic Consequences of Demographic Transition. *Paper prepared for G-20 Workshop on Demographic Challenges and Migration,* Sydney, 27-28 August 2005.

Münz, Rainer, and Heinz Fassmann. 2004. "Migrants in Europe and Their Economic Position: Evidence from the European Labour Force Survey and from Other Sources." *Paper prepared for the European Commission, DG Employment and Social Affairs,* European Commission, Brussels, and HWWA, Hamburg.

Munzele Maimbo, Samuel, and Dilip Ratha. 2005. *Remittances: Development Impact and Future Prospects.* Washington, D.C.: World Bank.

Neyer, Gerda. 2003. *"Family Policy and Low Fertility in Europe."* Max-Planck Institute for Demographic Research Working Paper 2003-021. Rostock, July.

OECD (Organisation for Economic Co-operation and Development). 2002. *Babies and Bosses: Reconciling Work and Family Life.* Vol. 1: *Australia, Denmark, and the Netherlands.* Paris. OECD.

————. 2003. *Babies and Bosses: Reconciling Work and Family Life.* Vol. 2: *Austria, Ireland, and Japan.* Paris: OECD.

————. 2004a. *Babies and Bosses: Reconciling Work and Family Life.* Vol. 3: *New Zealand, Portugal, and Switzerland.* Paris: OECD.

————. 2004b. *Trends in International Migration: SOPEMI 2003.* Paris: OECD.

————. 2004c. *Aging and Employment Policies: United Kingdom.* Paris: OECD.

————. 2005. *Babies and Bosses: Reconciling Work and Family Life.* Vol. 4: *Canada, Finland, Sweden, and the United Kingdom.* Paris: OECD.

Palmer, Eduard. 2005. "What is NDC?" In Robert Holzmann and Edward Palmer, eds., *Pension Reform: Issues and Prospect for Non-Financial Defined Contribution (NDC) Schemes.* Washington, D.C. World Bank.

Reitz, Jeffrey. 2005. "Tapping Immigrants Skills: New Directions for Canadian Immigration Policy in the Knowledge Economy." *IRPP Choices* 11 (1, February): 2–18.

Samuelson, Paul. 1958. "An Exact Consumption-Loan Model of Interest With or Without the Social Contrivance of Money." *Journal of Political Economy* 6 (December): 467–82.

Settergren, Ole, and Boguslaw Mikula. 2005. "The Rate of Return of Pay-as-You-Go Pension Systems." In Robert Holzmann and Edward Palmer, eds., *Pension Reform: Issues and Prospect for Non-Financial Defined Contribution (NDC) Schemes*. Washington, D.C.: World Bank.

Sinn, Hans-Werner. 2004. "The Pay-as-You-Go Pension System as Fertility Insurance and an Enforcement Device." *Journal of Public Economics* 88: 1335–57.

United Nations. 2005. *World Population Prospects. The 2004 Revision*. New York: UN.

World Bank. 2005. *Global Economic Prospects 2006: Economic Implications of Remittances and Migration*. Washington, DC.: World Bank.

INDEX

C

E

F

J

K

L

M

N

Q

R

S

U

V

W

Y

Z